SOURCEBOOK FOR
CHILD ABUSE AND NEGLECT

SOURCEBOOK FOR CHILD ABUSE AND NEGLECT

Intervention, Treatment, and Prevention
Through Crisis Programs

Edited by

OLIVER C.S. TZENG and JAMIA JASPER JACOBSEN

With Twenty-One Contributors

CHARLES C THOMAS • PUBLISHER
Springfield • Illinois • U.S.A.

Published and Distributed Throughout the World by

CHARLES C THOMAS • PUBLISHER

2600 South First Street

Springfield, Illinois 62794-9265

© *1988 by* CHARLES C THOMAS • PUBLISHER

ISBN 0-398-05419-3

Library of Congress Catalog Card Number: 87-18150

With THOMAS BOOKS *careful attention is given to all details of manufacturing
and design. It is the Publisher's desire to present books that are satisfactory as to their
physical qualities and artistic possibilities and appropriate for their particular use.*
THOMAS BOOKS *will be true to those laws of quality that assure a good name
and good will.*

Printed in the United States of America
SC-R-3

Library of Congress Cataloging-in-Publication Data

Sourcebook for child abuse and neglect: intervention, treatment, and
prevention through crisis programs/edited by Oliver C. S. Tzeng and
Jamia J. Jacobsen.
    p. cm.
  Includes bibliographies and index.
  ISBN 0-398-05419-3
   1. Child abuse—United States.   2. Abused children—Services for—
United States.   3. Crisis intervention (Psychiatry)—United States.
I. Tzeng, Oliver C. S.   II. Jacobsen, Jamia Jasper.
HV741.S692 1988
362.7'044—dc19   87-18150
                                                     CIP

CONTRIBUTORS

MICHELLE M. ALLISON, M.S.

Research Associate
Osgood Laboratory for Cross-Cultural Research
Indiana University — Purdue University
at Indianapolis, Indiana

ROBERT H. FORTIER, Ph.D.

Clinical Psychologist
Associate Professor
Indiana University — Purdue University
at Indianapolis, Indiana

BARBARA R. FURLOW, M.S.

Public Relations Assistant
U.S. Canoe and Kayak Team
School of Education, Counseling
Indiana University

ENA M. GOODRICH-SHELLEY, Ph.D.

Assistant Professor of Education, Early Childhood Education
Child Psychology, Elementary Education
Butler University
Indianapolis, Indiana

KEVIN J. GULLY, Ph.D.

Clinical Psychologist
Family Support Center
Salt Lake City, Utah
Utah Department of Correction
Sex Offender Division
Adjunct Assistant Professor
University of Utah

LINDA J. HANNER, DOCTORAL STUDENT

Research Associate
Osgood Laboratory for Cross-Cultural Research
Indiana University—Purdue University
at Indianapolis, Indiana

STUART N. HART, Ph.D.

Office for the Study
of the Psychological Rights of the Child
Indiana University—Purdue University
at Indianapolis, Indiana

ROBERTA A. HIBBARD, M.D.

Assistant Professor of Pediatrics
Department of Pediatrics
James Whitcomb Riley Hospital for Children
Indiana University School of Medicine
Indianapolis, Indiana

RUTH E. HOLLAND, Ed.D.

Associate Professor of Education
Indiana University—Purdue University
at Indianapolis, Indiana
Author: Children in Peril

BEVERLY R. HURD

Dietary Management I and II
House Manager
Indianapolis Propyleum Inc.
Kitchen Supervisor
Family Support Center
Indianapolis, Indiana

JAMIA JASPER JACOBSEN, Ph.D.

Administrator
Community Affairs Consumer Division
Blue Cross-Blue Shield, Indiana
Executive Director
Child Crisis Center 1981–1985
Adjunct Faculty
Indiana University—Purdue University
at Indianapolis, Indiana
Editor: Psychiatric Sequelae of Child Abuse

JUDY MANNING KENDRICK, M.S.W., A.C.S.W.

Coordinator
Family Life Education Program
Visiting Nurse Service
Indianapolis, Indiana

ELLEN R. LORCH, B.A.

Director
Volunteer Action Center of United Way
Supervisor of United Christmas Service
and Director of Leadership Giving
Indianapolis, Indiana

ROBERT S. NEVIN, M.P.H., M.S.W., Ph.D.

Associate Professor
Indiana University School of Social Work
Indiana University—Purdue University
at Indianapolis, Indiana

ROSANNE PIRTLE, M.S.

Associate Professor of Education
Marion College
Indianapolis, Indiana

ALBERT R. ROBERTS, Ph.D.

Associate Professor
Indiana University School of Social Work
Indiana University—Purdue University
at Indianapolis, Indiana

JAMES C. STROUD, DOCTORAL CANDIDATE

Early Childhood Education
Elementary Education at Indiana State University
Terre Haute, Indiana

JUDI E. STROUD, DOCTORAL CANDIDATE

Early Childhood Education
Elementary Education at Indiana State University
Terre Haute, Indiana

PAUL A. TURGI, M.A.

Director
Monroe County Guardian Ad Litem Project
Bloomington, Indiana
Counselor
Family Service Association
of Monroe County, Indiana

ANN H. TYLER, Ph.D.

Executive Director and Chief Psychologist
Family Support Center
Salt Lake City
Utah

OLIVER C.S. TZENG, Ph.D.

Director and Professor
Osgood Laboratory for Cross-Cultural Research
Department of Psychology
Indiana University — Purdue University
at Indianapolis, Indiana
Director of Consortium of Child Abuse
and Neglect Resources and Information Services

ROGER WARE, Ph.D.

Humanistic Psychologist
Industrial Organizational Psychology
Associate Professor
Indiana University — Purdue University
at Indianapolis, Indiana

To children everywhere.
May all children
Count their nights by stars, not shadows;
and
Count their life by smiles, not tears.

To caring adults everywhere.
May your work
Enrich your life with pride, not grief;
and
Enrich children and families with happiness and love.

PREFACE

This book is prepared under the impetus of desperate needs in practical social services and academic institutions for comprehensive resource materials related to the establishment, roles, and functions of a community-based crisis center in child abuse and neglect. Child abuse and neglect has been pervasive in threatening the well-being of children, the stability of families, and the development of pro-social community and institutional environments. Despite the fact that various agencies at the local, state, and national levels have been working diligently toward the development and implementation of various prevention, intervention, and treatment programs, the severity of child abuse and neglect is steadily increasing in all spectrums of family orientations. Due to the complex nature of the issues involved, the strengths of various community efforts have frequently been limited by: (1) a narrow focus on some specific issues, (b) the orientation of a single discipline, (c) separate or disjointed effort in services, (d) partial and frequently biased knowledge and skill in performance, and (e) a fragmental nature in program implementation. These limitations have severely undercut the efficiency and efficacy of the existing service efforts.

Since the child crisis center in each community represents the community-wide mechanism to intervene and prevent child abuse and neglect problems, it would be most effective for public and private sectors to start working on the development and improvement of community-wide crisis facilities. Therefore, we prepared this book as a guiding reference for this effort.

In preparation of this Sourcebook, we have used many aspects of resources that are directly related to community-based crisis intervention facilities. These resources include: (1) working experiences in a community-wide crisis center in metropolitan Indianapolis, (2) completion of many regional and statewide training workshops on child abuse and neglect for law enforcement and day care centers and other service providers, (3) consultation with various community service agencies working with abused and neglected children and families, (4) longitudinal analyses of child abuse and neglect cases at the local, state, and national levels, and (5) a comprehensive evaluation of documents and publications on child abuse and neglect.

This Sourcebook compiles comprehensive, integrated knowledge and information regarding the development, operation, and program implementation of child abuse and neglect crisis centers. The first part of this Sourcebook contains a theoretical development that addresses fundamental principles in combatting child abuse and neglect problems within each community. The theoretical development is followed by the presentation of a comprehensive operational model to study the etiology, dynamics, and consequential issues on child abuse and neglect. This model suggests the pursuit of a multidisciplinary collaboration of the strengths of all different approaches that have been currently prevalent in field applications. Our review of literature indicates that many professionals in various disciplines have adopted different, and frequently conflicting theoretical approaches as the basis for developing response strategies. Unfortunately, these individual approaches have not been self-sufficient: the **psychiatric approach** attributes child abuse/neglect to mental problems, but accounts for less than 15% of incidents; the **social approach** focuses on the improvement of social disparity issues (e.g., housing projects), but fails to reduce the abuse/neglect problems; the **situational approach** emphasizes a variety of situational causal factors, but cannot explain consistent child victimization patterns; the **legal approach** favors a safe guardianship, but frequently results in family discontinuity and compound damage on children; and the **criminal approach** punishes offenders through prosecution and incarceration, but still fails to deter the pervasive abuse/neglect problems in society. Therefore, our theoretical development addresses the importance of: (1) comprehensiveness in service functions, (2) coordination among all service intervention approaches, (3) community-based development of service systems and programs, (4) child and family-centered approach in service implementation, and (5) multidisciplinary considerations of all issues pertaining to the seven "W's" related to child abuse and neglect (**who** did **what** to **whom** and **when**, **where**, **how**, and **why**?).

In order to integrate the missions and functions of crisis centers within an effective community-based service system, the contents of this Sourcebook are organized under three broad categories: (1) organization of care facilities (including five specific topical chapters on national survey of service facilities, establishing a local crisis center, shelter care, volunteer corps, and kitchen program), (2) missions and functions of crisis centers (including six chapters on national phenomena and typologies, prevention through crisis intervention, counseling, emotional abuse, and sexual abuse), and (3) legal foundations and the role within the community-wide service system (including three chapters on historical perspectives of children's rights and abuse/neglect, national trends of state laws for protecting children, and cooperation between community agencies to foster legal rights of children). Individual chapters are written by professionals who have actively been involved with and have drawn heavily upon their individual areas of expertise and experiences.

As author-editors, we have tried to carefully integrate individual chapters in reference to the theoretical foundations and the model presented in the first part of the book. Evaluation of such an attempt is presented in the conclusion chapter. It is our hope and desire that those who work at the grassroots level can benefit from the material presented in this Sourcebook in their evaluation, improvement, and/or establishment of a community-based crisis center. Child abuse and neglect is no longer the problem of the child, or of the family, it is the problem of all the community. Therefore, we hope that all community officers and concerned individuals in various public and private—service as well as educational—institutions will benefit from reading this book and start their active contributions in each community. We believe that this book will provide theories, models, and strategies that can be used to reduce multiple gaps in current social service systems: between service needs of families and service capabilities of crisis centers, between service workers and service administrators, between service agencies and public institutions in supervision and policy formation, and between service professionals and social support groups and individuals. The ultimate goal of our effort is the reduction and/or elimination of child abuse and neglect problems such that children around the nation could feel safe to nourish and develop to their fullest potential.

Finally, we offer sincere thanks to many persons who helped make this work possible and to those who gave us continuing support and encouragement to see it through to completion. Specifically, we thank Linda Hanner for her dedication and patience in preparation of the entire manuscript. Her thorough and efficient typing and checking greatly expedited the completion of this book.

O.C.S.T. and J.J.J.

CONTENTS

SOURCEBOOK FOR
CHILD ABUSE AND NEGLECT

CHAPTER 1

NATURE AND ETIOLOGY OF HUMAN AGGRESSION AND VIOLENCE: A COMPREHENSIVE MODEL FOR STUDYING CHILD ABUSE AND NEGLECT PROBLEMS

OLIVER C. S. TZENG
LINDA J. HANNER
ROBERT H. FORTIER

INTRODUCTION

Child abuse and neglect are forms of human aggression and violent behavior. For this reason, scientific principles and a theoretical model identified as **Psychosemantic Process Model of Human Aggression** are introduced in the first part of this chapter to depict the dynamics of general aggressive and violent behaviors. In the second part of this chapter, the Model is used to specifically explain the nature and etiology of child abuse and neglect problems. The third part summarizes four topical issues related to the intervention and prevention of child abuse and neglect problems: (a) evaluation of child abuse and neglect phenomena from an ecological perspective, (b) evaluation of five major intervention approaches, (c) introduction of a holistic approach to combatting child abuse and neglect, and (d) an integration of seven comprehensive service domains in dealing with child abuse and neglect problems. Finally, the last section of this chapter presents an overall organizational plan of the subsequent 16 chapters of this book. The readers who are more interested in **application** of the theories and model presented in this chapter are encouraged to begin their reading in the third part of this chapter.

HUMAN AGGRESSION AND VIOLENCE

Aggression is generally viewed as a hostile action intended to dominate other persons or situations. Generally speaking, human aggression can be divided into two forms: behavioral and dispositional. **Behavioral aggression** of an individual usually manifests in verbal and nonverbal activities that cause physical and mental harm to others. **Dispositional aggression** represents attitudes and behavioral inclinations to dominate the situations or violate other persons' rights. Behavioral outcomes of such disposition may result in either an active **commission** (abusive) or passive **omission** (neglectful) act.

Aggression can be characterized in terms of the **targets** of its expression: **self** or **others**. For example, **suicide** is frequently considered in scientific literature as an aggressive act toward self, whereas aggression toward others is frequently characterized in terms of its targeted victims: either specific individuals (spouse, child, or any identifiable individual) or a specific social group or class of people with different backgrounds (such as income, sex, race, education, religion, and/or nationality).

In fact, aggression is not an all or nothing syndrome. It can be differentiated in terms of a four hierarchical step continuum ranging from **competitive, intrusive, domineering, to violent behaviors.** On this continuum, a competitive behavior is socially acceptable and, in fact, is commonly encouraged because of its representations of independence and self-reliance in contemporary social and occupational situations. On the other hand, the last three types (intrusive, domineering, and violent behaviors) are socially undesirable because of their inconsistency with social norms and values. Furthermore, it should be noted that different individuals may interpret the same behavior in terms of different types of aggression, and different groups of people may have different norm values regarding the acceptability of each type of aggressive behavior.

In short, the four aggressive types are continuous in nature, their manifestations in interpersonal interactions often possess different subjective interpretation ("**implicit meanings**") to the actors and observers. For example, the domineering acts of parents toward their children may be considered as abusive by outsiders, but the parents may interpret their own acts as perfectly acceptable disciplines.

In the literature of human aggression and violence, three broad categories of theoretical postulations have been most frequently mentioned to explain the etiology of an aggressive behavior against children.

1. The **Psychodynamic Approach,** led by Freud, generally assumes that aggression is an instinct of human species. It is a destructive energy that accumulates until it is discharged, either inwardly in self-destructive behavior, or outwardly in destructive acts towards others.

2. The **Social Learning Theory** asserts that aggression is a product of learning in social environment, because human beings have the ability to learn by observing the behavior of important others under the mechanisms of reward and punishment systems commonly used in society. Under this theory, a personal experience in any aggressive situation (as an actor, receiver, or pure observer) will induce the **learning** of the aggressive behavior and intention.

3. The **Frustration Aggression Postulation** assumes that human violent acts are usually associated with some unhealthy emotions such as anger, fear, and shame.

Each approach has its own validity and weaknesses. Therefore, no single approach is self-sufficient and universally acceptable in accounting for various aspects of aggression and violence.

PSYCHOSEMANTIC PROCESS MODEL OF HUMAN AGGRESSION AND VIOLENCE

In order to integrate all considerations and strengths of various approaches to the theoretical account of human aggression and violence, we have integrated a process oriented conceptual model. This model, identified as a **Psychosemantic Process Model for Human Aggression and Violence**, integrates various theoretical issues into a logical network that consists of many individual components. In order to identify the specific properties and nature of each component, some important theoretical concepts are first presented as follows.

Subjective and Objective Cultures

The characteristics of individual human beings and social environments can generally be dichotomized into two types of cultures: objective and subjective. **Objective culture** contains all visible characteristics of people and objects in a given social environment, such as materials, things, ethnicity, sex, housing, and cars. **Subjective culture**, on the other hand, contains various mental conditions of an individual or of a group of people that cannot be directly observed, such as thoughts, feelings, beliefs, hopes, and understandings. These two types of cultures are closely interrelated in human behavioral dispositions and life experiences.

Cognitive and Affective Evaluation Systems

In the process of social learning and interactions with life environments (people as well as inanimate objects), we human beings constantly go through a mental process of **evaluating** other people and/or objects we encounter. This evaluation process consists of five sequential stages: (1) perception of an input stimulus (verbal or nonverbal, animate or inanimate object), (2) uncoding (understanding) of the stimulus through analysis of its characteristics in reference to familiar references (e.g., age and sex in objective culture, and likes and attitude in subjective culture), (3) integration of the meaning in reference to the existing general mental status that was previously established about the similar stimuli, (4) formulation of behavioral disposition about the stimulus, and (5) decoding (expression) of dispositions as some overt reactions toward the objects.

Except for the expression stage in (5), all mental activities in perception, understanding, integration, and formulation of meaning are important mental functions that can further be differentiated in terms of two types of meaning systems. First is the **cognitive system** that represents a person's evaluation of events or situations through some objective criteria. Such criteria are usually observable and/or easily measurable with known properties within a given society. For example, a child can be evaluated in terms of body height, food intake, and physical strength. The key function of the cognitive system involves evaluation of content issues, integration of current and past conditions, and formulation of expectations or predictions regarding these issues and concerns.

The **affective system** represents an individual's feeling and emotional reaction to objects or situation. For example, people distinguish an event as being **fun** or **dull**, an object as being **good** or **bad**, and a person being **nice** or **not nice**. In daily life situations, the average individual will always judge new life events in terms of such affective system developed over a variety of life situations. Therefore, the affective system usually governs subjective emotional status of each individual across different times, situations, and life contexts. Such affective system significantly influences the generation of the individual's behavioral dispositions and overt coping behaviors.

Five Ecological Levels of Human Life Experiences

Human life experiences can further be characterized in reference to five system levels of human ecology.

Idiosystem of individuals. This system covers the characteristics of the environment that are specific to a given individual. The nature of these characteristics can be either **subjective**, such as personality traits, attitudes, interests, values and moral standards, or **objective**, such as age, sex, race, and physical features. The idiosystem comprises of all characteristics that are fundamental to individual identity and interactions with outside world.

Microsystem of family. This ecological system represents the characteristics of family structures, functions, and home conditions. The terms **family** and **home** are meant to include all types of living circumstances in the contemporary society; nuclear family, single parent family, cohabitants, and other arrangements. The characteristics of each family will include not only those that are common to other families, but also those that are specific to each household.

Exosystem of community and occupational environment. This system includes the environments of neighborhood, community, occupations, and various commercial/industrial facilities. These environments cover both subjective and objective conditions in each community that determine the total living situations of the individual under normal life functions.

Macrosystem of culture. This system represents an overall composition of people within a pluralized, heterogeneous country. The composition may be differentiated in terms of such objective cultural variables as ethnicity, sex roles, life styles, socioeconomic status, and political persuasion across different geographic regions. Within each macrosystem, the individuals prescribe some definite societal roles, subjective cultural values, attitudes, beliefs, and behavioral patterns that are homogeneous to all members of the same population.

Geopolitical System. This system represents the identities of different countries at the international level. Within this system, each nation will be perceived as a behavioral entity that has a set of identifiable characteristics (patterns or styles) in both subjective (e.g., values and perceptions) and objective cultures (e.g., national gross product and industries). Inter-communications between different nations will usually rely on such characteristics.

Culture Ecology Units

By separating subjective and objective cultures and by dividing human life experiences into five ecological systems, a two-by-five matrix can further be derived to detail the life conditions of human beings. As shown in Table I–I, each entry represents a **culture by ecology unit** which can describe specific issues and concerns of human behavior and interactions. For example, in daily family life and social interactions, we can use the **subjective by microsystem unit** to describe the attitude and beliefs of the people involved about various family issues. These family issues could be the perceptions of roles of individual family members and the priority of family values. Other examples for the ten culture-ecology units are given in Table I–I.

TABLE I-I
EXAMPLES OF HUMAN LIFE EXPERIENCES IN TEN CULTURE-ECOLOGY UNITS

Ecology/ Culture	Idiosystem of Individuals	Microsystem of Family	Exosystem of Community	Macrosystem of Culture	Geopolitical System
Subjective Culture	Needs Wants Perception of self	Family norms Values Expectations	Neighbor-hood values Career goals	Culture Values Taboos	Stereotypes of national issues
Objective Culture	Life style Leisure activities	Food Clothing Family activities	Crime rate Occupational relations	Transporta-tion Taxation	International trade, Tourism

Overview of the Theoretical Model

The theoretical concepts presented in the above sections can be applied to the evaluation of the nature, conditions, and consequences of human aggressive behaviors. Such an applications results in the development of the **Psychosemantic Process Model for Human Aggression and Violence** in Figure I-1. This model organizes various aspects of human behaviors, dispositions, and their backgrounds into ten individual content domains. Before the nature of each domain is discussed, the six functional steps that delineate the entire process of human aggressive behavior are presented.

Antecedent stimulus. This step represents the emergence of an aversive circumstance (i.e. immediate stressor) that causes an imbalance in feeling or thinking. This stressor requires attitudinal and/or behavioral adaptations through some form of aggressive or nonaggressive actions.

Supporting baseline characteristic. Each individual has developed some form of thinking and feeling patterns and behavioral adaptation mechanisms through a long-term social learning process. The results of such development becomes **implicit foundations** for social behaviors and interactions.

These foundations can further be divided into three categories in terms of their relative significance in daily life situations: (1) **background characteristics**; general conditions of each individual's subjective as well as objective cultures that do not have any negative impact on general life situations, (2) **long-term stressors**; certain life events and/or conditions that have a negative and relatively long-term impact on the individual (e.g., long-term illness), and (3) **short-term stressors**; events and/or conditions that have a relatively short but very significant impact on the individual (e.g., family car broke down, or a short-term hospitalization).

Evaluation processes. This functional step refers to the mental process used by each individual to evaluate antecedent stimuli (stressors). This process will rely on the use of supporting baseline characteristics of each individual to perform two types of evaluations: (a) **cognitive evaluation** will first perform an analysis of the antecedent stimuli objectively and then integrate all information and formulate expectations and response strategies, and (b) **affective evaluation** will determine each individual's subjective feeling and attitudes about the antecedent stimuli and related circumstances that will facilitate the cognitive system in formulation of coping strategies.

Behavior generation and monitoring process. This step involves three functional mechanisms in response to any short-term stressor: (1) retrieval of previous coping strategies from life history, (2) generation of behavioral dispositions, and (3) monitoring of a behavioral disposition through habits. This step represents the linkage between each individual's present behavioral plan and past behavioral tendency and habit in facing similar stressful events or situations.

Overt coping behavior. This functional step represents the **performance** of eventual, overt coping behavior that may be violent or nonviolent. Again, the behavior is initially stimulated by the antecedent stimulus, linked to the supporting baseline characteristics, evaluated by both affective and cognitive systems, monitored by prior behavioral habits, and finally carried out as an overt stress-coping activity.

Social consequences. Any social behavior is interactional in nature with

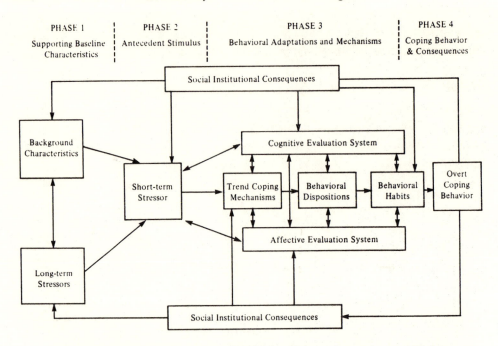

Figure I-1. **Psychosemantic Process Model for Human Aggression and Violence**

respect to various ecological circumstances. Therefore, each individual's stress coping behavior has social consequences in each ecological environment. These consequences will influence the subsequent social behaviors for all individuals involved, either positively or negatively, directly or indirectly. More detailed discussion of the contents and the dynamics of the above six functional steps will be made after the presentation of individual components as follows.

Nature and Dynamics of Individual Components

The proposed model in Figure I-1 is continuous in time and space. By **continuous in time** it means that all components in the model are constantly active and they are functionally linked from the first component of background characteristics to the last component of overt coping behavior. There are many components in between which all contribute to the eventual manifestation of overt behavior.

On the other hand, by **continuous in space,** it means that all the components in this Model deal with issues involved in the ten culture-ecology units at the same time in varying degrees. Although the structural characteristics of these components are independent of each other, their functions are not. Therefore, it is important to specify the structural characteristics of individual components and their functional relationships. For this reason, the major contents of each component and their dynamics are illustrated in the following sections.

Background Characteristics

Each individual has various kinds of background characteristics that are responsible for aggressive or nonaggressive behaviors. These characteristics can be illustrated in terms of the ten **culture-ecology units:**

1. **Idiosystem by objective culture** represents various social identifiers of each individual, such as sex, race, physique, behavior patterns, life styles, and routine activities;
2. **Idiosystem by subjective culture** contains the individual's values, beliefs, needs, expectations, and perception of self and others;
3. **Microsystem by objective culture** represents observable family characteristics such as housing, family members, activities, and socioeconomic status;
4. **Microsystem by subjective culture** covers family norms, values, identities, roles, and expectations;
5. **Exosystem by objective culture** covers issues on neighborhoods, crime rates, community development, and occupational opportunities;
6. **Exosystem by subjective culture** consists of neighborhood values, norms, perceived peer pressure, career goals, and need for achievement;
7. **Macrosystem by objective culture** covers such social indicators as transportation, taxation, energy, and national wealth and security;
8. **Macrosystem by subjective culture** contains cultural norms, values, taboos, and sex roles;
9. **Geopolitical system by objective culture** reflects various kinds of indices occurring through international interactions such as trade, conflicts, and travel; and
10. **Geopolitical system by subjective culture** represents various international stereotypes, cultural exchanges, and international ethics.

Each individual's background characteristics as mentioned above are identifiable through various sources. These characteristics usually determines the individual's competence and performance in interaction with other people. Generally speaking, each individual's behavioral patterns in normal life situations are predictable in terms of his/her background characteristics. Furthermore, members of any social group tend to share similar characteristics on the same issues that enable them to develop common goals, objectives, and activity patterns.

On the other hand, members from two different culture groups (which may be broadly defined in terms of race, age, sex, or other social issues) may have different background characteristics. In intergroup interactive situations, such differences frequently become stressful factors that might bring strain, conflicts, or prejudices.

Long-Term Stressors

Subjective background characteristics of each individual are acquired through a continuous social learning process in all five ecological environments. When some permanent changes occur at an ecological level, the changes may influence the stability of the subjective culture of the individual. For example, the loss of a job may induce changes in a person's value system and confidence in future job performance.

When an individual's objective characteristics change, they also become long-term stressors that may require new adaptations. These changes may be due to natural or accidental causes, such as the aging process or an unexpected physical handicap. Like subjective stressors, these objective changes also contribute to the development of aggressive behaviors.

Under usual circumstances, individuals have developed adaptive behaviors and habits as part of background characteristics that will facilitate "normal" interactions with the social environment. They will also facilitate a reasonable control of long-term stressors. This is especially true where the individual's baseline characteristics are compatible to the external circumstances in routine life situations.

Short-Term Stressors

Under some circumstances, the individual's life situation may undergo abrupt and possibly severe changes that require urgent behavioral adaptations (e.g. breaking in a new job or visiting a foreign country). Such changes are usually temporary in time and can occur in any one of the ten culture ecology units. These changes can be referred to as **short-term stressors.**

There are several measurement instruments that have been developed to evaluate the impact of various short-term stressors on the individual's mental health and coping behaviors. For example, Holmes and Rahe (1967) developed the Social Adjustment Rating Scale in which 43 stressors (life events) are ranked in order of their "life change units" (severity of stress-producing level). The events of death of spouse and divorce are the two highest units on the life change scale, whereas the events of vacation, Christmas, and minor violations of the law are at the bottom of the list.

When short-term stressors (life events) occur, they represent a "deviation" or "interruption" in the individual's routine behavioral patterns. **Deviation** implies an unusual change from expected characteristics of the individual or environment. Deviation changes can take a favorable or unfavorable direction. **Interruption** on the other hand implies the change from the current status to some new behavioral pattern. In either case, the individual, and possibly the environment, is required to change in order to overcome the acute nature of the short-term stressor.

Trend Coping Mechanisms

Each individual develops a set of behavioral strategies (mechanisms) from repeated coping with long-term and short-term stressors in life history. Theoretically, how well a persons's trend coping mechanisms work can be evaluated in terms of their capability to resolve various "pressures" in daily lives; whether new or old, familiar or unfamiliar, and/or similar or dissimilar events. When facing old, familiar, and generally similar situations, these mechanisms will automatically respond. When facing new, unfamiliar, and dissimilar short-term stressors, the individual usually uses cognitive and affective evaluation systems to determine if trend coping mechanisms can be applied to each short-term stressor.

Cognitive Evaluation System

Human cognition controls the processes of information identification, appraisal, and integration. According to Tzeng (1977), the process of human judgement involves at least three major elements: (1) the **individual** making the judgement, (2) the **objects** (events or stressors) being judged, and (3) the **criteria** the individual uses in making judgements. For any domain of life situations (e.g. cognitions about kinships) the individual formulates **implicit theories** about them. These theories serve as internal criteria in judgment of the objects or events involved.

With respect to any new short-term stressor, the individual will first employ relevant implicit theories to assess the nature and conditions of the stressors in order to select relevant coping mechanisms for responses. This cognitive evaluation process involves three major functions: (1) **appraisal** of the stressors in reference to the existing implicit theories in order to derive some meanings for the stressors; (2) **integration** of meanings of the **new** stressors and the **old** life experiences; and (3) **expectations** about the stressors in terms of their strengths, weaknesses, progressions, and consequences.

Again, the cognitive system is developed through long-term interactions with environments and situations. This system is relatively stable in time and space under normal social circumstances. However, when social ecologies change over time, they are also subject to continuous modifications.

Affective Evaluation System

This system represents the emotional aspect of evaluation about stressors and related issues. Like the cognitive system, the affective system is developed from lifelong learning processes through interactions with other individuals and objects (events, situations, and external environments).

The role of the affective evaluation system in human behavior has been investigated indepth by Osgood (Osgood, Miron & May, 1975). In the context of human aggression and violence, three affective components, identified by Osgood, are directly relevant: (1) **evaluation** is the attitude toward objects and events classified as **good** or **bad, desirable** or **undesirable,** and **nice** or **awful;** (2) **potency** refers to the intensity and strength of things being **potent** or **impotent, strong** or **weak,** and **heavy** or **light;** and (3) **activity** refers to the occurring frequency of things in life experiences identified as **active** or **passive, fast** or **slow,** and **noisy** or **quiet.** These three affective components play an important role in evaluating baseline characteristics, short-term stressors, and coping mechanisms.

Furthermore, human affect system generates three behavioral dispositions: (1) **approach,** the positive and readiness tendency in endorsing certain overt behaviors; (2) **retreat,** the passive tendency in withdrawing involvement from a given situation; and (3) **attack,** the aggressive tendency in attacking the counter parts or situations. Under normal, familiar life situations, the affective system tends to maintain the **approach** disposition. But under the pressures of severe short-term stressors, the individual might **retreat** or **attack,** depending upon what outcome was expected from the cognitive as well as affective evaluation systems.

Usually the attack disposition is the emotional arousal that generates such feelings as **anger, contempt, disdain,** and **hate.** These emotions have been frequently reported as causal factors in human aggression and violence. On the other hand, the retreat disposition is the emotional inhibition that might generate such passive emotions as **fear, shame, self-pity** and **grief.** These emotions have frequently been considered as major symptoms of depression and social withdrawal.

Social aggression and violence have been associated directly with **attack;** however, suicide and self-targeted destructive behavior can be linked with both **attack** and **retreat.** Specifically, suicide has been considered in the literature as an inward-oriented, aggressive behavior that might come from a global frustration in life. In addition, suicide has also been believed to be the ultimate means of escaping from reality. Such retreating behavior is the direct consequence of inhibition from the **approach** emotions of desire, affection, curiosity, and pride.

Therefore, to understand the generative process of human behavior, it is important to assess the nature and characteristics of the affective system of each individual or group. In short, the assessments should be done in reference to three affective components (evaluation, potency, and activity) and three behavioral dispositions (approach, retreat, and attack) toward general social environments and specific stressors.

Behavioral Dispositions

In facing an unfamiliar short-term stressor, the individual may have to produce new adaptations quickly. When this happens, the cognitive evaluation system identifies the intellectual/knowledge aspects of the conditions in relation to various baseline characteristics and trend coping mechanisms. The result from this cognitive evaluation forms strategies and procedures for overt coping behaviors. The **intended action** from this process is represented by the term **behavioral disposition** in the model.

This behavioral disposition is further facilitated positively or negatively by the affective evaluation system that will characterize the disposition as being good or bad, strong or weak, and active or passive. As a result, the individual tends to display either approach, attack, or withdrawal behavior.

Behavioral Habits

Behavior is made up of **routine responses** to familiar stimuli and situations. These responses range from the abstract level of mental activities to the concrete level of physical routines such as walking styles and physical gestures. Generally speaking, routine responses can be categorized in terms of: (1) the individual's familiarity with the stimulus, (2) the occurrance frequency of stimulus in general life situations, (3) the individual's response patterns under normal circumstances, and (4) the generality of the stimulus to other stimulus conditions. The linkage between stimuli and routine responses will increase when the stimulus is repeated frequently and is much like other familiar stimuli.

Such behavioral linkage is called a **trend habit.** Theoretically, all individuals have developed many trend habits in life situations. These habits will monitor all behavioral disposition after they are formed in response to various stimuli (or short-term stressors). The monitoring functions of a habit will intensify, neutralize, or block any intended action. Therefore, it is useful to identify the habits that a person responds with under specific situations and stimuli. Furthermore, if habits can be categorized, they can help in the evaluation, interpretation, and prediction of a person's aggressive behaviors.

Overt Coping Behaviors

Behavioral dispositions can be manifested through observable coping behaviors that are either verbal or nonverbal. These overt behaviors can be explained in terms of a four step hierarchy of human aggression: (1) **competition,** (2) **intrusion,** (3) **dominance,** and (4) **violence.** Labeling these coping behaviors depends upon the norm value of the community at the ecological level. For example, each family has its own values and expectations of behavior; each community has its own **rules of thumb** for relationships between people and groups; and each culture group has its own verbal and nonverbal **standards** for behavior.

The individual adapts to the environment when his/her observable behaviors agree with norm values of higher ecological levels. Disagreement between individual values and community values may mean that the individual needs to adjust within the environment. Of course, both individual behaviors and social norms may change continuously over time which means the definitions of the four levels of social aggressiveness behavior will change as well. Because an individual's overt behavior is usually stable over time, it is possible to trace the individual's adaptation mechanisms across different ecological levels.

Social Institutional Consequences

The behavioral norms, values and expectations for a group within a society can be identified. This is true even if the individual members vary in terms of economic status and political orientation. The identified norms, values, and expectations become the groups' standards for accepting specific behaviors. These standards can be formal such as laws, regulations, and rules, or can be informally passed through generations such as customs and traditions.

Each social institution at the individual, family, community, and cultural levels has its own standards for behavior. Standards of all the levels are not necessarily the same because they continually vary with time. Because of this variance, an individual's behavior is always compared to standards of higher ecological levels. For example, in **social evolution,** the standards are developed from the lower levels; but in **societal functions,** the standards are controlled and monitored by the processes of higher levels.

In the processes of setting standards, the behaviors of an individual can be controlled by social reinforcement systems. Social consequences of these behaviors can be separated into three general categories: (1) **"acceptable" approach behaviors** that are within the normal range of the standards of a given ecological level, (2) **"offensive" attack behaviors** that vary in levels of aggression and violence, and (3) **"insufficient" retreat behaviors** such as withdrawal, passivity and inhibition. These behaviors are usually labeled to help describe them. For example, **good, pleasant, and smart** describe acceptable behaviors; **agitating, frustrating, and rude** describe offensive behaviors; and **naive, timid, and insane** are used to describe insufficient behaviors.

Given feedback, an individual can increase a behavior or change the mechanism that controls the dispositions of behavior. Feedback from all ecological levels, therefore, can determine the direction and force of social movement in general. This could especially affect patterns of social norms, values, and expectations about interactions between people.

Relationships Between Components

Each of the ten components in Figure I-1 is independent regarding its structure, role, and content. On the other hand, all the components work together to determine an individual's behavior. By working together, components provide: (1) continuity in the content of components, (2) sequence of behavioral processes over time, (3) equal importance of all the components, and (4) integration of their functions.

These ten components are categorized into four **operational phases** in Figure I-1. These phases correspond with how daily life experiences are handled, including acute short-term stressors that might lead to aggression and violence. These phases are:

1. **Supporting baseline characteristics** which include background characteristics and long-term stressors;
2. **Antecedent Stimuli** such as short-term stressors;
3. **Behavioral Adaptations and Mechanisms** that includes cognitive evaluation system, affective evaluation system, trend coping mechanisms, behavioral dispositions, and behavioral habits; and
4. **Coping Behavior and Consequences** that includes overt coping behavior and social institutional consequences.

This model is comprehensive, dynamic, and process-oriented, and it can be applied to general social behaviors. It can explain **normal** circumstances as well as **deviant** functions of·different social institutions. Because this model proposes to handle the issues at different ecological levels at the same time, it can be applied to **individual** dispositions and to behaviors of **social institutions**. This includes handling issues at the microsystem, exosystem, and macrosystem levels. How the model can be applied to child abuse and neglect is illustrated in the following sections.

PSYCHOSEMANTIC PROCESS FOR CHILD ABUSE

There are a variety of conflicting, controversial, and difficult issues that affect the efforts to attack child abuse and neglect problems. These problems are briefly summarized and then explained in terms of the Psychosemantic Process Model.

Child abuse and neglect is a widespread social problem that affects all kinds of family structures and all parts of the population. This is true regardless of individual differences in cultural background, geographic location, or economic status. Statistics indicate that from one to six million children are abused and neglected each year in the United States (American Humane Society, 1986; Kempe & Helfer, 1972; Wolfe, 1985). Child abuse and neglect incidents are not dropping, but are increasing at an alarming rate. This is the case even though all fifty states have developed strict laws and reporting systems, and have increased money spent for child welfare and protection services. These increases clearly show the need for reassessment of basic issues about the etiologies and phenomena of child abuse and neglect problems at all ecological levels.

Many definitions of the term **abuse and neglect** have been reported in child maltreatment research. None, however, are accepted by everyone and none are free of ambiguity. This is because definitions are not comparable or reliable, and they lack operational standards. For example, the Federal Child Abuse Prevention and Treatment Act of 1974 defined maltreatment as "the physical or mental injury, sexual abuse, negligent treatment, or maltreatment of a child under the age of 18."

Some researchers have further categorized the specifications, by act of commission (abuse) and omission (neglect), (Halperin, 1979; Watkins & Bradbard 1982). These categories are: physical, sexual and emotional abuse; physical, medical, emotional, and educational neglect; abandonment; and multiple maltreatments that involve more than one type. Both federal and state definitions provide working guidelines for various public and private agencies to follow. However, because it is difficult to define terms such as **chronic** and **severe**, child abuse and neglect terminology remains well known for its complexity and ambiguity.

Application to the Psychosemantic Process Model

Definitions associated with the Psychosemantic Process Model focus on the maltreatments of children by adults or institutions at the **microsystem** and **exosystem** levels. Victimized children suffer **abnormal development** both **subjectively** (mentally) and **objectively** (physically). While abuse is usually the end result of the **attack** disposition, neglect is the end result of the **retreat** disposition. When considering the terms that are difficult to define, such as **chronic** or **severe**, the model suggests identifying factors in the repertoire of both victims and offenders that could be the cause. These factors can also be identified by both **subjective** and **objective** **indicators**.

Baseline Characteristics and Antecedent Stimulus

Two types of persons directly involved in child abuse and neglect are **victimized children** and **abusive adults**. Both of these types may be explained in terms of their objective and subjective baseline characteristics in the four ecological environments.

The objective characteristics of **victimized children** may include age, sex, physical health, medical history, behavioral patterns, siblings, and relationship to the abusive adult. Subjective characteristics may include intellectual levels, emotional maturity, developmental characteristics, and behavior patterns.

The objective characteristics of **abusive adults** include occupation, income, marital status, age, sex, family structures, childhood experiences, parenting competency, and relationship to the victimized child. Subjective characteristics include mental development, emotional condition, health, childhood experiences, values, beliefs, personality, and how they perceive themselves as a parent.

Baseline characteristics and short-term stressors that are directly related to child abuse and neglect must be identified to understand the nature of child maltreatment. Important baseline characteristics include family backgrounds, community activities, socioeconomic status, value systems, religion, and chemical substance use. Short-term stressors can include crises in physical, mental, and economic conditions as well as crises in other microsystem-related issues.

Interactions between baseline characteristics create specific **antecedent stimulus conditions** that may cause child abuse and neglect to occur. Study of the relationships between baseline characteristics and how they control individuals is important for a comprehensive understanding of the phenomena and etiologies of child abuse and neglect.

Components of Behavioral Adaptations, Mechanisms, and Social Consequences

It is necessary to observe behavioral adaptations and coping mechanisms of adults and children in their related microsystem to explain the processes involved in all components in the model. This identification must be done before intervention and treatment of child maltreatment. To accomplish this, the model defines **six** components under Phase 3 (Behavioral Adaptation and Mechanisms) and Phase 4 (Coping Behavior and Consequences) in Figure I-1. How these components can be used with aggressive or violent acts against children is explained here.

Identify Trend Coping Mechanisms

An adult may behave aggressively toward a child for reasons that fall into two categories: (a) frustration with the child's behavior, and (b) frustration with the adult's own short-term or long-term stressors. In either case, the abusive adult responds violently because his/her trend coping mechanisms are not sufficient or proper. Reasons for insufficient coping mechanisms include rigid standards for the child that are set by the parent, an inconsistent tolerance level for the child's behavior, or a wrong association between the adult's role in the exosystem and the role with the child in the microsystem (e.g. a submissive role in occupation may cause a parent to have an over-domineering role in the family).

Prevention and intervention of child abuse and neglect must deal with helping adults to develop sufficient and proper trend coping mechanisms. This development is especially important when it is the major reason for the abuse or neglect.

Cognitive and Affective Evaluation Systems

For some individuals, short-term stressors preoccupy the evaluation systems in daily life. When this happens, the thinking process in interactions with peers and children is not **normal**. As a result, undesirable emotions may easily occur which generate **attack** or **retreat** affective dispositions.

These processes are based on long-term social learning. Because of this, it is important to study the repertoire of the cognitive and affective systems for those individuals who fall in different typologies of child abuse and neglect. This must be done in order to identify why the cognitive and affective evaluations were processed as they were and what effect this had on coping behavior.

The Psychosemantic Process Model looks at the importance of cultures or groups being alike in cognitive and affective evaluations. It is desirable and possible to separate child abuse and neglect cases into many subgroups in terms of one, more, or all components used in the model. This can be done so that characteristics of individuals can further be separated into **victimization profiles**. This can help develop effective methods and strategies for intervention, treatment, and prevention of child abuse and neglect.

Behavioral Dispositions

The idea of **isomorphic attributes** between individuals that are involved in interactions has been used to help identify the contents and dynamics of communication. This is much the same in dealing with child abuse and neglect problems. The reactions of different adults to the same short-term stressors are usually guided by different implicit theories and behavioral dispositions. It is important to understand why certain aggressive behavior happens and how it can be corrected. As mentioned in the Psychosemantic Process Model, behavioral dispositions are the end result of cognitive integration and decoding processes. In order to stop **violent** dispositions, behavioral dispositions across individuals in different neglect or abusive categories must be separated and understood.

Behavioral Habits

There are different categories reported for abusive or neglected conditions of children. For example, some cases were labeled as being in the **habitual abuser** category. This category suggests that many behavioral habits of aggression and violence exists in the family structure. Furthermore, some aspect of the neglect problem is habitual in nature (e.g. malnutrition of children due to the parents' unhealthy habits of food intake). Because of this, behavioral habits are perhaps the easiest to detect in their association with child abuse and neglect problems. They are also the easiest to focus on for correction under the paradigm of behavior modification.

Under some unusual circumstances, an individuals' behavior can be habitually influenced by chemical substances. Psychoactive drugs or alcohol may be used as a way to cope with long-term or short-term stressors. However, the effect of using such substances frequently causes behavioral habits to appear in relation to the environment, including children. In some cases, this kind of behavioral habit may be aggressive and violent in nature. It would seem that removing the chemical substance would reverse the inappropriate behavior. However, this does not always remove the cause or existence of the stressors that initiated the chemical abuse. Therefore, only a change of behavioral habits may not be sufficient for long-term intervention or treatment of abusive adults.

Overt Coping Behaviors

A medical model has been used frequently to identify the types and severities of child abuse and neglect incidents. The judicial system, on the other hand, focuses on the abusive consequences in mental and physical damages. Both models stress identification of incidents and treatment of damages done to the children.

The Psychosemantic Process Model goes further than identification and treatment of damages. It attempts to find the possible **causes** and other **variables** that contribute to child maltreatment. In other words, the model stresses the understanding of roles and functions of all components in the model that are directly or indirectly related to the observable behavior of child abuse and neglect.

Social Institutional Consequences

The problems of child abuse and neglect have immediate and direct negative effects on the well-being of the children and adults involved. These problems also have long-term impacts on the development of harmony and prosperity at other ecological levels. These levels would include, the microsystem of family, exosystem of communities, and macrosystem of culture. History has shown that many social happenings are related to the unhappy childhoods of the individuals involved. Many cases in mental hospitals are also directly related to bad experiences in childhood.

Sexual abuse in particular has been reported to create the worst effect on adjustment of the victimized child later in life. This could effect the child both as an individual and as a member of institutions at different ecological levels. The most common effects include unsatisfactory marital life, inadequate parenting, and mistrust of social institutions. In any case, the social institutional consequences of child abuse and neglect are broad issues that are complex. It is necessary to define the whole picture of social institutional consequences. This must be done in order to identify the etiology, dynamics, and treatment for child abuse problems.

The Psychosemantic Process Model presented in Figure I-1 is made up of **four phases** of working procedures that should be followed in studying any child abuse and neglect problems. These phases are:

1. **Identification of baseline characteristics** that focus on the background characteristics and long-term stressors components;
2. **Identification of antecedent stimuli** that are defined by the short-term stressors;
3. **Investigation of the behavioral adaptation and mechanisms** that consists of five components (trend coping mechanisms, cognitive and affective evaluation systems, behavioral dispositions, and behavioral habits); and
4. **Categorization of coping behavior and consequences** that include overt coping behaviors, and social institutional consequences.

For the first two phases, each component should be further separated in terms of different topics under the ten **culture ecology units** defined by the five ecological levels and two types of cultures. Each component in the third and fourth phases has its own properties that should be dealt with independently, at the same time, and indepth. However, all the components in the model are functionally related and work with the roles and functions of the other components. They should be dealt with as integral parts of a single, process-oriented operational program.

Dynamics of Child Abuse and Neglect from Ecological Perspectives

From a social behavioral science point of view, child abuse and neglect are socially undesirable behaviors that involve the issues pertaining to a simple question of **who did what to whom**. The term **who** represents the individuals and/or institutions that act undesirable behaviors against children, the term **what** represents the undesirable behaviors manifested by the offenders against the children, the term **whom** represents the children who are victimized by the offenders. Each of these three terms; **who, what,** and **whom**; represents a significant domain of issues involved in the child abuse and neglect literature. They can be further delineated as follows:

1. Who: Offenders

As shown in Figure I-2, there are three general types of **offenders** that might be responsible for child abuse and neglect:

a. **System offenders**. Within each social ecology where children reside, there are numerous institutional systems that assist, govern, or monitor social behaviors and interactions (e.g. systems of education, welfare, transportation, health, marriage, religion, law enforcement, and economical structures, etc.). Each system has a significant impact on the individual members within the system, and also on other systems. Therefore, each system can positively serve the individuals and families, and also possibly generate negative impacts on some families and/or individuals which might lead to the direct or indirect consequences of child abuse or neglect.

b. **Program offenders**. Within each public and/or private social institution or system, there are always some kinds of ongoing programs (projects) that will generate impacts on individuals and other institutions. For example, within a child abuse and neglect crisis center, some programs may be for volunteer participation, parents anonymous activities, parenting assistance, or respite care for children. Of course, the intent of the general assistance program is always positive, but the consequence of the program implementation may not be always beneficial to all families and individuals involved. Due to various reasons, the objective of some

CONCEPTUAL INQUIRIES ABOUT CHILD ABUSE AND NEGLECT

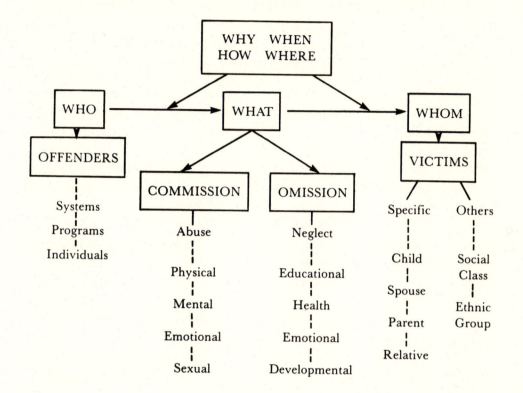

Figure I-2

programs may miss the anticipated remediation or improvement of some social problems related to children. Under such circumstances, improper or misguided program implementations may result in institutional offenses against children.

c. **Individual offenders.** The incident of child victimization is always associated with identifiable individuals who are directly responsible for the abusive or neglectful acts. These individuals may be family members, relatives, or workers in child service/education institutions. Additionally, other individuals who have no family or child care relationships may also be responsible for abusive acts against children (e.g. sexual abuse, physical and/or verbal attacks from strangers). Furthermore, according to child protection codes in most states, people who witness child abuse incidents are punishable if they do not report to proper child protection authorities. These individuals according to law are **responsible** for child victimization even though they do not contribute the direct abusive act.

2. What: Types of Offenses

While child abuse is the result of **commission** (action) of undesirable/unacceptable behaviors against children, neglect is the result of **omission** (inaction) of necessary behaviors for the benefit of children. It is clear that between active commission and passive omission, there is a continuum of behaviors that involve the interactions between children and adults (or child care/education institutions). On this continuum, excessive behaviors are not permissible (e.g. over punishment of children for running outside during the cold weather), whereas excessive inaction is equally harmful to children (e.g. letting children be exposed to cold for long periods of time without proper intervention).

Between abuse and neglect, there is a range of acceptable and desirable behaviors that are needed for the benefit of children. Therefore, the issue becomes apparent; where are the critical points to differentiate between acceptable and unacceptable behaviors on the part of adults and institutions? In most state laws, there are general criteria regarding the unacceptable abusive or neglectful behaviors against children. Victimization of such behaviors results in the so-called "children in need of services" (CHINS) code of law that requires the intervention and protection of children from various public protection services.

Therefore, adults in families and care institutions have a definite responsibility to take action within a certain permissible limit according to law for the well-being of children. Any individual working in child education, protection, and care institutions should know those requirements for performing such duties and also know their limits of activities related to children.

Due to the multifaceted nature of child development and behavioral needs, the types of abuse and neglect (the issue of **what**) can be broadly categorized in five areas: physical/health, emotional, educational, sexual, and social. Comprehensive presentation and intervention programs for child abuse and neglect should address these areas of needs simultaneously.

3. Whom: Victimizations

Generally speaking, child victimization of abuse and neglect involves two types of target persons; self and others. While **self-victimization** may be due to environmental stress from physical, mental, or emotional difficulties; victimization of others may be the result of inappropriate background characteristics and the inability of the perpetrator to adjust to norms of higher ecological levels. As discussed earlier, short-term stressors of the individual, either due to real or imaginary circumstantial conditions, may trigger the abusive or neglectful reactions that might be further intensified by improper coping behaviors and habits. On the issue of child abuse and neglect, a child's self-victimization (e.g. head-banging among emotionally disturbed children) is rarely reported. In fact, in most states it is **not** considered as a legal problem.

On the other hand, **victimization of others** can be divided into two subcategories: (a) specific individuals as target victims (e.g. children, spouse, old aged parents, siblings, and specific individuals in an institution), and (b) social classes or groups in a certain ecological system (e.g. victimization against a certain ethnic, low social economic, or the aged group). Child abuse and neglect is mostly under the subcategory of victimization against specific individual children. But it is also possibly under the subcategory of institutional maltreatment against all children (e.g. all children of a certain day care facility might suffer abuse and/or neglect under the maltreatment of system, program, and/or individual caretakers).

From a strictly behavioral point of view, the purpose of intervention is simply to sever the linkage of **who did what to whom;** the elimination of commission of abuse or omission of neglect (what) between the two counterparts **who and whom.**

Unfortunately, statistics have repeatedly suggested that the reoccurrence of child abuse and neglect had its recursive origin from the adult's own victimization in early age. It also has long-term impacts of the child's own abusive dispositions against the next generation. Therefore, it is clear that intervention of child abuse and neglect requires a comprehensive investigation of other important issues as proposed in the Psycho-semantic Model. That is, we have to address other issues surrounding the **who did what to whom** linkage. The issues include: (a) **why** the offender acts or doesn't act in certain ways, (b) **how** the incidents of child abuse and neglect occur, and (c) **where** and **when** the maltreatments happen. In short, we should address all of the issues that would answer the questions pertaining to **who, what, whom, why, when, how,** and **where** on child abuse and neglect incidents.

Five Intervention Approaches to Child Abuse and Neglect

The pervasiveness and severity of child abuse and neglect problems have aroused significant public and private attentions to the prevention, intervention, and treatment issues. There are five general models that have been most popularly used. They are briefly described as follows:

1. Psychiatric Model

This approach assumes that maltreating parents are abnormal or mentally ill. Traditionally, general neurotic or psychotic personality was considered to be a strong etiological factor in child abuse. Now, however, most researchers consider only the most violent parents to be psychotic. Followers of this model do agree that abusive parents have some type of personality defect that allows aggressive impulses to be expressed. Attempts at pinpointing the actual source of these aggressive impulses have been unsuccessful.

Generally, abusing parents were reported to have some abuse and/or neglect history in their own childhood. Raised without love and nurturance, maltreating parents are incapable of extending such protective care to their offspring. Therefore, the validity of the Psychiatric Model has been questioned in the literature because national statistics indicate that less than 15% of offenders have mental emotional difficulties. The remaining major proportion of incidents are due to other factors.

2. Sociological Model

This approach focuses on the causality of economic disparities, social instability, and functional deficiencies in the community rather than on the causality of individual differences among parents. Underlying this model are three basic assumptions:

a. Poor housing, unemployment, and lack of material resources are major contributing factors to higher incidents of abuse and neglect;

b. Child abuse in American society is partly due to the cultural sanction of physical force to resolve interpersonal conflicts; and

c. Parental stress and frustration in occupation and in maintenance of household generates unhealthy coping behaviors against family members especially young children.

Consequently, attempt has been made by various government agencies to improve social disparity issues (e.g. development of racially balanced urban housing projects, school desegregation and employment quota for minorities).

3. Situational Model

Child abuse and neglect are viewed as the result of compound effects or unhealthy parent and child personalities, patterns of reciprocal interactions among family members, and environmental stresses impinging on the family unit. This model stresses that abusive patterns may be the by-products of **physically punitive** and **inconsistent discipline techniques.** Parents who readily administer low-intensity corporal punishment in a disciplinary context may be prone to accelerate the intensity of punishment when confronted with the stress and frustration surrounding a highly volatile, anger-eliciting situation.

Furthermore, parental punishment is frequently divorced from the alleged misbehavior, and the reasons parents give for the severity of the discipline are often illogical and inappropriate. Characteristics of children that are more likely to be the target for maltreatment include: premature births, low birth weight, physical appearance, temperament, reactions to parents (children who react with defiance), and age (the older child being more susceptible to abuse).

4. Criminal Model

This approach emphasizes the prospect of criminal justice. Child abuse and neglect are considered to be the manifestations of criminal behaviors of the offenders. The offenders are assumed to display deviant behavioral conducts that are inconsistent with the social norms. Such deviant acts that violate the rights of children, may occur in various social situations and stimulus encounters. To maintain law and order of a given society, this model addresses the establishment of criteria and mechanisms to punish the unlawful act and/or isolate the offenders from the general public.

5. Legal Model

This approach emphasizes the rights of parents as the appropriate guardians of the minor. Within the acceptable limit of parenting, including discipline, the parent's right to have full guardianship for the child is protected according to law. On the other hand, the violation of proper guardianship (e.g. substantiated abuse and neglect), might result in readjustment or reassignment of guardianship for the child.

In many cases, child abuse and neglect by a parent frequently results in the separation of parents in divorce proceedings that lead to the subsequent battle over the custody of the child. Termination of parental rights under this model is one of the natural outcomes. Unfortunately, substitution of foster care or new assignment of guardianship (to a single parent or other relatives) frequently generates new and additional adjustment issues for all individuals involved. Such issues may have compound impact on the trauma experiences of the children under abuse and neglect.

Holistic Ecological Approach to Child Abuse and Neglect

It is clear that to address issues on seven "W's," each of the five currently predominant models are not self-sufficient. The incident of child abuse and neglect is well recognized as being pervasive across all types of families regardless of age, sex, race, economic status, education, and marital conditions of the adults. As such, the **psychiatric model** accounts for less than 15% of the incidents; the **social model** can not fully resolve the child abuse and neglect problems by merely working on social disparity issues; and the **situational model** can not predict many clear behavioral consistencies across various situations. The **legal model** usually fails to uphold family continuity and simultaneously fails to eliminate abusive cycles; and the **criminal model** fails to deter the occurrence of over 1.7 million cases per year, and in the meantime, the sheer emphasis on the criminal model would drain tremendous amount of human and economic resources without proven evident of cost efficient consequences.

Therefore, it is imperative to develop an integrated approach that will not only consider the strengths of individual models, but also their constraints and weaknesses. Under this objective, it is possible to identify five **fundamental principles** in combating child abuse and neglect problems within each community:

1. **comprehensiveness** in service functions,
2. **coordination** among all service providing **agencies,**
3. **community-based** development of systems, programs and activities,
4. **children and family centered** approach in implementation of services, and

5. **multidisciplinary** considerations of all issues as represented by the seven "W's."

Under these principles, the major characteristics of human behavioral dispositions and three associated basic emotions are specifically summarized below because of their direct pertinence to the intervention, treatment, and prevention efforts of child care personnel.

1. **Three Basic Behavioral Dispositions and Emotions.** Human behaviors are manifestations of three directional dispositions: (a) **approach**, readiness in positive and spontaneous actions that can be characterized as being friendly, helpful, happy and willing; (b) **attack**, readiness in aggressive or defensive actions that can be characterized as being unfriendly, hostile, critical, and damaging; and (c) **withdrawal**, readiness in retreat or inhibited actions that can be categorized as depressed, indifferent, ignoring, and unhelpful.

2. **Three Emotions.** Manifestation of behaviors through these dispositions are facilitated by three basic emotions that are most frequently cited in the child abuse and neglect literature: (a) **desire**, the positive attitudes toward self, others, and environment that will facilitate the individual's spontaneous and approaching behaviors in acting, reacting, searching, helping, and enjoying; (b) **anger**, the emotional status that derives from frustration or rejection of expressed or implicit desires, which can be characterized in terms of such attitudes as hostile, explosive, hot-tempered, domineering, and single-minded; and (c) **fear**, a status of isolation, depression, and uncertainty that will manifest in such behavioral patterns as inaction, wandering, avoidance, ignorance, and insecurity.

These three emotions are related to the three behavior dispositions in child rearing/disciplinary activities: **desire** elicits active and appropriate parenting behaviors, such as loving, caring, and guiding; **anger**, due to whatever internal/external reasons, might elicit critical, hostile, disciplinary actions that are abusive in nature; and **fear** might elicit passive and withdrawal parenting patterns that can be characterized by indifference, ignorance, and negligence.

Under normal circumstances, each individual (child as well as adult) has these three emotions exhibited in daily life. However, significant individual differences exist in: (1) the tolerance level of accepting rejection (of real or imaginary), (2) the persistence level in persuing desires, and (3) the level of recovering from inhibition and frustration. Due to such differences, each individuals may develop distinct coping behaviors and habits in handling life situations. Therefore, for some individuals, unfulfilled desires and needs might lead to severe frustrations and/or inhibitions that can generate abusive attack or neglectful withdrawal in child rearing practice.

Intervention, prevention, and treatment of child abuse and neglect problems will require indepth analyses of the underlying dynamics between these emotions, dispositions, general coping behaviors, and habits. Analyses of this nature will provide fundamental information to address issues on the previously mentioned seven "W's."

Theoretically, comprehensive analysis of the issues across all abuse and neglect cases will result in profiles for not only different homogeneous subgroups of perpetrators, victims, and offensive acts, but also for clear delineations of specific causalities and dynamics for each subgroup that may have unique profiles surrounding the why, when, where and how issues.

Comprehensive Seven Service Domains

Within each community, it is theoretically possible and also practically desirable to identify common profiles for families and individuals that have similar characteristics related to the seven "W's." With such information, a community-based and child/family-centered planning of programs becomes possible. From our indepth evaluation of the literature regarding the phenomenon, typologies, and social intervention/treatment systems, a comprehensive community network of services is proposed in Figure I-3. This network requires a simultaneous consideration of **seven service domains** as follows:

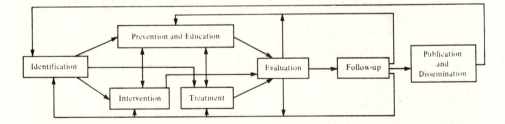

1. **Identification.** The identification domain focuses on the analysis of profiles of victimized children, offenders and their interactions with respect to three areas of the Psychosemantic Model: **background characteristics** (e.g. health and intellectual development of the child); **long-term**

stressors (health problems, emotional difficulties, etc.); and short-term stressors (family crisis related to abuse and neglect). In order to have a comprehensive understanding of all the issues involved, the analysis should involve the subjective and objective aspects of cultures across the ecological levels of individual victimized children and offenders, families, and the occupations and community status of the families. Such information is a prerequisite to the identification of the etiology of child abuse and neglect and also to the development of effective service delivery programs and strategies.

2. **Intervention.** This domain emphasizes the missions of immediate **rescue** of victimized children and also the deterrance of abusive or neglecting circumstances. Many programs have been established for these purposes, such as crisis centers for child care, crisis counseling, volunteer assistance, parent aides, parents anonymous, and telephone hot lines. However, an effective intervention effort will rely on the integration of all community resources across all service and support systems.

3. **Treatment.** This domain calls for the development and implementation of a comprehensive case treatment and management program that will utilize resources from both the public and private sectors (e.g. hospital, mental health centers, schools, juvenile court, child protection services, and private therapists). For this purpose, it is ideal to develop a multidisciplinary community-based treatment network that will coordinate the service functions of all individual providers. Separate efforts can then be united to work for each type of family.

4. **Prevention and education.** Due to individual and family differences as mentioned in the Identification Domain, it is necessary to develop many preventative services such that each will be most efficient for a subtype of victimizations or vulnerabilities. In addition, this domain emphasizes the implementation of various instructional programs for training professionals, paraprofessionals, volunteers, and the community at large regarding the issue of identification, intervention, and treatment of child abuse and neglect.

5. **Evaluation.** This domain includes two types of evaluation: (1) **process evaluation** of all implementation procedures and strategies across all service domains, and (2) **outcome evaluation** of the impact of various programs on changes in individuals, families and the community. For both evaluations, specific criteria should be established such that the degree of success of individual programs can be objectively analyzed.

6. **Follow-up.** Ideal operational procedures for intervention, treatment, and prevention of child abuse and neglect problems are always accompanied with positive changes in an individual's coping mechanisms, dispositions, habits, and overt behaviors. When the procedures are operated with suitability and efficiency, intervention in child abuse and neglect usually yields temporary modification of problematic circumstances. However, in some instances, the individual's habits may not be easy to completely replace with desirable behaviors. In either case, the effort of outcome evaluation is not sufficient to detect recidivism or qualitative improvement in circumstances. Thus it is necessary to follow the course of changes and related consequences on a long-term basis such that the process and outcome evaluations can continue to ensure the permanent improvement of the situation.

7. **Publication and dissemination.** This domain emphasizes the dissemination of the information on contents, issues and operational strategies for all seven domains of services. The literature has been criticized for its lack of comprehensive integration and presentations of all issues involved. Professionals in various service facilities frequently operate under the constraints of partial knowledge and narrow focused strategies. To reverse such deficiencies, it is necessary to integrate knowledge from multidisciplinary perspectives and to disseminate information to all practitioners in different service functions.

Under this premise, the following implementation strategies become important: development of regional resource centers, development of computerized data retrieval systems, organization of a community-based prevention and education network, development of constant in-service training/workshop programs, and publications of documentations in professional journals as well as in public media.

In an ideal community-based service network, the above seven service domains should be independent of each other in their missions, but interdependent in their functions. Therefore, the combination of their missions and functions possess all the necessary properties as advocated in the Psychosemantic Process Model: multidisciplinary orientation, comprehensive programs, coordination network, community-based planning, and family-centered approach.

Overall Plan of Sourcebook

The theoretical backgrounds of the model presented in this chapter are used to identify the content areas of this Sourcebook. In order to integrate the missions and functions of crisis centers within an effective community-based service system, the content areas of this Sourcebook are organized in Table I–II under three broad categories: (1) organizations of care facilities, (2) missions and functions, and (3) legal foundations and the role within the community service system.

TABLE I–II
ORGANIZATION OF BOOK CHAPTERS

Organizations and Facilities	Legal Foundations	Missions and Functions
	Historical Perspectives Ch. 2	
National Survey of Service Facilities Ch. 6	National Trends of State Laws Ch. 4	National Phenomena and Typologies Ch. 3
Establishing a Local Crisis Center Ch. 7	Cooperation Between Community Agencies to Foster Legal Rights of Children Ch. 15	Prevention Through Crisis Intervention Ch. 5
Shelter Care Ch. 8		Counseling Ch. 11
Volunteer Corp. Ch. 9		Emotional Abuse Ch. 12
Kitchen Program Ch. 10		Sexual Abuse Ch. 13, 14

The first category involves the implementation and maintenance of the child abuse and neglect crisis intervention facility. It contains basic information for developing a comprehensive, integrated child crisis shelter and intervention program. Five chapters were used in this Sourcebook to cover five different areas of structures in maintaining a child crisis center.

To identify the general trend of service facilities at the national level, a sample of 53 crisis centers from 26 states were studied indepth. The topics include the availability of the facilities, treatment methods used, staff numbers and content, how often the crisis center's services are evaluated, where their referrals come from, finances, and specific problems that exist. These are important epidemiological data that are important considerations when establishing a child crisis center.

Careful planning and management is necessary for a child crisis center to be a preventive service. The number one purpose of the center should be to create a safe environment for the child as well as a nonthreatening resource that parents can turn to when they recognize a crisis. Other goals of the crisis center include; providing the child with therapeutic aid, referring the child for emotional or medical screening or consultation, helping the parent to obtain assistance, and offering programs and workshops that teach the parent appropriate child care. These facilitative aspects are addressed as well as organizational aspects in the development of a new center such as funding, record keeping, program planning, organizing a Board of Directors and hiring staff.

Segments of a child crisis center include: administration, child care, volunteer staff, kitchen program, counseling and medical services, and maintanence of the center. These topics are introduced in chapter 7 and expanded upon in subsequent chapters, specifically, Chapter 8 (Shelter Care), Chapter 9 (Volunteer Corp.), and Chapter 10 (A Kitchen Program).

Another major column of the proposed plan of this Sourcebook is that of missions and functions. There are six chapters represented in this section beginning with the Phenomenon and Typology of Child Abuse and Neglect. This chapter provides descriptors for the different classifications of abuse and neglect that are often used in reporting or state laws.

Accurate reporting and classification of incidents of maltreatment can be a step toward better methods of prevention and intervention concerning identification of target groups, families with abusive potential, and children in danger of being harmed. National statistics of the growing trends in child abuse and neglect are presented and analysed, as well as the responses from child protective agencies. Society as a whole suffers when children are maltreated or families get caught up in abusive cycles. Growing up in such an unstable environment can manifest problems of violent behavior and juvenile delinquency. These topics are discussed in Chapter 3.

The best way to deal with problems of child abuse and neglect is the developing the ability to detect potential abusive behavior before it occurs. The next chapter (Chapter 5) in the missions and functions section of Table I–II introduces prevention in terms of: (1) primary, which is truly preventive measures, (2) secondary, which is stopping abusive cycles in families, and (3) tertiary, which is more accurately termed **intervention**. The child crisis center is noted as being the main source of services for families and children that are in need of respite care or counseling. The following four chapters in this section of Table I-II, (Chapters 11-14), expound upon methods of prevention and intervention used for different typologies of maltreatment (i.e., psychological maltreatment, and sexual abuse).

The third and much smaller category of this model is the **legal foundations** column. These two chapters (Chapters 4 and 15) are placed in the center of the Table to pull the structure together. Chapter 4 presents a summary of all 50 states' laws that deal with child maltreatment. Each state has different definitions of abuse as well as different restrictions within the courtroom and requirements for reporting. This makes cooperation between health professionals, crisis centers, and law enforcement personnel murky at best.

Chapter 15 stresses the need for cooperation between community services which is paramount for efficient, helpful, and individualized services that are to be offered to the child and family in need.

REFERENCES

1. American Human Society: *Highlights of Official Child Neglect and Abuse Reporting; 1984.* Denver, American Humane Association, 1986.
2. Halperin, M.: *Helping Maltreated Children: School and Community Involvement.* St. Louis, C. V. Mosby, 1979.
3. Kempe, C. H., and Helfer, R. E.: *Helping the Battered Child and His Family.* Philadelphia, Lippincott, 1972.
4. Osgood, C. E., Miron, M. S., and May, W. H.: *Cross-Cultural Universals of Affective Meaning.* Urbana, University of Illinois, 1975.
5. Tzeng, O. C. S.: A quantitative method for separation of semantic subspaces. *Applied Psychological Measurement, 1:*171-184, 1977.
6. Watkins, H. D., and Bradbard, M. R.: Child maltreatment: an overview with suggestions for intervention and research. *Family Relations, 31:*323-333, 1982.
7. Wolfe, D. A.: Child-abusive parents: an empirical review and analysis. *Psychological Bulletin, 97*(3):462-482, 1985.

CHAPTER 2

CHILDREN IN PERIL:
HISTORICAL BACKGROUND

Ruth E. Holland

INTRODUCTION

Child abuse has been an ugly phenomenon throughout mankind's written record, It is an age old problem. Early written records have reflected negative attitudes in general. These notations have indicated a prolonged and insidious history of man's cruelty to his progeny. Some of the means used to inflict pain are hard to believe in any century. Many physically abusive practices have ranged from starvation, beatings, scaldings, floggings to electric shocks, cigarette burns and mental tortures of all descriptions. From the beginning of human history to the present time, the abusive behavior toward children has been a continuously complex and emotive problem with which to deal.

Child abuse is not a by-product of the complex **modern** societies. Infants and children have been mistreated, according to recent standards, from the beginning of time. They have been treated as an expendable commodity by parents, caretakers and employers. The willful destruction of newborn babies and children through exposure, abandonment, smothering, starvation, exploitation and various forms of torture has been noted in written and oral records around the world.

HISTORICAL REVIEW

The Father's Decision

In ancient times, infanticide was not a legal matter. It was condoned by those in authority. The magistrates usually left the decision to do away with the new born to the head of the household. The dominant male figure, most often the father, was the absolute authority in all matters. Both groups, clergy and magistrates, gave full support to any decision the

39

head of the family made concerning the children under his jurisdiction. An overview of historical research clearly indicates that fathers frequently committed acts of physical abuse toward children, as well as being more apt to neglect or abandon them (Ryan, 1862). According to Aries (1962), in established institutions, leaders in the power positions have tended to demonstrate a greater insensitivity to the needs and rights of infants and young children.

Early written records often reflected negative attitudes toward children. DeMause (1975), indicated that cruelty to children has been practiced from the dawn of time. According to the Patria Protestas in 700 BC, fathers had a right to sell, mutilate, or kill infants.

In all early societies, infanticide has been regarded as an accepted means of disposing not only of deformed and atypical children, but also those born into families that were poor and ill equipped to handle additional members. From the humane point of view it is very difficult to understand the detached attitude of parents or heads of families toward their offspring. Babies were often regarded as burdens rather than a blessing.

In 450 BC, the Law of Twelve Tables modified the Patria Protestas. Beller and Solomon (1986) indicated, "In any case, there is much evidence to suggest that throughout history, fathers, as compared to mothers, have generally tended to be more neglectful and more physically abusive." A child could only be sold three times. The decision to keep or do away with a child was left to the decision of the father, as he was the responsible head of the family.

In the Beginning

The etiology of the noun **family** carries a revealing curious denotation. Originally the term was derived from **famulus** meaning domestic slave, and **familia** referred to the total number of slaves belonging to one man. This accumulation of a **clan** is the root of today's family. Many centuries passed before the concept changed to mean simply the male and female with their progeny. Until recently, most families, that is, women (wives), concubines, children, servants, and slaves, were literally the possessions of a head of a household.

Biblical References

The harsh treatment of children in ancient societies is an established fact. Cruel treatment is due, in part, to the definitions of children.

According to Walters (1975), **children** are obviously adults. Such references as "children of God," "children of Israel," "son of man," and "daughters of my people," further obscures the definition of young children. However, there are instances where many children, as well as adults, were made to suffer death. I Samuel 15 refers to the slaying of "both man and woman, child and suckling." This identical command was made in early civilizations, toward other peoples such as the Assyrians, Moabites, Canaanites and so on.

The book of Judges relates the story of Jephthah's victory over the Ammonites. A vow was made to slay the first person he saw upon his return home. With victory behind him, he met his only daughter and she was sacrificed. Other references to the slaying of first born children are found elsewhere in the Old Testament. The Feast of the Passover, as explained in Exodus 12:12, commemorates the passing of the plagues and "smiting the firstborn in the Land of Egypt, both man and beast".

References in the twenty-sixth chapter of Leviticus foretell of families being forced to eat the flesh of sons and daughters. Conditions of debilitating famine was the background for other references to children being boiled and eaten (II Kings, chapter 6).

Biblical examples have influenced child rearing practices in western civilizations. The basic concept that the infliction of pain was necessary for proper moral training has been widely accepted. "Thou shalt beat him with the rod, and shalt deliver his soul from hell," is an adage which has been an avid part of child rearing practice for centuries. Another biblical reference used by strict disciplinarians is, "He that spareth the rod, hateth his son: but he that loveth him chasteneth him betimes." For many centuries the prevailing belief and customs favored severe physical punishment as a necessary means to: (1) maintain discipline, (2) transmit educational, cultural, moral and religious ideas, (3) please certain gods, or (4) expel evil spirits (Radhill, 1974).

Whipping children has always been the prerogative of civic leaders, as well as parents, Justice (1976) used the term **cultural scripting** to describe the accepted patterns of interaction between individuals. The spoken and unspoken scripts have historically condoned child maltreatment between children and adults. A scriptural allusion in reference to Nimrod, King of Babylonia, learned that a boy born in Mesopotamia, would rule the country. He subsequently called for the death of 70,000 boys in an attempt to prevent this from occurring. This epitomizes the scripting idea.

In ancient cultures, children were considered miniature adults, thus they were entreated to honor and obey their parents and elders. Those who did not were destined to suffer grave consequences. Several biblical references are quite clear on this matter. In Second Kings, mention is made of Elisha going to Bethel and some children came out and mocked him. After he reprimanded the culprits, two bears came out of the wilderness and mutilated the youngsters. The book of Deuteronomy reminds parents of the custom of dealing with rebellious offspring. The men of the city would stone them to death, if they failed to obey.

Abuse: The Greek Connection

In ancient Greek history there are numerous notations of violence toward children. Many adult citizens tended to perceive children as an economic drain on the culture in general. In parts of Greek literature, the matter of infanticide is alluded to in some pronouncements by Aristotle. He wrote, "The justice of a master or father is a different thing from that of a citizen, for a son or a slave is property and there can be no injustice to one's own property," (Russell, 1945).

The early Greeks justified the killing of defective children. There was little regard for human life, and licentious procedures which allowed the destruction of defective children was commonplace. Socially unacceptable infants were frequently left exposed to the elements. Aristotle, as well as other prominent leaders, accepted the idea of killing retarded or deformed babies as a way of strengthening the society (Radhill, 1974).

With limited resources, the problem of increased population was a continual source of concern of the city/state leaders. The consequences of this policy makes it difficult to recapture the relative insensitivity of parents toward their newborn. Aristotle contended that the size of the population should be limited by law (Hands, 1986). In this way, abortion could be controlled and was preferable to other forms of infanticide as a method of controlling the size of the population.

Seneca and Phiny, the Elder saw nothing unreasonable about attempting to control and regulate the number of people in the city slums. The practice of abandoning infants was a sure way of regulating the number of citizens. Plato reflected the idea that population control should be approached by regulating sexual behavior. This was considered, and in some instances, implemented. This not only controlled the population, but would tend to **insure** a more perfect human body (Plato, Jowett Translation, 1937).

Abuse: The Roman Connection

The practice of the Hellenistic Greeks influenced the Roman attitudes in the matter also. According to legend, Rome itself was founded by two abandoned children, Romulus and Remus. Unwanted children continued to be disposed of in ways which the Romans found acceptable. Many families were overtly struck in a perennial state of hopelessness. Consequently, it followed that family masters thought it altogether natural that they should protect themselves from further responsibility.

Following the Greek pattern, many infants especially females, were either abandoned, drowned, or thrown over the nearest cliff. Gibbon (1932), denounced this exposure of children as, "the prevailing and stubborn vice of antiquity."

As noted earlier, the Patria Patestas gave a Roman father the legal right to sell, abandon, kill or offer in sacrifice some or all of his children. In 450 BC, the Law of Twelve Tables modified the Patria Protestas so a child could be sold only three times. During the time of the Caesars, children's eyes were gouged out to make them more realistic beggars. By AD 1, the fate of children had changed very little, as evidenced by the biblical account of the hostile action of King Herod against the newly born male children of that period.

The European Connection

The bloody practice of infanticide was slow to change. European cultures perpetuated the exploitation of children, although some deviations in attitude came with the advent of Christianity. Religious leaders were influenced by Judaic Law, which denounced and discouraged the exposure of children as murder. The clergy in Europe proclaimed infanticide as a pagan practice and insisted that all human life was more or less sacred.

Although the attitude of the Christian Emperors was ambivalent, Langer (1974), reports that in 318 AD, "The Emperor Constantine declared the slaying of a son or daughter by a father to be a crime." Only at the end of the fourth century it was noted that the Emperors Valentinian, Valene and Gratian made infanticide a crime punishable by death.

A more humane attitude toward the treatment of infants was gradually adopted, however slowly. The progressive depopulation of Europe, due to devastating plagues and epidemics, reoccurring famines and frequent wars, both **holy and non-holy,** helped to limit the population growth. Now there was no need to practice infanticide. On the contrary, large families were now encouraged by both church and civic leaders.

Although child murder was diminishing, the Middle Ages are noted for the continued practices of infanticide. Lecky (1869) indicates, "It was practiced on a gigantic scale with absolute immunity." The practice was noted with most frigid indifference, and at least in the case of destitute parents, it was considered a very venial offense.

In order to deal more effectively with the problem of infanticide during the Middle Ages, authorities attempted to regulate death by suffocation by discouraging parents of sleeping with infants. It was almost impossible to prove premeditated murder. However, if parents wanted to rid themselves of an unwanted child, they could suffocate it by **overlaying** during the night.

In any case, asphyxiation continued to be a perplexing problem for authorities. Texler (1973), noted that fines and penalties were meted out to parents who kept babies in bed with them. An Austrian decree of 1784 made it illegal to have a child under the age of five in bed with parents. In order to protect infants in Eastern Europe the age of the child was dropped to two.

In Europe during the eighteenth and nineteenth centuries, the poor families were still struggling with the problem of disposing with the unwanted offspring. During this time there was an increase in sexual promiscuity. Some evidence suggests that upper class predators freely exploited girls of the lower class, especially live-in servants.

Impecunious girls were at the mercy of their employers and fornication was viewed as an inevitable aspect of lower class life. If the girl became pregnant, she was left to shift for herself. This situation encouraged girls to settle the fate of the unwanted baby in devious ways. Starvation or a dose of opiates were common ways used to dispose of the waifs.

In order to deal with the problem of **illegitimacy,** foundling homes began to appear. Girls began leaving their offspring on the steps of a church or other public institutions. This led to the opening of asylums and homes to care for the children.

Foundling homes tended to become popular charitable causes for upper class dowagers. Wealthy women of this era often spent large sums of money for the construction and maintenance of foundling hospitals. Despite the good management and professional efforts of those in charge, most of these institutions were ineffective, as many children succumbed either through neglect or severe punitive measure which were in vogue at that time.

In France, Napoleon tried to diminish the number of child murders by a variety of means. When rural hospitals became overloaded with babies, the infants were transported to the larger cities. Relatively few survived the arduous journey over rough roads in crude carts. In 1818, of the 4,779 infants admitted to one Paris hospital, 2,370 died within the first three months (McCloy, 1957).

Infant mortality continued to plague France during the nineteenth century. Foundling hospitals were overcrowded with babies born to unwed mothers as well as babies from married couples. Deaths continued to mount as many of the infants were diseased or half dead upon arrival at the institutions. The government gradually embarked on a program of aide to unwed mothers in order to reduce the rate of infant mortality.

The English Connection

This saga of foundlings in Great Britain was no less tragic than on the continent of Europe. The London Foundling Hospital, which opened in 1741, was built for the children of London, but pressure for admission from other areas came soon after the opening. According to Brownlow (1868), Londoners witnessed, "The disgraceful scene of women scrambling and fighting to get to the door (with their babies) that they might be of the fortunate few to reap the benefit of the asylum."

Parliament was exhorted to open the doors of these institutions to all needy children, and other asylums were urged to open throughout the kingdom to take care of exposed and deserted youngsters. By 1760, the London Hospital was deluged with 4,229 newcomers, making the total of 14,934 admissions in four years. Because of the high rate of infant mortality, the hospital was generally regarded as a **charnel house for the dead.**

Infanticide continued as a major problem in the nineteenth century. Although by 1824, cruelty to animals was being noted and experienced, the crime of killing children was still considered murder. Proof, however, seemed to be illusive and very hard to substantiate. Juries tended to refuse to convict women offenders, as the real culprits were the girls' seducers. Only the most notorious cases were ever brought to trial where capital punishment was carried out for the offender. One coroner in Middlesex charged that law enforcers tended to consider no more of finding a dead child than finding a dead cat or dog (London Daily Telegraph, 1862).

Countless women in London were guilty of destroying their offspring without having to answer for the crime. By the mid-nineteenth century, this condition was a national scandal. Disraeli (1846), among other writers, maintained infanticide was, "hardly less prevalent in England than on the banks of the Ganges." Consequently, infanticide flourished during the years long after the **Dark Ages** in Europe.

Industrial Development

The industrial revolution put great stress on the lower working class mothers. Women who were employed in factories or on farms had no choice but to leave their babies in the care of, "killer nurses who made short shrift of their charges by general doses of opiates," (Brockington, 1965).

Even more abhorrent were the **burial clubs.** Upon payment of a small premium, three to five pounds of sterling, women could leave the child at these designated places. After a short interval of time, the child died of starvation, harsh treatment or poisoning.

The institution of **killer nurses** or **angel-makers** eventually became known as **babyfarming.** Both lay people and medical professionals began to speak out against this horrendous practice. Lord Boughham (1892), studied the problem and concluded, "We cannot ignore the fact that the crime of infanticide, as well as that of criminal abortion, is widespread and on the increase."

The British press became quite vocal about the flagrant abuses to infants. During the 1860's many news stories revealed the frequent finding of dead infants under bridges, in parks, in culverts and ditches, and even in cesspools and swampy areas. The country reacted in shock and horror when the news broke concerning two women from Brixton and Peckham who left sixteen corpses in obvious places. The women were tried for murder and one was convicted and executed. In parliament, the reaction to this execrable system of wholesale murder was that of outrage (London Daily Telegraph, 1862).

A committee was established to study various ways to prevent the flagrant destruction of young, innocent lives. The report of the committee was enough to convince Parliament to pass the Infant Life Protection Act in 1872. This act forced the compulsory registration of all houses in which more than one child under the age of one, was admitted for more than twenty-four hours. The license, issued by a justice of the peace, required the reporting of all deaths. Stiff penalties were administered for violations. As a result, less was heard or written about infanticide in the nineteenth and early twentieth century in Great Britain.

The industrial revolution also had debilitating effects of the lives of older children who had survived the early years. The development of the textile mills in the nineteenth century offered an unprecedented opportunity to use the children of paupers. Many youngsters as young as four years of age, were put to work in factories for long hours and under horrendous conditions. There was no legal limitations of their working hours and often **slappers** were employed to keep them awake by whipping them when the fell asleep.

Typically, the children got up at four or five in the morning and worked until five or six in the evening or later. This made the working day sometimes sixteen to eighteen hours long. Children of six or seven years were put to the spinning wheel or to the loom where their small, deft, flexible fingers could throw the thread quicker than adults. During working hours they had to stand and were not allowed to leave their work place, outside of meals, to relieve themselves or to get a drink of water. Any child who left his or her station was brutally punished by whipping. Some children were actually chained to their posts to insure the daily quota of work. The plight of children in Dickens' **Oliver Twist** and in Hugo's **Les Miserables**, reflected the growing sentiment for the unfortunate children of this period in history.

The first step in the direction of their protection was the Health and Morals Act of 1802, passed on the initiative of Sir Robert Peel, who objected to the use of young children in labor camps. This statute restricted the working hours of **pauper apprentices** to twelve hours a day and forbade night work for children. However, the law only applied to children leased out from the poor houses. Cotton mill owners who hired children directly from their parents could continue to exploit them.

Concerned about these conditions, Peel and others pursued the demand for protection or working children against mistreatment and overwork. This movement led to the enactment of the Factory Act of 1833, which prohibited the employment of children under nine in the textile industry and limited daily working hours for children. At the suggestion of Edwin Chadwick, The law introduced the appointment of factory inspectors under a central national office. An amendment of the Factory Act in 1847, ordered a daily maximum of ten working hours for women and children under eighteen years. Even though child labor laws were passed in both Great Britain and the United States, the insidious practice has not yet disappeared from societies in other parts of the world.

Child Abuse in the United States

Child abuse and neglect is a complex problem which encompasses all levels of society. Consequently it has been and still is, a problem for individuals, families, and communities. Child neglect is an act of omission while abuse is the act of commission; thus it has a debilitating, profound effect of society as a whole.

A Legal Beginning

The first recorded case of child abuse in the United States occurred in 1874 in New York City. Mary Ellen Wilson, a nine year old girl living with Francis and Mary Connolly was being grossly abused. Mary Ellen was the **illegitimate** daughter of Mrs. Connolly's first husband, Thomas McCormack and Fanny Wilson. A neighbor noticed that she was being beaten, chained to her bed, and fed only bread and water for extended periods of time. Her bruised body bore blow marks from a blunt instrument.

The concerned neighbor reported the situation to Mrs. Etta Angell Wheeler, a friend of the Connollys (Fontana, 1964). Mrs. Wheeler was frustrated in her attempt to find help for the child. The law enforcement officials indicated that no crime had been committed because parents had the right to discipline their children as they chose. The prosecuting attorney confirmed this opinion, but noted that should the child die of injuries, a manslaughter charge could be filed against the caretakers.

While contemplating the seriousness of the situation, Mrs. Whitter came upon the resolution of the problem. She contacted Henry Bergh, who in 1866 had organized the first protective agency which was The American Society for the Prevention of Cruelty to Animals. They concurred that Mary Ellen should be removed from the home of her cruel guardians. As a member of the animal kingdom, she deserved the same protection as an abused animal.

The case was brought to court. Mary Ellen was so ill she had to be carried to the courtroom on a stretcher. E.T. Gerry, Counsel for the defense had her removed from the custody of the Connolly's by a petition for a **writ de monie replegando** which is an Old English writ for removing a person from the custody of another. The foster parents were arraigned and charged with cruelty to an animal. They were convicted on the premise that Mary Ellen was indeed a part of the animal kingdom and was therefore entitled to at least the same justice as a common cur. Mrs. Connolly was given a prison sentence. The publicity generated by the case created a furor in the State of New York, and it resulted in the first law which recognized the rights of children.

Emergence of Child Laws

In the United States, the medical profession's recognition of the problem of child abuse was alluded to in 1888 in a paper on, **The Acute Periosteal Swelling in Infants** (Solomon, 1973). In 1889, the first juvenile court was established in Chicago, Illinois. The philosophy of this court tended to underscore and favor a reasonable and more rational treatment of children by their parents (Mason, 1972).

Efforts on behalf of mistreated children culminated in the first White House conference on Children in 1909. By 1912, beginning legislation was initiated to establish a Federal Children's Bureau to deal with pertinent matters pertaining to the welfare of children and the factors which effect their lives among all classes of people.

In the early part of the twentieth century, various professions which were concerned with children and family interaction were emerging. In this century, the recognition of children as a special class came into being. The fields of child psychology and social work were becoming recognized as viable resource areas. In 1902, Folks wrote of the destitute, neglected and delinquent children of that era. Unwanted children were devising subterfuge and delinquent means in order to survive. Many were left to flounder on their own.

In 1935, the Social Security Act aided the development of public programs in the area of child care. As social institutions emerged, the orphanage and foundling hospital declined.

The 1960's were marked by a heightened awareness of the plight of children in a complex, diverse society. A need was perceived to protect children at all cultural levels. The television media helped to sensitize the general viewing public. In 1962, amendments to the Social Security Act required each state, "to develop a plan to extend child welfare services, including protective services, to every political subdivision" (Thomas, 1972).

CONCLUSION

The sacredness of human life has been observed as a rather new phenomenon of the twentieth century. Only in recent years has life become recognized as a precious possession. Our complex society has been made up of myriad social innuendos and relationships which appear, at first glance, to be unrelated. Upon closer examination and study, it is found that many parts mesh together which, in turn, has great impact on the lives of children. The mores, social customs, manners, economics, humane attitudes, education, and class values have a profound effect on child rearing practices.

Rapidly changing societal rules of behavior are tenuous for children. Moral codes tend to be diffuse and general when there is an absence of behavioral guidelines. This has created, in certain areas of our society, an imbalance which has adversely affected children. As a result, a deteriorated level of parenting has been noted. This condition adversely affects young people and ultimately, all of society.

All societies consist of a myriad, a diverse social phenomenon and on interrelationship, all of which appear on the surface, to be unrelated. Upon closer scrutiny, it is found that mores, social customs, certain child rearing practices, disintegration of family structures, and poverty, are closely linked with abusive practices toward children.

Social disorganization, catastrophic wars, natural disasters, and other conditions which influence rules of behavior often lead to social disorganization. These conditions lead to imbalance that adversely affect children.

Ignorance Without Bliss

An ever increasing number of couples do not want to be parents. Others have children and are unable to offer the essential care of their progeny. The general decaying of family life may inadvertently lay a base for abuse and neglect. The idea of abuse is so abhorrent that many couples prefer not to notice it. Consequently, it **can easily be denied.** Inaction, compounded by indifference can be a breeding ground for abuse. Its presence is announced in unmistakable ways. When this situation occurs, all strata of society realizes the **damaging effects.** The low quality or level of parenting becomes dangerous for children and effects are debilitating to society in general (Polansky, 1981).

It is certainly a perplexing paradox of our time that in the accumulation of knowledge in all levels of human endeavor, a solution for reducing human suffering has not made a corresponding impact on the reduction of that suffering. In no other field of human activity has man's ignorance or indifference been more lamentable in its consequences than that of rearing children; the future parents in our society.

When moral codes become generalized without specific guidelines, this creates imbalances which adversely affect children. It is at this level that parenting becomes dangerous in terms of a child's survival, and consequently all of society is effected.

An attempt must be made to integrate myriad levels of child rearing dilemmas, which result in malevolent attitudes that lead to cover debilitating actions toward children. It is evident that unstable and conflicting ideas result in the maltreatment of children in complex societies where there is a history of shifting social values. Finding a solution to this dilemma may be the major task of the twenty-first century.

REFERENCES

1. Aries, P.: *Centuries of Childhood: A Social History of Family Life.* New York, Knopf, 1962, (Translated by R. Baldick).
2. Beller, H. B., and Solomon, R. S.: *Child Maltreatment and Parental Deprivation: A Manifisto for Research, Prevention and Treatment.* Lexington, Lexington, 1986.
3. Brockington, C. F.: *Public Health in the Nineteenth Century.* Edinburgh, 1965, pp. 225–226.
4. Brougham, L.: *Infanticide: Its Law, Prevelence, Prevention and History.* London, 1982.
5. Brownlow, J.: *The History and Design of the Foundling Hospital.* London, 1968.
6. *Daily Telegraph.* London, September 10, 1862.
7. *Daily Telegraph.* London, January 21, 1863.
8. DeMause, L.: Our fathers made childhood a nightmare. *Psychology Today, 8:*85–88, 1975.
9. Dickens, C.: *Oliver Twist.* London, New Oxford, 1949.
10. Disraili, B.: *Sybil.* London, Nelson, 1846.
11. Folks, H.: *The Care of Destitute, Neglected and Delinquent Children.* New York, Macmillan, 1902.
12. Fontana, V. J.: *The Maltreated Child: The Maltreatment Syndrome in Children.* Springfield, Thomas, 1964.
13. Gibbon, E.: *The Decline and Fall of the Roman Empire.* New York, Modern Library, 1932.
14. Hands, A. R.: *Aspects of Greek and Roman Life.* New York, Ithaca, 1986.
15. *Holy Bible.* Exodus 12:12, II Kings 6, Proverbs 13:24.
16. Hugo, B.: *Les Miserables.* New York, Literary Guild of America, 1954.
17. Justice, B.: *The Abusing Family.* New York, Human Sciences, 1976.

18. Langor, W.: Infanticide: a historical survey. *History of Childhood Quarterly,* 335, 1974.
19. Lecky, W. E.: *A History of European Morals from Augustus to Charlemagne.* London, 1869.
20. Mason, P. T.: Child abuse and neglect, part I: historical overview, legal matrix and social perspective. *North Carolina Law Review, 50:*305, 1972.
21. McCloy, S. T.: *The Humanitarian Movement in Eighteenth Century France.* Lexington, 1957.
22. Plato: *The Republic.* New York, Random House, 1937, vols. V, VII, 4, 16, Jowett Translation.
23. Polansky, N. A.: *Damaged Parents: An Anatomy and Child Neglect.* Chicago, University of Chicago, 1981.
24. Radbill, S.: History of child abuse and infanticide. In Kempe, C. H., and Helfer, R. (Eds.): *The Battered Child.* Chicago, University of Chicago, 1974.
25. Russell, S. B.: *A History of Western Philosophy.* New York, Simon and Schuster, 1945.
26. Ryan, W. B.: *Infanticide: Its Law, Prevelence, Prevention and History.* London, Churchill, 1862.
27. Solomon, T.: History and demography of child abuse. *Pediatrics, 51:*774, 1973.
28. Thomas, M. P.: Child abuse and neglect part I: historical overview, legal matrix and social perspectives. *North Carolina Law Review, 50:*293, 1972.
29. Trexler, R. C.: Infanticide in Florence. *History of Childhood Quarterly, 1:*98–115, 1973.
30. Walters, D. R.: *Physical and Sexual Abuse of Children: Causes and Treatment.* Bloomington, Indiana University, 1975.

CHAPTER 3

ABUSE AND NEGLECT:
TYPOLOGIES, PHENOMENA AND IMPACTS

OLIVER C. S. TZENG
LINDA J. HANNER

INTRODUCTION

This chapter will cover three topics of importance: (1) typologies of child abuse and neglect that have been most frequently referred to in state laws and also in relevant literature; (2) statistical summaries of child victimization from abuse and neglect at the national level during the past decade; and (3) detrimental impacts of child abuse and neglect victimization on traditional family unities and individual life progressions through childhood, adolescence and adulthood. Each topic will be discussed in detail. It will become clear in the conclusion section that child abuse and neglect is not only a child's problem, nor is it only a family's problem. Rather, it is a problem of the whole society that requires all our efforts (individuals, communities, and public/private agencies) to combat this severe societal problem together.

TYPOLOGIES OF ABUSE AND NEGLECT

The term child abuse has been defined in a rather comprehensive way in all 50 states laws. It covers all kinds of behaviors that have negative impact on a child's emotional, physical, education, and social development. The specific behaviors appearing in 50 state laws include: physical abuse, mental abuse, sexual abuse, negligent treatment, maltreatment, severe neglect, general neglect, abandonment, willful cruelty, unjustifiable punishment, corporal punishment, harm, imminent danger, threatened harm, institutional abuse or neglect, and withholding of medically indicated treatment. Major types of abuse and neglect are explained further:

1. **Physical abuse** is the nonaccidental injury of a child which may occur repeatedly or by a single episode.

2. **Physical neglect** includes failure to provide safe supervision, medical care, appropriate clothes, and housing.

3. **Sexual abuse** includes any sexual activity with a child and becomes more difficult to define as the child grows toward adulthood. Sexual abuse may be assaultive or nonassaultive, chronic or a one time incident. The violence of assaultive sexual abuse tends to be more stressful for the child than nonassaultive abuse and chronic encounters can cause serious disturbances in a child's development.

4. **Emotional or psychosocial abuse and neglect** are extremely difficult to define and manage. Emotional abuse cannot be seen as dramatically as physical abuse, however, specific effects on a child's behavior and growth have been documented. Emotional or psychosocial abuse and neglect have been acknowledged by the courts only when improvement in a child's growth and development is evident when the child is away from the home. Cultural differences add to the difficulty in documenting emotional abuse, because what constitutes abuse in one culture may be acceptable in another. Examples of emotional maltreatment depicted by the National Center on Child Abuse and Neglect include when the parent chronically:

1. Belittles the child so he/she is made to feel he/she can do nothing right, or criticizes the child harshly,
2. Blames the child for things over which the child has no control,
3. Ridicules and shames the child,
4. Threatens the child's safety and health,
5. Takes no interest in the child's activities or problems,
6. Treats the child coldly, withholding affection,
7. Treats the child differently from others in the family, and/or
8. Engages in bizarre acts of torture or torment such as locking the child in a closet.

Generally speaking, depicted types of abuse/neglect can be represented by a general term of **maltreatment** under which all types of harmful behaviors against children can be summarized in terms of the following five categories:

1. **Physical injuries** including: (a) brain damage/skull fracture, (b) subdural hemorrhage or hematoma, (c) bone fracture, (d) dislocation or sprains, (e) internal injuries, (f) poisoning, (g) burns/scalds, (h) severe or minor cuts/lacerations or bruises/welts, (i) twisting or

shaking, (j) other injuries, and (k) unspecified/mixed physical injuries;

2. **Sexual maltreatment** including: (a) incest, (b) exploitation, (c) rape or intercourse, (d) molestation, (e) other sexual maltreatment, and (f) unspecified/mixed sexual maltreatment;

3. **Deprivation of necessities** including: (a) neglects in providing nourishment, shelter, clothing, health care, (b) failure to thrive, (c) lack of supervision, (d) educational neglect, and (e) unspecified/mixed deprivation of necessities;

4. **Emotional maltreatment** including: (a) emotional abuse, (b) emotional neglect, and (c) unspecified/mixed emotional maltreatment; and

5. **Other maltreatment** including: (a) abandonment, (b) unspecified/mixed maltreatments, and (c) others.

NATIONAL STATISTICS

This section presents summaries of official statistics on reported cases of child abuse and/or neglect in the United States between 1976 and 1986. These results were obtained from a national project conducted by the American Association for Protecting Children which is a division of The American Humane Association (AHA). The information, gathered from child protective service agencies across the nation for this project, include three types of issues; (1) the nature and volume of reporting to child protective agencies, (2) the characteristics of the reported cases, and (3) the responses from child protective agencies concerning reported cases.

The purpose of presenting summary statistics at the national level is to keep a diverse group of professionals informed on the status of reported child abuse or neglect cases in all 50 states. It is hoped that through a close comparison of the data at state and local levels with those at the national level, local child service providers, as well as child protection agencies, will have some references to evaluate the consequential impact from their local intervention and prevention efforts.

Table III–IA presents two major indices regarding the national trend on child abuse and neglect. First, the **Estimated Nationwide Report Cases** indicate the number was 669,000 cases reported in 1976, and it increased steadily at an average of 12.95% per year over the nine year period. The reported cases (1,727 thousand in 1984) were almost **triple** over those in

1976. Second, the **Child Report Rate** (in reference to 1,000 children per unit) indicates that in 1976, 10 out of 1,000 children were reported to be victims of child abuse and neglect in some form, whereas in 1984, more than 27 children out of 1,000 were reported as victims.

Table III–IB specifically focuses on the national statistics in child sexual abuse. The data were initially obtained from the child population in 1976. About 6,000 children (or about 1 per every 1,000 children in the nation) were reported as victims of sexual abuse. In 1984, the reported cases increased over 15 times: over 100,000 children (or about 16 per 1,000 children in the nation) were reported as victims.

TABLE III-I
NATIONAL ESTIMATES OF CASES IN CHILD ABUSE/NEGLECT

	A. GENERAL CHILD ABUSE/NEGLECT			
Year	Report Cases (in 1,000)	Increase %	Child Reporting Rate (per 1,000)	Increase %
1976	669	—	10.1	—
1977	838	25.26%	12.8	22%
1978	836	.24%	12.9	0%
1979	988	18.18%	15.4	19%
1980	1,154	16.80%	18.1	17%
1981	1,225	6.15%	19.4	7%
1982	1,262	3.02%	20.1	4%
1983	1,477	17.04%	23.6	17%
1984	1,727	16.93%	27.3	16%

	B. CHILD SEXUAL ABUSE		
Year	Number of Children (in 1,000)	Case Rate (per 1,000)	Base Rate of U.S. Child Population*
1976	6	0.86	33%
1977	11	1.74	36%
1978	12	1.87	43%
1979	27	4.23	42%
1980	37	5.76	43%
1981	35	5.55	47%
1982	57	9.01	40%
1983	74	11.86	46%
1984	100	15.88	41%

*Base rate represents the percent of children in the entire U.S. child population from which case rates in column 3 were derived.

Sub-National Statistics

The data presented in the following sections are from the National Study Data Base that represents 61 percent of the total U.S. child population. However, it should be noted that since the data was collected from only 30 states and that some topics in the study varied from state to state according to policy, the resulting statistics may not be truly representative of national trends. With this in mind, interpretations of the statistics will focus on the description of individual issues.

Sources of Reports

The types of people who report suspected child abuse and neglect are depicted in Table III–II. Although case reports are evenly divided between professionals and nonprofessionals, the single largest group of reporters are the victim's own friends, neighbors, and relatives (36.2%). This represents a great deal of community concern and involvement in protecting the safety of children. Nonprofessionals may have a greater opportunity for observing the abused/neglected child. Between 1981 and 1984, professional sources have increased from 46% to 50% possibly from their increased awareness of signs of maltreatment.

TABLE III-II
SOURCES OF REPORTS

Sources	% of All Reports
Professionals:	
1. School Personnel	13.5%
2. Social Services	11.9%
3. Medical Personnel	11.3%
4. Law Enforcement	10.7%
5. Child Care Providers	2.3%
Total Professionals:	(49.6%)
Nonprofessionals:	
1. Friends, Neighbors, Relatives, Self	36.2%
2. Anonymous	12.4%
3. Other Sources	1.9%
Total Nonprofessionals:	(50.4%)
Total Sources	100.0%
	(N = 341,330)

Types of Reports

The reports made by various originating sources to child protective services are categorized in four types in Table III–III. The most frequent types of report in both years is neglect which accounts for about 42%–45% of all reports. Abuse is the second highest type of report (28%–34%); and abuse and neglect is the third type that accounts for 16% to 19% of total reported cases. There are only 7% to 8% of all reported cases that were not identified as abuse, neglect, or both abuse and neglect.

When both physical and sexual abuse statistics are combined, they represent approximately 58% of reports. Therefore, both abuse and neglect are over half of all reports. In comparison between 1983 and 1984, data indicates that while the neglect reports tend to decline, the abuse reports tend to increase.

TABLE III-III
TYPES OF REPORTS

| | Percentage of Reports | |
Types of Reports	1983 (N = 269,818)	1984 (N = 286,801)
Abuse	27.9%	33.5%
Neglect	45.7%	42.1%
Abuse and Neglect	19.0%	16.3%
Unspecified Type of Report	7.4%	8.1%

Characteristics of Substantiated Cases

A national estimate of 727 thousand reported children were considered **substantiated** for child abuse and neglect. This was based on data from 19 states and represents approximately 42% of the 1.7 million children who were reported in 1984.

Substantiation means that there is some basis of factual evidence about abuse or neglect and that the child protection agency will respond to this finding. However, such a definition, when used for statistical purposes, can easily involve misleading problems: (1) various states and counties frequently use different standards or criteria to determine the factual evidence, and (2) the term **substantiated** can easily be misinterpreted as a **true** representation of all abuse and neglect. But in fact, numerous **unsubstantiated cases** are not free from child maltreatment.

Approximately 60% of substantiated reports are received from professionals, while only 40% of unsubstantiated cases are from the same sources. This difference may suggest that professional reports provide the primary data base for substantiation decisions.

Characteristics of Reported Families

Major demographic characteristics of families who are reported to child protection service agencies as involved with incidents of child abuse or neglect are shown in Table III–IV. It is important to note that most of the perpetrators in 1984 are caretakers who have full time responsibility for a child, not including babysitters, teachers, etc.

Age Distributions

Table III–V illustrates the distributions of age of children involved in incidents of abuse or neglect. The average age of reported children is 7.2 years while the average age for all U.S. children is 8.6 years.

Characteristics by Substantiation Status

Characteristics between substantiated and unsubstantiated cases can be compared in terms of age, sex, and race of the child involved and the characteristics of the caretakers or perpetrators. Children in substantiated cases tend to be slightly older, more often female, and more often white than children in unsubstantiated cases. The most obvious difference appears in the sex of perpetrators. For all reported cases, males represent 43% in reports, however they account for 46% of perpetrators in substantiated cases and 40% in unsubstantiated cases. This may relate to the types of abuse/neglect associated with substantiated cases in which males are the perpetrators responsible for sexual abuse and physical injury.

Maltreatment

The types of abuse or neglect for children involved in substantiated cases are shown in Table III–VI. Percentages of changes in different types of maltreatment from 1983 to 1984 are also depicted in the Table.

Combining the three types of physical injury (major, minor, and unspecified), Table III–VI shows an overall decrease (in proportion to all maltreatment types) in physical injury with the largest single decrease (−1.6%) being in the area of unspecified physical injury.

The largest increase in all types of maltreatment between 1983 and 1984 was in cases of sexual abuse which jumped from 8.5% to 13.3%. In

TABLE III-IV
DEMOGRAPHIC CHARACTERISTICS OF CHILD MALTREATMENT IN 1984

Demographics		*Trends/Comments 1976–1984*
A. Characteristics of Victimized Children		
Age (N = 722,704 Children)		
Average Age	7.2 years	Gradual decline from 7.8 to 7.1 years of age from 1976 to 1983. Slight increase in 1984.
Sex (N = 727,292 Children)		
Males	48.0%	Decline in proportion of males reported from 50.0 in 1976 to 48.0% in 1984.
Females	52.0%	
Race (N = 505,837 Children)		
White	67.0%	Relatively consistent over time.
Black	20.8%	
Hispanic	9.6%	
Other	2.6%	
B. Characteristics of Caretakers		
Age (N = 238,232 Caretakers)		
Average Age	31.9 years	Fairly stable over time with a slight gradual decline in average age from 1976 to 1982. Slight increase from 31.4 years in 1982 to 31.9 in 1984.
Sex (N = 295,624 Caretakers)		
Males	38.5%	Gradual decline in proportion of male caretakers from 1976 to 1982. Increase from 36.2% male in 1982 to 38.5% in 1984.
Females	61.5%	
Race (N = 245,374 Caretakers)		
White	74.5%	Relatively consistent aover time.
Black	17.5%	
Hispanic	5.5%	
Other	2.5%	
C. Characteristics of Families		
Single Female Headed Families (N = 186,606 Family Reports)	37.4%	Gradual increase between 1976 and 1982 with declines from 1982 (43.4%) to 1984 (37.4%).
Average Number of Children in Household (N = 180,057 Reports)	2.17	Gradual decline since 1976, but relatively consistent since 1979.
Receiving Public Assistance (N = 87,600 Reports)	48.3%	No obvious pattern over time, but has increased from 1982 (43.4%) to 1984 (48.3%).

TABLE III-IV (Continued)

Demographics		Trends/Comments 1976–1984
	D. Characteristics of Perpetrators	
Average Age (N = 344,172 Perpetrators)	31.5 years	Relatively consistent over time.
Sex (N = 395,898 Perpetrators)		
Males	43.0%	1984 increase in percentage males from
Females	57.0%	40.4% in 1983 to 43.0%. Relatively consistent in prior years.
Ethnic Backgrounds (N = 361,110 Perpetrators)		
White	69.9%	Relatively consistent over time.
Black	19.1%	
Hispanic	9.3%	
Other	1.9%	

comparison with a trend identified in other National Study reporting data, including those reported in Table III–IB, estimate the number of sexually abused children have increased significantly between 1976 and 1984. Factors contributing to this trend include: (1) increase in public awareness of sexual abuse, (2) expansion of state law definitions to include extrafamilial abuse by nonfamily members, (3) increase in number of sexual abuse programs and protection agencies, and (4) state and local policy to increase emphasis on reporting and investigating child sexual abuse.

Characteristics of Deprivation of Necessities

The type of report received most often by child protection agencies is neglect which accounts for 58% of all cases recorded in 1984. Among various types of maltreatment found upon investigation, deprivation of

TABLE III-V
COMPARISON OF AGE DISTRIBUTIONS

Age	All U.S. Children	Abused and/or Ngelected Children
0–5	34%	43%
6–11	31%	33%
12–17	35%	24%
Total	100%	100%

TABLE III-VI
TYPES OF MALTREATMENT

Types of Maltreatment	Percent of Children		Changes in %
	1983 (N = 397,785)	1984 (N = 304,993)	
A. Physical Injury:			
Major	3.2%	3.3%	+0.1
Minor	18.5%	17.7%	−0.8
Unspecified	5.2%	3.6%	−1.6
B. Sexual Maltreatment	8.5%	13.3%	4.8
C. Deprivation of Necessities	58.4%	54.6%	−3.8
D. Emotional Maltreatment	10.1%	11.2%	+1.1
E. Other Maltreatment*	8.3%	9.6%	+1.3
Total	100.0%	100.0%	

*Abandonment and forms of maltreatment that are not included in other categories.

necessities is the main form that accounted for 55% of all reported neglected cases.

The importance of these deprivation of necessities cases are relatively similar to abuse cases that require intervention of child protection agencies in terms of investigation, description, analysis, and tendency to be identified as substantiated. Approximately 80% of the cases reported as deprivation of necessities were substantiated in 1984, and about 42% of those reports received court action.

Table III–VIII shows percentages of neglect cases that were opened for child protection services and a comparison between general maltreatment cases and neglect cases that received court action. Although not all cases were opened for protective services, there is an upward trend possibly indicating that families have more services available to them (such as casework counseling and crisis intervention services). Between the years 1979 and 1983 more neglect cases than maltreatment cases were sent to court for action.

Fatalities

Child fatalities in relation to abuse or neglect are under reported because the actual number of children who have died as a result of abuse or neglect is not available. However, some characteristics of known fatality cases can be described and compared to other cases in which a fatality does not occur.

Between 1976 and 1984, data shows 1,491 children were reported as

TABLE III-VII
DEMOGRAPHIC CHARACTERISTICS OF 1984 REPORTED CASES
IN SEVEN MALTREATMENT CATEGORIES

Demographics	Overall	Physical Injuries		
		Major	Minor	Unspecified
A. Reported Children				
1. Average Age	7.3	5.3	8.0	8.5
2. Sex:				
Male	47.2%	54.2%	51.4%	50.8%
Female	52.8%	45.8%	48.6%	49.2%
3. Race:				
White	64.8%	57.5%	64.3%	71.8%
Black	19.9%	21.9%	19.0%	17.8%
Hispanic	12.4%	11.2%	13.7%	4.2%
Other	2.8%	9.5%	3.1%	6.3%
4. Relationship to Perpetrator:				
Own Child	84.6%	82.9%	82.6%	86.6%
Other Relative	6.2%	5.1%	5.2%	4.7%
Other	9.2%	12.1%	12.2%	8.7%
B. Family				
1. Number of Children in Household:				
Reported	2.1	2.0	2.1	2.2
All in U.S. Population	1.9	1.9	1.9	1.9
2. Unemployment of Caretakers	36.6%	37.4%	27.4%	37.5%
3. Single Female Headed Families	37.1%	27.8%	26.2%	29.2%

Demographics	Sexual	Neglect	Maltreatment	
			Emotional	Other
A. Reported Children				
1. Average Age	9.3	6.4	8.1	7.3
2. Sex:				
Male	21.7%	51.5%	48.3%	50.0%
Female	78.3%	48.5%	51.7%	50.0%
3. Race:				
White	74.7%	62.5%	71.4%	49.3%
Black	13.0%	22.5%	12.8%	31.4%
Hispanic	8.8%	12.9%	13.2%	15.9%
Other	3.5%	2.2%	2.6%	3.4%

TABLE III-VII (Continued)

Demographics	Overall	Physical Injuries		
		Major	Minor	Unspecified
4. Relationship to Perpetrator:				
Own Child	55.6%	91.3%	90.3%	89.9%
Other Relative	18.7%	3.8%	3.4%	4.1%
Other	25.7%	5.0%	6.3%	6.0%
B. Family				
1. Number of Children in Household:				
Reported	2.0	2.3	2.3	2.2
All in U.S. Population	1.9	1.9	1.9	1.9
2. Unemployment of Caretakers	27.7%	43.3%	35.1%	38.0%
3. Single Female Headed Families	24.5%	51.1%	35.9%	37.8%

having died in connection with deprivation of necessities. Although only deprivation of necessities is recorded in these cases, other maltreatments are often suspected as being present.

In fatality cases, the average age of children involved is much younger (2.6 years) compared to the age of children involved in other abuse and neglect cases (7.2 years). Male children represent slightly more than half of the fatality cases. Both parents were reported as present for 69% of the fatality incidents and this percentage continues to climb in relation to all

TABLE III-VIII
NEGLECT AND MALTREATMENT CASES INVOLVING
PROTECTIVE SERVICES AND COURT ACTION

Year	Neglect Cases Opened for Protective Service	Maltreatments Receiving Court Action	Neglect Cases Receiving Court Action
1976	59%	22%	20%
1977	80%	21%	21%
1978	78%	20%	20%
1979	54%	15%	18%
1980	54%	14%	26%
1981	74%	18%	25%
1982	68%	20%	34%
1983	75%	24%	33%
1984	89%	30%	26%

other reported cases. Single mother families were reported at 28% for fatality cases compared to 37% in all other cases.

Major physical injury is the most frequently reported type of maltreatment associated with the fatalities, followed by deprivation of necessities and minor physical injury. In recent years the percentage of fatalities involving major physical injury has increased (from 40% in 1983 to 47% in 1984) while the fatalities involving neglect has declined from 52% to 44%. Professional sources report 80% of all fatality cases, with medical personnel accounting for 36% and law enforcement officials for 31%.

Case Status and Sources of Report

Table III–IX depicts various report sources and the comparison between cases closed after the investigation and the cases opened for protective services. The category of **Other** report sources includes anonymous reporters, and is the least likely group to generate the opened cases. This may be due to a biased reporting system which leans toward the nature and completeness of reports from professionals. The report resources from professionals (Medical and School Personnel, Social Services, and Child Care) show about equal proportions in closed cases (50%) and also in those given to protective services (44%–46%). Reports by law enforcement are most likely to result in protective services (55%).

Case Status and Types of Maltreatment

Table III–X shows the types of maltreatment reported in 1984, percentage for each type closed after investigation, and percentage for each type opened for protective service. The information was recorded after an initial investigation that indicated: (1) the specific type of maltreatment, and (2) whether to provide protective services.

Generally speaking, all seven types of maltreatment have extremely high ratios of **open for protective services** (between 2.2% and 95.4% with an average of 87.7%). Emotional maltreatment is the most likely to be opened for services, followed by sexual abuse and neglect. About 10% of reported cases were closed after the investigation.

Services Provided

The frequency of services provided to reported children and their families are shown in Table III–XI. The service category of **Casework Counseling** refers to continuing involvement of a social worker from a protection agency. **Court Action Initiated** refers to any action in court

TABLE III-IX
CASE STATUS AND SOURCES OF REPORT

Case Status	Report Sources			
	Medical Personnel	School Personnel	Social Services	Law Enforcement
Currently Under Investigation	1.2%	1.3%	1.1%	1.2%
Case Closed After Investigation	50.5%	49.7%	50.8%	40.5%
Protective Service	45.9%	46.4%	44.6%	55.2%
Other	2.4%	2.6%	3.5%	3.1%
Total	100.0%	100.0%	100.0%	100.0%
(N of Cases)	(N = 12,342)	(N = 15,559)	(N = 15,766)	(N = 12,123)

Case Status	Report Sources			
	Child Care	Non Professionals	Other	All Reports
Currently Under Investigation	0.7%	1.1%	1.2%	1.2%
Case Closed After Investigation	53.3%	61.2%	71.3%	57.1%
Protective Services	44.7%	34.6%	23.7%	38.7%
Other	1.3%	3.1%	3.8%	3.0%
Total	100.0%	100.0%	100.0%	100.0%
(N of Cases)	(N = 3,319)	(N = 54,444)	(N = 19,965)	(N = 133,518)

proceeding from filing a petition through criminal prosecution. Emergency medical and shelter care are included in the category of **Immediate or Short-Term Crisis Services.** The long-term or support services category includes foster care and day care services. More than half of the report cases received services from two or more categories.

The category that has increased the most from 1983 to 1984 (13.7% to 30.2%) is **Court Action Initiated Services,** which reflects a trend of more emphasis on law enforcement and legalistic approaches for child protective services.

Table III–XII shows the percentage of selected services (Court Action, Placement, and Health Care) provided for the cases opened for protective services in 1984. Placement services include foster care and out-of-home placement, and health services include both physical and mental health services.

The percentage at about 30% for court action in Table III–XII is quite consistent with the percentage in Table III–XI. The 18% receiving placement services seem to suggest a significant increase over the previous two years (1982 and 1983).

TABLE III-X
CASE STATUS AND TYPES OF MALTREATMENT

Case Status	Types of Maltreatment			
	Physical Injury			Sexual Abuse
	Major	Minor	Unspecified	
Currently under Investigation	0.8%	1.4%	0.2%	0.8%
Closed after Investigation	7.1%	10.3%	11.6%	7.7%
Open for Protective Services	84.9%	82.2%	87.7%	88.7%
Other Status	7.2%	5.1%	0.5%	2.8%
Total	100.0%	100.0%	100.0%	100.0%
(N of Cases)	(N = 4,299)	(N = 13,626)	(N = 14,153)	(N = 19,218)

Case Status	Types of Maltreatment			
	Neglect	Emotional Maltreatment	Other	Overall
Currently under Investigation	0.7%	1.1%	0.8%	0.7%
Closed after Investigation	10.1%	3.0%	12.9%	10.0%
Open for Protective Services	88.7%	95.4%	85.9%	87.7%
Other Status	0.4%	0.5%	0.4%	1.6%
Total	100.0%	100.0%	100.0%	100.0%
(N of Cases)	(N = 48,930)	(N = 7,957)	(N = 3,089)	(N = 99,780)

TABLE III-XI
SERVICES PROVIDED

Categories of Services	% of Reports
Investigation Only/Services Planned	3.56%
Casework Counseling	73.94%
Court Action Initiated	30.24%
Immediate or Short Term Crisis Services	10.25%
Long Term or Support Services	55.58%
Other Services	2.65%
(N of Reports)	(N = 29,138)

Note: Some cases received multiple categories of services. Therefor, sum of percentages of reports will be greater than 100%.

TABLE III-XII
RATE OF PROVISIONS FOR SELECTED SERVICES AMONG OPENED CASES

Court Action *(N = 138,852 cases)*	*Placement* *(N = 89,078 cases)*	*Health Care* *(N = 53,696 cases)*
29.8%	17.7%	30.2%

Summary

The rate of reports of child abuse and/or neglect increased from 10.1 children for every 1,000 U.S. children in 1976, to 27.3 children in 1984. In fact, this alarming rate is further magnified by the estimate based on the Louis Harris Survey Method that suggests the actual amount of children subjected to physical violence is **seven times** greater than the number reported by the child protective services.

Variations in reported rates of child abuse/neglect from state to state may indicate there are discrepancies in resources, public awareness, and legal policies across the nation. The amount of abuse/neglect incidents create an enormous demand on communities, child protection agencies, health crisis centers, law enforcement officials, and courtrooms. Although reports of child abuse/neglect has increased 158% since 1976, it is doubtful that resources for these and other selected services have proportionally increased to meet the service demands.

In general, analysis of about 43% of nationwide total reporting data from 1984 suggests a growth in knowledge and cooperation between state data systems and protective agencies in investigation, reporting, and legal provisions about the cases. Major patterns emerging from analytical results can be summarized as follows:

1. Reports of general abuse/neglect as well as sexual abuse continue to rise;
2. Neglect as the type of maltreatment is declining relative to abuse, although the total reporting of both is on the rise;
3. Reports received from professionals continues to increase;
4. Almost half the families reported are receiving public assistance;
5. The average age of perpetrators is 31.5 years;
6. Thirty-seven percent of the families reported are headed by a single mother;

7. Forty-three percent of the children reported are under six (6) years old;
8. Sexual abuse reports increased about 35 percent between 1983 and 1984;
9. The average age of children involved in abuse/neglect cases is seven (7) years old, and slightly more than half are female;
10. Whites are underrepresented in reporting cases, and racial characteristics of families are consistent over time;
11. Maltreatment profiles indicate distinct characteristics in children and families depending on the type of maltreatment indicated;
12. Court action has increased to 30% of all reports in 1984, as compared to only 14% in 1980;
13. Child protective services substantiate almost half of the cases reported and 90% of those are open for protective services;
14. Almost half of the reported cases were opened for protective services with those reported by professionals consistently more likely to be opened;
15. Ten percent of cases identified with maltreatments are closed after investigation by child protection agencies;
16. Emotional maltreatment, when identified, is most likely to be opened for protective services followed by sexual abuse and neglect;
17. Case counseling is by far the most prevalent service provided.

The above findings indicate that there is a clear need to identify types of abuse and also to classify characteristics of all cases as quickly and efficiently as possible. Continued collection of data concerning case profiles will improve the system of child protection services in terms of identification, intervention, treatment, evaluation, and prevention.

In conjunction with estimated 1.7 million children subjected to physical abuse in 1984 and a significant increase of reported incidents by 158% in nine years, a continued increase in reported abuse/neglect cases must be anticipated. Therefore, greater increases in resources and their service efficiencies must be made in every state to accommodate for the protection of children.

Specifically, the increasing response of the child protection agency is to utilize the court in decision of placement services, such as foster care and out-of-home placement. The impact of court action on children and families has not been documented in the literature. It will need further investigations in the future.

IMPACTS

The impacts of child abuse and neglect are multifaceted and can affect individuals, families, communities, and cultures. In this chapter, we will summarize the negative impacts from three perspectives: (1) family unities, (2) psychosocial perceptions of family dysfunctions, and (3) societal problems. Finally, a short summary will be made to integrate negative impacts specifically from sexual abuse on victims.

Family Unities

The incident of child abuse or neglect represents one aspect of family dysfunctions. Each member of the family has psychological needs in the crisis of abuse or neglect. Therefore, the incident of child abuse and neglect will usually generate negative impacts upon not only victimized children, but also other family members including the abusive parents or adults. Literature has repeatedly documented that etiology of child abuse and neglect has historical roots associated with long-term or short-term stressors.

In fact, victimization of abuse and neglect itself is generally considered as a cause of subsequent abusive behaviors in the so called **abusive cycle** in the history of the family. The following is a list of observations from relevant literature that illustrates some of the negative impacts of child abuse and neglect on family development:

1. The parents were themselves victims of abuse/neglect as children or had no parent model to teach them about parenting.
2. A serious mental illness is manifested in the abusive family or a family member has encounters with the law for violent or assaultive behaviors.
3. Past abuse has occurred within the family unit or there have been inadequately explained deaths of their children.
4. Frequent job changes occur which may induce sudden temper outbursts, violent, or impulsive behavior.
5. Marital discord exists.
6. The family has a lack of friends or social activities, and is often isolated from contacts outside the family.
7. Extremely high expectations or rigid standards are set for children.
8. Harsh or unusual punishment is used or allowed at home or at school.

9. Children were unwanted by the parents or were seen as a burden or punishment for previous behavior.

Psychosocial Perceptions of Family Dysfunctions

Researchers as well as service providers have attempted to theorize the etiology and treatment principles for various types of abuse and neglect. From partial observations of incidents, specific types of abusive family units have been identified. Consequently, some theories or approaches have been developed under this procedure, but they do not address the multifacet nature of problems involved. For example, two theoretical models (psychological and sociological) are most frequently cited in the literature to explain the phenomenon and etiology of the battered child syndrome; (a) the **psychological model** is based on the idea that abusive parents were themselves abused as children, and (b) the **sociological model** is based on the idea that abuse happens out of frustrations in disadvantaged families that have low income, low educational backgrounds, lack of employment, little stability and live in cultural poverty. This model also suggests that society in general condones and unconsciously encourages aggressive and violent behaviors.

Although neither model is entirely correct in itself, the emphasis remains that child abuse is a collection of symptoms that has no single etiology. In reality, abusive families have been found to vary greatly in terms of education, occupations, lifestyles, and expectations. Characteristics of some abusive cycles can be illustrated in terms of three commonly known categories:

Flash point. These are parents that were expected by their parents to achieve rigid standards to the point of extreme emotional stress. They are encouraged to conform to middle class standards, to have a good job, to be a good citizen, a good neighbor, and to keep an immaculate home beyond average expectations. Without warning, one parent (usually the father) assaults the baby. This group of child abusers usually are found to have a psychiatric stress, as it is difficult for them to be aware of mounting stress before they explode.

Spare the rod. These are lower class, blue collar families that are likely to be arrested or convicted for child abuse. There is no target child, but everyone in the family, including the spouse, is chronically beat upon. These parents think they are rearing their children correctly by giving them a sound beating because that is how they had been raised. Incidents are often brought to attention because the parents openly admit they were the source.

Highly unstable motherhood. A previously abused girl may grow into a mother with very low self-esteem and find herself with numerous unstable marriages or boyfriend arrangements. When children are involved, the mother may relinquish child rearing to a man who has little experience with children, and the children may already resent his presence. Intentions are usually good in this case and abuse is not extreme. A mother who has a succession of boyfriends and gives babies as presents to boyfriends creates a lethal situation for the child. The court may see the situation as amenable if the boyfriend is ordered out, but he or someone like him will soon return.

Societal Problems

Child abuse and neglect problems have generated many societal instabilities. Most frequently cited impacts associated with child abuse and neglect include: (1) juvenile delinquency, (2) violent behaviors, and (3) aggressive behavior in younger children.

Juvenile Delinquency and Child Abuse/Neglect

Several observations have been made regarding the relationship between child abuse/neglect and juvenile delinquency:

1. Community agencies (i.e. hospitals) are used more often by families of delinquents due to the abuse or neglect of their children,
2. Children referred for abuse or neglect have a greater chance of subsequent contact with juvenile court, and
3. Children rejected by their parents tend to have a higher rate of recorded delinquency.

These observations have been supported by four empirical studies. In the first three studies, a sample of delinquent youths were identified and background characteristics were checked to determine if these youths had previously been involved with incidents of abuse or neglect.

In reference to the greater utilization of community facilities by families of delinquents, Lewis and Shanok (1977) did a retrospective hospital records check on 109 delinquents and 109 nondelinquents. They found 8.5% of the delinquents had been seen for services directly related to child abuse compared to only 1% of the nondelinquents. By utilizing community agency records, a positive relationship between abusive families and families of delinquents was established.

Children involved with abuse or neglect have a likely chance for contact with juvenile court shown by a study in which 16.2% or 873 out of 5,392 abused children had been subsequently referred to juvenile court (Gutierras and Reich, 1981). This is supported by the research of Alfaro (1978) who found 17.2% of 4465 children had at least one contact with juvenile court after referral for child abuse/neglect.

In the fourth study by McCord (1983), the case records of 232 males, originally compiled between 1939 and 1945, were categorized according to parental treatment in childhood. Tracing these men, McCord found that rejected children had a higher juvenile delinquency rate than the children that had been loved. Fifty percent of the children rejected by their parents had been convicted as children for serious crimes (i.e. theft, auto theft, breaking and entering, burglary or assault) in contrast to only 11% of the loved children.

Violent Behaviors and Child Abuse/Neglect

Several studies have substantiated a direct relationship between violence in sample populations (i.e. delinquents, psychiatric patients, and murderers) and previous child abuse or neglect history. Some findings can be summarized as follows:

1. Delinquents who were abused were more likely to commit violent offenses than those who were not abused,
2. The more the violent offenders were abused, the more violent were the crimes they committed,
3. Assaultive delinquents were more likely to come from families that used physical punishment, while socialized delinquents were more often from neglectful families,
4. Violent delinquent boys were more likely to have witnessed extreme physical abuse than nonviolent boys,
5. Psychiatric patients who had been abused were more violent than nonabused patients, and
6. Young murderers have slightly more evidence of abusive backgrounds than nonviolent youths.

In studying a relationship between violent criminal behavior and experience of child abuse/neglect, may studies examined differences between abused and nonabused populations. Many researchers, such as

Geller and Ford-Somma (1984); Tarter et. al. (1984); and Jenkins (1968) obtained supportive results. Lewis et. al. (1979) also states that violent boys were more likely to have experienced abuse or witnessed extreme physical abuse and that 15% of the violent youth studied had suffered from child abuse, and 2% had been sexually victimized in the home.

In the case of psychiatric patient subgroups, Monane et. al. (1984), found that 72% of abused child and adolescent hospital patients were extremely violent compared to 46% of nonabused patients. There was a high overall history (42%) of physical abuse in patients studied.

Young murderers or juveniles charged with homicide were researched by Lewis (1985) who noted 78% of the young murderers studied had been severely abused by one or both parents while 60% of the nonviolent youths had experienced abuse. This difference between subgroups is slight; however, Sorrells (1977) in studying the correlation between child abuse/neglect and violent behavior found that families of 31 youths charged with murder were **violent and chaotic.**

Aggressive Behavior in Young Children

Determining a direct link between abuse/neglect and aggressive behavior in young children has been mixed with many empirical issues, such as problems in research methods, definitions of abuse/neglect, and direct supportive evidence. Many studies combine abuse and neglect into a category of maltreatment suggesting that the abused and neglected children have generalized behavior difficulties. There is very little specific information available about type of abuse, duration of abuse, and the age at which abuse took place. The omission of such information in studies may obscure important findings.

Despite problems and shortcomings, findings of unwanted behavioral and emotional characteristics have been documented. Undesirable or maladjusted characteristic of abused young children include:

1. frequent physical assaults toward peers,
2. verbal and nonverbal harassment of caregivers,
3. assault or threatened assault of caregivers,
4. avoidance of other children,
5. different scores than nonabused children on psychological tests
6. more negative self-concepts,
7. tendency to handle aggressive impulses in a more aggressive way,

8. demonstrating fewer positive behaviors such as verbal and nonverbal affection and play behavior, and
9. more overall aggressive behavior such as physical, verbal and vocal aggression.

In a study by Martin & Beezley (1977), 50 abused children with mean age of six (6) years old were rated based on behavioral observation in context of physical examination, intellectual testing, interviews and neurodevelopmental assessment. The number children displaying nine major problematic behavioral characteristics are shown in Table III–XIII.

TABLE III-XIII
MAJOR PROBLEMATIC BEHAVIORAL CHARACTERISTICS

Types	*Frequency*
1. Impaired ability for enjoyment	33
2. Behavioral symptoms	31
3. Low self-esteem	26
4. Withdrawal	12
5. Opposition	12
6. Hyper-vigilance	11
7. Compulsivity	11
8. Precocious behavior	10
9. School learning problems	9

George and Main (1979) observed 10 abused toddlers and 10 nonabused toddlers during social interactions in a day care setting. It was found that abused toddlers revealed more of the undesirable behavioral characteristics, especially on avoidance and aggression toward caregivers and other children. Not only did the abused children harass and assault caregivers, but they were also less likely to approach caregivers in response to friendly gestures.

Psychological testing of 30 abused and 30 nonabused children (Kinard, 1980) showed abused children suffered in all five areas of emotional development tested. These areas were: (1) self-concept, (2) aggression, (3) socialization with peers, (4) establishment of trust in people, and (5) separation from mother. The research concluded that abused children had significantly more negative self-concepts and handled aggressive impulses in more aggressive or nonviolent ways.

Fewer positive behaviors and more aggressive behaviors were also observed by Bousha and Twentyman (1984) in comparative studies across

12 abused child/mother pairs, 12 neglected child/mother pairs, and 12 control child/mother pairs. Naturalistic observations in the home for three consecutive days for 90 minutes per day showed that neglected children had less verbal and nonverbal expressions, and much fewer social interactions.

Consequences of Sexual Abuse

Research is not extensive concerning the long-term effects of sexual abuse, but some indication of low self-esteem, mistrust, and depression have been seen in children that were maltreated. Other effects may include; sexual dysfunction, suicide, antisocial behaviors, prostitution, drug and alcohol abuse, psychosomatic illnesses, and multiple phobias.

Immediate consequences of sexual abuse are more apparent and may include regression to earlier behaviors such as fear of the dark or thumbsucking, enuresis, acting out behaviors, and possibly sleeping and eating disorders. Young children are often less affected by sexual abuse than older children due to not understanding the significance of the incidence and it is suggested that incest promotes more serious consequences for boys than for girls.

Besides age and sex of the child, other factors can influence the consequences of sexual abuse for the victimized child. Some factors include: (1) the child's developmental status, (2) the relationship of the perpetrator and the child, (3) the nature of the sexual act, (4) the duration of the incident or incidents, (5) the degree of shame felt by the child, and (6) the reaction of others once the incident has been revealed.

In sum, the victimization from abuse and neglect creates multiple impacts that usually have long-lasting negative impositions on children from cognitive development, physical health, emotional stability to social adjustment. Knowledge of such impacts is important to the development of effective intervention and treatment service programs.

REFERENCES

1. American Humane Association: *Highlights of Official Child Neglect and Abuse Reporting; 1984.* Denver, American Humane Association, 1986.
2. Bousha, D. M., and Twentyman, C. T.: Mother-child interactional style in abuse, neglect, and control groups: naturalistic observations in the home. *Journal of Abnormal Psychology, 93:*106–114, 1984.

3. Geller, M., and Ford-Somma, L.: *Violent Homes, Violent Children. A Study of Violence in the Families of Juvenile Offenders.* New Jersey State Department of corrections, Trenton. Division of Juvenile Services. Prepared for: National Center on Child Abuse and Neglect (DHHS). Washington, D.C., February, 1984.

4. George, C., and Main, M.: Social interactions of young abused children: approach, avoidance, and aggression. *Child Development, 50:*306–318, 1979.

5. Gutierres, S., and Reich, J. A.: A developmental perspective on runaway behavior: its relationship to child abuse. *Child Welfare, 60:*89–94, 1981.

6. Jenkins, R. L.: The varieties of adolescent's behavior problems and family dynamics. *American Journal of Psychiatry, 124:*1440–1445, 1968.

7. Kinard, E. M.: Emotional development in physically abused children. *American Journal of Orthopsychiatry, 50:*686–696, 1980.

8. Lewis, D. O.: *Neurological, Psychiatric, and Abuse Factors in Delinquents and Nondelinquents.* Paper presented at the American Society of Criminology meetings, San Diego, California, November, 1985.

9. Lewis, D. O., and Shanok, S. S.: Medical histories of delinquent and nondelinquent children. *American Journal of Psychiatry, 134:*1020–1025, 1977.

10. Lewis, D. O., Shanok, S. S., Pincus, J. H., and Glaser, G. H.: Violent juvenile delinquents: psychiatric, neurological, psychological and abuse factors. *Journal of the American Academy of Child Psychiatry, 18:*307–319, 1979.

11. Martin, H. P., and Beezley, P.: Behavioral observations of abused children. *Developmental Medicine and Child Neurology, 19:*373–387, 1977.

12. McCord, J.: A forty year perspective on effects of child abuse and neglect. *Child Abuse and Neglect, 7:*265–270, 1983.

13. Monane, M., Leichter, and Lewis, D. O.: Physical abuse in psychiatrically hospitalized children and adolescents. *Journal of the American Academy of Child Psychiatry, 23:*653–658, 1984.

14. Sorrells, J. M.: Kids who kill. *Crime and Delinquency,* pp. 312–320, 1977.

15. Tarter, R. E., Hegedus, A. M., Winsten, N. E., and Alterman, A. I.: Neuropsychological, personality, and familial characteristics of physically abused delinquents. *Journal of the American Academy of Child Psychiatry, 23:*668–674, 1984.

CHAPTER 4

NATIONAL TRENDS OF STATE LAWS FOR PROTECTING CHILD VICTIMIZATION

OLIVER C.S. TZENG
LINDA J. HANNER

INTRODUCTION

Protection of child victimization from abuse and neglect has its humanistic and legal foundations. Each individual as a human being should receive maximal benefits from family and social resources. Child abuse and neglect are violations of each child's privilege of being a human being in association with family and social environments. From a religious, educational, and a human decency point of view, protection and rescue of victimized or abused children is an unquestionable mission of loving adults.

From a legal standpoint, child abuse or neglect is an act that violates basic human rights set forth in the constitution of the United States. Intrusion and violation of such legal provisions requires intervention and remediation of our government's judicial system. Operationally, each state has various rules and regulations for protecting the rights and privileges of its citizens, including children.

To identify national trends of state laws, we analysed the provisions of 50 states that specifically focus on protection of minors. Across different chapters, articles, sections, and codes of different state laws, a total of 31 categories are identified, and each represents a topic issue that covers similar provisions related to child protection in different states. These 31 categories were further organized under 7 sections as shown in Table IV–I.

*The authors appreciate the evaluations of the contents presented in the chapter by Mr. Gary Hanner who is attorney at law in private practise with expertise in family law.

TABLE IV-I
CONTENT CATEGORIES IN 50 STATES LAWS
REGARDING CHILD ABUSE AND NEGLECT

I. *General*	IV. *Protection*
1. Definitions	1. Protective custody
2. Purpose	2. Protection and assistance teams
	3. Protection of rights of suspected
II. *Records and Reporting*	perpetrators
1. Mandatory reporting	4. Reunification and rehabilitation
2. Permissive reporting	
3. Contents of reports	V. *Evidence and Examinations*
4. Reporting procedures	1. Evidence of abuse
5. Report on postmortem	2. Photographs and X-rays
investigations	3. Admissibility of evidence
6. Falsified reports	4. Exemption due to religion
7. Unfounded reports	5. Emergency medical treatment
8. Penalty for failure to report	
9. Immunity for liability	VI. *Penalty*
	1. Penalty for abuse
III. *Administration*	2. Ordinary punishment protected
1. Central registry	by law
2. Confidentiality	
3. Duties of departments	VII. *Courts*
4. Cooperation of agencies	1. Right to counsel
5. Waiver of investigation	2. Termination of parental rights
6. Regulations for changes	3. General proceedings

Explanations of 31 Content Areas

The meanings of the 31 category names in Table IV–I are briefly summarized as follows:

  I. **General**

    1. **Definitions:** Meanings ascribed to terms used throughout chapter or terms pertaining to child abuse/neglect.

    2. **Purpose:** Provisions and intent of chapter and of legislature in dealing with problems of child abuse/neglect.

  II. **Records and Reporting**

    1. **Mandatory reporting:** Who is required to report either written or orally, a known or suspected case of abuse/neglect to authority.

    2. **Permissive reporting:** Authorization of anyone not listed in mandated reporting statutes to report of suspected child abuse/ neglect.

3. **Contents of reports:** Information written reports shall contain if known.

4. **Reporting procedures:** When and how (written, orally) a report is to be made and to whom it is presented.

5. **Required report for postmortem investigation:** Person who has reasonable cause or suspects that death is due to abuse/neglect is required to report.

6. **Falsified reports:** Penalties for any person who knowingly makes a false report.

7. **Unfound reports:** Any report made which is not supported by some evidence of abuse.

8. **Penalty for failure to report:** Punishment for persons who knowingly fail to make report and who are mandated to do so.

9. **Immunity from liability:** Persons making report are immune from civil or criminal liability.

III. **Administration**

1. **Central registry:** Definition and duties of state established central registry for reports.

2. **Confidentiality:** All records and reports are confidential, section also includes disclosure authorization and penalties.

3. **Duties of department upon receipt of report:** Responsibility of action (investigation) by appropriate law enforcement agency or social service upon receiving a report and to whom that agency will report.

4. **Cooperation between agencies:** Responsibility of state, political subdivisions and agencies to cooperate with agencies which provide protective services.

5. **Waiver of investigation:** Circumstances under which a protective service can waive investigation of report.

6. **Regulations for changes:** Provisions for the administration to implement necessary changes.

IV. **Protection**

1. **Protective custody:** Persons authorized to keep child in custody and conditions in which a child can be kept in custody if believed to be in imminent danger.

2. **Protection and assistance teams:** Authorization and conditional status for protection agencies to organize teams for assistance in abuse/neglect and protection from abuse/neglect.

3. **Protection of rights of suspected perpetrators:** Rules and regulations for protection of suspected offenders of child abuse/neglect.
4. **Reunification and rehabilitation:** Provisions for reuniting family, establish reasons for abuse/neglect and removal of child, scheduled monitoring of agreed upon changes.

V. **Evidence and Examinations**
   1. **Evidence of abuse:** Definition of what must be evident before a child abuse/neglect report can be done.
   2. **Photographs and X-rays:** Authorization for officials to take photographs of areas of trauma visible on a child who is the subject of a report.
   3. **Admissibility of evidence (Evidence not privileged):** Provision stating privileged communication such as the doctor/patient is not grounds for exclusion in a proceeding of alleged abuse/neglect.
   4. **Exemption due to spiritual means:** Provision for child under treatment by spiritual means alone not considered medically neglected.
   5. **Emergency medical treatment:** Definition of emergency medical treatment, when it is authorized, and who is authorized to treat child.

VI. **Penalty**
   1. **Penalty for abuse:** Description of punishment by imprisonment or fines for proven guilt of abuse/neglect.
   2. **Ordinary punishment protected by law:** Provision for not prohibiting ordinary force in punishment enforced by parent, teacher, or other persons.

VII. **Courts**
   1. **Right to counsel (Guardian ad litem):** Provision for any abused or neglected child to be appointed an attorney to represent childs' rights and serve as guardian ad litem.
   2. **Termination of parent rights:** Proceeding to terminate rights of parents who are guilty of child abuse/neglect.
   3. **General proceedings:** Procedures for hearings, jurisdiction, venue, summons, etc.

SECTION I. GENERAL

Definitions

A category of definitions is included in most state's laws to explain or further clarify the provisions that government has set forth. A sample of terms that were defined in the 50 law chapters include child, child abuse and neglect, mental injury, physical injury, parent, guardian, physician, and indicated report, etc.

The term **child,** similarly defined across all 50 states, refers to a person who is under, or reasonably presumed to be under, a certain age limit. However, this age limit varies throughout the United States with 18 years being the most common age in 38 states. The remaining states list the age of a **child** to be: 19 years in one state (Wyoming), 17 years in one state (Louisiana), 16 years in seven states, 14 years in one state (Texas), and 10 years in one state (Oregon).

A summary of the definition of **child abuse and neglect** is as follows: when a person responsible for a child's welfare, knowingly, intentionally, or negligently causes or permits a child to be harmed or threatened with harm of physical injury by other than accidental means, injury resulting in a mental or emotional condition, negligent treatment, sexual abuse, maltreatment, mistreatment, nontreatment, exploitation, or abandonment.

Purpose of Child Protection Law

In order to protect children's health and welfare from abuse and neglect, the following are generally adopted goals by the 50 states:

1. encourage prompt, effective mandatory reporting processes of suspected or known incidents of abuse/neglect to the appropriate authorities, and provide effective child protection service to quickly investigate received reports,

2. establish a legal framework conducive to the judicial processing of child neglect, abuse and abandonment and neglect cases,

3. safeguard and enforce the general welfare of physically and mentally abused/neglected children, and take such actions as necessary and feasible to prevent further abuse/neglect,

4. encourage cooperation among the states as well as to coordinate efforts by state and local public agencies, in cooperation with private agencies and organizations,

5. provide care, guidance, and control for the child, for his/her own

welfare preferably in his/her own home but also if removed from the control of his parents or guardian, and

6. preserve and strengthen the privacy and unity of family life whenever possible and to provide rehabilitative services for abused/neglected children and families.

SECTION II. RECORDS AND REPORTING

Persons Mandated to Report Suspected Abuse and Neglect

Required by law and under subject to penalty, certain persons are mandated, in accordance with rules and regulations of each state to report the following:

1. suspected or known incidents when a child has been physically abused/neglected, has had injuries inflicted upon him/her by other than accidental means, or has been subjected to incest, molestation, sexual exploitation, or sexual abuse, and

2. observations in which the child is being subjected to conditions that are likely to result in abuse or neglect.

Persons required to report include but are not limited to: (a) any medical, dental or mental health professional (including osteopathic physician, resident, intern, nurse, emergency medical service, and hospital administrator), (b) religious personnel (including christian science practitioner and religious healer), (c) child educator and care service personnel (including school teacher or other school personnel, social service worker, child care or foster care worker), and (d) social services and child protection officer (including social service worker, peace officer, and law enforcement official).

Permissive Reporting By Any Person

In addition to those persons, firms, corporations and officials required to report, **any person may make a report** if such person has reasonable cause to suspect that a child:

1. has had physical injuries inflicted upon him/her by a parent or caretaker by other than accidental means,
2. has been sexually assaulted or sexually exploited, and
3. has been neglected or exploited by a parent or caretaker.

Contents of Reports

The reports provided for in each state's child abuse/neglect chapter shall contain, to the extent known to the reporter, the following information:

1. the names and addresses of the abused child and his/her parents or other persons responsible for his care,
2. age, sex, and race of the abused child,
3. other children threatened by the abusive conduct,
4. the nature and extent of the injuries, including any evidence of previous injuries to the child or his/her siblings, and any other information that the reporting person believes might be helpful in establishing the cause of the injuries,
5. the family composition,
6. the identity of the perpetrator,
7. the source of the report,
8. the name, address, and occupation of the person making the report and where he/she can be reached,
9. the actions taken by the reporting source, including the taking of color photographs or the making of radiologic examinations,
10. incidence of removal or protective custody of the child,
11. notification of coroner or medical examiner, and
12. any other information that the persons making the report believes may be helpful.

Reporting Procedures

Persons who are reporting mandatorily or voluntarily must follow procedure that complies with each state's rules and regulations. In general:

1. an oral report shall be made immediately by telephone or personal contact with the appropriated agency such as a county child welfare agency, the department of social welfare, or a sheriff or city police department, and

2. a written report to the appropriate agency is usually required to follow the initial oral report as soon as possible, and some states have deadlines such as 72 hours to report, or 24 hours for police departments to refer all cases reported to them.

Mandatory Reporting For Postmortem Investigation

Persons required to report or any other person who has reasonable cause to believe that a child has died as a result of child abuse or neglect must report that fact to the appropriate authority such as the district attorney, medical examiners, coroner, local welfare agency, police department, or county sheriff.

Some states require persons to report to more than one source and mandated reporters who fail to report may be subject to penalty.

Penalties of Falsified Reports

Any person who intentionally or recklessly files a false report may be subject to penalties according to each state's rules and regulations. Penalties may include:

1. criminal or civil liability for any actual damages suffered by the person or person so reported,
2. liability for any punitive damages set by the court or jury, and
3. in cases of one parent filing a report which lacks factual foundation against the other parent, the report may be deemed knowingly false.

Unfound Report

As a result of an investigation conducted pursuant to a state's law, an alleged report of abuse/neglect is determined as **indicated** or **unfound**. Unfound report implies there was no credible evidence of the alleged abuse or maltreatment and all information identifying the subjects of the report will be expunged from the central register and from the records of all local child protective services. The result of the investigation must be determined within a given time period, usually 90 days.

Penalty For Failure To Make Required Report:

All but four states (Maryland, Mississippi, North Carolina, and Wyoming) carry penalties for failure to report when mandated to do so, and some include penalty for willfully preventing another person from reporting child abuse/neglect incidents. The following Table is a classification of all penalties for failure to report child abuse/neglect.

TABLE IV-II
PENALTIES FOR NONREPORTING OF CHILD ABUSE/NEGLECT

Penalty	State
None	Maryland
	Mississippi
	North Carolina
	Wyoming
Misdemeanor	Georgia
	Hawaii
	Idaho
	Minnesota
	Nevada
	New Hampshire
	Oklahoma
	Virginia
Disorderly person	New Jersey
Class A Misdemeanor	Illinois
	Missouri
Class B Misdemeanor	Alaska
	Indiana
	Kansas
	Kentucky
	North Dakota
	Texas
	Utah
Class 1 Misdemeanor	South Dakota
Class 2 Misdemeanor	Arizona
	Florida
Class 3 Misdemeanor	Colorado
	Nebraska
Misdemeanor of the Fourth Degree	Ohio
A Gross Misdemeanor	Washington
First offense no penalty; subsequent offense is a Third Degree Misdemeanor.	Pennsylvania
A Misdemeanor; civil liability for damages resulting from failure to report.	Iowa
	Michigan
	Montana
	New York
Fine of not less than $25 nor more than $100	New Mexico
Fine of not more than $500	Connecticut
	Maine
	Vermont
Fine of not more than $1000	Massachusetts
	Oregon
Fine of $100 and up to five days imprisonment civil liability for damages resulting from failure to report	Arkansas

TABLE IV-II (Continued)

Penalty	State
Fine of $100 or imprisonment of not more than 10 days or both..........	West Virginia
Fine of not more than $100, imprisonment of not..................... more than 15 days or both.	Delaware
Fine of not more than $50 or imprisonment .... not more than three months or both.	Tennessee
Punishable by a fine of not more than $500......................... or imprisonment of not more than six months	Alabama Louisiana South Carolina
Punishable by a fine of not more than $500 or imprisonment .... of not more than one year or both; civil liability for damages resulting from failure to report.	Rhode Island
Punishable by a fine of up to $1000 or .... imprisonment of up to 6 months or both	California Wisconsin

Immunity From Civil Liability of Criminal Penalty

Any person, including those voluntarily making reports and those required to make reports, are in many states immune from any civil liability or criminal penalty that may be incurred or imposed as a result thereof, if the report was made in good faith.

Tennessee also provides that a person will have civil cause for punitive damages against any person who causes detrimental change in employment status of the reporting party because of the report.

SECTION III. ADMINISTRATION

Establishment of a Central Registry

Provisions to establish and maintain a central registry vary in requirements and in facilities. A state agency with various names such as Department of Pensions and Security, Department of Human Services, or Department of Public Welfare, may house a central telephone and reporting service. It is designed to receive reports of suspected cases of child abuse/neglect, in some cases, on a twenty-four hour a day, seven day a week basis. The central registry may contain but not be limited to:

1. all information in the written report,
2. record of the final disposition of the report, including services offered and services accepted,

3. the names and identifying data, dates and circumstances of any persons requesting or receiving information from the registry,
4. the plan for rehabilitative treatment,
5. any other information which might be helpful in furthering the purposes of that state's child abuse/neglect chapter, and
6. a department to organize and staff the registry and adopt rules for its operation.

Cases maintained in the central registry may be classified in one of the following categories:

1. court substantiated,
2. petition to be filed,
3. investigation inconclusive, and
4. unfounded report.

Confidentiality of Reports

The names of subjects of child abuse/neglect reports, names of reporters, records, and working papers used or developed in an investigation are confidential and may be disclosed only for purposes consistent with the rules and regulations of that department. It is unlawful to disclose, receive, make use of, or knowingly permit the use of any information and many departments enforce penalties for doing so. Exceptions for disclosure may include:

1. when determined material to an indictment or conviction by the court in which the investigation is filed,
2. to a health practitioner who is examining, attending or treating a child whom he/she believes had been the victim of abuse,
3. to the employees of the department having responsibility for the investigation of a child abuse report,
4. to a law enforcement officer having responsibility for the temporary emergency removal of a child from the child's parent or legal guardian,
5. for use by any person engaged in bona fide research who is authorized to have access to such information, and
6. for use by an attorney or guardian ad litem in representing or defending a child or his/her parents or guardians in a court proceeding related to abuse or neglect of that child.

Duties of Departments Upon Receipt of Report

Upon receipt of a report of abuse/neglect of a child, the appropriate department has duties provided for in each state's law some of which include:

1. an immediate investigation of the report (some states within twenty-four hours, some within seven days), which may include a visit to the child's home, an interview with the child, a physical, psychological or psychiatric examination of any child or children in that home,
2. submission of a written report after the investigation including determination of the nature, extent, and cause of the abuse, identity of the person responsible therefore, and evaluation of the parents, home environment, and all other facts found to be pertinent,
3. take necessary action toward preventing further abuses and offer protective social services when necessary, and
4. notify the police or prosecuting attorney if report is founded.

Cooperation Between Agencies

Any agency which provides protective services to children must receive cooperation, assistance, and information from the state, every county, municipality, and school district, the Division of Family Services, the Department of Health and Welfare, the Division of Mental Health, the State Board of Education, and state and local law enforcement officers to fulfill its responsibilities. Specific duties include:

1. full cooperation with the department in conducting activities,
2. transmitting reports of abuse and sharing pertinent information,
3. protecting the welfare of other children potentially subject to abuse detected by a report, and
4. making all reasonable efforts to minimize the number of interviews of any child victim which may be necessary.

Waiver of Full Investigation of Report

Nevada allows for a protective service agency to waive a full investigation of a report of abuse/neglect if it is satisfied that:

1. the person or agency who made the report can provide services to meet the needs of the child and the family, and this person or agency agrees to do so, and

2. the person or other agency agrees in writing to report periodically on the child and to report immediately any threat or harm to the child's welfare.

Regulations for Changes

The power to adopt, amend, or repeat rules and regulations necessary to implement and govern departmental procedures is often mentioned specifically in a state's law. Regulations may be fixed according to that section of the law, or allowed to be further defined or clarified by the appropriate department, such as, Director of Social Services, the State Department of Pensions and Security, or the Department of Social and Rehabilitation Services.

SECTION IV. PROTECTION

Protective Custody

In many states, a law enforcement official, attorney, trial judge, physician, or person in charge of any hospital or similar institution may retain temporary custody of a child when he believes it necessary for the health of the child. This can be done without a court order under two circumstances which are: (1) the child's physical or mental condition will be seriously impaired or endangered if he is not taken into immediate custody, and (2) there is no reasonable opportunity to obtain an order from the court. Each state has specific provisions for who is allowed to issue the necessary orders to protect the child and regulations for protective custody. Examples include:

1. an agency may hold a child for 24 hours or longer, not to exceed 48 hours excluding weekends or holidays, after which, the child must be released or a hearing must be held,

2. an agency must immediately notify the parent, guardian, and the court that it is holding the child in physical custody, where the child is and why he/she is being held,

3. a hospital may hold a child until the next regular weekday session of court, regardless of whether additional medical treatment is required and whether the child's parent/guardian requests the return of the child during that period,

4. a law enforcement official, or physician may retain temporary protective custody without the consent of the child's parent/guardian, and

5. if a parent/guardian requests the release of a child, the presiding

judge may authorize to keep that child in custody if he/she believes release would be detrimental to the child's health or safety.

Protection and Assistance Teams

An agency which provides protective service may, in many states, organize one or more protection/assistance teams to assist the agency in the investigation of abuse/neglect reports, diagnose treatment, and coordinate responsibilities. Members of these programs are usually appointed, must meet requirements, and may be given police powers. In their law, some states account for the appropriation of moneys to these programs and specifically list responsibilities such as:

1. informing persons mandated to report of their duties, options, and responsibilities,
2. informing the public of the nature, problems, and extent of abuse and neglect,
3. informing the public of the therapeutic services available to children and their families,
4. encourage self-reporting and voluntary acceptance of therapeutic services available,
5. conduct ongoing training programs for the agency staff about the law,
6. publicize the existence and the number of toll free telephone service to receive reports of abuse or neglect,
7. investigate and screen complaints, and
8. offer counseling services to parents or other caretakers to prevent abuse or neglect, improve the quality of child care, and to preserve and stabilize family life.

Protection of Rights of Suspected Perpetrators

Maryland allows provisions for protection of the rights of persons suspected of child abuse/neglect. Rules and regulations include:

1. the person suspected of child abuse/neglect must be given notice before his/her name is entered in the child abuse/neglect registry,
2. on request, the department must hold an administrative hearing for the person suspected of abuse/neglect to appeal the entry of his/her name in the registry, and
3. this hearing must be held in the county in which the suspected perpetrator lives.

Reunification and Rehabilitation

Some states provide for a reunification plan to children and their families for purposes of:

1. averting a disruption of a family which could result in the placement of a child in foster care,
2. enabling a child who has been placed in foster care to return to his family at an earlier time than would otherwise be possible, and
3. reducing the likelihood that a child who has been discharged from foster care would return to such care.

The department may be required to develop a rehabilitation plan which specifically includes:

1. identifying the reasons for the child's removal from his/her home,
2. indicating changes which must occur for the child to return home,
3. providing the parents with notice of the child's residence and any serious injuries or medical care received,
4. making good faith efforts to cooperate with the parents in pursuit of the rehabilitation plan,
5. periodical review of the plan making any appropriate changes, and
6. petitioning for judicial review.

Upon the return of the child to the household, the appropriate department may be required to establish proper supervision and monitoring of the household on a regularly scheduled basis for a set period of time.

SECTION V. EVIDENCE AND EXAMINATION

Evidence of Abuse

Before a report of child abuse/neglect is required or will be classified as **indicated**, there must be clear and convincing evidence found for burden of proof. Some states specify abuse or neglect to be evidenced by, but not limited to:

1. the presence of characteristic distribution of fractures, a disproportionate amount of soft tissue injury, internal or external bleeding, and/or swelling,
2. evidence that injuries occurred at different times or are in different stages of resolution,
3. evidence of malnutrition,

4. evidence of emotional injuries which may hinder the physical or emotional development of the child,
5. indication of a suspected cause of recent trauma in question,
6. indication of a family history of such episodes, and
7. no occurrence of new lesions during the child's hospitalization or removal from custody of a parent/caretaker.

Photographs and X-Rays

Less than half of the 50 states provide that, any person mandated to report incidents of suspected child abuse/neglect may take or cause to be taken, at public expense, photographs of the areas of physical trauma visible on a child and, if medically indicated, cause to be performed radiological examinations of the child. Requirements for persons causing to be taken, or taking photographs/x-rays include:

1. sending photographs/x-rays to the appropriate child protective service as soon as possible,
2. taking photographs in a manner consistent with professional standards, including minimizing trauma to the child,
3. notifying the department as soon as possible if he/she is unable to take, or cause these photographs to be taken, and
4. no requirement of gaining consent from the parent/guardian to take photographs/x-rays.

Admissibility of Evidence

Only the attorney/client doctrine of privileged communication will be upheld pertaining to any civil or criminal litigation in which a child's neglect, dependency, abuse, or abandonment is in issue.

Any other legally recognized privileged communication including doctor/patient privilege and husband/wife privilege will not be grounds for excluding any evidence regarding a child's injuries or their cause in any judicial proceeding.

Exemption Due to Spiritual Means

A parent or guardian legitimately practicing his/her religious beliefs, who selects and depends upon spiritual means alone for the treatment or cure of disease or remedial care of his/her child, will not be considered a negligent parent or guardian. Although many states carry this section in their law, few add amendments such as:

1. the spiritual means of treatment must be in accordance with the tenets and practice of a recognized church or religious denomination,
2. this exception shall not preclude a court from ordering medical services by a duly accredited practitioner who relies solely on spiritual means for healing be provided to the child when his/her health requires it, and
3. this exemption shall not preclude a court from ordering medical services be provided to the child, when his/her health requires it.

Emergency Medical Treatment

When any physician, law enforcement officer, social service representative, or court, indicates that a child believed to be abused or neglected is in need of immediate medical treatment, they may order the indicated treatment with or without the consent of the child's parent or guardian.

Some states require a petition to the court if the child's custodian is unable or unwilling to consent to treatment, while other states waive the court order otherwise required in situations of immediate risk of serious injury to the child.

SECTION VI. PENALTY

Penalty for Child Abuse/Neglect

A person commits child abuse if he or she knowingly, intentionally, or negligently causes or permits another to cause:

1. serious bodily injury, serious physical or mental deficiency or impairment to a minor,
2. a child to be placed in a situation that endangers his/her life or health,
3. a child to be deprived of necessary food, clothing, shelter, or care, or
4. a minor to be exposed, tortured, tormented or cruelly punished in a manner which does not constitute aggravated assault.

If a person commits a child abuse offense intentionally, penalties may be (a) Class E Felony, (b) Felony of the Second Degree, or (c) Class 4 Felony.

If a person is guilty of an offense done with criminal negligence, penalties may be (a) Class A Misdemeanor, or (b) Class I Misdemeanor.

Ordinary Punishment Protected by Law

Oklahoma and Washington include provisions that nothing in the law should be construed to authorize interference with child raising practices. The law will not prohibit any parent, teacher, or other person from using ordinary force as a means of reasonable discipline, including spanking, switching, or paddling, which are not proved to be injurious to the child's health, welfare, and safety.

SECTION VII. COURTS

Right to Counsel and Guardian Ad Litem

In cases involving children who are alleged to be neglected or abused, the child, his parents or custodian, are entitled to be represented by counsel at every stage of the proceedings. If the parents cannot afford an attorney, one will be appointed. In most jurisdictions the judge determines at the initial stage whether or not the child should have a guardian ad litem appointed for him. The guardian ad litem may also hire counsel. Many states have instituted programs to supply persons to act as guardian ad litems who have expertise dealing with children alleged to be abused or molested.

The guardian ad litem, if one is appointed, and the welfare department will:

1. be advised of any significant developments in the case, particularly any further abuse/neglect of the child involved, as well as the parents,
2. make any investigations he/she deems necessary to ascertain facts,
3. talk with or observe the child involved,
4. interview witnesses and parents/guardians of the child,
5. examine and cross-examine witnesses in hearings and may introduce and examine his/her own witnesses,
6. make recommendations to the court concerning the child's welfare, and
7. participate in the proceedings to the degree necessary to adequately represent the child.

Termination of Parental Rights:

The finding that a child is delinquent, mistreated, or neglected does not always deprive the parents of their parental rights of that child, but a court may terminate the rights of a parent to a child in situations set forth by a state's law. Some circumstances include:

1. termination will be valid only if acknowledged by the court and parent who is ordered to terminate his/her parental rights under circumstances free from duress and fraud, any termination must be ordered by the court, one parent cannot voluntarily terminate his rights and responsibilities,

2. finding that a parent who is entitled to custody has abandoned his/her child for one year (time period may vary), or failed to provide support for a specific statutory period,

3. finding that a parent who is entitled to custody has failed to give his/her child the parental care or protection necessary for that child's physical or mental health, or has willfully neglected to provide the child with the necessary support or education,

4. finding a parent unfit by reason of debauchery, intoxication, habitual use of narcotic drugs, repeated lewd or lascivious behavior, or other conduct that is detrimental to the physical or mental health or morals of his/her child, or

5. establishing the parent as a perpetrator of child abuse/neglect.

General Court Proceedings

Some state's laws include the general proceedings of the presiding court (i.e. juvenile court, probate court, family court) that is designated by that state to process hearings concerned with child abuse and/or neglect. These general proceedings vary from state to state according to the structure of the legal system, but in general:

1. the court has exclusive original jurisdiction in proceedings concerning any child living or found within that same state,

2. a petition to invoke jurisdiction or the court must be filed pursuant to the appropriate state's law, usually the petition is referred to the attorney general or prosecuting attorney,

3. any person who has evidence of abuse, neglect or abandonment as recognized in terms of the state, may request a petition to be filed,

4. after a petition is filed, the court will summon the parent/guardian, the suspected perpetrator, the child, or anyone else the court deems necessary to appear in court, and set the time and place for the adjudicatory hearing,

5. the adjudicatory hearing's purpose is to determine the truth of the allegation in the petition filed and the possible cause, and

6. if at the adjudicatory hearing the child is determined as abused/neglected, the court will set a date for a **disposition** hearing to ascertain the best interests of the child, such as remaining with his/her parents or vesting legal custody to another individual or authorized agency.

CONCLUSION AND EVALUATION

Completeness

States currently define abuse and neglect in broad, sometimes vague language and these statutes are often susceptible to various misapplications. This is true especially for families with atypical cultural norms. Such broad definitions may cause problems such as: (1) misuse of the definitional term, (2) increasing the likelihood of unnecessary or inappropriate intervention, and (3) permitting arbiters and social workers to make subjective decisions. Based on these contentions, states are urged to further delineate the legal codes and statutes associated with identifiable characteristics about children victimization.

The current legal system emphasizes intervention and treatment modes of child abuse and neglect issues. The prevention and follow-up modes have been mostly neglected. Therefore, state legislation may be used to mandate that education and prevention programs be made available to all professionals in the community working with children and their families. Beyond the statutory roles and duties of intervention and treatment of victimized children, social service providers and criminal justice system investigators should be trained in a broader perspective of victimization: the background stressors, trigger mechanisms, profiles of victims and needs for comprehensive services, etc.

The ultimate goal of legal intervention of child abuse and neglect cases is to provide a healthy environment for children to grow. Therefore, to the abused and/or neglected child, treatment and rehabilitation are extremely important, unfortunately they are not available to the victimized child in most states. Specifically, the current state laws do not require the person convicted of child victimization to pay for the treatment (with the exception of Colorado and South Dakota), and most social services and state and local programs do not automatically provide these services to all victimized children.

Enforcement

There are two major concerns in the handling of child abuse and neglect cases. The first is the protection of the child, and the second is criminal prosecution of the perpetrator when necessary. In the decision of whether to initiate criminal proceedings, two aspects are frequently considered: (1) the rights of a criminal defendant are closely guarded, and (2) prosecution requires evidence **beyond a reasonable doubt** that the defendant was responsible for the offense. In child abuse cases, evidence may not be sufficient to indicate which individual was truly responsible although the incident of abuse is evident. Generally speaking, the judicial intervention on child abuse and neglect cases is required to follow the same prosecuting procedure in trying other criminal cases. Therefore, various rules must be followed in prosecution of the perpetrator (e.g. right to a jury, adherence to rules of evidence, right to cross-examination, right to appointed counsel, right to a public and speedy trial, and the highest standard of proof). The prosecutor must prove that the defendant intentionally committed the offense, and without proof, the prosecution will be unsuccessful. The constitution prohibits placing a defendant in double jeopardy, so there is no second chance to prove guilt.

Unfortunately, the legal/prosecution mode of intervention could yield results that frequently put the child in a no win dilemma. For example, the unsuccessful prosecution can place the child in further danger if the perpetrator's frustration over the criminal charges is directed toward the child, whereas the successful prosecution may break up the family unit. Therefore, alternative intervention programs other than criminal proceedings may be considered to better meet the child's needs.

One recurring difficulty in prosecuting cases of child victimization is that many cases go unreported for years. Children involved with abuse incidents may be very young, confused, responsible for the incident, or unaware that it is a crime. Because of the time lapse, many cases cannot be tried. Many states are extending their statue of limitation for crimes involving children from the average three year limitation to seven to eight years.

Interstate Differences

Establishment of legal standards for state intervention of child abuse and neglect is a very difficult undertaking. The absence of much data and the strong emotions involved with children victimization make it difficult for everyone to adopt a specific set of standards. A state law reflects the views of the people drafting that law, and people across different states have different opinions as to the extent of intervention their government should be allowed to make and the approach of that intervention when it comes to family matters. Therefore, under the concerns with the right to privacy and the freedom to bring up children as parents think best, most legal standards assume it is best to intervene only when essential (i.e. when a child is in danger), and to intervene successfully when necessary.

Some court issues remain to be resolved in different states. For example, some experts consider the use of videotaped testimony of the child can lessen the child's stress in the courtroom and can also establish a stronger case to bring a guilty charge. However, the Sixth Amendment to the United States Constitution guarantees that the accused person shall enjoy the right to be confronted with the witnesses against him.

Normally, out of courtroom statements (heresay) are excluded as evidence from any trial, but recently there have been provisions that would allow any out of court statements made by a child that describe any act of sexual contact. This provision would make it easier for the child to provide all necessary information in the court proceedings.

As mentioned previously, many states have the provision to exclude all privileged conversations except the lawyer/client privilege. This allows the lawyer to obtain as much information as possible concerning the welfare of the child. On the other hand, this provision also poses a problem with therapists and counselors working with family members. When it is known a case will go to court, the therapist/counselor must warn the parent(s) their conversation may end up in court. As a result, the effort of counseling might be seriously hampered.

The above issues are some examples of differences across states. Such differences may reflect different legislative philosophies across the nation. However, all legal systems are common in maintaining the rights of all parties involved including children, parents, and alleged perpetrators.

Qualifications of an Expert Witness

Determining whether a witness is qualified to testify as an expert in a proceeding is a decision that is left to the trial court. The trial judge must decide whether the expert's knowledge of the subject matter is enough that his opinions will most likely assist the court in arriving at the truth.

A witness may qualify as an expert by reason of knowledge, skill, experience, training, or education. An expert is not required to have certificates of training or memberships in professional organizations, nor does he need to be an outstanding practitioner in the field in which he professes expertise. Three general principles are important: (1) a witness' qualifications must be based on the nature and extent of his knowledge and not on his title; (2) an expert's testimony must relate to the subject matter on which he is qualified; and (3) a witness may be an expert at using an instrument of measure, but not in interpreting the meaning of the results.

A primary argument for excluding expert testimony in abuse/neglect cases is that lay jurors are likely to overvalue the expert testimony. Therefore, the court should admit only opinions that are entitled to the weight the jurors are likely to attach to it.

Another consideration is that expert opinions are often discredited in cross examination because the opinion is usually based on heresay (what the child tells the expert) than on fact.

Regardless of either consideration, an expert witness is often used in sexual abuse cases to explain to the jurors: (1) the dynamics of interfamily child sexual abuse, (2) why the child delayed reporting the alleged incident, (3) the opinion on how the child is suffering from stress or had suffered sexual trauma, and (4) the opinion relating to the child credibility. Regarding the credibility of a child's testimony, a study of 287 cases of alleged sexual assault on children found that children do not fabricate claims of sexual assault (Colo. App. 1984).

CHAPTER 5

ABUSE AND NEGLECT PREVENTION THROUGH CRISIS INTERVENTION

Jamia J. Jacobsen
Oliver C. S. Tzeng

INTRODUCTION

America's children and their families are in trouble, trouble so deep as to constitute a serious threat to the future of our society. The major source of that threat is bureaucratic "benign neglect." We have failed to recognize that the problems of the multi-troubled family in a changing society are the problems of the entire society in the midst of moral and economic crisis and cannot be solved except in that context (Fontana, 1986).

Today, our families are facing multiple problems. The problems of child abuse and neglect do not stand alone in American society. There are problems of wife abuse, family alienation, multiple marriages in both of the child's parents and grandparents. There are also problems of divorce which leaves mothers to raise children alone, teenage pregnancies, the involvement of AIDS, and drug and alcohol abuse. In the midst of this barrage of problems, the main difficulty facing families is maintaining family stability, and thus preventing child abuse and neglect.

The best strategy for dealing with violent or unstable families is to prevent the violence or instability from occurring in the first place. A major part of the battle of preventing child abuse is to spread knowledge to the community, parents, children, social service workers, law enforcement officials, or anyone that may come into contact with child abuse.

Other prevention strategies include, training child protection workers, implementation of hotlines, new and better investigative procedures, treatment programs and self-help groups.

Prevention in the Past

Certainly, prevention programs are not new, for they date to the 1960's when prevention efforts were included as part of the mental health programs. However, prevention activities for child abuse have been slow to materialize even though great effort and amounts of money have been spent on identification, reporting, and intervention. It has been only recently that research has facilitated the realization that child abuse **prevention** is vital.

Too often, efforts to establish prevention programs have been resisted due to high costs and lack of funding. The projection that prevention could not be measured for statistical purposes existed, therefore, funding of such projects could not be substantiated. Added to these problems have been the **turfism** or mind set of professionals in the field. Many were so busy with treatment issues or were trained only in aspects of the treatment level, that they viewed prevention as an entity that should not or could not be dealt with. Therefore, in the past, serious attention has not been given to the area of child abuse and neglect prevention.

APPROACHES TO PREVENTION

Prevention can be found on three distinct levels which are primary, secondary, and tertiary. The community, however, often deals with the three levels in a singular effort. It must be recalled that primary prevention refers to efforts aimed at positively influencing caregivers before abuse or neglect occurs. Secondary prevention is the supportive services offered to parents **at risk.**

Tertiary prevention (or treatment) is services offered to families after the child abuse and neglect has occurred. Prevention here is in the form of keeping families from developing abusive cycles in which children are repeatedly abused or neglected. Presently, most efforts are aimed at tertiary prevention with little development of primary or secondary levels. Adequate community prevention programs must develop strategies on all three levels.

Garbarino (1986), refers to two basic approaches to prevention which are: (1) the **patchwork prevention** or working with distinct problems of child abuse in isolation, and (2) the **total reform prevention** or altering families within a community. From these approaches, he drew the following conclusions:

1. We should be as precise as possible in stating the prevention goals and limits of these claims;

2. We should recognize that prevention efforts may operate only under specific conditions. For example, some prevention programs may only

work for certain distinct ethnic or social classes. Thus we must focus on abuse in target populations by using different approaches;

3. Statistical comparison for lowering child abuse across the whole society must be measured on like indices;

4. A complete strategy will involve both generalized primary prevention and programming targeted at comparable high risk groups using random assignment to assist in preventative interventions;

5. Comparable communities can be the targets for intervention to facilitate research attempts;

6. Evaluation efforts must utilize multiple measures; and

7. Prevention efforts including measures designed to restrain destructive patterns and measures designed to replace destructive patterns with positive patterns that are incompatible with abuse.

Garbarino stresses that to reach these propositions, the work of program design and evaluation must be linked to a research base in order to set goals for reduction and prevention of child abuse. The same holds true when considering what programs to implement in a community. With over one million children abused in 1984, implementation strategies must be looked at to prevent this problem from continuing.

It is also important to stress that more research needs to be conducted on these newly emerging prevention efforts. While the child abuse syndrome was identified as early as 1974, little research has been done in the area, (Grave, 1983).

Child Protective Services

A child protective service is the agency with primary responsibility for child abuse and neglect prevention and treatment in each county. An agency can take many different approaches to offering service to abusive or potentially abusive families as well as offering primary prevention education. A description follows of various types of services available.

Child Crisis Centers

These centers are beneficial to families and children caught in the abuse cycle. They may differ in approach, some offer therapeutic schools, some offer crisis stays for children, and others offer peer support services and/or education programs.

Depressed or overwhelmed parents may bring their children to a 24 hour crisis center for respite care. This is one concrete method to help reduce stress for parents and provide a loving nurturing stay for their children. Families may leave their children for short-term (1–3 days) or long-term (1–6 months) care depending upon the situation. Goals are usually set for reducing stress and helping the family with its current situation. These centers also help families learn positive child rearing behaviors and assistance in obtaining needed resources through other social service programs.

Most crisis centers have developed multiphase and multidisciplinary approaches for intervening directly with parents and children. A counselor or counselor aide screens calls to the center to interview the parent calling in. This helps assess that persons need or appropriateness for the crisis center service.

Drop-in Centers

These centers permit the parent to place children for short periods of time without detailed explanations or preparation. They offer short-term crisis care or respite.

Home-Based Family Services

These services provide the worker or paraprofessional the opportunity to assess the family in its own habitat. This allows observation of a family's strengths and weakness in operating as a unit.

Support Groups

Support groups or self-help groups can reduce the family's social isolation. They provide an opportunity for the victim and/or perpetrator of the abuse or neglect to talk and receive counseling in a nonjudgemental way.

Extended Family Centers

These centers are designed to offer parenting programs in a nonresidential mode that combine day care and family treatment programs. Families remain intact in these centers but allow the counselor and staff an opportunity to intervene and teach.

Live-In Treatment Centers

These centers offer live-in treatment to the whole family. This facilitates the use of a controlled environment during treatment, and although it is costly, it allows families to stay intact while protecting the child from danger. Families work directly on intervention methods and positive parenting techniques.

Emergency Homemaker Services

Homemaker services offer the assistance of a caregiver or surrogate parent to families in times of crisis or emergency. This allows a new role model to be present in the home to teach techniques of positive parenting.

Comprehensive Emergency Services

These services are a system of coordinated services designed to meet emergency needs of children and their families in crisis. They can provide options in care which will protect children and reduce trauma induced by crisis. Integrated in the services may be emergency foster care, emergency shelter for families, emergency shelter for adolescents, outreach and follow-up.

Working With the Child Protective Service
for Prevention of Child Abuse

Because of the vast responsibility and the complex nature of child maltreatment problems, the prevention of child abuse and neglect cases should be handled by coordination of a child protective service staff and various social services such as specially trained law enforcement officers, educational systems, and medical treatment organizations, as well as community members or organizations.

This teamwork should have multiple functions, such as: the protection of the child, reduction of friction between agencies, streamlining of the investigative process, and enhancement of all services for the children and their families with a focus on prevention.

A cooperation between agencies includes coordination of programs within each organization. Duplication or competition of services must be controlled as much as possible under the direction of the child protective service. Examples of prevention programs that can be supported in a number of different agencies include:

1. Parent education and support groups;
2. Education and support groups for teenage parents, inexperienced parents, single parents and parents to be;

3. Information about services for handicapped and developmentally delayed children;
4. Bibliography lists to provide professionals with information that can help protect hearing impaired children from abuse and neglect;
5. Support groups for victims of abuse and neglect;
6. Development of self-study manuals, for use by individuals and groups which focus on the assessment, intervention, and prevention of adolescent abuse and neglect. These manuals stress continuing education and provide outlines for workshops. They provide a series of exercises in experimental learning, and include how to define and identify family malfunctioning;
7. Skits, both video and live drama, which teach prevention and increase awareness of abuse and neglect;
8. Parent education projects that give street theater performances directed toward hard to reach parent populations;
9. Prenatal and perinatal programs including infancy and early childhood factors relating to the prevention and occurrence of child abuse;
10. Child stimulation and parent stimulation training;
11. Specific child abuse prevention programs for teachers;
12. Specialized programs directed toward prevention among ethnic populations such as Mexican, American, Hispanic, and American Indian;
13. Implementation of family life education to help break the cycle of child abuse by teaching positive discipline strategies to future parents; and
14. Stress/crisis intervention programs intended to prevent or intercede in the development of abusive patterns of family interaction.

Law Enforcement Agencies and Child Protective Services

Law enforcement agencies should be involved in primary preventive efforts as well as the typical secondary or tertiary role of the police officer. For the most part, these approaches to helping the community in prevention efforts involve better education and services.

Officers can advocate for prevention of child abuse and neglect both professionally and individually. Individually, they can advocate through clubs, churches, civic organizations, and other groups to which they belong. Professionally, they can work through leaflets, lectures, and public relation sections. They can even provide space at the police station for discussion groups or for lectures.

Community advocacy should be aimed at:

1. Educational programs for parenthood, child development, perinatal care, and problem solving skills;
2. Community services for families such as day care, homemaker services, employment counseling, and Police Boys and Girls Clubs or camps; and
3. Community coordination in planning, administration, and service delivery among all agencies.

In addition, law enforcement agencies should advocate for higher priority and funding to be allocated for the development and implementation of new types of preventive programs and for the improvement of already existing ones.

The law enforcement agency's first task in providing secondary and tertiary preventive support should be the establishment of policies and procedures about the investigation and intervention of suspected child abuse and neglect cases. Establishing policies and procedures can demonstrate law enforcement's commitment to assisting the protection service. In terms of secondary or tertiary preventative measures, law enforcement can assist by:

1. Responding to situations of abuse and neglect;
2. Helping to make decisions about suspected cases of family violence;
3. Reporting and intervening with cases of abuse and neglect that can prevent a recurrence of the problem in a family;
4. Monitoring systems such as a statewide central registry designed to record and trace families in an abusive cycle; and
5. Train officers to identify children and families who might be potentially abusive or neglectful.

Specially trained Child Abuse Units can work routinely with community agencies besides the child protection service such as schools, hospitals, and mental health centers. They can respond quickly at any hour of the day or night to family crises that may or may not be confirmed cases of child abuse and neglect. These officers help the child protection service seek prevention and treatment solutions rather than criminal prosecutions.

Even when no special Child Abuse Unit is available, child protection services and law enforcement officials must work cooperatively to seek more treatment and prevention solutions. This partnership is logical as in most states, both organizations have responsibility for dealing with child abuse and neglect. By working together, families can be better served and the chance of serious error in the handling of a case can be reduced.

Open and continual communication, team work, support meetings, and a leadership role by the child protective service are important to both organizations for effectively handling child abuse and neglect cases.

Educational Systems and Child Protective Services

Schools have a primary role in primary prevention of child abuse and neglect. Education regarding abuse and what the child can do about it should be started as soon as possible because experts say abuse is starting at younger and younger ages. The education system must work cooperatively with child protective services in the referral of suspected cases of neglect. Schools can also make use of prevention ideas and educational programs that are available through protective services.

School administrators should adopt options that can be taught by trained volunteers from child protection services, police officers, or teachers such as:

1. Teaching **good touch, bad touch** programs,
2. Teaching children they can say **no** to an adult,
3. Where children can safely turn for help,
4. Teach children how to deal with threats, bribes, and force, and
5. Include in programs the possibility of molestation by strangers as well as loved ones.

Teachers usually come into contact with their students on a daily basis, and they should be trained to discern any change in the child's physical and/or emotional well-being. Teachers that generate trust with their students may be able to know more about their personal life than other professionals.

Teachers must be trained and prepared to report suspected incidents of abuse or refer children that come forth after programs such as **good touch, bad touch.** They should know what services are available through child protective services and how to report their suspicions.

The educational system is often bombarded with criticism to improve children's academic performance, however, many studies have suggested that children who are recipients of abuse tend to have lower verbal and performance scores. Kim Oates and Anthony Peacock (1984), compared scores of thirty-eight children hospitalized because of physical abuse with scores of a control group. They found the abused children showed significantly lower mean academic performance scores than the comparison children on verbal performance and full scale scores. Scores were measured on the Wechsler Intelligence Scale for Children-Revised and the Wechsler Preschool and Primary Scale of Intelligence.

Prevention in the school system includes devising methods for teachers and counselors to deal with problems of low academic performance in abuse children.

Experts say the best way to break a generational cycle is to work with the very young children. They must be taught how to defend themselves and where to turn for help. They must be given the best chance possible to succeed in society with good academic performance. Children must be taught coping techniques such as how to deal with angry and violent feelings without resorting to violence.

Health Facilities and Child Protective Services

An effective way to prevent child abuse and neglect is to educate people at risk of becoming an abuser. Hospitals, newborn health facilities, mental health centers, and counseling centers are ideal settings for prevention education.

Hospitals come into contact with almost all new parents, and parenting classes can be very effective when a new mother or father is entering this role for the first time. Most people are more determined to be a good parent right after the birth of their child and they are more responsive at this time to instructions or accepting advise.

Many times when a parent fears they are losing control they will seek the advise of their doctor or their child's pediatrician. It is very important for doctors to take these incidents seriously and respond with help. Parents may be referred to self-help counseling groups or classes offered through a child protective service. Physicians should know what services are available through the child protection service and contact the service when abuse or neglect is suspected.

Well-balanced clinics may provide more detailed information on parenting skills, methods of caring for children, and alternative forms of discipline. The clinics can let parents know what to expect from children at different stages so they will not have unrealistic expectations.

Mental health clinics can also assist the child protective service by identifying persons who are potentially abusive. A perpetrator may seek help from mental health facilities for help with problems other than abusive behavior. A staff member who is alert may detect signals and intervene with therapy that would not have been thought to be necessary.

Counseling services should be designed to keep careful records in coordination with child protection agencies. This can bring to attention families that have potential to fall into abusive cycles and to isolate cases that may have idiosyncratic needs. Many times, families bring their children to a crisis center and begin to get involved in the system, only to cease coming after one or two visits.

Benjamin Lahey (1984), compared eight matched controls and eight middle class abusive mothers on three measures of emotional and somatic distress. They found that abusive mothers showed far greater depression and physical distress than controls. These abusive mothers also used more physical punishment than controls. Based upon studies such as this, it becomes clear that continued counseling in conjunction with services provided by child protective agencies is needed. Ongoing help and intervention is needed to prevent further abuse and to achieve family stability.

Communities and Child Protective Services

In earlier chapters, it has been noted that intervention of child abuse and neglect cases is found at the community level. Likewise, in order to establish effective prevention programs, the community which instills its attitudes, values, mores, and resources must become involved.

Only through cooperative community planning can a child abuse and neglect program be developed which will be efficient, and cost effective. An efficient program must avoid duplication of effort and operate to the advantage of the families it is designed to serve. Problems of establishing such programs include: (1) maintenance cost, (2) the large number of diverse programs needed, and (3) the broad community base needed to support those programs. These difficulties can be overcome if programs are approached as a business effort and presented as a much needed effort within in each community.

Many communities are turning to a multidisciplinary approach by developing child abuse and neglect case conference committees and community child protection teams or task forces. This will assure that planning and service delivery will be integrated. All teams or committees include representatives from child protective agencies, as well as health, mental health, law enforcement, and education agencies. This ensures members will have a wide range of backgrounds, diverse skills and experience. The group can also call upon many different services, resources, and programs because of their diverse backgrounds.

Committees address broad community issues such as the resources that are available, where funding for programs will come from, training, and public awareness. They discuss individual cases to try to develop the best treatment program possible for the individual family.

Another important contribution of community teams and committees is in resolving the issues and conflicts that arise between public and private agencies. Addressing social problems between agencies is a vital link in child abuse and neglect prevention processes.

Community involvement at last is being recognized as vital in preventing child abuse and neglect. Society has become only too aware of the need to utilize trained specialists such as social workers, teachers, physicians, nurses and others in these community based prevention and intervention programs.

Federal and State Governments and Child Protective Services

There is a lack of understanding of the nature of family violence or the extent of the problem. Violent families hide in secrecy and victims are often silent because they don't know where to get assistance. Neighbors try not to get involved and teachers and doctors ignore tell tale signs of child victimization. This general confusion, whether intentional or not, stems from a misperception of the dynamics of family violence. A national public awareness and prevention campaign supported by the federal government could do much to overcome this misconception.

A national campaign should publicize:

1. Information directed toward very young children,
2. Where victims can get information for local help,
3. The criminal consequences of child abuse and neglect,
4. Ways to prevent family violence, and

5. The cost of family violence for both the persons involved and the economy.

A national campaign could reach many people and be directed at various target audiences. It could make professionals aware that they are in the best position to detect possible abuse and neglect, and it could instruct parents on how to warn their children about molestation from strangers.

Working with state and local governments, the federal government can play a useful role by helping to finance production costs. There is precedent for this. The Department of Justice already is cooperating with private agencies on the development of a national public awareness campaign for crime prevention. The Department has been active and shared the costs of the National Crime Prevention Council's successful McGruff campaign. This campaign has over 100 national and state sponsors and reaches an audience of several million persons.

Effective national awareness campaigns such as prevention of child abuse and neglect, need a great many organizations working together. The federal government's role should not be a dominant one because family violence is more than a federal issue. The government should contribute only by providing funds for the production costs of a national public awareness campaign.

Each state should work with private organizations to develop and maintain a 24 hour toll free hotline for victims of family violence. By using a single state wide number, it is easier to publicize, and more people will become aware of its availability. It provides a quick method of reporting incidents of abuse and a place for victims to call for help. For the hotline to be of adequate help to victims however, there must be community resources available to meet the needs of the victim.

Media and Child Protective Services

Publicity by way of printed words or broadcast can quickly influence many people. By advertising what local services and resources are available for child abuse and neglect victims, abusive families, or what prevention programs can be found, radio and television stations can make a very valuable contribution. Documentaries, news stories, and movies about child victimization can encourage victims to call for help or generate many volunteers from the community.

Unfortunately, as a result of emphasizing child abuse and neglect only in certain aspects, too many people still respond to instances of reported child abuse as simply belonging to the welfare department, police and courts. Too many community members do not want to learn about or help prevent the abuse and neglect from happening, and the idea still exists that child victimization is someone elses problem. Such a view may be quite harmful to our society in general and specifically to the families and children caught up in the abusive process.

Local television services, newspapers, and magazines can make the public aware of the extent and seriousness of family violence and what can be done to reduce the problems involved. The media also plays another role in the reduction and prevention of child abuse and neglect which is that it must realize the power it has upon those who absorbed its information. There is much concern among experts that violence in the news influences further violent acts. Media must work to avoid depictions of violence that can exacerbate unwanted aggressive or antisocial behavior.

SUMMARY

Laws and public policies affirm the principle that every American child should have the opportunity to realize his or her full potential (Apter, 1982).

Yet, far too many children suffer from abuse or neglect and far too few services are being provided. Too many American children are growing to adulthood distressed, apprehensive about their own ability, displaying low self-esteem and often showing mental disabilities. Many of these problems may have been addressed through earlier intervention with appropriate prenatal input and early childhood programs. All to often, services that are needed for children and adolescents with unique needs are unavailable in the community.

In reference to the difficulty of agreeing on a definition of prevention, Cowen (1978) described **prevention** as, "a beautiful, mushy, abstract term". Despite problems, prevention efforts for abused and neglected children must be instituted in order to: (1) provide strength for our basic societal units, (2) provide more community education and research, and (3) utilize the total community strengths.

Families involved in abuse and neglect are likely to be cut off from prosocial support systems and as a result of this, intervention and prevention efforts must reach beyond the family by enlisting the services of individuals and groups who help to create the family's social contact. Understanding the pathology involved in child abuse and neglect is not enough. To date, history has taught us that one of the most effective ways to help the child is to understand and help the parent.

Perhaps, the best tool to give children is the ability to learn how to function with the support system provided to them. They need to be taught about the community services and resources available and how to use teachers, family, and friends when they need assistance.

Communities can and must provide continuing support to improve family functioning. America's children and families are in trouble, and a major building block in American society is strength of its families. Prevention and education provide hope for our future in producing healthy families and promoting healthy communities, however, many government programs and much community-based help is needed.

Barth Hackeng (1986) states that child abuse prevention programs are growing rapidly in response to a national uprising against domestic violence. All experts agree that close relationships between health, legal and social services are essential, but it must be stressed that the prevention of child abuse and neglect truly depends on jointly building family and community strength.

REFERENCES

1. Apter, S.: *Troubled Children, Troubled Systems.* New York, Pergamon, 1982.
2. Barber, P., and Burns, G.: An alternative approach to the prevention of child abuse: pre-service training. *Education Canada, 26*(1):18–23, 1986.
3. Barth, R., Hacking, S., and Ash, J.: Identifying, screening, and engaging high-risk clients in private non-profit child abuse prevention programs. *Child Abuse and Neglect: The International Journal, 10*(1), 1986.
4. Buried, S., Collins, R., and Divine-Hawkins, P.: Employer supported child care: everybody benefits. *Children Today,* May–June, 1983.
5. Cohn, A. H.: *An Approach to Preventing Child Abuse.* Chicago, National Committee for the Prevention of Child Abuse, 1980.
6. Cowen, E.: Prevention in the public schools: strategies for dealing with school adjustment problems. In Apter, S. J. (Ed.): *Focus on Prevention: The Education of Children Labeled Emotionally Disturbed.* Syracuse, Syracuse University, 1978.
7. Downing, C. J.: Parent support groups to prevent child abuse. *Elementary School Guidance and Counseling, 17*(2):119–121, 1982.
8. Fontana, V. J.: *The Maltreated Children.* Springfield, Thomas, 1979.

9. Fontana, V. J.: *Somewhere a Child is Crying.* New York, MacMillian, 1983.
10. Fraley, Y.: The family support center: early intervention for high-risk parents and children. *Children Today,* Jan–Feb, 1983.
11. Gale, N.: *Child Sexual Abuse in Native American Communities.* Washington, D.C., Children's Bureau, 1986.
12. Garbarino, J.: Can we measure success in preventing child abuse? Issues in policy, programming and research. *Child Abuse and Neglect: The International Journal,* 10(2):143–56, 1986.
13. Graves, J.: *Early Interventions in Child Abuse: The Role of the Police Officer.* California, R & E Publishers, 1983.
14. Helfer, R.: A review of the literature on prevention of child abuse and neglect. *Child Abuse and Neglect: The International Journal,* 6(3):251–261, 1982.
15. Iscoe, I.: *Opinions About Child Abuse Survey: An Assessment of Professional Attitudes Concerning Child Abuse.* Austin Research Institute, Texas University, 1986.
16. Jacobsen, J. J.: *The Psychiatric Sequelae of Child Abuse: Reconnaisance of Child Abuse and Neglect, Evaluation, Prospects, Recommendations.* Springfield, Thomas, 1986.
17. Lahey, B. B., et. al.: Parenting behavior and emotional status of physically abusive mothers. *Journal of Consulting and Clinical Psychology,* 52(6):1062–1071, 1984.
18. Marion, M.: Primary prevention of child abuse: the role of the family life educator. *Family Relations,* 31(4):515–582, 1982.
19. McCrone, W.: Preventing child abuse: a bibliography of information professionals should know to protect deaf children. *Perspectives for Teachers of Hearing Impaired,* 3(5):11–13, 1985.
20. Meier, J. H.: *Definition and Dynamics of Child Abuse: A Multifactorial Model.* Monograph Series No. 3, 1983.
21. Oates, K., and Peacock, A.: Intellectual development of battered children. *Australia and New Zealand Journal of Developmental Disabilities.* 10(1):27–29, 1984.
22. Rotartori, A.: A multidisciplinary approach to assessing the abused youngster. *Early Child Development and Care,* 14:93–108, 1984.
23. Selinske, J.: Practice: models for implementing child abuse and neglect legislation. *Journal of Children in Contemporary Society,* 15(4):71–78, 1983.
24. Small, D. L.: Child abuse and neglect prevention project. *Annual Report: Innovations in Protective Services.* Washington, D.C., Office of Human Development Services (DHHS), 1985.
25. Vinyard, E.: The problem of child sexual abuse and approaches to prevention. *Early Child Development and Care,* 19(3):133–149, 1985.
26. Wolfe, D., MacPherson, T., Blount, R., and Wolfe, V.: Evaluation of a brief intervention for educating school children in awareness of physical and sexual abuse. *Child Abuse and Neglect: The International Journal,* 10(1), 1986.
27. Ziefert, M.: *Adolescent Abuse and Neglect: Prevention and Intervention Continuing Education Manual,* Washington, D.C., Administration for Children, Youth and Families (DHHS), 1985.

CHAPTER 6

A NATIONWIDE SURVEY OF
SERVICE FACILITIES FOR INTERVENTION
OF CHILD ABUSE AND NEGLECT

OLIVER C. S. TZENG
MICHELLE M. ALLISON
JAMIA J. JACOBSEN

INTRODUCTION

This study was designed to evaluate the facilities and programs available on a nationwide basis related to crisis intervention and treatment of child abuse and neglect problems. Many facilities existing in all parts of the country differ from each other in many aspects, from size, focus, and capacity, to treatment orientation. It is quite difficult for an individual who plans to initiate a new facility to comprehend the needs and requirements for the facility in order to optimize its future service functions and crisis intervention programs. For this reason, and in order to demonstrate the different types of crisis facilities, we report in this chapter, a cameo study of 53 crisis centers in 26 states, and a more indepth analysis of 20 crisis centers that responded to our follow-up survey. Hopefully, from such analysis a nationwide trend of facilities, programs, issues, and concerns can be depicted. Such information will provide interested professionals to compare their facilities with the profiles from our survey. At the end of this chapter, we will synthesize some major issues and recommendations that are necessary for future designing, establishing, monitoring, and evaluating service facilities.

PURPOSE

There is a national rate of 23.8 children **reported** as maltreated for every 1,000 children living in the United States, and that rate may actually be as high as 75 children being abused and neglected out of every 1,000 children. These statistics reflect the scope and severity of the problems of child abuse and neglect which are becoming more and more visible in America. They also illuminate the necessity for a comprehensive evaluation of the social systems/institutions that are currently providing services to victims and/or perpetrators of abuse and neglect.

A type of social institution which provides services to victims, often on an emergency basis, is the crisis center. Generally speaking, crisis centers or shelters have as their primary goal the prevention of child or wife abuse. They may be utilized by families in times of stress or to seek relief from an oppressive situation. They are essential in order to divert or relieve potentially damaging situations.

The areas of concern are diverse and complex. This is true because of the enormous geographic distances in the United States, as well as the variety of issues and problems interrelated in the phenomena and etiology of child abuse and neglect. In attempting to provide a comprehensive analysis of national status on intervention and treatment of child abuse and neglect problems, we first list the major concerns as follows:

1. What kinds of facilities are available for victims of abuse and neglect? How effective are they for protection and prevention purposes? Who are the clients? Are there counseling/rehabilitation services available for perpetrators of child abuse and neglect?

2. What kinds of service programs are available for children who have been abused or neglected? How much are these services used? How many of the services are directly provided by an average institution, and how many are provided by a different agency through referrals?

3. How much are these service facilities used? What proportion of children are treated on a residential basis? What proportion are treated in a nonresidential capacity? For what period of time is service available?

4. How many staff members are needed for operation of an average facility? How many are paid staff and how many are volunteers? What kinds of staff are needed and employed?

5. How often are the services evaluated? What are the contents and criteria for the evaluation?

6. Where do the service facilities refer their clients? What are the sources which refer clients to these facilities? What is the frequency of referrals?

7. What are major financial sources for operation of the facilities? How much (in proportion) do different sources contribute to the total budget? What is the total budget?

8. What are the major issues of concern that are facing various service

facilities? What are some major conditions that are required to run various service facilities effectively? What suggestions can be made for improvement of current systems and programs?

The above questions reflect major issues and concerns about prevention and treatment facilities for child abuse/neglect problems. The major purpose of this chapter is to report our survey results which can provide empirical evidence to address these questions. Furthermore, since our evaluation will depict the national status of service facilities and their functions, we will identify major deficiencies, problems, and needs that are confronting various service organizations. In this regard, we will also discuss the recommendations and strategies for future development of an efficient and cost-effective facility.

ANALYSIS OF 53 SERVICE FACILITIES

Descriptions of 53 service facilities from 26 states (see Table VI–I) were analyzed in terms of seven categories: services, capacity, staffing, clientele, organization, coordination, and funding.

TABLE VI-I
STATE IDENTIFICATIONS OF 53 SERVICE FACILITIES

States	Number of Facilities		States	Number of Facilities
Alabama	1		Michigan	3
Alaska	1		Missouri	1
Arizona	2		Nebraska	3
California	3		New Jersey	1
Colorado	1		New York	2
Florida	2		Ohio	2
Hawaii	3		Oklahoma	2
Illinois	2		Pennsylvania	2
Indiana	5		Tennessee	2
Iowa	2		Texas	2
Kentucky	2		Utah	2
Louisiana	2		Wisconsin	1
Maine	2			
Massachusetts	2	Total	26 States	53 Facilities

Descriptions of these facilities were obtained initially by on site visits and/or telephone interviews conducted by Jamia Jacobsen. The current questionnaire was administered by phone interviews. The format of the interview included questions on the seven categories of issues. Results from the interview were used as the base for constructing the questionnaire for a follow-up study. Findings from both the phone interviews and the follow-up study questionnaire yielded information about the general trends of child abuse and neglect shelters and programs throughout the United States. The following is the summary of our analyses of the information obtained from both the telephone interviews and the questionnaire survey.

Services

Services can be dichotomized as either **direct** or **indirect services**. While **direct services** are various assistance programs for victimized children and/or accused perpetrators, **indirect services** are various programs that are directed to the development, evaluation, and maintenance of various social systems regarding the problems of child abuse and neglect.

Furthermore, in the area of direct services, most facilities made a distinction between services offered for children (usually more treatment oriented), and adults (usually more prevention oriented). The most common direct services offered for children were emergency and medical services, therapy, foster care, and residential care in the form of crisis nurseries and 24 hour care. For adults, counseling and therapy were by far the most common direct services offered, with assistance in the form of legal, housing, employment, and transportation often being provided as well. The complete listing of services offered to parents and children in order of frequency is given in Table VI–II

The other area of services offered were the indirect services. Referral was the most common indirect service provided by the respondent facilities, with efforts to increase public awareness of the problems of child abuse and neglect also being very frequent. Information and library services were reported often as a means of raising the public level of awareness.

Table VI–III presents a complete listing of twelve indirect services that are the most popular functions of various service agencies. Generally speaking, notification of child abuse and neglect cases was by far the most common indirect service mission for agencies. Other indirect services fall in three general areas: **system services** (reporting, training, coordination and planning), **client assistance** (technical, volunteer and legal), and **public dissemination** (advocacy, awareness and information services).

TABLE VI-II
DIRECT SERVICES TO CHILDREN AND ADULTS

Children's Services		Adults' Service	
Service Types	*Frequency*	*Service Types*	*Frequency*
Emergency services	21	Parent/family counseling	24
Medical services	16	Social work counseling	17
Art/play therapy	13	Group/indiv./lay therapy	17
Individual therapy	13	Crisis counseling	12
Foster care	11	Legal/job/housing assist.	10
Diagnostic services	8	Transportation	9
Crisis nursery	7	Parenting skills	8
24-hour care	5	Medical care	7
Recreation	4	Respite child care	4
Education	4	Parent support groups	4
		Drug/alcohol counseling	3

Capacity

The capacities for intaking clients had a broad range and a great deal of variability among service facilities. As seen in Table VI–IV, the number of clients who could be served on a daily basis ranged from 4 persons to 60 persons, with an average of 17 persons. Of the 36 facilities that responded to the question of capacity, 10 facilities reported having space for 4 to 8 clients per day; 9 facilities reported having space for 9 to 14 clients per day; 9 facilities reported having space for 15 to 26 clients per day; and 8 facilities reported having space for 27 to 60 clients per day.

TABLE VI-III
INDIRECT SERVICES

Service Types	Frequency
Referral	24
Professional/public awareness	23
Child abuse and neglect reporting	17
Advocacy	16
Information and library services	13
Training	11
Service coordination	11
Needs assessment	8
Program planning	8
Technical assistance	8
Volunteer services	3
Legal services	3

TABLE VI–IV
CAPACITIES OF SERVICE FACILITIES

Number of Clients Served Per Day	Number of Facilities Having the Capacity
60	1
40	1
36	1
32	1
30	4
26	1
25	1
22	1
20	2
16	2
15	2
14	1
12	4
10	3
9	1
8	2
7	2
6	4
4	2

Staffing

Staffing considerations were categorized into two major groups: paid staff and volunteers. Table VI–V presents a listing of distributional frequencies for both positions.

The staff of the service facility is a vital element in its ability to perform the designated mission to serve the clientele. The most common positions for paid staff are those who are responsible for day to day operation responsibility (i.e., administration director and clerks), and also the staff members who perform direct services for victimized children (e.g., child care and social workers). Other staff members are specialists to cover many aspects of service (e.g., psychological, education, medical, and nutritional care).

For the volunteer workers, there were generally lower ranking positions where there was a need for many people. The use of volunteer aide is an important way to increase the effectiveness of a facility without increasing the cost, so it is rather surprising that the overall volume of volunteer help is much lower than that of the paid staff. It is also interesting to note that very few professionals in a higher occupational status (i.e., law, medicine, psychology and education) are active in volunteer corps.

TABLE VI-V
FREQUENCY DISTRIBUTION OF STAFF

Paid Staff		Volunteers	
Position	*Frequency*	*Position*	*Frequency*
Administrator	38	General volunteer	10
Child care	30	Receptionist	9
Clerical	23	Child care	4
Support staff	15	Therapist	4
Social worker	15	Transportation	4
Case coordinator	9	Student/intern	4
Counselor	7	Teacher/speaker	4
Supervisor	7	Clerical	3
Houseparents	6	Social counselor	2
Psychologist	6	Medical	2
Nurse/medical	4	Legal	1
Teacher	3		
Cook	2		
Housekeeper	2		
Dietician	2		
Advocate	2		
Receptionist	1		

Clientele

The clientele services provided by various facilities are discussed in two categories: (1) geographic regions, and (2) age categories of victimized children. The geographic regions or areas served by the facilities were separated in terms of five levels of living environment, from local community to national circumstances. First, **county** citizens were the primary service focus (11 facilities). **Multi-county** areas were also served (by 9 facilities), followed by provision to **local community** members. On a less frequent basis, **entire state populations** made up the clientele (3 facilities) and in two cases the service facilities accepted clients from anywhere in the **nation**. Although many facilities included services for both children and parents, most residential facilities were primarily for children. The ages of the children served ranged from infants to 18 years. Four facilities took children only to age 7, four took children to age 11, six took children up to age 17, and three took children up to age 18.

Organizations

The great majority of the facilities were run as voluntary private nonprofit organizations (29 facilities). The other, much less frequent, categories were church related (4 facilities), state department (4 facilities), Salvation Army (1 facility), and public county run (1 facility). It is clear that nonprofit organizations are the most common type of agency for intervention and/or treatment of child victimization.

Coordination

One of the most distinctive features in intervention and treatment is the use of service agreements, or the purchase of services from other agencies. Therefore, the referral of clientele has been the most important aspect of coordination across different agencies. The two categories of referral covered in the survey were: (1) the **referral sources** where the service facilities receive their clients, and (2) the **outreach of referrals where the service facilities sent their clients for more complete services. Both sources and outreach are listed in order of frequency in Table VI-VI.**

TABLE VI-VI
REFERRAL RELATIONSHIPS

Referred by	Frequency	Referred to	Frequency
Social service agencies	31	Public agencies	8
Law enforcement	29	State agencies	7
Self referral	25	County agencies	5
Courts	23	Nonprofit agencies	4
Family member/neighbors	22	Federal	1
Hospitals	11	City	1
Schools	10		
Sources within agency	7		
Welfare Department	6		
Churches	6		
Medical personnel	5		
Probation Department	2		
Child Protection Service	2		
County Health Department	1		

By the nature of crisis intervention for victimized children, the respondent facilities **received** more referrals than they **sent** clients elsewhere. The five major referral sources are: children service agencies, law enforcement, courts, family/neighbors, and self-referral. Hospitals and schools are two additional important sources for referral. On the other hand, the outreach agencies for referrals were mainly public institutions at different government levels.

Funding Sources

An important issue for all service facilities was the source of funding. In this first step of the study, the exact budget wasn't requested, but the financial resources for maintaining the facility were emphasized. Generally speaking, the facilities have multiple sources of financial income that will cover areas from private donations to public funds. As shown in Table VI–VII, the total number of funding sources is 167 which yielded an average of 3.17 sources per facility. Private donations from individuals and nonprofit organizations were by far the most common type of funding, and account for 27% of the total funding sources. Local and state funds (i.e., state, United Way, and county) were the major sources, which accounted for 32% of income requirements. It should be noted that this figure reflects only the **sources,** rather than the **actual amount,** of dollars involved in operation of facilities.

Federal monies, through Title XX and other funding mechanisms, also contributed to the operations of service programs. Other funding sources included church, client fees, fund raising, revenue sharing, and township funds. These sources can, in theory, be characterized in terms of two general (public and private) categories. However, in order to familiarize the readers with the funding possibilities, they are kept under separate sources.

ANALYSIS OF NATIONWIDE QUESTIONNAIRE SURVEY

Development of the Questionnaire

The questionnaire which was sent to individual service facilities was developed using the results from the previous section and other literature on the topic of child abuse and neglect. The questionnaire was designed as a detailed follow-up study on various issues that are related to the seven areas of concern mentioned earlier. As a result, a 15 item questionnaire was sent to each of the 53 service facilities that were interviewed by phone in the first phase of this study. The first twenty returned questionnaires were used as the basis for data evaluation and

TABLE VI-VII
SOURCES OF FACILITY INCOME

Funding Sources	*Frequency of Facilities*	
Private/personal donations	31	(19%)
State	21	(13%)
United Way	18	(11%)
County	14	(8%)
Private, nonprofit organizations	13	(8%)
Title XX	9	(5%)
Federal	9	(5%)
City	7	(4%)
State administered federal funds	7	(4%)
Church	6	(4%)
Client fees	6	(4%)
Fund raising	5	(3%)
Foundation	4	(2%)
Revenue sharing	4	(2%)
Mental health center	3	(2%)
Jr. League	2	(1%)
Corporate donations	2	(1%)
Endowments	2	(1%)
Welfare Department	1	(1%)
Consultation fees	1	(1%)
Township funds	1	(1%)
Total:	167	(100%)

analysis in this section. These twenty facilities represent a sample of fourteen states in the Nation, with one facility each from ten states: Arizona, California, Tennessee, Iowa, Kentucky, Louisiana, Nebraska, New Jersey, Ohio and Wisconsin; and two facilities each from four states: Hawaii, Illinois, Indiana, and New York. A sample of the questionnaire is in Appendix VI-A.

The following are summaries of responding frequencies (and percentages) on each questionnaire item from the twenty facilities:

1. Types of Facility Functions

The functions or programs for child abuse and neglect as indicated by the returned questionnaires can best be represented by social service agencies and shelters for abused children, women, and teenagers. Other functions included family counseling (longer term treatment), and crisis intervention centers (shorter term). In general, most facilities reported more than one function, for example, being a social service agency which also offers emergency shelter to those in need.

The hierarchical order of 29 total identified service facility functions are summarized in Table VI–VIII. These 20 facilities were further differentiated in terms of three general categories of service organizations: public vs. private, profit vs. nonprofit, and residential vs. nonresidential.

TABLE VI–VIII
TYPES OF FUNCTIONS

Types of Services	Number (%)	
Social service agencies	12	(45%)
Emergency shelters	5	(17%)
Crisis nurseries	4	(14%)
Family counseling centers	3	(10%)
Community center	1	(3%)
Child protective investigation	1	(3%)
Temporary group home	1	(3%)
Diagnostic services and shelter	1	(3%)
Residential treatment	1	(3%)
Total:	29	(100%)

In six combinations of the three categories with the possibility of multiple distributions, 17 facilities (85%) are private nonprofit organizations, 10 facilities (50%) are residential organizations, 4 facilities (20%) are nonresidential and 2 facilities (10%) are public nonprofit. The two categories of **private profit** and **public profit** were not reported in the sample.

2. Provided Services

The provided services were defined on the basis of whether an organization or program has made services available in the **past six months**. From the literature review and analysis of the telephone interviews, available services were divided into three categories: **Child Services, Adult Services, and Indirect Services.** As a result, 15 common service programs were listed under Child Services, 31 programs under Adult Services, and 13 programs under Indirect Services.

For each service program listed, the facility was first asked to respond to the question: "Is it part of your Services?" The facility would select either **yes** or **no** as the response. If the answer is **yes**, the facility is then asked to indicate the **activity level of service** in terms of one of the four frequency levels (i.e., always, frequently, sometimes and never). Table

VI–IX summarizes available services for children. The relative importance of these programs were identified in terms of their **activity level** reported under the two positive response alternatives: **always** and **frequently.**

Child Services. The Child Services provided most frequently can be categorized into three main domains: shelter, counseling, and emergency services. The most common service provided by service facilities is shelter, both emergency and residential, that account for a total of 23% of the available services. Case management (12%), diagnostic services (8%), and individual therapy (6%) were the most reported counseling services. Emergency services (14%) and medical services (8%) were both listed by the majority of respondents as being offered. Services offered with a lower frequency included: crisis nurseries (4%), recreational therapy (4%), tutorialship (6%), and play therapy (4%).

TABLE VI-IX
RELATIVE FREQUENCIES OF CHILD SERVICE PROGRAMS

Available Services	*Frequency (%)*	
Emergency shelter	16	(14%)
Emergency services	16	(14%)
Case management	14	(12%)
Residential shelter	10	(9%)
Medical services	9	(8%)
Diagnostic services	9	(8%)
Tutorialship	7	(6%)
Individual therapy	7	(6%)
Crisis nursery	5	(4%)
Recreational therapy	5	(4%)
Play therapy	5	(4%)
24 hour crisis line	3	(3%)
Advocacy	2	(2%)
Group home living skills	2	(2%)
Therapeutic day care	2	(2%)
Delinquency prevention classes	1	(1%)
Therapeutic foster care	1	(1%)
Residential treatment	1	(1%)
Counseling	1	(1%)
Food and clothes	1	(1%)
Drama	0	(0%)
Total:	117	(100%)

Note: Frequency was based on two positive response alternatives (always and frequently) in the rating of "Activity Level" for each program.

Adult Services. There were fewer adult services reported, with lower frequencies, as shown in Table VI–X. The services can be divided into three areas of discussion: counseling/therapy, crisis management, and aid to parents. In the area of counseling/therapy, the main services included family counseling, group counseling, individual therapy, mental health services, social work counseling, and consultation. In the area of crisis management, two major services included help lines and crisis intervention. In the area of aid to parents, major programs in practice were child management classes, transportation, respite child care, 24 hour counseling, parent/child bridging, residential care, etc. It is apparent that aids to parents can be multifaceted in nature, ranging from the competence of parenting skills and employment assistance, to home education. Under this conceptualization, services to adults become interdisciplinary in nature and multidimensional in context.

Indirect Services. Sixteen indirect services were reported as active service programs (cf. Table VI–XI). The services most commonly reported were referrals, (i.e. case referral, reporting of child abuse and neglect, and information services). These three services account for 32% of the total indirect services. The remaining services fall into three general categories: (1) **Research and Training,** including program planning, training, need assessment, and training advocacy; (2) **Institutional Assistance,** including service coordination, technical assistance, library service, consultation and case review; and (3) **Public Awareness,** including advocacy, public awareness programs, and professional awareness programs. These results are quite consistent with the findings from the first phase of the study (i.e., Table VI–III), but we used different names to characterize a broad nature of service orientation.

In summary, the above three types of services depict a dominant trend in attacking child abuse and neglect problems: (a) the services deal more with emergency intervention for the children affected by child abuse and neglect, (b) the services offer short-term assistance to parents in facing emergent needs or crises, and (c) the services provide referral services between various agencies and individuals. Deviations from this trend are programs that focus on other aspects of needs in mental, physiological, economical, social, and political perspectives. Unfortunately, due to various reasons, no comprehensive programs were developed and implemented within a single facility that would simultaneously cover all important aspects of service needs.

TABLE VI-X
RELATIVE FREQUENCIES OF ADULT SERVICE PROGRAMS

Types		Frequency (%)
Respite child carea	8	(7%)
Transportation	7	(6%)
Social work counselors	7	(6%)
Family counseling	7	(6%)
Mental health services	6	(6%)
Crisis intervention	6	(6%)
Help line	5	(5%)
Child management classes	5	(5%)
Consultation	5	(5%)
Group therapy	5	(5%)
24 hour counseling	4	(4%)
Couples counseling	4	(4%)
Individual therapy	4	(4%)
Education	4	(4%)
Parent/child bridging	4	(4%)
Needs assessment	4	(4%)
Lay therapy	3	(3%)
Residential care	3	(3%)
Housing assistance	3	(3%)
Alcohol counseling	3	(3%)
24 hour hotline	3	(3%)
Legal assistance	2	(2%)
Employment assistance	2	(2%)
Recreational activities	2	(2%)
Parents Anonymous	1	(1%)
Residential care	1	(1%)
Homemaker service	1	(1%)
Financial assistance	0	
Parental aid counseling	0	
Senior citizens	0	
Medical care	0	
Total:	109	(100%)

3. Service Intake

Under the issue of service intake, we asked four types of questions: the capacity of children cared for per day, the average number of children cared for per day, the average length of stay, and the maximum length of stay. Table VI–XII presents a summary of responses to these questions. For the intake of children, the range of capacity across different facilities

TABLE VI-XI
INDIRECT SERVICE PROGRAMS

Types	Frequency (%)	
Referral	15	(13%)
Reporting child abuse/neglect	12	(10%)
Information services	11	(9%)
Program planning	11	(9%)
Service coordination	11	(9%)
Advocacy	10	(8%)
Training	9	(8%)
Public awareness	8	(8%)
Professional awareness	8	(8%)
Needs assessment	6	(5%)
Legal services	4	(3%)
Training advocacy	4	(3%)
Technical assistant	3	(3%)
Library services	3	(3%)
Consultation	2	(2%)
Case review	2	(2%)
Total:	119	(100%)

is from seven children per day to 77 children per day, with an average of 31 children under care. The capacity for adults was much lower, only 36 maximum per day, with an average of 25 adults under care. The average number of children actually being cared for is in the range between 4 and 72 (with 27 as the average per day), and for adults, the number was 6 to 25 (with 13 as the average per day).

TABLE VI-XII
CAPACITY OF SERVICE INTAKE

Types	Range in Days	Average Days
(A) Intake of Children:		
Capacity per day	7–77	31.06
Average # per day	4–72	27.33
Average length of stay	1 hr–240 days	72.28
Maximum length of stay	3 hrs– 5 days	213.67
(B) Intake of Adults		
Capacity per day	14–36	25.00
Average # per day	6–25	13.20
Average length of stay	1 hr–270 days	180.00
Maximum length of stay	3 hrs–730 days	410.00

In terms of the length of time staying at the facility, there was a great deal of variation for both adults and children. Average length of stay for children ranged from one hour to eight months across different facilities (with an average length of 27 days). For adults, the range was one hour to a nine month stay. For maximum length of stay, the time span was from three hours to five years for children, and from three hours to three years for adults.

Another area of interest covered by the questionnaire was the **geographic boundaries of the clientele.** Many agencies have multiple boundary levels for the clientele. In computing the number of facilities serving at each boundary level, it was found that the majority (55%) of the facilities provided services primarily for county residents. The next highest frequency was for city residents (45%), then multi-county residents (35%). The lowest frequency of service areas was for state residents (20%). In terms of the types of clientele population, most facilities also serve multiple target groups: 80% of the facilities served children, 50% served families, 40% served parents, and only 15% offered services for lay audiences and various professional populations.

4. Staff Organization

Information about the paid and volunteer employees was sought to examine the quality and quantity of staff for the service facilities sampled. For all the responding facilities, the size of the staff varied from 5 to 185 (with an average of 52) paid workers, full and part time. The volunteer staff was smaller in size, ranging from 5 to 120 with an average of 33 volunteers.

There was a total of 41 different staff positions reported by the respondents, with varying numbers of personnel. The number of staff for each position ranged from 1 person to 25 persons, depending on the size and capacity of the facility. A summary of different types of paid staff reported by the 20 respondents is given in Table VI–XIII.

The information given in Table VI–XIII depicts a general trend as to which positions were seen as the most important for the overall needs of the service facilities. The positions and the staff listed in the Table can also shed light on the core group of personnel needed for all facilities. Administration and management seem to be the priorities in staff that all responding service facilities share. Therefore, the first eight types of positions that are required for day to day operations of a child care service facility accounted for over 57% of all positions listed. It is interesting to note that there is an apparent lack of emphasis on the prevention/

TABLE VI-XIII
STAFF INFORMATION

Number of Paid Staff				*Number of Volunteers*	
Range	Mean			Range	Mean
5–185	51.89			5–20	33.08

(A) Paid Staff		
Types of Positions	*Total # of Facilities with Positions Filled*	*Average # of Positions per Facility*
Administrators	19	1.63
Secretaries	14	3.47
Social workers	12	2.87
Cook	10	2.14
Child care persons	10	13.75
Custodians	10	2.18
Managers	10	3.20
Office managers	10	1.82
Nurses	8	1.25
Shelter staff	8	7.56
Receptionists	8	1.13
House managers	5	2.20
Outreach counselors	4	2.40
Community involvement coord.	4	1.00
Interns	3	2.30
Laundry	3	3.00
Transportation aides	3	2.50
Pediatricians	3	2.00
Children's interns	2	1.50
Teacher	2	1.00
Clerical aides	2	2.00
Kitchen helpers	2	1.50
Parent aides	2	1.00
Therapist	1	1.00
Physician	1	1.00
Account clerk	1	1.00
Staff training coord.	1	1.00
Personnel safety program	1	1.00
Psychologist	1	1.00
Attorney	1	1.00
Voluntary foster homes	1	24.00
Women advocates	1	2.00
Family counselors	1	1.00
Child programmer	1	1.00
Lay therapist	1	2.50
Babysitters	2	4.00
Child advocates	0	

TABLE VI-XIII (Continued)

Types of Positions	Total # of Facilities with Positions Filled	Average # of Positions per Facility
Shelter advocates	0	
Recreational aides	0	
Homemakers	0	
	Total: 108 (100%)	
	(B) Volunteers	
Types of Positions	Total # of Facilities with Positions Filled	Average # of Positions per Facility
Child care persons	5	24.00
Secretaries	2	1.50
Clerical aides	2	2.50
Interns	2	1.00
Outreach counselors	1	5.00
Receptionists	1	4.00
Shelter staff	1	50.00
Custodians	1	1.00
Lay therapists	1	6.00
Nurses	1	13.00
	Total: 17 (100%)	

treatment staffing position. The total number of facilities with counselor/therapy positions filled was less than ten.

Another area of interest in analysis of the staffing profile is the number of persons employed for each position. This analysis gives an idea on how comprehensive the service facilities are, and where the priorities are in each organization. The greatest number of paid employees were reported as being child care and shelter staff, with a range of 1 to 25 persons employed for each. The average number of the child care staff was the highest, at 14 persons; the average number of shelter staff was 8. Administration was also a priority, evidenced by the relatively high number of managers and secretaries (average of 3 staff members each), and counseling was represented with an average of 2 outreach counselors, 2 women advocates, 3 social workers, and 3 lay therapists. An area where staffing was also high priority was in the management of the service facility. House managers, custodians, and cooks (average of 2 persons) and laundry workers (average of 3 persons) were vital to all of the service facilities.

Some of the volunteer staff positions were counselors, secretaries, clerical aides, receptionists, shelter staff, child care staff, therapists, nurses and interns. In most cases, the volunteer staff was concentrated in just one or two areas, usually child care or clerical. All service facilities had a much greater percentage of paid workers than volunteer workers.

5. Program Evaluation

Program evaluation is an important aspect in examining the strengths and weaknesses of service facilities. Our survey focused on evaluation information during the past two years and also the respondents' evaluation plans for the next two years. Three topics were addressed: internal evaluation, external evaluation, and the contents of evaluation. A total of 14 service facilities (70%) have been evaluated by outside sources in the past two years, and 12 facilities (60%) had conducted interior evaluations. In looking ahead for the next two years, 12 service facilities (60%) expect to have outside evaluations, and seven facilities (35%) are anticipating internal evaluations. The average number of evaluations for both internal and external evaluations is seven for the past two years, and two for the next two years.

The contents of evaluation generally fall into three categories: (a) organization evaluations of needs and staff requirements, (b) satisfaction in inter-agency coordination and referrals, and (c) evaluation of staff performance. Generally speaking, most evaluation emphasizes the **product** aspect of services, rather than the **process** and dynamic aspect of service institutions.

TABLE VI-XIV
SUMMARY OF EVALUATION STATISTICS

	Past Two Years			Next Two Years		
No. of Facilities	% of Eval.	Average # of Eval.		No. of Facilities	% of Eval.	Average # of Eval.
External 14	70%	6.57		12	60%	2.08
Internal 12	60%	7.33		7	35%	2.29

6. Referrals

A major function of the service facilities surveyed was in referring clients to appropriate organizations or agencies for help. This is especially true in the smaller facilities that did not offer a diverse range of services. Survey responses to referral frequencies were divided into three levels: high, medium, or low referral rates. The highest outreach referrals were to public and private social service programs. Referrals directed to public schools, child protective services, and sources within the agency were also high. Medium referral rates were reported to law enforcement agencies, public hospitals, courts, family members and churches. A summary of the outreach of low, medium and high outreach referrals is given in Table VI–XV.

TABLE VI-XV
OUTREACH OF REFERRALS

Outreach Agencies	Number and Referral Rates	
Child protection services	16	(80%)
Public social service programs	14	(70%)
Private social service programs	14	(70%)
Sources within the agency	14	(65%)
Public schools	11	(55%)
Family members	9	(45%)
Law enforcement agencies	9	(45%)
Public hospitals	9	(45%)
Courts	7	(35%)
Churches	7	(35%)
Neighbors	4	(20%)
Federal organizations	1	(5%)
Housing organizations	1	(5%)
Employment agencies	1	(5%)
Alcohol abuse treatment	1	(5%)

*Note: Referral rate was based on the percentage of agencies making referrals in the time frame of *always, very often, frequently,* and *occasionally.*

The other important aspect of referral is in the **referral sources** that represent agencies, programs, or organizations from which the survey facilities received referrals. Again, we divide the referral sources into three (high, medium, and low) referral rates. The responses were very interesting in their similarity with the outreach of referrals, (i.e., the existence of a clear pattern of simultaneous and concurrent referrals between outreach and referral sources). The high referral sources were child protective services, public social service agencies, and public schools. The medium referral sources were private social service agencies, public hospitals, law enforcement agencies, courts, family members, neighbors, self-referrals, churches, and sources within the agency. These two categories of referral sources are listed in order of frequency in Table VI–XVI.

TABLE VI-XVI
REFERRAL SERVICES

Source Agencies	Number and Source Rates	
Child protective services	16	(80%)
Public schools	15	(75%)
Public social service agencies	14	(70%)
Private social service agencies	12	(60%)
Courts	11	(55%)
Self referrals	9	(45%)
Law enforcement agencies	8	(40%)
Family members	8	(40%)
Public hospitals	7	(35%)
Neighbors	6	(30%)
Churches	6	(30%)
Sources within the agency	6	(30%)

The referral rate is very important in a service facility, especially in the case of child abuse and neglect. Since there are so many aspects to the problems, it might be difficult for one agency to provide comprehensive treatment programs in all possible areas. Therefore, by a strong interaction of community referrals, better services can be designed for the special needs of individual victims and perpetrators of child abuse and neglect.

7. Funding Sources

An important area of investigation in the questionnaire was the financial resources for service agencies. The size and effectiveness of an organization is usually dependent on the amount of money available to maintain and improve it. Thus, funding is a crucial factor for the quality of service facilities. There is a great deal of variety in funding resources, and the total reported budgets for 1986 ranged from $88,602.00 to $3.5 million.

In order to give a better perspective of the amounts involved, the total budgets from 1985 and 1986 have been grouped in eight hierarchical categories by thousands of dollars, and the percentage of responding facilities falling into each category is displayed in Table VI–XVII.

The questionnaire also examined the sources of funding for these service facilities. Nearly every facility reported multiple sources, and there was a wide variety in the principle funding organizations. In 1985, the most common source of funds was the state, which was reported as a

TABLE VI-XVII
TOTAL BUDGET

Yearly Budget (thousands)	% of Facilities	
	1985	1986
$ 0–$100	5%	5%
$101–$150	15%	10%
$150–$200	10%	10%
$201–$500	15%	20%
$501–$750	5%	5%
$751–$1 million	15%	15%
$ 1–$1.5 million	15%	10%
over 1.5 million	5%	10%
	85%	85%

major funding source by 70% of all responding facilities, followed by the county (55% of the facilities) and personal donations (50% of the facilities). Other sources were: United Way (30%), Title XX (25%), client fees (25%), private foundations (20%) and churches (20%). Table VI–XVIII is a complete listing of funding sources and percentages of facilities using those sources.

The sources that have the frequencies of zero, one or two in the listings as funding resources are interesting, because they represent some potential financial sources that are being left untapped. The last column in Table VI–XVIII indicates the range of monies obtained from each funding source by different service agencies. Variations between agencies might suggest that some facilities are perhaps more creative, more resourceful, or more persevering in the search for funds to improve the facilities. A sharing of this knowledge and motivation could improve the situation of all services for child abuse and neglect.

Issues of Concern, Effectiveness and Cost Efficiency

The most informative topics on the strengths and weaknesses of current facilities are: (a) issues of concern, (b) conditions for increasing the effectiveness of services, and (c) methods for improving cost efficiency of service facilities. To the question, "What are some of the problems that your organization might be facing right now?" the responding facilities were asked to first identify the appropriateness of each possible problem and then to indicate the level of severity for the item that was conceived as a problem area. Responses from all agencies were aggregated and ranked from high to low in terms of the perceived severity and urgency

TABLE VI-XVIII
FUNDING SOURCES

Sources	Number of Facilities Using Source		Range of Funding (thousands)
State funds	14	(70%)	$20– $ 823
County funds	11	(55%)	20– 1,674
Personal donations	10	(50%)	2– 566
United Way	6	(30%)	15– 250
Title XX	5	(25%)	3– 72
Client fees	5	(25%)	2– 124
Private foundations	4	(20%)	10– 20
Churches	4	(20%)	1– 293
Salvation Army/fund raising	3	(15%)	5– 96
Revenue sharing	2	(10%)	12– 104
Federal/State grant	2	(10%)	15– 46
Endowment/benefits	2	(10%)	21– 100
Youth Association	1	(5%)	93
Per diem allowance	1	(5%)	55
City funds	1	(5%)	53
Miscellaneous agencies	1	(5%)	32
School lunches	1	(5%)	20
Medicaid	1	(5%)	20
Special events	1	(5%)	9
USDA	1	(5%)	2
Township funds	0		
Local funds	0		
Local mental health board	0		
Consulting contracts	0		
Other nonprofit org.	0		

for improvement. These responses reflect a general trend of where the strongest areas of concern lie.

As shown in Table VI–XIX, the biggest issue of concern is financial difficulties, with five facilities ranking it as high in severity as a concern, and seven facilities ranking it as moderate in severity. Two other areas of concern are limited capacity, and limited resources. Both were ranked as a high concern by three facilities, and as a moderate concern by six facilities.

To the open ended question about five major conditions that would make a crisis center become most effective, over fifty responses were elicited. These responses were organized into some 20 categories in Table VI–XX. These suggestions are ways to ameliorate the current services. Eight facilities (40%) stressed the importance of financial support/funding,

TABLE VI-XIX
ISSUES OF CONCERN

Issues of Concern	Number of Facilities with High or Moderate Concern
Financial difficulties	12
Limited capacity	9
Limited resources (other than financial)	9
Cooperation with outside service providers	3
Political	3
Lack of emergency care	1

and the value of a good staff. Six facilities (30%) suggested that good marketing techniques are a way to bring in higher numbers of clients. Five facilities indicated that high quality training programs for staff would increase the effectiveness of the facility or programs. Four facilities cited good accessibility and cooperation with referral services as important factors to a far reaching effect. Other conditions to improve effective services include: good community support, adequate staff, networks with other service providers, availability of services, good design, counseling and child service care, and 24 hour care programs.

To the question, "How do you think crisis centers can be more efficient?", responses were summarized in Table VI–XXI. The most commonly suggested measures for improving the **cost effectiveness** of service programs were: the use of volunteers, effective funding, and noncentralization of the organization. Other suggestions included effective strategic planning, help from the state government, combination of smaller agencies with larger agencies, and reduction of staff. These measures are all related to the financial condition of a service facility. However, in some cases, steps taken to reduce costs may reduce quality as well. For example, cutting down on staff will cause expenses to go down, but there will be less aid available for the clientele. This a double bind situation which exists for nearly every organization.

When asked for a list of **three major issues concerning crisis centers today**, certain situations came up repeatedly as they are summarized in Table VI–XXII. Predictably, the financial and funding limitations were mentioned most often (by 55% of the respondents) and problems of space limitations were next frequently mentioned (by 30%). Staffing was a commonly reported issue, relating to both training of staff and the

TABLE VI-XX
MAJOR CONDITIONS FOR EFFECTIVENESS

Conditions	Number of Responding Facilities	
Financial support	8	(40%)
Capable staff	8	(40%)
Good marketing of facility	6	(30%)
Good training for staff	5	(25%)
Cooperation with reference service	4	(20%)
Good accessibility	4	(20%)
Good community support	3	(15%)
Adequate staff	3	(15%)
Network with other service providers	3	(15%)
Availability	2	(10%)
Good design	2	(10%)
Counseling and child care	2	(10%)
Holistic approach	1	(5%)
Contract for services	1	(5%)
Programs beyond physical care	1	(5%)
Placement options	1	(5%)
Adequate space	1	(5%)
Efficiency	1	(5%)
Simple, quick intake procedures	1	(5%)
Good communication	1	(5%)

problem of low pay for highly qualified individuals. Other issues are more specific to individual crisis facilities, (e.g., care management, increases of referrals and replication of programs).

Finally, when asked if they thought a national crisis center newsletter would be helpful to their organizations, eight facilities responded **yes,** six responded **no,** and six did not respond. If the content of newsletters was specified in more detail, the uncertain responses would most likely be reduced.

TABLE VI-XXI
IMPROVEMENT OF COST-EFFECTIVENESS

Measures	Number of Facilities Making Suggestions	
Use of volunteers	3	(15%)
Noncentralized administration	2	(10%)
Effective funding	2	(10%)
Effective strategic planning	1	(5%)
State government help	1	(5%)
Combination with larger agencies	1	(5%)
Reducing staff	1	(5%)

TABLE VI-XXII
MAJOR CURRENT ISSUES CONCERNING CRISIS CENTERS

Issues	Number of Responding Facilities	
Financial/funding limitations	11	(55%)
Space limitations/length of stay	6	(30%)
Programs for needs of children	4	(20%)
Legal/political system	3	(15%)
Staff training	3	(15%)
Low pay for staff	2	(10%)
Case management	1	(5%)
Future growth & expansion	1	(5%)
Children's complaints against staff	1	(5%)
Misuse of funds	1	(5%)
Increase of referrals	1	(5%)
Lack of parent attendance for programs	1	(5%)
Condition of facility	1	(5%)
Shortage of foster homes	1	(5%)
Increase of functioning level	1	(5%)
Crisis response	1	(5%)
Replication of programs	1	(5%)

SUMMARY OF NATIONAL TRENDS AND PROSPECTS

From the nationwide responses presented in this chapter, certain patterns can be found which would help to understand the current conditions of service facilities in the United States. It is also feasible to identify the strengths, weaknesses and desirable changes.

The majority of the responding facilities were social service agencies for children, and many had shelter facilities for crisis intervention. Other services are mainly in the form of counseling and emergency treatment. The most common form of indirect service was referral which was a cooperative effort, involving interactions between the service facilities and child protection services, public/private social service agencies, and public schools. Funding was most often provided by state resources, county sources, and personal donations.

There were three main issues of concern which were most commonly mentioned by the responding service facilities. They were: (1) financial difficulty, usually related to the lack of funding; (2) staffing problems, usually due to lack of quality staff caused by lower pay scales and benefits; and (3) service limitations, due to the lack of space which necessitated shorter stays and less than comprehensive treatment. These concerns clearly center around the issue of public commitment to the problem of child abuse and neglect.

In examining these and other national trends and concerns, the most important suggestion that can be made is to form a comprehensive community cooperation program for improved services.

The literature of child abuse and neglect repeatedly calls for simultaneous efforts on the prevention, education and treatment of child victimization. By educating and training parents, it is highly possible that a great percentage of child abuse and neglect incidents can be reduced. This can be accomplished by creating more volunteer and assistance programs for the adult population, along with good marketing to assure that those in need are aware of the available services. Children can also be educated to realize what constitutes abuse and neglect and to understand their right to ask for help. This could be established by local programs incorporated into the network of public schools and community organizations such as churches and neighborhoods.

In order to reach the above goal of greater education and prevention efforts for both adults and children, two areas are required for future concentration. The first, and most obvious area, is that of financial resources. It is logical that more funding may be necessary for expanding the services already offered, and the improvement of cost efficiency for the existing resources is equally important. For this reason, service facilities in different states are encouraged to work together in order to share strategies and resource information. Since most funding is on a state, county, or personal level, there is little or no real chance for agencies from different states to compete for the same local funding sources.

The second area for improvement of current services is related to inter-facility coordination at the community level. Many methods can be used to establish a network system which will link all service providers together in such as a way that all agencies and organizations are benefited by close interactions and coordinations. By increasing referrals between various facilities within a given community, effective services can be offered, and cost efficiency can be guaranteed. There are also many sources in each community that can be used for a variety of programs. By working together, different service facilities can concentrate on development of respected expertise areas of service programs. This will improve the quality of staff in each facility. In addition, if the possibility of referring clients to other community service agencies was an option, the problem of duplicated programs and space limitations can easily be resolved.

In sum, there is a great deal of potential for improving the quality of services offered to victims and perpetrators of child abuse and neglect. According to the results from this national sample, the single area of concentration that is receiving the most attention at this time is treatment of child abuse and neglect. While the importance of treating those affected by abuse and neglect cannot be underestimated, this report suggests a desperate need of effective programs for prevention and education purposes. In this regard, all facilities need to participate in developing a comprehensive, community-wide system for treatment, prevention, and education on child abuse and neglect problems. Communication on a regional and national level is also suggested for identifying resources and designing comprehensive cooperation efforts. Only by working together, communities and the nation as a whole can reduce, and hopefully someday eliminate, the problems of child abuse and neglect.

APPENDIX VI-A

Nationwide Survey of Service Facilities
Related to Child Abuse and Neglect

1. Your facility or program for child abuse and neglect can best be described as:

   _____ Day Care Center　　　　_____ Crisis Nursery
   _____ Mental Health Hospital　_____ Family Counseling Center
   _____ Private Practice　　　　 _____ Social Services Agency
   _____ Community Center　　　　_____ Advocacy Program
   _____ Other (Please Specify _____)

2. Please indicate (by circling) whether your organization provides the services below or not and also indicate the average activity level of each service during the past six months. Please note that services are divided into three categories: Adult Services, Child Services and Indirect Services.

   For rating the activity level, use 1 = always, 2 = frequently, 3 = sometimes, and 4 = rarely.

A. Child Services Is it part of your your services? Activity level of the service

		always	freq.	some-times	rarely
emergency shelter care _____ yes no _____		1	2	3	4
residential shelter care _____ yes no _____		1	2	3	4
crisis nursery _____ yes no _____		1	2	3	4
recreational therapy _____ yes no _____		1	2	3	4
art therapy _____ yes no _____		1	2	3	4
drama _____ yes no _____		1	2	3	4
tutorialship _____ yes no _____		1	2	3	4
medical services _____ yes no _____		1	2	3	4
emergency services _____ yes no _____		1	2	3	4
play therapy _____ yes no _____		1	2	3	4
individual therapy _____ yes no _____		1	2	3	4
diagnostic services _____ yes no _____		1	2	3	4
case management _____ yes no _____		1	2	3	4
therapeutic day care _____ yes no _____		1	2	3	4
education _____ yes no _____		1	2	3	4
other specify: _____ yes no _____		1	2	3	4
other specify: _____ yes no _____		1	2	3	4
other specify: _____ yes no _____		1	2	3	4

B. Adult Services Is it part of your service? Activity level of the services

		always	freq.	some-times	rarely
couples counseling _____ yes no _____		1	2	3	4
family counseling _____ yes no _____		1	2	3	4
24-hour counseling _____ yes no _____		1	2	3	4
group therapy _____ yes no _____		1	2	3	4
lay therapy _____ yes no _____		1	2	3	4
legal assistance _____ yes no _____		1	2	3	4
residential care _____ yes no _____		1	2	3	4
employment assistance _____ yes no _____		1	2	3	4
housing assistance _____ yes no _____		1	2	3	4
transportation _____ yes no _____		1	2	3	4
respite child care _____ yes no _____		1	2	3	4

B. Adult Services	Is it part of your service?	Activity level of the services			
		always	freq.	some-times	rarely
recreational activities _____ yes no _____		1	2	3	4
financial assistance _____ yes no _____		1	2	3	4
prenatal aid counseling _____ yes no _____		1	2	3	4
senior citizens counseling _____ yes no _____		1	2	3	4
mental health services _____ yes no _____		1	2	3	4
alcohol counseling _____ yes no _____		1	2	3	4
social work counseling _____ yes no _____		1	2	3	4
individual therapy _____ yes no _____		1	2	3	4
consultation _____ yes no _____		1	2	3	4
education _____ yes no _____		1	2	3	4
Parents Anonymous _____ yes no _____		1	2	3	4
parent-child bridging _____ yes no _____		1	2	3	4
child management classes _____ yes no _____		1	2	3	4
needs assessment _____ yes no _____		1	2	3	4
help line _____ yes no _____		1	2	3	4
crisis intervention _____ yes no _____		1	2	3	4
medical care _____ yes no _____		1	2	3	4
residential care _____ yes no _____		1	2	3	4
homemaker services _____ yes no _____		1	2	3	4
24-hour hot line _____ yes no _____		1	2	3	4
other specify: _____ yes no _____		1	2	3	4
other specify: _____ yes no _____		1	2	3	4
other specify: _____ yes no _____		1	2	3	4

C. Indirect Services

		always	freq.	some-times	rarely
referral _____ yes no _____		1	2	3	4
training advocacy _____ yes no _____		1	2	3	4
reporting child abuse and neglect cases _____ yes no _____		1	2	3	4
information services _____ yes no _____		1	2	3	4
library services _____ yes no _____		1	2	3	4
training _____ yes no _____		1	2	3	4
public awareness _____ yes no _____		1	2	3	4
advocacy _____ yes no _____		1	2	3	4
needs assessment _____ yes no _____		1	2	3	4

C. Indirect Services	Is it part of your service?	Activity level of the services			
		always	freq.	some-times	rarely
professional awareness _____ yes no _____		1	2	3	4
program planning _____ yes no _____		1	2	3	4
services coordination _____ yes no _____		1	2	3	4
technical assistance _____ yes no _____		1	2	3	4
legal services _____ yes no _____		1	2	3	4
other specify: _____ yes no _____		1	2	3	4
other specify: _____ yes no _____		1	2	3	4
other specify: _____ yes no _____		1	2	3	4

3. Please answer the following questions that deal with your intake of cases.
   a. capacity of **children** your faculty can serve per day?
      _____ children.
   b. average number of children per day under care? _____ children.
   c. average length of childrens' stay?   _____ days.
   d. maximum length of childrens' stay?   _____ days.
   e. capacity of **adults** your facility can serve per day?
      _____ adults.
   f. average number of adults you serve per day?   _____ adults.
   g. average length of adults' stay?   _____ days.
   h. maximum length of adults' stay?   _____ days.

4. Staff Information:
   How many paid staff members do you have
   currently?   _____ members
   How many volunteers do you have currently?   _____ volunteers
   Please specify the number of staff and volunteers
   in each of the following categories:

| | PAID STAFF | | | NON–PAID STAFF |
	Number of full time	Number of part time and **average** per cent time)		Number of Volunteers in each position
	N:	N:	%	N:
administrators _____	____	____ ___ %		____
managers _____	____	____ ___ %		____
outreach counselors ___	____	____ ___ %		____
office managers _____	____	____ ___ %		____
secretaries _____	____	____ ___ %		____
receptionists _____	____	____ ___ %		____
clerical aides _____	____	____ ___ %		____
child advocates _____	____	____ ___ %		____
women advocates _____	____	____ ___ %		____
shelter advocates _____	____	____ ___ %		____
family counselors _____	____	____ ___ %		____
pediatricians _____	____	____ ___ %		____
social workers _____	____	____ ___ %		____
child programmer ____	____	____ ___ %		____
shelter staff _____	____	____ ___ %		____
child care persons ____	____	____ ___ %		____
cook _____	____	____ ___ %		____
kitchen helpers _____	____	____ ___ %		____
children's interns _____	____	____ ___ %		____
house managers _____	____	____ ___ %		____
custodians _____	____	____ ___ %		____
recreational aides _____	____	____ ___ %		____
transportation aides ___	____	____ ___ %		____
parent aides _____	____	____ ___ %		____
lay therapists _____	____	____ ___ %		____
baby sitters _____	____	____ ___ %		____
homemakers _____	____	____ ___ %		____
visiting nurses _____	____	____ ___ %		____
telephone receptionists _	____	____ ___ %		____
interns _____	____	____ ___ %		____

	PAID STAFF		NON–PAID STAFF
	Number of full time	Number of part time and **average** per cent time)	Number of Volunteers in each position
	N:	N: %	N:
other specify: _____	____	____ ____ %	____
other specify: _____	____	____ ____ %	____
other specify: _____	____	____ ____ %	____

5. Who are your clientele? (Check as many as they are applicable)

	Your clientele?	Number of target population	Estimated number served in 1985.
a. Geographic boundaries			
State residents _____	yes no	____	____
Multi-County residents _____	yes no	____	____
County residents _____	yes no	____	____
City residents _____	yes no	____	____
b. Types of populations			
parents _____	yes no	____	____
children _____	yes no	____	____
families _____	yes no	____	____
lay audiences _____	yes no	____	____
professional groups _____	yes no	____	____
other specify: _____	yes no	____	____
other specify: _____	yes no	____	____
other specify: _____	yes no	____	____

6. Type of Organization? (check all that apply)

_____ private nonprofit   _____ public nonprofit

_____ private profit   _____ public profit

_____ residential   _____ nonresidential

7. Assessment/evaluation regarding your organization.

	Number performed during the last two years.	Number planed for the next two years.	Contents of the evaluation.
external evaluation/ assessment	_____	_____	_____ _____ _____
internal evaluation/ assessment	_____	_____	_____ _____ _____

8. **Outreach of your referrals:** Please indicate your referral frequency to each agency (or person) in terms of the following categories:

	always	very often	frequently	occasionally	rarely	never
to public hospitals	1	2	3	4	5	6
to private social service agencies	1	2	3	4	5	6
to public social service agencies	1	2	3	4	5	6
to public schools	1	2	3	4	5	6
to law enforcement agencies	1	2	3	4	5	6
to child protective services	1	2	3	4	5	6
to courts	1	2	3	4	5	6
to family members	1	2	3	4	5	6
to neighbors	1	2	3	4	5	6
to churches	1	2	3	4	5	6
to sources within the agency	1	2	3	4	5	6
to other specify:	1	2	3	4	5	6
to other specify:	1	2	3	4	5	6
to other specify:	1	2	3	4	5	6

9. **Referral source for your agency:** Please indicate the source from which **your agency receives referrals** in terms of their frequency. Please also include the percentage of referrals you receive from each individual source such that the total percentages from all sources will equal 100%.

Frequency

Relative percent

	always	very often	frequently	occasionally	rarely	never	Relative percent
public hospitals _____	1	2	3	4	5	6	___ %
private social service agencies _____	1	2	3	4	5	6	___ %
public social service agencies _____	1	2	3	4	5	6	___ %
public schools _____	1	2	3	4	5	6	___ %
law enforcement agencies _____	1	2	3	4	5	6	___ %
child protective services _____	1	2	3	4	5	6	___ %
courts _____	1	2	3	4	5	6	___ %
family members _____	1	2	3	4	5	6	___ %
neighbors _____	1	2	3	4	5	6	___ %
self-referrals _____	1	2	3	4	5	6	___ %
churches _____	1	2	3	4	5	6	___ %
sources within the agency _____	1	2	3	4	5	6	___ %
other specify: _____	1	2	3	4	5	6	___ %
other specify: _____	1	2	3	4	5	6	___ %
other specify: _____	1	2	3	4	5	6	___ %
					TOTAL		100 %

10. **Funding Sources of Your Organization.** Please specify the total amount of your 1985 budget and the percentage of each of the following categories contributing to your 1985 total budget:

Sources:	Total Dollar Amount in 1985	Relative percent in 1985 Budget
Title XX _____	$ _____	___ %
Revenue Sharing _____	$ _____	___ %
State funds _____	$ _____	___ %

Sources:	Total Dollar Amount in 1985	Relative percent in 1985 Budget
County funds _____	$ _____	___ %
City funds _____	$ _____	___ %
township funds _____	$ _____	___ %
local funds _____	$ _____	___ %
United Way _____	$ _____	___ %
personal donations _____	$ _____	___ %
client fees _____	$ _____	___ %
local mental health board funds _____	$ _____	___ %
consulting contracts _____	$ _____	___ %
interest contracts _____	$ _____	___ %
private foundations _____	$ _____	___ %
churches _____	$ _____	___ %
other nonprofit organizations __	$ _____	___ %
other specify: _____	$ _____	___ %
other specify: _____	$ _____	___ %
other specify: _____	$ _____	___ %
		TOTAL 100%

What was your total budget for 1985? _____

What is your total budget for 1986? _____

11. **Issues of Concern:** What are some of the problems that your organization might be facing right now? Please check all appropriate, and indicate their severity in terms of the following levels: 1 = high, 2 = moderate, 3 = somewhat, and 4 = low.

Possible Problems/issues:	Is it a problem?		Level of severity.			
			high	mod	some-what	low
cooperation with outside service providers _____	yes	no	1	2	3	4
financial difficulties _____	yes	no	1	2	3	4
political _____	yes	no	1	2	3	4
no crisis nursery _____	yes	no	1	2	3	4
no emergency care _____	yes	no	1	2	3	4
limited capacity _____	yes	no	1	2	3	4

Possible Problems/issues:	Is it a problem?		Level of severity.			
			high	mod	some-what	low
limited resources other than financial _____	yes	no	1	2	3	4
other specify: _____	yes	no	1	2	3	4
other specify: _____	yes	no	1	2	3	4
other specify: _____	yes	no	1	2	3	4

12. Would you please list **five major conditions** that you feel would make a crisis center become most effective?

    1. _____
    2. _____
    3. _____
    4. _____
    5. _____

13. How do you think crisis centers can be more **cost efficient?**

14. What are the **three major issues** concerning your crisis center today?

    1. _____
    2. _____
    3. _____

15. Do you think a national newsletter would be helpful to your organization? _____

16. Other comments or suggestions: _____

    _____

    _____

    _____

Thank you for your assistance. Please fold on the dotted line, staple, and return to us.

CHAPTER 7

ESTABLISHING A LOCAL CRISIS CENTER ORGANIZATION: FORMAT, PROCEDURES AND MATERIALS USED

JAMIA J. JACOBSEN
OLIVER C. S. TZENG
LINDA J. HANNER

INTRODUCTION

Social problems such as poverty, sickness, child abuse and family dysfunction have existed throughout history. Violence has always been a part of the lives of families and individuals. Only recently have we begun to deal with the whole family and the violence perpetuated therein. For every family and child helped, we assist the next generation to build a more solid family foundation (Jacobsen, 1986).

The magnitude of the child abuse and neglect problems and of the surrounding family dysfunctions makes it necessary to organize social services for children under public and private initiatives (Friedlander and Apte, 1980). Today, more children are in need of services from child crisis center facilities. Crisis centers have as their primary goal the prevention/intervention of child abuse and neglect. These centers are to provide for each needy child a temporary shelter for safety and also to assist a child's parent(s) or guardian to obtain some economic and social necessities. Often times parenting education programs are also provided to abusive or neglectful parents for learning various skills and competency in child rearing and stress-coping behaviors.

The purpose of this chapter is to present the principles, methods, strategies, and implementation steps for developing a crisis center for intervention and prevention of child abuse and neglect. For such purposes, this chapter will cover five general topics in sequence: (1) principles and strategies for developing a child crisis center, (2) identification of financial resources and fund raising, (3) organizational structures of the crisis center, (4) program planning and implementation of the crisis center,

157

and (5) staff recruitment, education and evaluation. Each topic will be discussed and illustrated with exemplary materials from a crisis center in Indiana (i.e. The Family Support Center Inc., Indianapolis).

DEVELOPING A CHILD CRISIS CENTER

Child abuse can be viewed from three perspectives: (1) the individual problem of the abusive family, (2) the one time only happening of abuse within a family, and (3) the abuse which occurs because the community or culture encourages such practices.

Intervention of child maltreatment may begin with providing immediate care to the abused child with eventual family counseling to protect the child from further injury. Formulation of a crisis center can help a community deal with such abusive patterns. Many communities have attempted to work on programs related to identification, intervention, and treatment for victimized children. It has only been within the last few years that crisis-intervention programs have been emphasized for children.

Working Together To Meet a Community Need

Community-wide cooperation must be stressed to accomplish the goals of crisis intervention and to develop a safe, nurturing atmosphere for children. Individuals and private businesses in the community area must be involved, as well as local welfare departments, lawyers, juvenile court officials, law enforcement officials, school personnel, various social service agencies, and the community-based child abuse and neglect teams.

With cooperation and community backing, a crisis center can begin to set goals. Wolfe (1981) states, "Active groups have goals, and members must help achieve those goals." A sample of the major goals that a group must agree upon in the process of formulating a crisis center include: (1) when the center will be established, (2) the ages of children the center will care for, (3) the length of stay a child will have, (4) if the parents and family will be housed as well as the target child, (5) the funding of the center, and (6) amount of interaction between the crisis center board and the staff.

It is of major importance when deciding goals, that all members of the discussion work together. It is best to let one person rise as a leader, and all members should guard against letting egos or petty jealousies interfere with the work of establishing a center. All members should have input in decisions, but not overwhelm other members with suggestions. Extensive commitment, sometimes without recognition, may be required to accomplish the goal of opening a center. Plant the seeds and let them generate.

> Learning to put a break on your enthusiasm or distress when you don't have the group with you, learning to quietly educate, learning to be patient when you feel that something cries out for attention, is absolutely required. Don't ever assume that everyone agrees with you, (Wolfe, 1981).

Problems in formulation of a child crisis center may occur when the leader is unaware the consensus of the group is not with his/her decisions, or when all ideas aren't allowed to surface and be reviewed. A group leader must keep an open, honest atmosphere and be able to effectively work with other members of the group.

Charity

> It must be recalled that anyone can start a charity. All that is really needed is a cause (whether or not you believe in it), time, effort, dedication, (if only lining your pockets), and gall. (Liston, 1977, p. 37).

Once the crisis center ideas has been established, a name to represent it must be devised. The name should be simple and easy to recall. It must clearly state the purposes and the procedures of the project to the public. In this case the name should make reference to children. The logo will make an impact on the general public and most specifically on those targeted for fund raising.

To obtain working capital, funds need to be raised through a statement letter that can be sent community-wide. This letter should include: (1) a statement of what funds are needed, (2) the purpose of the child crisis center, (3) an explanation of what the center is seeking to accomplish, (4) who the center will benefit, and (5) information or statistics of child abuse relevant to that community. This letter may include an appeal for monetary support and/or volunteer services.

Professional fund raisers who are designated members of the fund raising society are available for hire. These individuals can assist with the statement-of-need letter, or volunteers may be willing to help. Mailing lists may be purchased, or one may be compiled from area volunteer organizations, country clubs, and churches. An enclosed self-addressed envelope will encourage donations and costs can be saved if a first class permit is acquired from the Post Office which will charge only for envelopes returned. Thank you notes written for all donations will encourage future funding. Careful records must be kept of all donations, including who donated money and how much was given. (See Appendix VII in the back of this book).

Laws concerning the start-up of a charity are weak, but it is best to file for the 501-C-3 tax exempt category status, and possibly engage help from an accountant. Forms may be acquired from the IRS as well as a booklet called, **How to Apply for and Retain Exempt Status for Your Organization.** Check with local and state laws concerning their charitable solicitations requirements. Registration or a complete report of the center's activities may be necessary. Many states today impose a limitation on the amount of money spent for the cost of fund raising.

Many nonprofit charitable institutions hire an executive director to police costs and to show the public that donated money is being put to designated use. However, a crisis center's board and staff members must be actively involved in fund raising as well to create the faith necessary from the community that donations are being put to their best use.

Accurate and careful records must be kept of all income and expenses. This is necessary for the annual report and for proving to the inquiring public that funds are spent properly. Chances are that the faith of Americans in the goodwill and effectiveness of charity organizations is well founded, but there have been enough proven instances of abuse in the name of charity (some of them gross abuses) to add a large element of chance to this faith (Liston, 1977).

Do's and Don'ts of Starting a Crisis Center

Speculation and fear are not abnormal feelings when first formulating a crisis center, but the best method is to jump in and get it going. A crisis center is a remarkable institution and a viable method of helping abusive parents and their children. It may be that the community under consideration truly needs a 24 hour long-term care facility or a day care crisis facility. Flanagan (1981) lists advice for starting a center, such as:

1. Be realistic about lacking talents, and look for help from others who can fill in those weaknesses;
2. Dare to be different and if a new idea doesn't work the first time, try it again;
3. Plan strategically and take time to think, move from A to B to C;
4. Keep program activities going while organizing, and don't lose the interested members, (a speakers bureau has proven helpful);

5. Focus and listen to new ideas, but don't try to do every one;
6. Ask for funds from the start, don't wait to accomplish something first because donations and involvement are critical;
7. Choose a program that is a reasonable goal, (read about monetary support and programs that are available);
8. Trust the group process and listen to others' suggestions, members may detect people or situations which have been overlooked;
9. Ask the best leaders to join the project, don't accept assigned people from a company or the buddy of a board member;
10. Set standards of hard work, even a leader should be prepared for cleaning, painting, taking care of donated clothing, etc.; and
11. Keep priorities straight, organize categories of work and plan for each.

Flanagan also lists advice of what **not** to do when starting a center. This advice includes:

1. Don't wait to set up books, a qualified accountant can eliminate the many headaches of a partially started accounting system and will keep a good audit trail;
2. Don't think it can all be done alone, others are needed to support and carry out ideas;
3. Don't be afraid to ask for help, an auxiliary group may be needed to provide funds, time, and talents;
4. Don't put money into furniture or equipment too early because many businesses will donate furniture, office space, typewriters, etc.;
5. Don't depend on just one source of money for funds, the loss of one main fund drive or donor can cripple a center financially;
6. Don't waste time on somebody else's meeting, as a leader it is impossible to spend hours sitting in a committee meeting and also be overseeing staff and raising funds at the same time. If it won't benefit the center, send a social or staff member as a delegate;
7. Don't be stalled by a lack of certain skills, recruit people that have and use these skills;
8. Don't expect to be appreciated, the reward is a job well done and in the long run it will be well recognized; and
9. Don't give up, changes and set backs should be expected, but should not end the project's goals.

The well-being and protection of abused children, as well as the assistance to abusive families in the community is the goal to keep in mind while difficulties in formulating a crisis center are undertaken and overcome. Flanagan's lists of success and failure are provided in Table VII–I to be placed where it can be seen daily.

TABLE VII-I
TEN POINTS FOR THE SUCCESS OR FAILURE OF A CHILD CRISIS CENTER

Factors Most Likely to Cause Success	*Factors Most Likely to Cause Failure*
Clear goals	Unclear or contradictory goals
The will to succeed	Lack of the will to succeed
Focus on a limited number of goals	Too many goals
Plan and time table to reach goals	No plan or time table for goals
Tangible victories	Lack of paid staff
Exciting programs	Boring programs
Dependable income	Too little money
Strong board of directors	Lack of dedicated leaders
Up to date bookkeeping	Inaccurate bookkeeping
Fun	Conflict of interests

Public Recognition For the Center

To gain recognition and funding for a crisis center, search for the most effective ways to provide news for the media. It is not as difficult to get the media's attention as one might think. Educate the general public about the center to generate and maintain a feeling of closeness between the community and the child crisis center. Guidelines to help gain recognition include: (1) explaining what the agency is about, (2) opening the clinic to the public, (3) showing what is being done in a different manner than other groups, (4) publicizing speakers for the clinic and their credentials, (5) becoming a special resource to provide accurate and sound information to the media, (6) building good relationships of trust, and (7) being honest and helpful.

Some pragmatic suggestions for getting the media's attention include: (1) keep news station addresses and contact persons on file, (2) know how much time is needed to release a news story, (3) research the many books written about publicity and the press, (4) ask for help from a public relations professional to develop a media campaign.

Honest communication and open meetings create an atmosphere of trust. Flanagan advises groups to let their members, friends, neighbors, donors, and enemies know what they are doing.

Publicity consists of factors other than the press including, internal communications, internal publications, and external publicity. Internal communications among the staff, board, and other members is important. The grapevine method (having one person call 5 or 6 others, etc.) is being implemented in many organizations and is an excellent way to inform people of a quickly called and/or cancelled meeting.

Internal publications should be prepared in the following ways: staff guidelines, counseling and admission procedures, board notebooks, etc. Clear, attractive and easy to read publications can reduce confusion and encourage readers.

External publicity in the form of a newsletter is an excellent method of keeping active members well informed and excited about the crisis center. Some agencies send newsletters to paid members only, while others sell subscriptions. Suggestions in publishing a newsletter include: (1) ask a bank or business to underwrite the printing as a donation, (2) always include a notice asking for donations in each newsletter, (3) ask a volunteer auxiliary to handle the mailing and labeling, (4) buy or trade mailing lists to be cost efficient, and (5) give some newsletters away for promotional efforts or to large donors.

Designing a newsletter to be interesting and eye catching will encourage more readers. Print such items as: (1) thank you columns, (2) names of those who run the center, (3) advice on how to become a member, (4) board presidents' and executive directors' names, (5) messages and quotes from community or agency leaders, and (6) articles or cover issues on all phases of the center.

Another method of reporting to organization membership is through annual reports. Flanagan suggests groups should publish annual reports to record their history and recognize their supporters. It is a good way to publish financial reports and gain fund raising assistance from corporations and foundations. Reports can be as plain as typewritten budget reports with graphics, or a fancy presentation. Using color for the newsletter or the crisis center logo on the cover will attract attention and promote the center's theme. Annual reports should begin with remarks from the Board President, followed by the Executive Director's report, and should be not more than six to eight pages. Keep in mind that distribution of the annual report is much narrower than for the newsletter.

A speakers bureau is another cost efficient way of publicizing a crisis center because it is free. Volunteers can be trained to schedule requests which can be generated by a list of availability in the newsletter. Free public service announcements (PSA) time can be used to gain recognition of the speakers bureau. There may be no charge for listening to the speakers, but donations should be requested in some form. This is an excellent means of publicizing the program and communicating its needs, for both financial needs and for the childrens' needs.

Speakers must be trained and informed about the group to whom they will speak. (See Appendix VII–U for a Speaker Bureau Assignment Sheet). A volunteer from a public relations firm may be available to train speakers. Volunteers can be responsible to call service groups to schedule initial speeches. A speaker's bureau should be one of the first volunteer groups initiated because it will make the public aware that the center is in the community, as well as bringing name recognition.

A logo is a graphic representation which makes it visually easy for the public to recognize the crisis center. An artist or designer may donate his/her time to create it professionally for the center. It is cost efficient and helpful to design the logo so it can be copied. When used consistently on all printed materials, a logo will provide instant recognition and will come to represent the meaning of the center.

Letterhead is important and is often overlooked. Select good quality paper and feature the name of the executive director and affiliated board members in the margin. Legal size envelopes with return address and printed logo will create a more professional image for the center.

Brochures are another good means of publicizing the crisis center and can be made attractive with photos of the center. Due to monetary constraints, it may be necessary to use clip art and a typewriter, but a business may be willing to underwrite the copying. It is important to consider the use of the brochure and how it will be distributed before investing money. Boxes full of brochures, stored in a dark room, will help no one.

The person answering the phones for the center often is the first contact with general public, and that person represents the organization. Have the telephone company train volunteers on the proper way to answer the phone politely, and use an answering device when no one is available to answer the phone.

The use of display boards and/or bulletin boards is also important to publicize the crisis center. Exterior displays can be used for educational purposes and an inhouse bulletin board is a good place to honor a staff member or volunteer. Keep the displays fresh, clear, and professional looking.

Slide shows can be an effective and cost-efficient method of publicizing the center. Slides can be borrowed from other crisis centers and slightly modified. A television announcer might be recruited to narrate the show for free. Short presentations, usually five to seven minutes, allow enough time to tell the story and still hold the attention span of the viewers. Whether a slide show is used for publicity in a mall, to call on corporations, or to train an audience, it is a valuable method of crisis center publicity.

> Coaches say that the best defense is a good offense, and the best offense against negative publicity is to tell your own story to the public. Proud publicity will tell your story the way you want it told (Flanagan, 1981).

Remember that all key members of the public should know what the crisis center is doing. A democratic organization with honest intentions will never need to worry about harm being done to them if they are open and honest in their methods and communications.

Finally, keep in mind that the best method of getting attention for the crisis center is to do **something important**. Most nonprofit organizations are afraid of using publicity. It is truly a missed opportunity.

> ...the most important asset of any public relations campaign is a compelling organizational mission. If your organization has a clear sense of purpose, then public relations will consist of making sure that it's communicated in all written materials, enlivened by a consistent graphic image, and reflected in the behavior and attitude of everyone involved in the organization (Setterburg and Schulman, 1985, p. 109).

Strive constantly to keep the crisis center's name and accomplishments in the news and therefore, in people's minds.

Raising Money for the Crisis Center

Liston has said that a sure fire way to appeal to the American public's generosity is through children. This thought, however mercenary, is true. "Basil O'Conner and the National Organization showed the way by calling polio 'infantile paralysis' and depicted children rather than adult victims," pointed out Liston. Appeals using children strike at the heart of Americans because they don't want to see a child being abused and neglected. Using children as the central focus of publicity does work.

Throughout the years, children have been exploited in fund raising. However, this is not what should be done in starting a child crisis center. Tell the story of the center to the public tastefully, objectively, and with honesty. It is one thing to picture a child in fund raising material or use children in a special project, but quite another thing to transport children to a strange neighborhood miles away from where they live or are housed.

Reading some of the many books available on fund raising and talking to professionals are good ways to get started with a plan. Some major principles of fund raising include: (1) finding volunteers who are creative and have follow-through, (2) reviewing all green-light ideas with certain guidelines in mind, (3) setting a budget before beginning any fund raising project, and (4) knowing what goals need to be accomplished.

Joan Wolfe (1981, p. 70–71) lists five very reasonable guidelines which are important in fund raising for a crisis center. They are as follows:

1. The project should take as little time possible for the most dollars raised, or should be a project in which the service provided is more important than the profit per hour;
2. The project should require no large financial risks, or should involve risks which can easily be borne by the organization if the project fails;
3. The project should be relevant to the aims of the center, or the project should make so much money that relevance is unimportant;
4. The project should help publicize the organization and its purpose, if publicity is important to the group; and
5. The project should be fun and help members get to know each other better, or the project should be a service which gives members self respect and an opportunity to be useful to others.

With these guidelines in mind, remember that what is started one year may be expected to grow, thus involving more money and more people each following year. Start with a base, and plan towards both one year and five year goals. Each year has the potential to challenge new leaders and volunteers as they learn that they can succeed by participating.

As Flanagan stresses, independence comes from a diversity in fund raising. It does, and many different sources can be put to work. Some examples include government funds, foundation funds, corporate money, church money, and grass roots money.

Government funds are not as plentiful as they once were. It takes a knowledgeable writer to compose a grant proposal, but funding is still available. The biggest hurdles are in making sure that the grant fits the project goals, that the staff can handle the project, and that an accurate accounting system is in place.

Guides for foundation funds can be found at the library. Research to find out who is interested in children and who will donate within the area (some foundations only give locally). It may be beneficial to call the funding institution for the guidelines and due dates, then write them a letter of introduction telling them of the crisis center or a specific area within the center relevant to their interests. (See Appendix VII–S). When all the criteria is obtained, write a grant proposal (usually not more than three pages), explaining why the money is needed and how it will be used. With local foundations, it may be possible to call on the person in charge personally to express interest and discuss the crisis center.

To raise funds from corporate money it is helpful to compile lists of the major corporations, including banks, in the local area of the crisis center. A good project for volunteers is to gather information from these corporations including the name of the Chief Executive Officer. Once the list is compiled, review it with the community leaders directly involved with the center. Some of these leaders may know certain of the executives personally and be willing to make the call on behalf of the center. Corporations may be willing to give gifts other than money, such as furniture, coping, paper, equipment, and supplies. It must be remembered, however, that corporate donations will not build the crisis center, so the larger donor must be recruited.

Many churches have foundations and this good source of money should not be overlooked. Besides monetary donations, many local churches and synagogues are also sources of food and clothing for the children in the center. Churches are also useful as training sources and for help in fund raising.

Grass roots money is the area in which the membership of the center should be built. The base for recruitment should be as large as possible. Requesting smaller amounts ($15 to $20) will invite personal commitment into the center. Use every newsletter to ask people to become members. This will encourages growth of the agency and promote publicity and dependable forms of future donations.

Joining United Way can guarantee the center a set amount of money per year and can increase the legitimacy of the project. However, the paper work and curtailment of other funding may be harmful. United Way does not build the organization. Be aware that by joining the United Way, a center becomes accountable to United Way rather than to its own members. There is a risk of the board becoming dependent on what United Way wants rather than what is truly good for the crisis center.

A relatively new idea to provide an excellent stable income for the project is to back the center with a personal business. This option is often overlooked by nonprofit organizations.

The following six methods for building financial self-sufficiency are suggests by Flanagen (1981, p. 164).

1. Be democratic. Financial self-sufficiency is produced by the work of the membership and the value of the organization, not by the skills or relationships of a few people. Most important, self-sufficiency is not dependent upon the relationships of any paid staff, because they can easily work somewhere else tomorrow.

2. Form a variety of sources. Independence comes with diversity.

3. Control finances internally. Know how and when money comes in and goes out. This requires sound business management and rigorous record keeping. The bookkeeper is a key person, and computerized equipment is vital to keep track of this information.

4. Be honest. Nothing is more important than this point because the respect of the community is needed for financial support. People will give for a while but their donations are likely to dwindle if an agency always seems near extinction.

5. Be renewable. This results from having sources that produce donated income year after year. There is no vulnerability to fads, politics, or economic fluctuations. Corporate gifts and grants are flexible since they are often one or two year donations. A planned donation program can escalate funds as membership builds, while annual donation campaigns can continue to make wider use of capital campaign techniques.

Some ideas to raise money are through: (1) sales such as cookbooks, auctions, rummages, raffle tickets, or articles made by the membership, (2) services provided by the center such as serving meals or tutoring, and (3) passive entertainment such as speakers, children's programs, or health fairs. Other events to raise money could include selling items in a store on commission or games such as "Bingo".

All fund raising is based on good sales technique. This technique includes publicizing the crisis center in a positive manner, planning the amount of money needed, and practicing what speakers and staff will say to the public. Evaluate every fund raising effort and thank everyone who donates money to the center. Remember, there are many charities to choose from when donating money.

Fund raising experience seems to indicate that people give to organizations which provide worthwhile services and are lead by leaders they respect. People also tend to give to organizations with which they are involved. Fewer people will be available to help raise funds than in the past because more women are joining the workforce. More ingenious methods will be needed to attract and keep volunteers in the future.

Forming a Board of Directors

While most crisis centers usually begin with an informal structure, it is important to plan ahead to form a Board of Directors. Many nonprofit agencies rely on a hierarchical structure. Generally, the final decision making is vested in a Board of Directors who also hires the Executive Director. The Executive Director is then empowered to hire the staff to oversee the tasks of the crisis center. To fulfill its duties, a Board selects a strong Executive and the staff reports to the Director, never to the Board. The Director mediates between the Board and the staff and he/she belongs at every Board meeting and committee meeting. "The Board meeting is the primary location in which bonding is forged with the Director," says Settelberg and Schulman (1985).

The positive aspect of top-down management is that the Executive Director can make decisions quickly while the staff can concentrate on their jobs and areas of specialization. In reality, however, the small nonprofit organization will most likely have to be a collaborative effort.

Board of Director members of nonprofit agencies are usually comprised of volunteers who assume legal, fiscal and ethical responsibilities of the crisis center. They should be people from many different areas of expertise, such as accounting, legal, corporate, education and volunteer recruitment. The number of members can range from three to fifty, but around twelve members function best as a group. Members should elect officers and draw together bylaws and articles of incorporation. These articles should be reviewed annually and the correct forms must be filed with the state and federal governments.

Selection of the top-level personnel can be accomplished by talking with prospective leaders to gain their commitment to the center. Top candidates are those who have real experience in their field and who are interested and aware of the true crisis center cause. In discussing a Board, attendance should be stressed. If a person can't attend don't ask him/her to be a member even if the name is impressive. This could keep another person who is just as capable and able to attend from being a member. Attendance is important to keep power from becoming concentrated with only a few members and resulting in tunnel vision.

Each Board member has a specific term of office usually lasting one to three years. In starting a new crisis center Board, a co-president relationship may be more beneficial than a single presidency because this will double leadership. A vice president, secretary, and treasurer should also be elected. Board members should eventually rotate off the Board to open new places for new talent. Members should plan for around five to ten hours a month to devote to crisis center business.

The Board should list committees when writing its bylaws. Often these committees include fund raising, membership, publicity, nominating, finance and planning.

The Board may decide to incorporate the center which will force the group to think about the organization structure. Most crisis centers are tax exempt nonprofit corporations. This means they don't have to pay corporate income taxes. Forms are available from accountants or from the Internal Revenue Service (IRS) who should be made aware of the decision to incorporate. Joan Flanagan in **The Successful Volunteer Organization** provides an excellent table on filing for tax exempt status.

The Board must file for a federal employer identification number even though no workers are employed. It takes approximately six weeks to actually be assigned a number which can be obtained by sending an SS-4 form to the IRS.

Boards of Directors are made strong through education and a clear understanding of what is expected. This is important because programs come and go, staff leave and must be replaced, and goals are constantly being reevaluated. The Board must be educated as to how to read the current financial statement, what the committees have done, and what they are accomplishing.

Board members must know that part of the job is to help solicit funds. The crisis center needs help and guidance to keep operating and if the Board does not raise funds, it may be wise to consider an outside committee to undertake fund raising, and then report to the Board. Board members should also be aware that if a member is not attending or fulfilling his or her role, the means to remove that person are in place and will be used. Nonattendance is a dangerous condition because it causes the group to atrophy.

It is important to note that the purpose of the Board of Directors is to set policy and oversee the crisis center's progress and action. Committee action must be brought to the Board in an open and honest method and the Board must respond in a creative and innovative tone.

PROGRAMMING AND PLANNING FOR A CRISIS CENTER

Planning provides the opportunity for guidance of the crisis center. Flanagan states that planning is the chance to find new ways for the organization to solve problems and get results. It is a tool for keeping the crisis center on track and it must be used by both the Board and the staff. Planning provides the means to expand, grow, and become innovative.

Begin planning both one year and five years ahead from the first time the idea to establish a center is conceived. Establish a statement of purpose (i.e., why the center should be started and what the center will be for). Evaluate and write a plan for the money, time, and other resources needed for a crisis center.

Long-range plans give depth and purpose to the center as well as helping to determine what can be accomplished on a short-term and long-term basis. Board members as well as staff should be involved in planning and all plans should be reviewed by the Board of Directors. If it is an active, quality Board, the members will look at what has been proposed and carefully think through all possible actions.

In crisis centers as in other nonprofit agencies, recognition is usually too little, rewards are often insufficient, and power is spread too thin or concentrated among a few individuals. Just as in other nonprofit organizations, the mission of preventing or intervening with child abuse and neglect is the true catalyst which holds the group together.

Plan the ages of children to be accepted at the center, such as from birth to legal adulthood. Set objectives, such as the hours of service that will be offered, the type of crisis counseling or situational intervention that will be provided. Consider the possibility of becoming a central point in the network of services available to abused or potentially abused children and their families.

Segment the center into areas such as administration, child care, volunteer, kitchen, counseling, medical and maintenance. Each area will have its own paperwork and records, but they all will be tied together by common goals. A crisis center should be a nondiscriminatory agency that can make referrals to and from other agencies.

Personnel should be employed under administration VII–B for Job Descriptions) and employment applications can be general operation forms. Each employee must have a current health examination on file. Doctors who are Board members may agree to give each staff member a free yearly physical. Injections such as TB shots may be required in different states and volunteer nurses may agree to give them to the staff.

Many job applications may be received and a response should be returned to each person. Use a plan for each employee's probationary period and performance reviews. Vacation and sick leave records should be kept as well as absence reports that can be sent to the Executive Director for daily review.

Payroll time sheets should be kept by hand or on a computer and turned into the Executive Director either monthly or weekly. Long distance calls may be restricted to use from the Executive offices. Records for short-term travel and trips to conventions should be kept. Weekly expense sheets kept by each department are good practice as well as requests by in-house staff members for printing. Petty cash should be maintained by the Executive offices and by the kitchen staff. A careful record should be kept of all donations made. A process for employee grievances to be heard may also be appropriate.

Each employee should be given a personnel manual, at which time they should sign a form stating that they have received and read the manual. This will protect the crisis center from any employee stating that he/she was not told the rules.

Statistical records can be maintained by both counseling and child care departments.

Evaluation

All staff should be evaluated annually for a raise by the Executive Director and shift supervisors. These evaluations are important and should be treated as priority items and marked on the calendar for the date of review. The Board of Directors should annually evaluate bylaws, program plans, the Executive Director's yearly record, the budget and fund raising strategies.

Staffing The Crisis Center

Hiring a leader. A leader needs to be hired in order to get the crisis center up and running. Flanagan states that a great leader is someone who will be present, someone who will pay attention to detail, someone who will listen, and someone who will work as a team member.

This person also must have a philosophy in which everything that is done has the ultimate goal of helping the crisis center and its cause. A leader needs to know when to be resourceful, competent and confident.

He or she will have to make decisions alone and handle responsibility well, but also know how to reward the team members. A leader for a crisis center will be needed to give reassurance to the staff and to laugh and joke especially in situations where stress abounds. No true leader tries to do it alone, but will delegate the task of making the crisis center successful in the eyes of the staff. Consistent delegation infuses the organization with lasting strength. Nonprofit agencies are notorious for their poor working conditions, insecure employment, miserly salaries and cavalier responses from Board members who should care the most.

Hiring staff. Before interviewing the first person for employment, the Board should know what its functions will be, and the Director should know what the hired staff is expected to do. Total costs of staffing should be projected. These costs include: (a) federal and state taxes, (b) health or disability insurance, (c) salaries, (d) retirement plan, (e) paid vacations, (f) training and expenses such as travel and meals, and (g) costs of fund raising. Once the staff is hired the budget will at least double, and the money must be available to pay them. Flanagan also recommends that if a staff employee can't be paid for a two year period, that person shouldn't be hired.

Decide if positions will be part time or full time and clarify roles as to authority and accountability. Develop hiring practices such as advertising for open positions or hiring from within. Affirmative action and equal employment opportunity statements must be in place. Other policies must be delineated such as: (a) salaries and benefits, (b) overtime, (c) merit or cost of living raises, (d) working hours, (e) allowance for flexible working time, (f) sick leave, and (g) vacation holiday schedule.

Each person hired should have the goals of the center explained to him or her, with emphasis on the concept of teamwork. Paper work needed should be completed such as an IRS Form W-4 if applicable to that state and any other forms that need to be signed by the new employee. Every new staff member should be given a copy of personnel policies including rules for termination. Once the policies have been read, it should be signed by each new staff member. Explain if there is a trial period for new employees, or a certain amount of time an employee will be needed.

Training Staff

The budget should include funds for staff training from which a formal education plan can be devised for each new staff member. Each crisis center department, including the kitchen and maintenance departments, should have staff and inservice meeting schedules for further training within specific areas. Informative books or videotapes are good training aides that may be borrowed at little or no cost from the public library.

Goals should be written clearly so the staff will know what to do when a new employee joins the team. This includes the manner in which the new member will be introduced to other staff as well as crisis center policies. Written plans should be available defining work that the new employee is expected to do, and assessments of that work.

Evaluating Staff

It is a good policy to conduct individual evaluations of staff performance. Staff members should know before the evaluation process how their performance is to be measured and who will be the evaluator. A written job description and work plan can provide an objective and accurate way to measure quality of work, as well as assessing more clearly which staff members are fulfilling their individual work duties. During evaluation it is important to set a comfortable tone. The most successful evaluations will give the employee the feeling that they have been talked to rather than judged. Some managers like to issue lists of topics to be discussed before the meeting. These topics may include new information or ideas, disagreements, or opinions. The sandwich effect: a compliment; a discussion about what is wrong and then ending with a compliment; is a good way to build on strengths and praise a person for accomplishments. The staff person should be given opportunities to train in areas where his work is below standards and should be questioned to be sure he or she understands what is expected.

If a person must be fired, do it in a pleasant manner and try to avoid letting the person leave angry. Unfair or unfriendly terminations may reverberate around the community and will do neither the crisis center or its members any good. If a program is being phased out, the staff should be told in sufficient time to look for work elsewhere.

EVALUATING THE CRISIS CENTER

Evaluation is important for the staff, but it is also vital for every phase of the crisis center. Each program and project must be evaluated to determine what changes can and should be made. New and different theories are constantly being made available concerning working with and caring for abused children. Discretion and measurement for progress are the appropriate tools to use in evaluating each and every phase of the crisis center.

It is often better to face the unpleasant truth if the continued existence of a program may not be feasible or appropriate. Use the **organized abandonment** approach to the dissolution of any part of the center. Give the staff and volunteers open and honest appraisals of what is occurring instead of trying to sneak something by. Setterberg and Schulman state several reasons for stopping a project which include: (1) it has fulfilled its mandate, (2) it has outlived its usefulness, (3) there is no money to support it, and (4) the organization has disintegrated beyond repair.

Don't confuse the end of a project with the end of personal commitment and the values and vision which led to their formation and contribution.

SUMMARY

Family violence and child abuse are complex phenomena. As a result of such behavior and the attitudes associated with it, intervention programs and strategies have been developed.

Family therapy, lay therapy, and self-help groups have all been recognized for their service to human beings, and to supplement these programs there is an emerging trend to open child crisis centers. Families may utilize these centers in times of stress or to seek relief from oppressive situations. A crisis center can be essential to divert or relieve potentially damaging situations. Child crisis centers are an important resource for children and parents in order to prevent and intervene with abusive situations.

To open a child crisis center, funds must be raised, publicity generated. Board members, volunteers and staff persons must be recruited and hired. Programming must be decided upon for the particular community in which the crisis center will be established. In earlier times, individuals citizens gave alms to people in need and charities were established in churches. Today we look to crisis centers as a means to help victimized children and families with abusive tendencies.

The unawareness of the general public of the extent of child abuse and neglect helps explain the lack of adequate resources for measures to protect children against neglect, cruelty, and abuse, especially sexual abuse (Erikson, 1983). The job of the child crisis center is to make people more aware of such needs and to ultimately make life safer and healthier for all children.

Some of the tools, ideas, and knowledge needed to start a child crisis center are provided in this chapter. Not all of these pointers will work in every situation of establishing a center, but careful choices can be made that will reduce making mistakes. The job of starting a center is not easy and some plans may go awry, but rest assured there is no way to have all the knowledge required to set up a center without error.

A crisis center can make a difference to the children who walk through its doors, to the parents who are in need of guidance, and hopefully to all citizens in the community.

FROM THE OSGOOD LABORATORY OF CROSS-CULTURAL RESEARCH

Those readers desirous of having these following general descriptions of a crisis center with related personnel and related procedures, and with necessary forms as examples of illustration purposes, may request this information from Dr. Oliver C. S. Tzeng; Osgood Laboratory for Cross-Cultural Research; Department of Psychology; P.O. Box 647, KB22; Indiana University; Indianapolis, Indiana 46223.

1. Organization:
   Appendix A. Structure and personnel of crisis center
   Appendix B. Job descriptions
2. Personnel Recruitment:
   Appendix C. Nondiscriminatory policy
   Appendix D. Response to a job application
   Appendix E. Employee agreement form
   Appendix F. Employee work plan
3. Administration and Operation:
   Appendix G. Weekly expense sheet
   Appendix H. Petty cash requests
   Appendix I. Payroll timesheet
   Appendix J. Long distance calls
   Appendix K. Travel forms
   Appendix L. Printing request form
4. Supervision and Benefit of Employees
   Appendix M. Absence report
   Appendix N. Record of vacation and sick leave

Appendix O. **Employee** health record
Appendix P. **Employee** performance review
Appendix Q. **Grievance** procedure
5. **External Fund Raising Activities:**
Appendix R. **Letter** of need
Appendix S. **Foundation** request letter
Appendix T. **Crisis** center contribution form
6. **Outreach Programs:**
Appendix U. **Speaker** bureau assignment sheet
Appendix V. **Referal** policy

REFERENCES

1. Abbot, G.: *The Child and the State.* Chicago, University of Chicago, 1938, vols. I and II.
2. Banfield, E.: *The Heavenly City: The Nature and Future of Our Urban Crisis.* Boston, Little Brown, 1970.
3. Delliquadri, F.: An overview of the next two decades. In Trecker, B. (Ed.): *Goals For Social Welfare 1973-1997.* New York, Association, 1973.
4. De Schweintz, K.: *England Road to Social Security, 1349-1947,* 3rd ed. Philadelphia, University of Pennsylvania, 1947.
5. Erikson, E.: *Children and Society.* New York, Norton, 1963.
6. Flanagan, J.: *The Successful Volunteer Organization: Getting Started and Getting Results in Nonprofit, Charitable, Grass Roots, and Community Groups.* Chicago, Contemporary Books, 1981.
7. Friedlander, W., and Apte, R.: *Introduction to Social Welfare.* New Jersey, Prentice-Hall, 1947.
8. Frost, R.: The road not taken. In Frost, R. (Ed.): *The Poetry of Robert Frost.* New York, Rinhart & Winston, 1967.
9. Jacobsen, J.: *The Psychiatric Sequelae of Child Abuse: Reconnaissance of Child Abuse and Neglect. Evaluation, Prospects, Recommendations.* Springfield, Thomas, 1986.
10. Liston, R.: *The Charity Racket.* New York, Nelson, 1977.
11. Setterberg, F., and Schulman, K.: *Beyond Profit. The Complete Guide to Managing the Nonprofit Organization.* New York, Harper & Row, 1985.
12. Wolfe, J.: *Making Things Happen: The Guide for Members of Volunteer Organizations.* Massachusettes, Brick House, 1981.

CHAPTER 8

CRISIS INTERVENTION
SHELTER CARE FOR VICTIMIZED CHILDREN

Ena M. Goodrich-Shelley
James C. Stroud
Judi E. Stroud
Rosanne Pirtle

INTRODUCTION

The Crisis Intervention Shelter is often the difference between the repeat of child abuse, or even the onset, and returning to a more functional family setting. While the emphasis is on meeting the needs of the children involved, the needs of the family unit must be considered.

A comprehensive facility provides protection and immediate care for the child/children who are or may be abused or neglected. Parents needs in addition to respite **breathing time** are also met. Adults caught in the situation of being abusers first need to have the object(s) of their attacks protected and then need time to regroup. These parents are usually so overwhelmed with their own problems and needs that the added responsibility of child care is just too much. They may need time to keep appointments with health professionals, counselors or to do a multitude of errands. They also need guidance in dealing with all of these demands in such a way that their children do not become the target of their frustration and anger. Parents who can afford to pay for help in dealing with their problems still may not know how to organize and manage their time and lives to do this. The adults involved may need help and direction in dealing with many aspects of their lives such as employment, finances, marriage/relationships, and health. In addition, they may need specific support and guidance in understanding and dealing with their abusive behavior toward their children. A trusted counselor at the crisis shelter can play this role.

The primary concern at the time of the crisis is, however, for the child/children. First, these children need a safe place to stay, good food, adequate rest/sleeping space, a schedule or routine, opportunities for appropriate activities and unconditional love and affection.

Admittance to the facility is usually on a emergency basis and little planning for such a step is done. The referral may come through various sources such as law enforcement, judicial, social service agencies, health professionals, schools, etc. Parents should also be able to admit their children themselves if they need to do so. While the center is operated to care for children in a time of crisis either following abuse or to prevent abusive action, it will in all probability be used by some as a care facility when there is simply no other place to turn.

The children involved as well as their parents, must feel as comfortable as possible in the setting from the time that they enter the facility and throughout their stay. If a child is brought by someone other than the parents, he will already be somewhat in a state of uneasiness in addition to the possible trauma of the abuse suffered. Therefore, while appropriate admission procedures are necessary, care must be given so the needs of the child are taken care of without lengthy waits for the intake. A variety of admission forms will probably be used during the initial hours of a child's stay. This chapter presents examples of such forms and discusses the environment in general by suggesting what is necessary to meet the needs of the child most effectively. It also discusses equipment and materials, including toys.

The appropriate environment, including physical space, use of space, color, and personal environmental adequacy will be discussed as well as effective personnel, direct services (program), and support services (non-program) in regard to meeting the needs of the abused and neglected child.

The culmination of efforts is accomplished through appropriate daily programming so that a child is not only safe at the crisis center but actually benefits from the stay there. Obviously such a program (a quality facility and program) will be very expensive. Some needs, costs, and possible funding sources are also explored in this chapter.

Admission Forms and Records

Records should provide the personnel with pertinent information for each individual child. Some records can be completed in written form by the parent at the time of admission while others may be completed in a direct questionnaire format between the personnel in charge and the parent. The latter often aids in opening the lines of communication, and both approaches are recommended for use in gathering initial intake information.

Information which should be collected at the initial intake should include background information, the health history of the child, and emergency information. Information such as the child's legal name, home address, telephone number, birthdate, birthplace, number and ages of siblings, name(s) of parent(s) or guardian, home address, telephone number, occupation, place of employment, business address and business telephone should be a part of the background information.

The health history of the child should be general in scope if the program he/she will be entering is short-term. However, if the program is one in which the child would be enrolled for a period of weeks and/or months, medical forms completed by a physician must be obtained (see Appendix VIII–A). The types of items which should be included on a general health history form are: a history of the child's illnesses, especially childhood communicable diseases; frequent illnesses such as earaches, colds, sore throats; general evaluation of the health of the immediate family members; and any physical, social or emotional handicapping condition(s). Appendix VIII–B is an example of the general health history form.

Information on the child's personal/social history is often a part of the initial intake information. This type of information lends itself well to the questionnaire format described earlier where the personnel in charge collects the data by asking the parent the question and recording the responses given. Many times the nonverbal response of the parent provides as much, and in many cases more, information than does the verbal response. Data which may be obtained would include items on toilet training, child rearing practices, child's physical and language development, self-reliance, previous experiences in a group setting, interests, problems, and the current family situation. One of the most thorough family and social history forms is the one developed by Clare Cherry (1978) shown in Appendix VIII–C.

Finally, a report form with the information needed in case of an emergency or accident should be completed and readily available for use if needed. Some of the items such as the names of the parents and child are duplicates of previously gathered data but the important differences are the items regarding physician and hospital preference and other adults who could be notified if the parents cannot be reached or located at the time of the emergency. Two examples of emergency forms can be found in Appendix VIII–D.

One other form of record keeping recommended is anecdotal records. This type of record is based upon direct adult observation of the child as he/she participates in the program. Decker and Decker (1984) have identified the following five characteristics as necessary for a good anecdotal record:

1. It gives the date, the place, and the situation in which the action occurred;
2. It describes the actions of the child, the reactions of other people involved, and the responses of the child to these reactions;
3. It quotes what is said to the child and by the child during the action;
4. It supplies **mood cues** such as postures, gestures, voice qualities, and facial expressions that give cues to how the child felt, and it does not provide interpretations of feelings, but only the behaviors by which a reader may judge the situation; and
5. The description is extensive enough to cover the episode. The action or conversation is not left incomplete and unfinished but is followed through to the point where a little vignette of a behavioral moment in the life of the child is supplied.

Even though anecdotal records are subject to bias because of the adult observer's assumptions, opinions, etc., anecdotal records collected over a period of time with the child in many peer play situations can give the teacher a great deal of insight to the reasons for the child's behavior. Through the careful collection and interpretation of behavior by the use of anecdotal records, caregivers should be able to better understand the needs, interests and development of the individual child.

Environment

There are several important factors to consider when designing the facility. Safety factors and state regulations should be given first priority. Special plans and room arrangements are needed for children with special needs such as the physically handicapped or visually impaired child. Flexibility is also essential.

Housing should be planned to accommodate both individual and group pursuits. The early childhood program requires that the site and the space, as well as the furniture and equipment, be so adaptable as to permit activities to expand, shrink, disappear completely or even move outdoors (Decker and Decker, 1987).

Six factors to consider in designing the interior of the physical environment are: color, lighting, acoustics, floor coverings, ventilation, and room arrangements. A brief description of items to consider for each of these follows, however, for further information the reader should consult the resources cited in the references at the end of this chapter.

In selecting colors it is best to use restful, subdued tones on the walls. Too bright of colors overstimulates children and too dark reinforces gloomy feelings (Cherry, 1982).

A balance of fluorescent, incandescent and natural lighting is best. In general, a southern or eastern exposure is better than a western one. Window coverings which can easily be adjusted for proper lighting such as adjustable window blinds are recommended.

Acoustical problems are directly related to the type of floor coverings, size of the room and the ceiling height. The recommended ceiling height is ten to eleven feet. In order that the adult can provide supervision, but at the same time minimize his presence during the childrens' free play, there should be some play areas with low-ceilinged spaces, approximately four feet, which exclude the adult (Decker and Decker, 1984).

Many states require a minimum of thirty-five square feet per child for indoor space, however, forty to sixty square feet is preferable. There are ways to stretch space when the existing floor space is small and ceilings are high. Building lofts or balconies, with railings for safety purposes, can utilize vertical space.

Maintenance, durability and drafts should all be considered when selecting floor coverings. State fire regulations also dictate the fire retardant standards which must be adhered to. The most widely used floor coverings in centers for children are carpeting, vinyl, and linoleum. Carpeting absorbs sound better but can be a problem when it comes to cleaning up spills and in terms of static electricity and retention of germs. Vinyl or linoleum are easier to clean and keep more germ free but are not practical for warmth and comfort for the many occasions children are either playing or sitting on the floor. Many times both types of surfaces are used to accommodate these needs. For example, vinyl or linoleum would be good to have in restrooms, water supply areas and the art area, while carpeting would be best in the block building area and the area where children are gathered as a group for activities such as a story or singing.

Ventilation affects the behavior of children. Too much humidity or heat will make them lethargic and irritable, while too cool of a room will cause them discomfort and inattentiveness. Floors and windows should be well insulated and as draft free as possible.

A well-planned room arrangement provides children with both private and busy areas, and a smooth flowing traffic pattern which encourages positive or **prosocial** behavior. It also conveys a child-centered learning environment. There should be no hidden areas so that all children can easily be seen by an adult for safety and supervision reasons. Flexibility of wall space, such as portable dividers and shelves, makes possible adaption to changing needs and interests of the children being served. Again accommodations for children with special needs must be considered.

Equipment

Play is an essential learning medium (Sponseller, 1974) which contributes to the physical, intellectual, social, and emotional development of young children; as such, it is commonly recognized as the **work** of childhood. Children, like adults, need good **tools** to accomplish their **work.** Those who develop programs for young children must carefully select a variety of materials which will promote productive play experience for the children entrusted in their care.

Table Toys

These materials are most generally associated with four activity categories: coordination, construction, reconstruction, and classification activities (Whiren, 1979). Coordination activities, designed to develop small muscles and eye-hand coordination, utilize toys such as sewing cards, stringing beads, and pegboards. Interlocking blocks, small colored cubes, and magnetic shapes are often used in construction activities which allow children to explore the dimensions of space and to combine pieces to create a new structure. Typical materials used in reconstruction activities are shape boards, puzzles, and stacking cups or rings. These toys are self-correcting, can be taken apart and reassembled, and require visual memory and assessment of color, size, and shape for task completion. Reconstruction toys should represent a variety of difficulty levels to insure continued challenge for children who are mastering skills and competencies. Toys which require matching and grouping are used for classification activities. Examples are dominoes, lotto, and other board games. Table toys should be displayed on open shelves at the children's eye level. They should be rotated on a regular basis and offered in a setting which provides comfortable seating and good lighting.

Construction Materials

Blocks are the most common construction material found in programs for young children. Their value is demonstrated by their ability to develop muscles, problem-solving, creativity, and social skills. While large sets of wooden blocks are expensive, their purchase is easily justified as a one-time expenditure because they last for generations. In addition to wooden block units, large hollow blocks and building boards are recommended to expand opportunities in construction play. Block building can be further enhanced by the addition of props such as miniature cars, trains, people, road signs, animals, trees, etc. Blocks should be displayed on low, open shelves in an isolated, carpeted area. Shapes of unit blocks may be painted on the shelves to assist children in cleanup tasks.

Woodworking is a satisfying construction activity for many children. Commercial workbenches are desirable, but not essential; a firm, steady surface of approximately 24 inches in height is recommended. Real tools such as hammers, saws, screwdrivers, files, drills, planes, etc. accompanied by vises, c-clamps, large-headed nails, screws, and soft wood will insure children's success. Small brooms and dustpans will assist the children's cleanup efforts.

Sensory Materials

Water play provides sensory pleasure, intellectual stimulation, and opportunities for emotional and social growth (Eggleston & Weir, 1979). Commercial water tables are available, but can be substituted with plastic wading pools or dishpans placed on tables. Standard equipment for water play includes: floating objects, sinking objects, measuring cups and spoons, plastic containers of various sizes, sponges, egg beaters, squirt bottles, small pitchers for pouring, funnels, and sections of clear plastic tubing. In addition, water wheels and water pumps may be purchased, plastic smocks may be provided, and liquid dish soap or food coloring may be added to the water for variation. A floor mop and towels should be nearby for use at cleanup time.

Sand play expands understanding of logical mathematical thinking (McIntyre, 1982) and develops skills in the language arts (Barbour, Webster, & Drosdeck, 1987). Sand tables, like water tables, may be commercially made or substituted with other types of containers. Equipment for sand play includes: scoops, sifters, funnels, measuring cups and spoons, containers of various sizes, sand molds, and sand wheels. Water may be added to the sand for variation. In addition, the sand may be replaced by rice, salt, flour, corn, or beans. Small brooms and dustpans should be available for children's cleanup tasks.

Clay may be purchased or made from a variety of homemade play-doh recipes. Rolling pins (or cylinder blocks), cookie cutters, and wooden mallets may be provided for added interest.

Dramatic Play Materials

Dramatic play develops and provides opportunities to practice important cognitive, social, and emotional skills (Griffing, 1983). Traditional house play requires child-sized furniture (e.g., stove, sink, refrigerator, table and chairs), dolls and accessories, dress-up clothing for both sexes, and dishes. Additional props such as telephones, toasters, ironing boards, food models, mops, and brooms may be added to enhance the play. Thematic props may be provided to encourage other forms of dramatic play (e.g., grocery store, dentist's office, restaurant).

Large-Muscle Equipment

A variety of equipment should be provided to allow vigorous use of many muscles. Climbers, slides, swings, rocking toys, and balance beams are suitable for climbing and balancing. Riding toys, including tricycles, scooters, and wagons, should be matched to the sizes and abilities of children. Large wooden vehicles on which a child may sit or ride may be used indoors for large-muscle play.

Art Materials

Art experiences foster creativity and develop prereading and writing skills. Representative media appropriate for use with young children include: tempera paint, finger paint, crayons, chalk, watercolors, and water-based markers. A variety of paper types and application techniques should be employed. Additional equipment for art activities may include paintbrushes, paint easels, scissors, and glue.

Summary

Table toys, construction materials, sensory materials, dramatic play materials, large-muscle equipment, and art materials are necessary for the social emotional, physical, and intellectual development of young children. Good toys are attractive, well-constructed, durable, safe, useful in various ways, and matched to the abilities of children (Feeney & Magarick, 1984).

Staffing

Three categories of personnel are needed when staffing a program for young children; direct service or program personnel, support service or nonprogram personnel, and volunteer service personnel. Direct service or program staff includes a director, an assistant director, a nurse, counselor, teachers, and aides. Support services or nonprogram personnel includes kitchen staff, drivers, maintenance workers, and secretaries. Volunteer service personnel (an important nonbudgeted, nonpaid part of the program) includes parents, community resource people, and students from local high schools, colleges, and universities.

Recommended adult/child ratios should be considered when budgeting for direct service personnel. Professional early childhood education associations and state licensing regulators have suggested adult/child ratios based on ages of children served which are presented in Table VIII–I

TABLE VIII-I
ADULT/CHILD RATIOS

Infants (0–12 mos.)	1: 4
Toddlers (12–24 mos.)	1: 4
Two-year-olds	1: 8
Three-year-olds	1:10
Four-year-olds	1:12
Five-year-olds	1:15
Six to eight-year-olds	1:18

Salaries and (Minimum) Requirements

The following is a list of minimum educational and experiential requirements and suggested salaries to assist in hiring crisis center staff.

1. Director: Master of Arts degree in early childhood education/child development; three years teaching experience in day care/preschool setting; 21 years of age; $20,000.

2. Assistant Director: Bachelor of Arts degree in early childhood education/child development; three years teaching experience in day care/preschool setting; 21 years of age; $17,500.

3. Teacher: Bachelor of Arts degree/Associates degree in early childhood education; experience working with young children; 21 years of age; $15,000.

4. Nurse: Bachelor of Science degree in nursing; experience in a school setting; 21 years of age; $15,000.

5. Counselor: Bachelor of Science in school psychology/counseling; experience in a school setting; 21 years of age; $15,000.

6. Aides: High school diploma; experience working with young children; 18 years of age; $10,000.

7. Kitchen Staff: High school diploma; experience in large group food preparation; 18 years of age; $8,000.

8. Maintenance Workers: High school diploma; knowledge of equipment; 18 years of age; $8,000.

9. Secretary: High school diploma; secretarial skills; 18 years of age; $8,000.

10. Drivers: High school diploma; chauffeur's license; excellent driving record; experience transporting children; 21 years of age; $4,000 (part-time position).

Meeting the Needs of the Abused and Neglected

Children and young people of all ages will be served at the crisis center. The younger a child is, the more vulnerable he/she is to abuse and neglect, however, abuse and neglect have no boundaries. Infants, toddlers, preschoolers, school age children and adolescents each have their own special needs, as well as the common need for safety and security/protection.

The infant (0 to 12 or 15 months) presents a special challenge and set of needs to the crisis caregivers. Infants will need their own comfortable, clean, quiet sleeping area and they will need to be kept warm, dry, clean, and receive proper feeding. Besides this, the baby will need much individual physical attention. The baby will need to be held, rocked, touched, talked to (by the same person preferably) as much as possible or the bonding that the infant is developing with whoever is taking care of them will be interrupted. To thrive emotionally and physically the infant needs this individual care and stimulation. Extended confinement to crib or other area is not conducive to proper development and the youngest infant will need to be rocked and talked or sung to while his physical needs are met. Older infants will need an opportunity to interact at the appropriate level with adults and the environment.

While the physical, social, and emotional needs can begin to be met by the personal attention of one person, the older infant needs to see others as well as to begin to meet his needs and must have appropriate environmental stimulus such as toys to meet his cognitive needs.

The infant and especially the older infant, while responding to care from a nurturing adult, may/will be aware that he is in a strange setting and needs extra support.

The toddler (1 to 2 1/2 years) needs the security of an attentive individual as well as exposure to peers and others. The toddler is a more social being. Starting with a child's first birthday, experiences oriented toward people begin to increase at the expense of experiences not oriented toward people (White, 1985). The toddler then needs the opportunity to interact with people as well as to be stimulated by the environment, to explore his surroundings and to interact with objects, toys, and materials.

The child of this age will also be much more aware of changes in his surroundings. He may be fearful of the very people who are protecting and caring for him because he is used to the familiar adults in his life no matter how inadequate they may be in caring for him or how abusive. The toddler will need lots of comfort and support but will also need to have an opportunity to get used to the new adults and surroundings. There may be difficulties with mealtime and bedtime. Common, simple foods should be offered in pleasant, attractive surroundings. Adequate adult care must be provided to help the child who is not completely self-fed and to allow him to eat at his own pace. Appropriate seating and the correct size utensils also need to be provided. A number of children at this age may use the bottle some or a lot and being away from home may increase this need.

The toddler will also need individual attention and ritual at bedtime, bathing, and/or snack time. Even the child who has indicated no difficulties through initial entry and a long day may experience fears at bedtime. This may be his first realization that he has been left for longer than he may be accustomed to. Time and patience will be required to meet the needs of the toddler.

The preschooler (ages 3 to 5 years) will have all of the needs of the younger child; the need for physical care, emotional support, socialization opportunities and opportunities to experience a variety of activities that are age appropriate for his cognitive development. The preschooler will also need good food, proper clothing, an appropriate place to rest and sleep, and a place that is his own. Additionally he will need the opportunity and the space to engage in active play, both alone and with others. Both indoor and outdoor space should be provided for these activities, for example, playground equipment must be safe and adequate supervision must be provided. The preschooler is more aware of ownership, etc. and may have questions or feel uncomfortable using strange toys, wearing unfamiliar clothing, etc.

Emotionally, this age group will need lots of support and comfort. The child will be aware of being in strange surroundings and that he suffered harm; the preschooler will be confused, being both fearful of the parents and yet missing them. Crisis center personnel need to be gentle but provide structure for the child who may not be used to doing things in any orderly fashion.

Reversion to immature behavior is common and the child may suck his thumb, wet or soil his clothing, cry a lot, etc. Understanding caregivers are a must. The preschooler may have difficulty concentrating on the activity at hand. He may become sad and cry at mealtime or he may be extremely hungry and need to eat often.

The preschooler may exhibit fear at staying overnight in unfamiliar surroundings and may have his greatest difficulties at bedtime. Any familiar routine or objects will be helpful to his comfort as well as a routine that is established at the crisis center. Certainly the child will need attention and reassurance, including physical contact such as hugs, a goodnight kiss, perhaps his back rubbed and gently "tucked in". Even though the center may have a number of children in this age group at any given time, each one will need to feel special and cared about.

Children in this age group need opportunities to play and be with peers. They are learning to cooperate, to engage in group activity, to share. While supervision is necessary, the children need freedom to explore, work things out, solve problems and talk with one another. Appropriate toys and materials should be available. Children of this age are learning rapidly; they learn from their play, from activity directed by adults, from toys, from their surroundings, and from each other.

Perhaps the adolescent (12 to 17 years of age) has the most difficult time when admitted to a crisis center. Outwardly many of these young people would seem to be able to take care of themselves but they usually have a low level of self-esteem and are in need of adult acceptance and caring about them. They will need privacy, opportunities for socialization, understanding and encouragement in educational activities. Here again a structured day with time for tutoring and study is important. The adolescent is questioning his own identity, his abilities, and his sexuality; the abused adolescent may be fearful, aggressive, sad or angry. He needs support and understanding.

Regardless of age, children who come to the center may be in need of medical or dental care. Children who are sick need immediate attention and isolation. Less pressing are the long-term needs which also must be attended to. Children should also be helped to learn good health habits and hygiene themselves.

This area would not be complete without mentioning the special needs child. This child is even more vulnerable at any age to abuse and neglect and more likely to be the victim of either. Children with mild or moderate handicaps can easily be served in the setting with additional consideration of their needs, time and attention. Severely handicapped children's needs will need to be assessed on an individual basis to determine the best setting for them.

Programming

A good early childhood program does not happen by accident! Careful planning and scheduling are critical if a quality program is to be designed to meet the needs of all the children to be served.

In designing the program the first step is to identify the philosophy and goals. These will be determined by the purpose(s) of the program, ages of the children to be served, beliefs as to how children learn and the corresponding role of the teacher/caregivers, grouping policies, funding, size and location of the facility, and the training and size of the program staff.

From the works of well-known early childhood educators and educational theorists such as Jean Piaget, James L. Hymes, Jr., John Dewey and David Elkind, as well as many others, it is known that the best setting for young children is one which promotes active learning through a child-centered approach. In other words, the teacher helps to plan the environment based upon the needs and interests of the children. The children then act upon the environment so that learning comes from within, or as it is often referred to as **self-directed**, rather than the child being acted upon by the adult where the belief is that learning can be imposed upon children.

A child-centered program is flexible and therefore responsive to the changing needs and interests of children. A rich learning environment is created to stimulate physical, social, emotional and cognitive development. There are a variety of activities and materials to select from as well as a balance of busy and quiet times for children.

The following areas should be included in the indoor environment: (1) art center, (2) block building area, (3) housekeeping/dramatic play area, (4) shelf games and small motor/manipulations (puzzles, pegboards, etc.), (5) language arts and listening center, (6) science center, (7) music area, (8) sand and water areas, and (9) large motor area. For further information and details the reader should consult the references for this chapter.

It is important to be flexible in planning the daily schedule, but equally as important is the need to provide children with a routine. A routine makes children feel secure and more in control of the situation. Many children today lack any routine in their lives and the result is seen in their stressful behavior (often described by adults as **aggressive behavior**). Providing a calm and relaxed daily routine will help alleviate stress in children. Variations in the routine should be gradual and when abrupt changes are necessary, a restful period should be provided to recreate the serene setting.

The following examples of schedules should provide the reader with a general plan for the day. The first schedule would be appropriate for three, four, and five year olds.

The most flexible and adaptable schedule must be the one for infants and toddlers. Due to individual sleeping and feeding periods, the following times are only guidelines and would be adapted to the child's individual needs.

Funding

The financial planning by a program can either cause the program to be a success or a failure in its educational component or in its entirety. An assumption can be made that quality and cost correlate positively.

TABLE VIII-II
GENERAL SCHEDULE FOR FOUR AND FIVE YEAR OLDS
IN A CRISIS CENTER

Time	Activity
7:00–9:00 AM	Arrival, breakfast for children who have not eaten or who want additional food, sleep for children who want more rest, and child-initiated play (which should be relatively quiet) in the interest centers.
9:00–9:30 AM	Toileting and morning snack.
9:30–11:45 AM	Active work and play period, both indoor and outdoor. Field trips and class celebrations may be conducted in this time block.
11:45 AM–12:00 noon	Preparation for lunch, such as toileting, washing, and moving to dining area.
12:00 noon–1:00 PM	Lunch and quiet play activities.
1:00–3:00 PM	Story, rest, and quiet play activities or short excursions with assistants or volunteers as children awaken from naps.
3:00–3:30 PM	Toileting and afternoon snack.
3:30 PM until departure	Active work and play periods, both indoor and outdoor, and farewells as children depart with parents.
5:00 PM	Evening meal for those remaining in center, and quiet play activities until departure.

More often than not, programs for young children have a very limited income. The financial management of the program must be carefully planned and monitored.

Many options for program funding have been identified by Finn (1982):

1. Individual support, finding a person or persons who are willing to invest in part or all of the program;
2. Corporation support, large corporations offer support to groups or individuals both through monetary and in-kind donations;
3. Foundations support, large foundations such as the Ford Foundation, corporate foundations within the community, and private family foundations;
4. Government support, grant monies such as Title XX;
5. Fund raisers, events arranged by the individual program, for example, an annual auction, or several events through out the year such as promotional sales or garage sales.

TABLE VIII-III
GENERAL SCHEDULE FOR INFANTS AND TODDLERS
IN A CRISIS CENTER

Time	Activity
8:30–8:45 AM	Greeting of group, opening exercises, sharing of experiences, and planning for the day.
8:45–9:45 AM	Active work and play in interest centers (with small-group learning episodes in some kindergarten programs) and cleanup. Field trips and class celebrations may be conducted during this time block.
9:45–10:15 AM	Outdoor activities.
10:15–10:45 AM	Music and rhythmic activities.
10:45–11:00 AM	toileting and preparation for lunch.
11:00–11:45 AM	Lunch.
11:45–12:15 PM	Rest and toileting.
12:15–12:45 PM	Outdoor or indoor activity.
12:45–1:30 PM	Active work and play in interest centers and cleanup.
1:30–1:45 PM	Toileting and snack.
1:45–2:00 PM	Evaluation of day, preparing for next session, cleanup of room, and farewells.

The funding of a program could be through any one of, or a combination of, the above options.

Start-Up Costs

The initial costs of a program can be overwhelming and seemingly out of reach. Start-up costs are those costs that occur before the program opens its doors. In fiscal planning, it is necessary to have a self-contained start-up budget. Areas that need to be addressed in the start-up budget are: capital costs, working capital, and labor and miscellaneous costs (Click, 1981, pp. 124–125).

Capital costs include land and building, an enormous amount of the start-up budget. The available monies are used either to construct a new building, renovate an existing building, or purchase an abandoned program facility. Some programs may choose to rent or lease space. With renting or leasing there is still a large amount of initial cost due to owner's requirements of first and last month's rent and a security deposit.

Also included in capital costs are all supplies and equipment needed to begin operation of the program. This includes indoor equipment such as kitchen appliances, office machines and furniture, and classroom tables and chairs, plus outdoor equipment such as swings, climbers, and slides.

Working capital is the amount of money needed on hand at the opening of the program and during the next few months. Generally, maximum income is not received during the first few months of operation; the start-up budget must include funds to cover program costs for at least four to six months.

Since the director is usually employed during the initial planning stage, labor and miscellaneous costs must be included in the total start-up budget. Others involved during the planning stage may include a secretary, an accountant, a lawyer, and an architect. The services of teachers, aides, cooks, and janitorial staff are employed as needed.

Additional start-up costs include license fees, permit fees, and inspection costs. These fees vary between different regions and programs. It is important to provide monies for additional unexpected costs in the start-up budget (Click, 1981).

Operating Costs

The following items have been identified by Click (1981) as important operating costs:

1. Staff salaries, the largest portion of the operating costs. All employees from director to cook are included in the salary schedule which accounts for approximately 75% of the operating costs.
2. Fringe benefits, including social security, unemployment compensation, retirement plans, medical and life insurances, sick leaves, vacation leaves, and professional development programs.
3. Consultation services, including people who provide occasional services such as inservice for staff. Consultation fees vary according to the length and type of service provided.
4. Equipment, including permanent equipment such as computers, cots, and educational toys. Click (1981) groups equipment into the following categories: education or curricular equipment, caretaking and housekeeping equipment, office equipment, and kitchen equipment.
5. Supplies and materials, including items such as art materials, office supplies, and cleaning supplies.
6. Transportation, including vehicles for transporting children on field trips and to and from school. Transportation costs may also

include staff reimbursement for travel expenses associated with professional conferences and other activities.

7. Food, usually includes two snacks and two meals each day per child (programs open past 6:00 PM, also include dinner; programs open past 8:00 PM include a bedtime snack). The budget should reflect the number of snacks and meals per day to be served.

8. Space costs, including maintenance of all indoor and outdoor areas. The cost varies greatly from region to region.

9. Utility costs, including expenses for telephone, water, heat, and electricity.

10. Other costs, including charges for yearly licenses, marketing, and insurance (insurance cost is sometimes listed as a separate line item).

11. Income, including income from tuition, registration fees, fund raising events (estimated), government grants, gifts and donations, and all other income-producing sources. A 10% loss of total income should be allowed for program vacancies and nonpayment of fees.

Summary

The completed budget must be approved by the board of directors. Points to remember are:

1. Have one person in charge of buying all equipment and supplies;
2. Have one person in charge of issuing all checks for purchase of equipment and supplies;
3. Issue a monthly statement showing all transactions and balances for each account;
4. Keep within budgeted amounts for each area and seek board approval for overspending and underspending; and
5. Maintain records of the budget, contracted services, receipts, and annual reports for a minimum of four years.

With good financial planning and management, program operation and budgeting become progressively easier each year.

REFERENCES

1. Barbour, N., Webster, T. D., and Drosdeck, S.: Sand: a resource for the language arts. *Young Children, 42*(2):20–25, 1987.

2. Butler, A. L.: *Early Childhood Education: Planning and Administering Programs.* New York, D. Van Nostrand, 1974.
3. Carmichael, V. S., Clark, M., and Leonhard, B.: *Administration of Schools for Young Children.* Southern California Association for the Education of Young Children, 1972.
4. Cherry, C.: *Nursery School and Day Care Center Management Guide,* rev. ed. Belmont, David S. Lake, 1978.
5. Click, P.: *Administration of Schools for Young Children,* 2nd ed. Albany, Delmar, 1981.
6. *Community Coordinated Child Care: Guidelines for Comprehensive Service.* State of Indiana, Governor's Office of Community Affairs, Indianapolis, IN, 1972.
7. Decker, C. A., and Decker, J. R.: *Planning and Administering Early Childhood Programs,* 3rd ed. Columbus, Merrill, 1984.
8. Eggleston, P. J., and Weir, M. K.: Water play for pre-schoolers. In Adams, L., and Garlick, B. (Eds.): *Ideas That Work With Young Children.* Washington D.C., National Association for the Education of Young Children, 1979, pp. 155–161, vol. II.
9. Feeney, S., and Magarick, M.: Choosing good toys for young children. *Young Children, 40*(1):21–25, 1984.
10. Finn, M.: *Fundraising For Early Childhood Programs.* Washington, D.C., National Association for the Education of Young Children, 1982.
11. Griffing, P.: Encouraging dramatic play in early childhood. *Young Children, 38*(2):13–22, 1983.
12. McIntyre, M.: Early childhood discovery through sand play. *Science and Children, 19:*36–37, 1982.
13. Sponseller, D. (Ed.): *Play as a Learning Medium.* Washington, D.C., National Association for the Education of Young Children, 1974.
14. Stevens, Jr., J. H., King, E. W.: *Administering Early Childhood Education Programs.* Boston, Little Brown, 1976.
15. Sunderline, S. (Ed.): *Housing For Early Childhood Education.* Washington, D.C., ACEI, 1968.
16. Weiser, M. G.: *Group Care and Education of Infants and Toddlers.* St. Louis, C.V. Mosby, 1982.
17. Whiren, A.: Table toys: the underdeveloped resource. In Adams, L., and Garlick, B. (Eds.): *Ideas That Work With Young Children.* Washington, D.C., National Association for the Education of Young Children, 1979, pp. 97–104, vol. II.
18. White, B.: *The First Three Years of Life.* New Jersey, Prentice-Hall, 1985.

APPENDIX VIII-A

Physical Examination

Child's name _____

Comment on any significant findings:

Eyes: Right _____ Left _____ Squint _____

Ears: Right _____ Left _____ Discharge _____

Nose _____ Throat _____

Glands _____ Tonsils _____

Heart and Circulation _____

Lungs _____

Abdomen _____

Bones and joints _____

Reflexes _____

Nutrition _____

Posture _____

Hernia _____ Neurological _____

Hemoglobin (if physician indicates) _____

Urinalysis (if physician indicates) _____

Does the school program need to be adjusted for this child? _____

_____

_____

Date _____ Signed: _____ M.D.
                                                  D.O.

Immunization Record

Child's name _____

Diphtheria-Tetanus (since age 3)

_____ _____ _____

    (1st date)   (2nd date)   (Booster)

Poliomyelitis (since age 3)

_____ _____ _____ _____

 (1st date)   (2nd date)   (3rd date)   (booster)

Measles (Rubeola): Disease or Immunization _____
                                                (date)

T.B. Test
   Tine _____ Reaction: Pos. _____ Date: _____

   Mantoux _____   Neg. _____ Date: _____

   Chest X–Ray __ Results: _____ Date: _____

Date _____ Signed: _____ M.D.
                                               D.O.

Dental Report

Child's name _____

Cavities _____ Gums _____

Malocclusion _____

Please explain any abnormal findings or deformities _____

Please indicate care given:

Prophylaxis _____   Cavities filled _____

Extractions _____   Orthodontics _____

What additional care do you plan for this child? _____

_____

Date: _____ Signed: _____ D.D.S.

APPENDIX VIII-B

Health History

Child's name _____

General evaluation of family's health: _____

_____

Family deaths (causes): _____

Child's illnesses. If your child has had any of these diseases, please state the age at which he had them.

_____ measles   _____ smallpox
_____ mumps   _____ diabetes
_____ whooping cough   _____ heart disease
_____ poliomyelitis   _____ Chorea
_____ rheumatic fever   _____ epilepsy
_____ scarlet fever   _____ chicken pox

_____ diphtheria   _____ pneumonia

_____ serious accident   _____ asthma, hay fever

Has your child ever had tests for tuberculosis? _____

Skin test? _____ Date _____ Chest X–Ray? __ Date _____

Please check any of the following which you have noted recently.

_____ frequent sore throat   _____ short of breath

_____ persistent cough   _____ freq. nose bleeds

_____ freq. headaches   _____ allergy

_____ poor vision   _____ freq. urination

_____ dizziness   _____ fainting spells

_____ freq. styes   _____ abdominal pain

_____ dental defects   _____ loss of appetite

_____ speech difficulty   _____ hard of hearing

_____ tires easily   _____ four + colds/year

Describe your child socially and emotionally _____

_____

Are there any matters which you would like to discuss with the school

staff? _____

Date _____ Signed: _____

                                     (Parent or Guardian)

APPENDIX VIII-C
PERSONAL INFORMATION FOLDER FOR CHILD

Family and Social History   Telephone _____

Name of child _____ Date of birth _____

Mother (or Guardian) _____ Age _____
                    (include maiden name)

Father (or Guardian) _____ Age _____

Marital Status of Parents: If Child is Adopted:

Living together _____ Stepfather _____ Age at adoption? ____
                                (how long?)

                                        Does child know he is

Separated _____ Stepmother _____ adopted? _____
          (how long?)   (how long?)

Divorced _____ Remarks: _____
         (how long?)

Custody/visiting arrangements: _____

Brothers and Sisters of Child:

Name _____ Date of birth _____ Grade in school _____

Name _____ Date of birth _____ Grade in school _____

Other members of the household: (include relationship and age) _____

_____

If both parents are away from home during the morning, please state

arrangements for child's care when he is not in school: _____

_____

Does child have room alone? _____ If not, with whom? _____

Who has cared for child other than his parents? (State whether adults or teen-agers) _____

Has child had group play experience? _____ Where? _____

Does child have neighborhood playmates? Specify. _____

_____

When and with whom does child watch TV? _____

Developmental History of Child

Age at which child: Crept on hands and knees _____ sat alone _____

Walked alone _____ Named simple objects _____ Repeated short

sentences _____ Slept through night _____ Began toilet training _____

Word child uses for: Urination _____ bowel movements _____

Usual time for B.M. _____

Does child dress self? _____ Undress self? _____

Is child right or left handed? _____

When does the child usually eat breakfast? ___ Lunch? ___ Dinner? ___

Is family vegetarian? _____ Other Dietary Restrictions _____

What time does child usually go to bed at night? _____ Awaken? _____

Does he sleep well? _____ What are child's favorite:

  Indoor play activities? _____

  Outdoor play activities? _____

Does child play with water? _____ Go barefoot? _____

Does child have any special fears that you are aware of? _____

_____

Does child have any speech problems? _____

Does child have any other problems that we should be aware of? _____

What method of behavior control is used in your home? _____

What is child's usual reaction? _____

How would you describe your child's personality? _____

Health History of Child

What past illness has he had? At what age?

Chicken Pox _____ Scarlet Fever _____ Diabetes _____

Mumps _____ Measles _____ Hepatitis _____

Does child have frequent colds? Explain. _____

Tonsillitis? _____ Ear aches? _____

Stomach aches? _____ Does he vomit easily? _____

Does he run high fevers easily? _____

Has he had any serious accidents? Explain. _____

Is child allergic? _____ If so, how does it usually manifest itself?

Asthma _____ Hay fever _____ Hives _____ Other _____

Do you know what his allergy is caused by? _____

Has he ever been to a dentist? _____ Has he had his vision tested? _____

Hearing tested? _____ Does he wear corrective shoes? _____

Please give a statement of your evaluation of your child's overall health:

For school use only:

Illness _____ Date _____ Illness _____ Date _____

Illness _____ Date _____ Illness _____ Date _____

Accidents: _____

Other Health Information: _____

Cumulative Record

Date started school _____

Attendance Records: Excellent ____ Good ____ Irregular ____ Poor ____

Health Record while in school: Excellent __ Good __ Irregular __ Poor

Comments on school progress:

APPENDIX VIII-D.1

Emergency Information

Child's name

Home address   Phone number _____

Father's name _____

Place of business _____ Phone number _____

Mother's name _____

Place of business _____ Phone number _____

Give name of another person to be called in case of emergency, if parents cannot be reached:

Name _____ Phone number _____

Address _____ Relationship _____

Physician to be called in case of emergency:

1st choice _____ Phone number _____

2nd choice _____ Phone number _____

Name of hospital to be used in emergency:

1st choice _____

2nd choice _____

Other comments: _____

_____

_____

Date _____ Signed _____

(Parent or Guardian)

APPENDIX VIII-D.2

Identification and Emergency Information

Name of child _____ Date of birth _____

Last   First   Nickname

Address _____ Zip _____ Phone _____

Mother or guardian _____

(Include maiden name)

Employment _____ Phone _____ Hours _____

Father or guardian _____

Employment _____ Phone _____ Hours _____

(If either parent is a student, please list name of school, phone and current schedule)

_____ Phone _____ Days _____

Persons authorized to pick up child:

_____ _____ _____

(Under no circumstances will child be released to anyone not known to the school without authorization from parents or guardian.)

Persons to be Called in Case of Emergency

(Be sure to include someone who will usually know your whereabouts)

Name _____ Relationship to child _____

Address _____ Phone _____

Name _____ Relationship to child _____

Address _____ Phone _____

Child's physician _____ Phone _____

Emergency hospital preference _____

School Use Only:

Date of interview: Date of Child's Visit: Starting Date:

Class Assignment: No. of Days/Wk: No. of Hours/Wk:

CHAPTER 9

ESTABLISHING A MULTIFACETED VOLUNTEER CORP

Ellen R. Lorch
Jamia J. Jacobsen

INTRODUCTION

A carefully planned volunteer program can substantially improve the care of abused and neglected children by expanding the services that are already offered by a child crisis center. A volunteer program can also increase community knowledge and support of an organization by promoting a positive attitude about the agency and publicly advocating children's rights. However, to establish and maintain a successful volunteer program, careful planning is necessary.

The board of directors and the child crisis center staff must both be willing to make a commitment to a volunteer program and be actively involved in its development. A careful analysis of the agency's needs and an understanding of volunteers' needs and motivations is necessary to implement and perpetuate a successful program. This chapter will address the considerations involved in establishing and maintaining a volunteer corp within a child abuse and neglect crisis center by taking a look at: guidelines for training and supervision, targeted recruitment, careful interviewing, appropriate placement and recognition and, last but not least, evaluation tools. These and other strategies all must be decided on and in place before the first volunteer reports for work.

Volunteerism: Past and Present

Volunteering, or people helping people, is as old as man's first kindness to his fellow human being. Certainly giving freely of one's time and energy for the good of others has been an integral part of American history and American society. No other country in the world has such proliferation of voluntary organizations founded by volunteers who recognized a need and banded together to fill the need, resolve the problem, and/or advocate for the cause.

209

A historical view of volunteerism travels through the days of the early settlers who helped each other build communities, through the times when quarantines were set up by volunteers in response to yellow fever epidemics. The gift of giving continues on into the days of noblesse oblique when middle and upper class women ministered to the poor and more recently through the late 20th Century's complex high tech, high powered society. In spite of a society that has changed throughout history and continues to change, volunteerism and volunteering still flourish.

Volunteerism has taken on a new look. In the past, women's auxiliary's flourished due to the fact that most women worked in the home. After children left home, more women would occupy their extra time by volunteering. Today, women have many occupational options and responsibilities in and out of the home. According to the Statistical Abstract of 1979, 43% of working women are single heads of households and it is estimated that by 1990, 61% of all adult women will work outside the house. These changes are sure to impact the nature and memberships of the volunteer corps of today's society.

Today, volunteer corps consist of women and men, both young and old who enjoy intrinsic rewards for volunteering in their communities. Many people from the working sector oftentimes volunteer in addition to a paid vocation. In some of these instances, companies may give time off during the work day to employees who participate in volunteer duties. Also, persons with excess time due to retirement offer many volunteer services. The older volunteer population may be searching for friendships and a continuing societal role as well as filling the desire to help others who are in need of their assistance. There is the potential for a large reserve of volunteer power here, as the 1979 Statistical Abstract estimated that by 1990, one out of eight people will be over the retirement age of 65.

What does all this mean to us who believe volunteers bring an extra dimension, a caring presence to the many human problems that society is dealing with these days? It means that, like all successful enterprises in a highly competitive society, leaders have to organize and lay careful plans for a meaningful volunteer program. To flourish and accomplish goals of serving clients in the best manner possible, programs must be well organized, efficiently run, and effectively meet the needs of today's volunteer. For example, volunteers should be given clear expectations or guidelines, rewarded for their time, and shown consideration from the paid crisis center staff.

Volunteers are a much needed and necessary component of a child crisis center. They can offer the center and particularly the children housed there, a special love and attention which the staff may not have time to give. While not taking the place of staff, volunteers may enhance the quality of care by assisting staff in duties of basic care or spending time interacting with the children.

Volunteers can, and do, save the crisis center thousands of dollars by offering free services of which the center could otherwise not afford. In today's world of cost containment, tight budgets, and the vying of not-for-profit organizations for the donated dollar, volunteers may offer a partial solution to these problems by assisting in almost all aspects of the center.

On the other hand, the crisis center must meet certain obligations in order to have the volunteer program run smoothly and successfully. Although guidelines may have been set, the director and staff must adhere to their basis philosophy and implement them in an orderly fashion.

THE FIELD OF VOLUNTEER ADMINISTRATION

The field of volunteer administration is being recognized as a viable profession. Colleges and universities are offering courses and seminars in volunteer administration. The Association of Volunteer Administrators (AVA) which is a national organization, offers certification for directors of volunteers and awards the initials CAV (Certified Administrator for Volunteers) to individuals who have successfully completed the requirements for certification.

In addition, the Association of Volunteer Bureaus, Inc. (now merged with VOLUNTEER: The National Center) developed standards and guidelines for volunteer programs which have served as a basis for certifying those programs through volunteer centers across the nation.

To develop and manage a good, professional volunteer program that satisfies the missions of the child crisis center and the expectations of the board, staff, volunteers and clients, it is important to define exactly what is to be done and then decide how it is to be accomplished. Good organizational structure is needed, such as knowing who will be in charge of the volunteer program and who a volunteer reports to. Other major decisions include: designing a realistic budget, offering appropriate job descriptions to possible future volunteers, and setting appropriate time frames or work schedules in order to complete each task necessary in the establishment and maintenance of the program.

The Volunteer Coordinator

The first task in the development of a volunteer program in a crisis center is for the board of directors to carefully review what the objectives of such a program would be. Then the board must give approval for the hiring of a volunteer coordinator and allocate the funds for doing so. These decisions should be followed by a written job description by the executive director of the center who then begins the task of finding the best person for that position.

In hiring a volunteer coordinator, it is important to look for an individual who has experience as a volunteer, in addition to personnel management and public relation skills. Specific qualifications may include: (1) experience in managing volunteers, (2) ability to teach and communicate with others, (3) have a valid driver's license, and (4) have access to, or own a functional automobile.

In **Up the Organization**, Robert Townsend has stated, "First-rate people hire first-rate people; second-rate people hire third-rate people. Hire the best you can." Good employees are always available to work for good organizations. Jean Flanagan (1981) states, "The people who choose to work for nonprofit groups are often the most idealistic, energetic, and creative workers around."

The volunteer coordinator must be a person who is truly interested in people and enjoys being involved in a multifaceted program. This person cannot display rigidity when working with many different people in many different situations because flexibility is the **name of the game**. Not only must this volunteer coordinator be flexible but must also be the type of person who demonstrates initiative, can focus on the effects that decisions will have on both volunteers and the community as large, build on people's positive contributions, and most importantly, be able to make solid and wise decisions.

Marlene Wilson (1976, p. 27) stresses, ". . . (a volunteer coordinator) must have a solid peer relationship with other paid staff in the agency (and other agencies); be a backer, helper, decision-maker, and, if need be, a disciplinarian to the volunteers. (A volunteer coordinator) must be a leader or consultant as the expert in the field in any of these roles, but feel comfortable with them all."

Duties and Responsibilities of the Volunteer Coordinator

The volunteer coordinator is the person who works with staff to decide for what jobs volunteers should be recruited and writes the job descriptions for them. S/he is the **boss** to whom volunteers report to for work assignments, the person they consult when they are unsure how to handle a given situation, when they need consultation or information, and if they can't come in for their volunteer time. In other words, the volunteer coordinator is very much like the supervisor in the office. On the other hand, s/he never forgets that these hard working people are volunteers that require flexibility in scheduling and respect for their time. For example, if the volunteer coordinator can foresee a certain day or week when there is a hiatus in the volunteer's assignment, s/he must notify the volunteer as far as possible in advance (think how it would feel to hire a babysitter or give up a dinner engagement only to find out there was no work to do when arriving at the job).

The volunteer coordinator must think in terms of management functions and responsibilities. Responsibilities may include any of the following:

1. **Planning** goals, objectives and the implementation of board policies;
2. **Organizing** interviews, the development of job descriptions, the use of community resources, and resources for volunteer programs;
3. **Staffing** needs identification, scheduling and providing opportunities for volunteer service while utilizing various recruitment techniques;
4. **Directing** volunteer orientation and training programs while supervising existing volunteers and volunteer recognition programs;
5. **Controlling** volunteer programs by utilizing written evaluations of individual job performance and ongoing evaluation of the program;
6. **Interpersonal Roles** within the structure by assuring communication between the staff and volunteers, working as a liaison between the agency and the community while promoting volunteerism;
7. **Informational Roles** within the center by enlisting the support of the staff for volunteers, maintaining records and being knowledgeable about trends and issues; and
8. **Decision Making** by hiring, firing and assigning volunteers to jobs within the center.

Specific duties and responsibilities that may be listed on a job description for hiring a volunteer coordinator may include:

1. Select volunteers with talents and interests of value to the center;
2. Survey various departments for areas where a volunteer can work in parallel with employees;
3. Arrange meeting between volunteer and department manager for indoctrination into duties;
4. Schedule volunteers to work during their own available time and at a time most needed by the individual department;
5. Speak before various groups which might include potential volunteers;
6. Maintain records of hours worked by volunteers for future recognition;
7. Evaluate effectiveness of volunteers in various departments;
8. Arrange annual recognition luncheon and appropriate awards;
9. Rotate and/or dismiss volunteers who are not satisfactory or do not represent the standards of the center;
10. Select unique pins and/or articles of clothing which would identify an individual as a volunteer of the center;
11. Keep abreast of directives and procedural changes and transmit this information to the volunteers as required; and
12. Perform other duties as requested by the center.

THE VOLUNTEER PROGRAM

As mentioned above, the board of directors of the crisis center must establish the level of commitment that the agency has towards maintaining a successful volunteer program and the capability of the agency to institute it in an efficient and timely manner. These are important goals that must be hurdled before other implementation steps can be attempted. Because of their importance, the following check list provides some of the necessary questions that a crisis center board of directors must ask themselves before attempting to establish a program.

1. Is there a readily observable need for volunteer services and can this be translated into clearly defined jobs for volunteers?
2. Are we clear enough as to our professional tasks so that we may understand our own roles in relation to the volunteers?
3. Can we budget the staff time which must be allocated to the effective implementation of volunteer programs?
4. Have paid staff members at all levels been involved in thinking

through the proposal to use volunteers in the agency program and will they give support to the activities?

5. What are our expectations of the level of volunteer performance? Are we prepared for unevenness of service, and turnover of workers almost always a part of such programs?

6. Will we be able to assign responsibility to one central staff person for supervision of volunteer activities?

7. Are we willing to make available supervision and training for the new recruits?

8. Are we ready to accept the volunteers as colleagues and to give them appropriate recognition for their services?

9. Will we welcome volunteers from all social classes in the community so that our volunteer group will be truly representative of the total community which supports us?

10. Is there readiness to use volunteer participation at every appropriate level of agency service up to and including policy making?

11. Are we prepared to modify agency program in the light of volunteer contributions and possible enrichment of program?

12. Will we help the volunteer see the implications for the whole community of the programs on which he is working? Will we be comfortable with and able to encourage the social action of volunteers which should come from enlightened participation in social welfare and health programs?

Once the goals of the volunteer program have been determined, the budget has been established, and the volunteer coordinator has been hired, the next steps can be taken in the establishment of the program. There are nine basic elements to keep in mind to make the volunteer program work which are: (1) job design, defining positions within the center that could effectively be filled by volunteers, (2) staff involvement, (3) recruitment, (4) interviewing process, (5) placement or assignment of volunteers to jobs, (6) training, (7) supervision of volunteers, (8) evaluating individual volunteers and the volunteer program, and (9) giving recognition to volunteers who have given of their time and for a job well done. These nine elements will each be addressed in the following sections.

Job Design

To start off on the right foot and make sure volunteers will be welcome in the shelter, it is very important to work with the staff in deciding exactly what jobs volunteers will be asked to do. Only with full staff acceptance of the volunteer program can it hope to succeed. Sometimes professional staff look askance at the use of volunteers and it is up to the volunteer coordinator to make sure that the staff understands that volunteers enrich and extend the work of paid staff but never replace it.

The following questions may be of assistance for developing some basic criteria when defining volunteer positions or job descriptions.

1. Is this a real job? Can its usefulness be made clear and concrete to the volunteer?
2. Can this job be done satisfactorily on a part-time basis?
3. Will time required for training and for support be in proportion to the volunteer time needed in actual service?
4. Can essential supportive staff work be provided?
5. Can staff work adjustments be made of **backstops** be built in if the volunteer's other priorities make this necessary?
6. Does the job consider the varied interests and skills the volunteer may bring and the value of his community relationships?
7. Are there possibilities for volunteer satisfaction in doing his job?
8. Is it probable that the kind and/or number of volunteers required for this job be recruited?
9. Can you imagine a person really **wanting** to do this job?

After locating and defining the jobs available and appropriate for volunteers, a volunteer job description should be formally written. This form should include the job title and name the **supervisor** that the volunteer would answer to on the job. Objectives should be listed such as why the job is necessary and what the volunteer may hope to accomplish from volunteering his/her time for that position. Other topics that should be included are; specific responsibilities, qualification, training that can be expected, how and when evaluations are done, and the level of commitment that is needed from the volunteer such as time requirement and scheduling flexibility.

Staff Involvement

It is important that staff accept volunteers as part of the team to deliver the services for which the agency was established. The key is communication and involvement of staff at the very beginning. If staff understands that volunteers can increase their services to clients, perform some mechanical tasks for which professional expertise is not needed, and devote that extra measure of time that may be so crucial to an abused child, then the agency can move forward to serve the community. Staff and volunteers must work together as a team and each half of that team can bring a special dimension to the delivery of human services.

To facilitate communication between professional staff and the volunteer corp, suggested actions and attitudes for the staff to take include:

1. Do not describe the volunteer's job as it is not, and don't minimize the time or ability it takes;
2. Offer a well-planned program of training and supervision;
3. Concern yourself with the volunteer as a person, not an object;
4. Expect basic ability and reliability from the volunteer and then build on these talents; sharing understanding, not confusing them with technical jargon;
5. Be ready to place when you recruit;
6. Give the volunteer a significant task, don't equate volunteers with untrained persons;
7. Inform the volunteer by making him an inside member of the staff;
8. Evaluate with the volunteer;
9. Trust the volunteer; if your expectancy and faith are high, so will be his response; and
10. Give proper recognition for volunteered time.

In addition, volunteers can be offered suggestions for actions and attitudes toward the staff and their position in the crisis center which include:

1. Understand the job you undertake to do;
2. Accept training appreciatively and contribute your knowledge and experience;
3. Match your interests to the needs about you and therefore, the job;
4. Serve with faithfulness and continuity, listen for and report new insights about your work;
5. Discover its meaning to the total program of which it is a part;
6. Open yourself to opportunities for growth in skills, sympathy, self-confidence and responsibility;
7. Value your special two-way role as community interpreter;

8. Contribute to supervision by self-evaluation and a willingness to ask;
9. Give loyalty to your institution, it staff and its program; and
10. Take pride in the volunteer's career, it pays handsomely in treasures of the spirit.

Recruitment

As it was noted at the beginning of this chapter, Americans have always volunteered and even in today's changing society they are volunteering still. According to the Gallop poll, 50% of Americans 14 years or older, volunteer an average of 3.5 hours a week. If 89 million individuals still volunteer, we may ask, "Why is it so difficult to find volunteers these days?" The answer may be in the increased working force of this society and the decreased amount of extra time available to those working people. With so many more working people, it is important to tailor volunteer jobs to suit work schedules.

In addition to work, there are many options for use of time available to everyone. It is difficulty for agencies wanting and needing volunteers to compete with time for work, families, tennis, aerobics, self-improvement programs, and many more activities. Once job descriptions have been designed and definitions have been completed for exactly what jobs volunteers are needed, it is time to reflect on who will want to do these jobs.

A person who works from 8:00 AM to 5:00 PM will more than likely not be available during daytime hours; however, they may find time during evenings or weekends. Students often look at some jobs as career readiness training, as will people who are changing careers. Another possibility is a newcomer to town who may volunteer to meet people and begin to make friends. Deciding to whom the available jobs would appeal to, then targeting that group will get a much better response than a general appeal.

Pinpoint what type of volunteer is needed and desired and make an honest appeal for that population's services. Don't try to fool the general public because the volunteer will not have to be on the job long to know if an agency has misrepresented their needs. Particular care is needed in targeting the people that will be selected for childcare, especially when working with abused children because they have very special needs that are often diverse. Careful development is also needed when designing recruitment procedures for speakers bureau advocates, hot line operators, and counseling helpers. State what type of volunteers are needed for each area and why they are needed.

An example strategy for recruiting volunteers for a particular job title at a child crisis center may involve defining criteria specific to that position and the desired target population such as:

1. **General target population** or the kinds of volunteers desired (One-to-one Parent Aides);
2. **Specific target population** that is sought (women, 20 to 45 years old, mature);
3. **Product** or what the agency has to offer the volunteer (satisfactory volunteer experience);
4. **Competition** or what other agency wants this kind of volunteer (those involved with family services, adoption or foster care, and welfare departments);
5. **Research** or what are these people live and where can they be located (church groups, graduate school, women's groups, social work affiliations);
6. **Benefits** or what the agency has to offer in exchange for volunteer services (friendship or mentor role, making a difference in other's lives, increased parenting skills);
7. **Costs** or what is required of the volunteer (6 months commitment, weekly visits and use of their car); and
8. **Promotion** or how to get this message to this analyzed market (speakers, news media, university departments, church newsletters, and one-to-one correspondence).

Planning for recruitment is essential and it is best to develop a year long plan of recruitment activities which utilizes a variety of sources. Methods for promotion of the need for volunteers includes: newspapers, bulletins and newsletters, radio and TV spots, posters, brochures and flyers, information or orientation meetings, speaking engagements, university courses, slides and films, and billboards if they can be donated or if there is sufficient funds budgeted for this purposes. Community activity groups such as volunteer action centers, community service days, and year round public relations programs are often willing to donate promotion time and assistance, and satisfied volunteers that are currently donating their services are a vast recruiting resource when they advocate to friends and neighbors on a one-to-one basis. Table IX–I gives a more

TABLE IX-I
WHERE TO MARKET RECRUIT

- Word of mouth
- Classified ads in newspaper
- Feature stories in newspaper
- Information/Orientation meetings
- Bulletins and newsletters
- Bulletin Boards (laundromats, gyms, beauty shops, diet centers, bowling alleys, grocery stores, pet shops, etc.)
- Billboards
- Bumper stickers
- Courses (Law, Counseling, Health Education, Nutrition, etc.)
- Professional Associations and Publications
- Slides, Films, Video
- Open Houses
- Display in Corporation lobbies
- Buses and Taxis
- Brochures
- Posters
- Volunteer Bureaus
- Community Service Days (shopping centers)
- Radio and T.V. spots
- Year-Round Public Relations Program
- Publicize Recognition Ceremonies
- Radio and T.V. Talk Shows
- Personal letters/phone calls
- Presentations/Speeches
- Churches
- Service Clubs (Rotary, Lions, Kiwanis, Elks, Optimists)
- Retired Clubs (retired teachers, Senior Citizen Clubs)
- Retirement Homes
- Carpenters Union & other unions
- Alternative Sentencing Program
- PTA

- Community & Youth Centers
- Manpower & Employment offices
- Regional Occupation Program
- Chamber of Commerce
- Libraries
- Other child abuse agencies
- Teach a university course
- Press parties
- Career Counselors
- College Employment Bulletin Boards
- Newcomers Clubs
- Real Estate Offices
- Schools ("Career Day" presentations)
- Volunteerama
- Invitation or open lunches
- Be on emergency speaker's list of local community groups
- Junior Leagues, AAUW
- League of Women Voters
- Ask local politicians for names of prospective volunteers
- Recruitment booth at local schools, fairs, shopping centers
- Ads in large local industries' periodicals
- Contact local corporations about "release time" or "consulting"
- Train representatives from corporations, unions & minorities to recruit for you
- Recruitment drives with other organizations in community
- Ask successful volunteer organizations how *they* recruit . . . then follow their examples
- "Tupperware-style" coffees . . . where satisfied volunteers inspire friends and tell why they volunteer
- Local Boards & Commissions
- Grocery store lines—talk it up!!

complete list of methods and sources to use for marketing or recruiting for the volunteer worker.

Frequently, motivating volunteers can be a perplexing problem for a crisis center that is not easily solved. Much of the motivational research that has been done, such as that with Abraham Maslow, has determined that every individual has needs that have to be satisfied and the satisfaction of those needs is what motivates that person. Therefore, if one can't motivate someone, it may be possible to build upon the motivational needs of people.

Targeted marketing is a strategy for recruiting volunteers that involves an exchange between two parties (the agency and the volunteer) that is a mutually satisfying exchange that meets both parties' needs. The following is a list of factors that can build upon the motivation of people and are examples of the many varied reasons why we do what we do. There are no value judgments implied here and none of the factors are either good or bad. This is important to keep in mind when looking for the right person to perform a given task. If work does not meet a volunteer's motivational needs, it probably won't get done.

1. The volunteer needs to belong.
2. The volunteer needs to share in planning for what other volunteers and staff are doing.
3. The volunteer needs to understand what's expected of him or her.
4. The volunteer needs to feel that what s/he is doing is important.
5. The volunteer needs to know and understand his/her goals and objectives.
6. The volunteer needs to feel that the job is needed and not a waste of his/her time.
7. The volunteer needs to know the outcome of what his/her contribution is accomplishing.
8. The volunteer needs to know the important changes as they effect his/her job.
9. The volunteer needs to be able to trust the staff with whom s/he is working.

Undoubtedly there are programs which are not well-planned, efficiently organized, properly staffed, under-supervised and lack effective and helpful evaluation. When this unfortunate situation exists, the following results will inevitably occur:

Why I'm Not A Volunteer!

(A not-so-tongue-in-cheek confession of a former volunteer). Somehow, I get the feeling that not to be a volunteer in someone's program today is to be uncivilized. But, like many of my fellow sitter-outers, I have my reasons for letting opportunity pass me by. You, the program operator, the professional, have supplied me with them. Do you really want to know why I am not a volunteer?

1. For a long time I never knew you wanted me. You communicated quite well, "I'd rather do it myself, mother." You are articulate in expressing your needs in dollars and decimals. Your silence on service, I figured, was your last word.

2. Once you did call for help, and I stepped forward. But you never told me how to get started. I later thought that maybe what you actually said was, "Why don't we have lunch. . . . sometime?"

3. I persevered however, I reported for duty. You turned me over to a department head, and he in turn, sent me down to the section chief. He was out, and the secretary did not know what to do with so rare a species as a volunteer, so she suggested that I get in touch next Tuesday. I called, but my message got lost.

4. I might have overlooked the runaround. People cannot be blamed for doing the best they can, and the worst and best are hard to distinguish in the emptiness of a vacuum. For some reason, I thought you as their leader would have given a bit of thought beforehand to what you would do with me, a volunteer, or at least let someone else know I was coming and give them the worry of organizing the situation.

5. Come time for the spring mail-out, and I and my neighbor appeared on the scene. We worked; for two days we licked stamps and envelope flaps, until the steak at supper tasted like tongue. Then I learned from the slip of a clerk that before our coming you had turned off the postage machine. I really cannot blame; if you had not gone out of your way to make work for us what could a couple of volunteers have done for two whole days?

6. I tried again a number of times. But you really did not expect much from me. You never trained me, not insisted that my work be to a standard. A particularly tough day was coming up for the crew, and I cut out—it was a perfect day for golf. On my return, you said nothing of my absence, except to ask about my score. I never learned if my truancy made any difference.

7. In spite of it all, I think I did make a contribution. But the only real thanks I got was a letter from you—a form letter. I know how "demanding" this letter was on you. My neighbor had typed the master copy, I had copied it and together we forged your name, stuffed the envelopes, sealed, stamped, and mailed them. (Reprinted from—Voluntary Action News, Vancouver, B.C., March 1976.)

Interviewing

Before people begin applying for volunteer positions, it is best to decide who will conduct the interviews of the potential volunteers. It could be the volunteer coordinator or another volunteer trained for the techniques involved in the interviewing process. This is a most important part of the process of initiating or perpetuating a volunteer program and must be undertaken with great care, particularly when dealing with abused children.

Each volunteer applicant should be asked to fill out an application form such as the sample application form in Appendix IX–A. Additional information may be obtained from the applicant by asking questions either through the interview process or a more detailed application. Such information requests may include:

1. Please give your reasons for seeking participation in this particular volunteer activity;
2. Have you had precious interviewing experience? If yes, please indicate agencies, organizations or businesses you worked with, and briefly describe your activities;
3. Are you familiar with this community's service agencies in terms of programs, services and needs? Please indicate how knowledge was gained;
4. Have you done volunteer work previously? If yes, please indicate where, when, what duties you performed, and how you feel about your volunteer experience;
5. Please list any employment, previous or current, that you consider pertinent to the job described, give the name of the company or agency, and describe your duties;
6. Please list any other special interests, skills, schooling or experiences that you would consider useful in interviewing and referring volunteers;
7. Because of the time involved for orientation and training of interviewers, we ask for a least a six month commitment of three to four hours a week from you, are you willing and able to make this commitment? and
8. Please list three references, one personal, one from previous volunteer experience, and one from previous or current employment.

The interviewer should give the volunteer applicant a chance to ask about the volunteer opportunities and the job expected of the volunteer as well as any other questions that may arise. Effective interviewing is a task that requires some tact and experience, however with practice it can become an enjoyable experience for the interviewer as well as the applicant in question. Some general principles for interviewing a prospective volunteer include:

1. Conduct the interview in a quiet and private location;
2. Review the application to get an overview and to determine what additional facts will be needed;
3. Put the applicant at ease;
4. Keep the objective of the interview in mind;
5. Know your available assignments so that you can weigh the volunteer's qualifications against the personal and skill requirements of the jobs;
6. Be honest with the applicant;
7. Make your questions work for you (questions that can be answered YES or NO rarely advance the interview);
8. Give the volunteer time to talk; a good interview is a discussion, not a cross-examination;
9. Use questions to help evaluate motivation, interests, skills, values, emotional stability and attitudes;
10. Weigh and evaluate the facts;
11. Give the volunteer a decision or explanation of planned future action; and
12. Respect the volunteer's right to confidentiality.

In Peter Druker's **The Effective Executive**, p. 86, he suggests asking, "What has he or she done well? What does he or she have to learn? If I had a son or daughter, would I be willing to have him or her work under this person?"

Marlene Willson, p. 122, states, "We also owe it to our agencies and organizations to interview well. When we are about the business of human services we must be responsible about our efforts or we and our volunteers may do more damage than good."

Always thank your volunteer applicants for their time and tell them you will get back with them within a short time frame to let them know about their future volunteer placement. Remember that every volunteer should be accorded the rights and privileges of the Bill of Rights for Volunteers.

Bill of Rights For Volunteers

1. The right to be treated as a coworker; not just as free help . . . not as a prima donna.
2. The right to a suitable assignment . . . with consideration for personal preference, temperament, life experience, education and employment background.
3. The right to know as much about the organization as possible including its policies . . . its people . . . its programs.
4. The right to training for the job . . . thoughtfully planned and effectively presented training.
5. The right to continuing education on the job such as a follow-up to initial training . . . information about new developments . . . training for greater responsibility.
6. The right to sound guidance and direction . . . by someone who is experienced, well informed, patient and thoughtful . . . and who has the time to invest in giving guidance.
7. The right to a place to work such as an orderly, designated place . . . conducive to work . . . and worthy of the job to be done.
8. The right to promotion and a variety of experience through advancement to assignments of more responsibility . . . through transfer from one activity to another . . . through special assignments.
9. The right to be heard and to have a part in planning . . . to feel free to make suggestions . . . to have respect shown for an honest opinion.
10. The right to recognition in the form of promotion . . . and awards . . . through day-by-day expressions of appreciation . . . and by being treated as a bona fide co-worker.

Placement

It is most important that the right job is found for the volunteer. As Wilson (1976, p. 131) states, "To make sensible and imagination placements involves matching the interests, skills and personal characteristics of the volunteer with the requirements outlined for a specific job."

Personnel practices that are effective with paid staff are also basic for volunteers. In addition, there are special considerations which arise out of the nature of volunteering. Some of these which relate to planning to start a volunteer on a job are:

1. Since the volunteer has no "pay" other than satisfaction in his work,

his enjoyment of his work should be considered in whatever ways are possible. In training, **avoid being pedantic or heavy-handed,** use humor, informality, sensitivity.

2. The volunteer's time is limited; s/he wants to get to work. **Cover only what s/he must know to begin.** S/He will be ready for additional training when s/he sees a need for it.

3. Because volunteers come from widely varying backgrounds, an individual may have much or little experience related to the kind of job and work setting in which he now finds himself. **Be sure your assumptions about his/her experience** or lack of it **are correct** as you start him/her on the job.

4. The volunteer may now find himself not only in a new job, but also in a whole new setting. **Be sure to use language with which he is familiar** (no professional jargon); and to **clarify any routines** and practices that may affect his job (e.g. staff schedules, use of phones, etc.).

5. The volunteer should know the people with whom he will work and his relationship with each.

6. The nature and extent of an individual volunteer's responsibilities may be quite different from those of career or home life. **Be sure the volunteer and the staff** with whom he will work **have a clear common understanding** of what these responsibilities are and what each person may expect of the other.

7. The volunteer must know the tools and resources for doing his job, to whom he goes for specific help, and mechanics relating to his job.

8. The volunteer should be assured that there are plans for his growth and development as well as opportunities to assess his performance.

9. The volunteer should know the goals of the unit in which he is working and should understand how he contributes toward these.

Explain why this particular position was selected for this volunteer and explain how the volunteer will fit into the center. Give the volunteer background information about the position, other volunteers and staff persons with whom s/he will be interacting. Ask the volunteer to read all of the informational materials and make sure that the system will be right for both of the volunteer and the agency. Explain that there will be training, supervision and evaluation and that if for some reason the position is not working, changes can be made. Have the volunteer read the "Code of Responsibility for Volunteers (Journal of American Hospital Associations, 1958) in which it lists the following:

Code of Responsibility for Volunteers

1. **Be sure:** Look into your heart and know that you really want to help other people.
2. **Be convinced:** Don't offer your services unless you believe in the value of what you are doing.
3. **Be loyal:** Offer suggestions but don't "knock".
4. **Accept the rules:** Don't criticize what you don't understand. There may be a good reason for it.
5. **Speak up:** Ask about things you can't understand. Don't coddle your doubts and frustrations until they drive you away, or turn you into a problem worker.
6. **Be willing to learn:** Training is essential to any job well done.
7. **Keep in learning:** Know all you can about your hospital, or agency and your job.
8. **Welcome supervision:** You will do a better job and enjoy it more if you are doing what is expected of you.
9. **Be dependable:** Your word is your bond. Do what you have agreed to do. Don't make promises you can't keep.
10. **Be a team player:** Find a place for yourself on the team. The lone operator is pretty much out of place in today's complex community.

Training

While it is important to stress to volunteers that training is a means to help them increase their knowledge, it is also important to stress how volunteerism helps the organization.

There are three areas of training which are vital to a sound volunteer program.

Preservice training. This involves training a volunteer before he begins to work. It helps the new volunteer take a look at himself and his skills, at the job that needs to be done, and at the organization's philosophy and services. Preservice training begins with the recruitment process by acquainting the potential volunteer with the organization's program and philosophy. Examples of such training might include: (1) structured observation of the operation of the organization; (2) apprenticeship observation; (3) group meetings of volunteers; and (4) anticipatory practice, (e.g., role play);

Start-up training. This is assistance given to the volunteer as he begins his service. It is a critical period and a period of greater openness than preservice training for the volunteer to ask questions and become more familiar with his position. The volunteer will need to feel recognized and accepted by people already in the system and should be introduced to everyone he will be working with. Examples of such training might include: (1) a supportive chat with his supervisor, trainer, or coworker; (2) pairing the new volunteer with an experienced volunteer; (3) organizing a short meeting of new volunteers shortly after beginning work; (4) placing the volunteer in a variety of spots with experienced people; and (5) listening to recorded instructions or scenarios that will assist the new volunteer to effectively perform his duties.

Maintenance-of-effort training. This can also be referred to as in-service training which provides regular opportunities for the volunteer to ask questions and gain additional knowledge. It is an opportunity for the worker to increase his skills, get out of ruts, answer questions and deal with his or someone else's concerns. This provides a time to refine practices both informal and formal, those flexible and those subject to change. Examples of such training might include: (1) regular co-volunteer meetings for volunteers to interview each other about knowledge, resources, and questions; (2) input sessions and reading of program material; (3) organizing problem clinics on a regular basis; (4) exchanging ideas with organizations having different ideas or methods; (5) holding mini-sabbaticals in the community; and (6) providing adult education opportunities.

It is important to involve everyone in training who could possibly confront a particular situation through their volunteer position. Prior to the orientation and training the following list of questions should be reviewed.

Orientation and Training

1. Are time and personnel for the orientation of volunteers included in planning for your volunteer program?
2. Do all volunteers working in your agency understand why the job they are doing is necessary and how it fits into the total agency picture?
3. Are they given a place to work and to keep their belongings?
4. Are they introduced to staff members and volunteers with whom they will be working?
5. Do your volunteers know what is expected of them in terms of,

performance, confidentiality, appearance, behavior and attitude toward clients or patients?

6. Can volunteers differentiate between the role of the volunteer and that of staff?

7. Have you prepared manuals or other literature to help volunteers keep in mind the things they need to know?

8. Do you acquaint volunteers with the agency's total facilities and with the names of its various department heads?

9. Are your volunteers sufficiently informed as to the agency's purpose, program and philosophy; when to share these intelligently with their families and friends, and when not to discuss outside the agency for confidentiality purposes?

10. Do you give the volunteer an opportunity to acquire the skills needed for a particular assignment through formal training programs and consistent on-the-job training?

11. Have you explored community resources for types of training that your agency is unable to provide?

12. Do you keep the orientation process from becoming static through periodic volunteer meetings, invitations to pertinent workshops, organizing discussion sessions, and offering reading material?

The training room and atmosphere should be carefully scrutinized in order to be sure it is bright, comfortable, the correct temperature, well equipped and ready to conduct the training. Remember, volunteer training should be pertinent, informal, interesting, challenging and ongoing. As Wilson (1976, p. 155) states, "Our purpose in training should be to extend horizons, encourage competency, build confidence, and finally to share the exhilaration of new discovery."

Supervising

Once a good volunteer is in a correct placement, the volunteer coordinator must continue contact through careful supervision in an ongoing effort to provide the agency with properly trained volunteers, the volunteers with their individual needs, and a clear communication between board members, staff and volunteers.

Decide how the new volunteer will fit into the current structure of the existing workers and be sure they know that they are ultimately responsible to the volunteer coordinator.

Every volunteer should know the answers to the following questions to which the volunteer coordinator should have established answers.

1. Has the agency administration designated one person, staff member or volunteer, as the overall director of the volunteer program?
2. Is the chain of command in the volunteer program clearly established?
3. Do volunteers know to whom they are immediately responsible to, report to for work, turn to for help and advice, and call when unable to be present?
4. Do volunteers know when and where they can find their supervisor?
5. Is there always some experienced person available to work with new volunteers and show them what to do?
6. Is there knowledge of how volunteers are getting along in their jobs through an adequate system of records or personal conferences?
7. Do the volunteers who are doing well know that they are appreciated?
8. Is an attempt made to help the volunteer who is not doing well by building up interest, increasing skills, and/or instilling confidence?
9. Are the channels of communication always open between the volunteer coordinator and the volunteers?

Since all supervision is a basic three-step process, it is not difficult for the volunteer or the staff to become confused.

1. Set goals and prepare a work plan.
2. The volunteer and staff do the work required to complete the plan.
3. Evaluation of the work is necessary.

When volunteers and staff succeed, give praise lavishly. Tell them good things have been heard about their work and focus on the successes. Working in a child crisis center is not an easy task, however, the rewards are there if successes are found and verbal praise is given for a job well done.

Evaluation

Flanagan states that, "evaluation is a essential part of planning," and it is the volunteer coordinator who must judge what works and what doesn't work through careful evaluation. Questions must be posed such as: (1) how well is this situation working for the volunteer, the staff and the organization, (2) what can be done to better enable the volunteer to become an even more effective volunteer, and (3) how well did the volunteer meet the goals set out for him or her?

Program evaluation is important as well as individual evaluation and this assessment can begin by reviewing the program's goals. This can be done by collecting information about the portion of the program under question, reviewing it, and then reacting to it. If the program is functioning well it may be beneficial to expand it, however, if is not working well, serious consideration should be given to revising it or abandoning it altogether.

Outside evaluation is an important consideration and it can be very helpful to an organization. The Volunteer Action Center in Indianapolis offers such assistance for nonprofit agencies and there are similar groups in every city nationwide.

Evaluation, when used correctly, can be the means to greatest growth. It can be a new beginning.

Recognizing

People are happy and grow fastest when they are rewarded. Plan for each person to be rewarded each volunteer time by using tangible rewards or verbal praise. It may be as simple as saying "thank you," "you did a beautiful job," or "keep up the good work." Most people do not volunteer to be given things, but to offer their services to those who need help, to meet knew friends and know new experiences. Although gifts or tangible rewards are not one of the main objectives of volunteering time and energy, cards or holiday treats are an acceptable way to let the volunteer his or her actions have not gone unnoticed or unappreciated. Some suggestions on ways to give recognition to volunteers are listed as follows:

1. Smile, greet the volunteer by name with a pleasant good morning;
2. Provide good preservice training by adequately orienting them to the agency and then continue to provide substantive inservice training;
3. Carefully match volunteer with job;
4. Invite participation in team participation and policy formulation by putting up a volunteer suggestion box and/or holding rap sessions;
5. Persuade "personnel" to equate volunteer experience with work experience, motivate agency VIP's to converse with volunteers,

invite them to staff meetings, welcome them to staff coffee breaks, and defend against hostile or negative staff;

6. Arrange for discounts and reimburse for assignment-related expenses;

7. Be familiar with the details of assignments and give additional responsibility if possible such as asking for a report or for assistance in an emergency situation;

8. Maintain a safe working condition and provide useful **tools** such as methods of handling a situation;

9. Recognize and try to accommodate personal needs and problems;

10. Provide a baby sitter or a nursery;

11. Maintain a coffee bar within the agency, surprise them with cake or treat to a soda;

12. Send cards for birthdays, Thanksgiving, Valentine's Day, Christmas, and just thank you or impromptu fun cards;

13. Post an honor roll in the reception area, nominate for volunteer awards, color code name tag to indicate particular achievements (hours, years, unit, etc.), and/or give service stripes;

14. Plan annual ceremonial occasions to celebrate outstanding projects and achievements that can be community-wide, inter-agency cooperative events, such as a public reception;

15. Plan staff and volunteer social events such as informal teas and wine and cheese tasting parties;

16. Facilitate personal maturation by challenging them with new situations such as enlisting them to train other volunteers, offering advocacy roles, or utilizing them as consultants;

17. Help develop self-confidence by enabling them to grow on the job and also allowing them to grow out of the job;

18. Praise a sponsoring group or club by awarding plaques, and distinguish between such a group and an individual volunteer;

19. Have a "Presidents Day" for new presidents of sponsoring groups;

20. Send commendatory letters to prominent public figures for their group's participation;

21. Accept people's individuality, respect their sensitivities and try to honor preferences;

22. Utilize purchased newspaper space or send newsworthy information to the media;

23. Rent billboard space for public laudation;

24. Promote a "Volunteer-of-the-Month" program;

25. Plan a "Recognition Edition" of the agency newsletter;
26. Award special citations for extraordinary achievements;
27. Provide opportunities for conferences and evaluation such as the volunteer evaluating himself or asking clients to evaluate the volunteer services they have received;
28. Create pleasant surroundings by promoting staff smiles and saying "we missed you" when someone returns from an absence;
29. Recommend a volunteer to a prospective employer or commend their work to the supervisory staff;
30. Admit to partnership with paid staff;
31. Provide scholarships to volunteer conferences or workshops;
32. Send a letter of appreciation to the volunteer's employer, and praise them to their friends;
33. Plan occasional extravaganzas such as planning a theater party, attending a sports event, or having a picnic;
34. Instigate client planned surprises for the volunteers;
35. Take time to explain things fully, be verbal, and take time to talk to volunteers;
36. Say good night and thank them for a job well done.

With recognition, it becomes a win-win situation. While a volunteer's reward is a job well done, recognition creates that special pat on the back. When a yearly Volunteer Recognition Day is planned for the center's volunteers it should have a meaningful theme that will promote the best for all of the volunteers. The most important goal for such an event is for volunteers to feel that the volunteer coordinator, staff, executive director, and the board of directors recognizes what an important job the volunteer has provided to the center.

SUMMARY

Today with greater numbers of people joining the work force makes extra time a precious commodity and with the cost of running child abuse programs rising into triple figures or higher, the volunteer has become an even more important commodity. Good planning, organization, staffing, supervision and evaluation must take place in order to ensure the successful placement of volunteers and a successful volunteer program.

Concerned individuals have involved themselves in meeting the needs of the Child Crisis Center by donating their extra time and energy.

Indeed, volunteers have involved themselves in meeting the needs of communities for as long as America has existed as a nation. In order to retain and keep this precious commodity, the volunteer program must attempt to meet the individual needs of the volunteer and at the same time offer the best services possible to the clients seeking help from the agency. This is a difficult but not impossible goal that many crisis centers attempt. Without the help of the volunteers in many agencies, the cost of services would be extremely high and agencies may find that they could not accommodate the number of persons seeking assistance with the same quality of services.

Many volunteers could chose a different road such as staying at home or devoting time only to their personal work, however, they have not done so. They have chosen to give freely of their time so that abused and neglected children and families may benefit.

> *Two roads diverged in a wood, and I; I took the one less traveled by; and that has made all the difference.*
>
> Robert Frost
> The Road Not Taken

REFERENCES

1. Druker, P.: *The Effective Executive.* New York, Harper & Row, 1967.
2. Flanagan, J.: *The Successful Volunteer Organization: Getting Started and Getting Good Results in Nonprofit, Charitably Grass Roots and Community Groups.* Chicago, Contemporary Books, 1981.
3. Mason, G., Jensen, G., and Ryzwocz, C.: *How to Grow a Parents Group.* Western Springs, C.D.G., 1979.
4. Naylor, H.: *Volunteers Today: Finding, Training and Working With Them.* Dryden, 1967.
5. Townsend, R.: *Up the Organization.* New York, Knopf, 1970.
6. *Voluntary Action News,* Vancouver, British Columbia, March, 1976.
7. Wilson, M.: *The Effective Management of Volunteer Programs.* Boulder, Volunteer Management Consultants, 1976.

CHAPTER 10

ESTABLISHING A FOOD SERVICE CENTER IN A NOT FOR PROFIT AGENCY

BEVERLY R. HURD AS TOLD TO BARBARA R. FURLOW

INTRODUCTION

Nutrition is important for all people, especially children. Good nutrition can be linked to high energy, good health and better classroom performance. In the young infant, nutritional balance has proven to be essential in the prevention of certain forms of retardation. Poor nutrition can be a contributing factor in some emotional disturbances in the older child, the teenager and the adult. In their book, **Normal and Therapeutic Nutrition,** Robinson and Lawler (1977) state:

> Food influences each stage of physical, mental, and emotional development. The infant's earliest relationships are associated with food, and throughout the growing years food continues to be a major factor in the development of the whole person. Food becomes a language of communication; it has cultural and social meanings; it is ultimately associated with the emotions; and its acceptance or rejection becomes highly personal.

Food is not only a necessity, but also an opportunity to contribute to the physical, mental and emotional well being of all who come to a family service agency. Therefore, the goal of planning the kitchen and dining area and the establishment of a proper nutritional program is to create a positive learning experience and balanced diet. This chapter will present information to aid in planning a kitchen at a not-for-profit center. It will provide both a checklist of necessary steps to accomplish this goal and a more detailed discussion of action necessary to complete each task. It will include a floor plan and a list of equipment and utensils to complete the kitchen, as well as a list of dining room furnishings. Besides several suggested strategies for the operation of the kitchen and the dining facilities, the final section of this chapter will focus on several ways in which the food program might be incorporated into a learning program for the welfare of these children and their families.

235

PLANNING STEPS AND STRATEGIES

1. Contact the State Board of Health (SBH) to obtain a list of requirements for food service and storage areas and for food purchasing.
2. Make initial contacts with possible contributors or donors of food items.
3. Shop for equipment, utensils and furnishings in compliance with SBH requirements.
4. Contact the local food bank. Check on the center's eligibility for commodity foods. Get a list of available commodities. Apply for the appropriate applications for authorized credentials.
5. Hire a supervisor or a kitchen coordinator.
6. Attend a seminar or workshop with the supervisor provided by the School Lunch Program Department or similar agency.
7. Select vendors and suppliers needed. Establish a credit line.

Food Service Requirements

It cannot be emphasized too strongly or too frequently that any action taken in the planning of a kitchen for a not-for-profit agency must begin by contacting the state agency which licenses and approves such facilities. The State Board of Health (SBH) can provide the proper booklets containing rules and regulations which must be met in the operation of a food service facility. Time and money can be saved in the planning stage by becoming familiar with these sanitation requirements and incorporating the needs of such requirements into the physical layout of the kitchen and storage area. For example, Section 4 (b) of the **Indiana Food Service Sanitation Requirements** (1983) states that containers of food shall be stored a minimum of six inches above the floor . . . except that; (1) metal pressurized beverage containers . . . need not be elevated when the food container is not exposed to floor moisture, and (2) containers may be stored on dollies, racks, or pallets, provided such equipment is easily movable.

This section goes on to include provision for: (1) storage of food away from exposed sewer or water lines, (2) protection against cross contamination, (3) the refrigeration of foods, and (4) so forth. It is understandable that awareness of these types of requirements influence the way in which the kitchen and the food storage areas are arranged. State Board of Health regulations also effect certain areas of purchasing and should be carefully studied.

Food Donors

Although it may seem premature to contact contributors or donors of food items as a next step, it is important to have available any sources of food which might be used by the center. Knowing the schedules of distribution and the types of food to be distributed are important factors in planning menus and purchasing requirements. If donations from bakeries, produce vendors or fast food chains are successfully solicited, frequency and amounts of donations need to be factored into the menu and purchasing program. Since publicity about such a facility as that for abused and neglected children reaches a peak when the center is opened, a good opportunity is provided for publicly thanking such donors. (Check with the donors before using individual or corporate names in publicity releases.) Such mass media coverage may cause other interested donors to come forward. Of course, such public thank you's do not take the place of personally written letters or continued correspondence with comments and words of appreciation from the children themselves.

Kitchen and Dining Room Equipment

Budgetary allowances will help you determine how and where to shop for your kitchen equipment, utensils, and furnishings. Remember these must meet the guidelines established by the SBH. Price listing the kitchen with all new equipment will be a guideline to determining which items might provide the largest cost reduction if available for purchase used. Explore liquidation sales, salvage sales, and demolition sales for needed equipment. Always state the agency's name and purpose, and request an item be donated or discounted, if possible. Remember to have the agency's tax number which should be included on all purchases. Table X–I lists equipment needed to establish a complete food service center. Table X–II lists necessary utensils and small appliances.

Commodity Foods

The local food bank, school lunch program, or commodity distribution center are all possible sources of staple supplies, meats, and cheeses. Contact these agencies to determine the eligibility requirements for inclusion. Get the necessary document substantiation and applications completed for participation in these programs. Get the schedule of foods which can be expected and the times and quantities of distribution. These sources may also supply a chart of nutritional values, sizes and

TABLE X-1
EQUIPMENT NEEDED

  6- Large (full) stainless steel steamtable pans with lids
12- Half stainless steel steam table pans with lids
12- ¼ stainless steel steam table pans with lids
  6- Slotted spoons, 4 short handles, 2 long handles
  4- Solid spoons, 4 short handles, 2 long handles
  4- Pairs of locking stainless steel tongs, 3 short, 1 long
  6- Short wooden handled rubber spatulas
  2- Long wooden handled rubber spatulas
  2- Pair kitchen shears
  1- Pair of scissors
  6- Assorted sizes butcher knives
  1- French or chopping knife
  6- Paring knives
  2- Meat forks
  2- Potato peelers
  1- Small cake decorator spatula
  1- Set basic cake decorating tips and bags
  6- Nine inch cake pans
  6- Nine inch pie tins
  8- Nine by thirteen cake pans: use for casseroles, too
  3- Sets assorted sizes stacked stainless steel mixing bowls
  2- Small wire whisks
  1- Large wire whisk
  1- Large stainless spoon rest
  6- Two quart pitchers (stainless with lids)
40- Plastic refrigerator and freezer containers with lids
  6- Stainless cookie sheets
  8- Large stainless sheet pans
  6- Stainless half sheet pans
  6- Nine by five stainless bread pans
  6- Short wooden handled egg turners
  2- Long wooden handled egg turners
  1- Egg poacher
  6- Assorted sizes ladles for gravy, soup, etc.
  3- Large well covered trash containers on wheels with liners
  2- One hundred pound covered bin on wheels for sugar and flour
  6- Large covered plastic containers with labels for salt, coconut,
     chocolate chips, rice, etc.
  1- Microwave oven

---

*These numbers are based on a maximum census of 20 clients. The kitchen also provides meals for the staff and volunteers.

TABLE X-II
UTENSILS AND SMALL APPLIANCES

Large Cooking Pots	*Sauce Pans (Long Handles)*
1-Ten gallon with lid	2-Six quart with lids
2-Five gallon with lids	4-Two quart with lids
2-Three gallon with lids	4-One quart with lids
3-One gallon with lids	

Small Appliances

1-Heavy mixer with slicing, grinding and shredding attachments (i.e., dough hook, whisk and mixing blades and 2 bowls)
1-Small hand mixer
1-Commercial blender
1-Four slice commercial toaster
1-Commercial food processor
2-Fifty to seventy-five cup coffee pots
1-Small commercial coffee maker (usually furnished from supplier for coffee)

Dishes

40-Four ounce juice glasses
40-Six ounce milk glasses
40-Ten ounce milk glasses for teens, adults, and staff
1-Heavy duty dishwasher
Proof plastic
Assorted flatware including: soup spoons, small and toddler spoons, forks, knives and feeding spoons for infants
Weighted cups for toddlers (with two handles and lid)
Weighted bowls; divided and plain for toddlers
Baby bottles, nipples, rings, stoppers made of dishwasher safe plastic
Divided baby food dishes that hold hot water to keep food warm

servings per container of food distributed. Such charts are helpful in menu planning.

The Kitchen Coordinator

The **kitchen coordinator** is the key person in the efficient operation of the food service for this type of facility. It is now time to hire this person. The qualifications needed for successful management of the food program are: (1) the ability to know and understand the federal programs available, (2) knowledge on how to best utilize their benefits, (3) the ability to accurately work with numbers, (4) the ability to understand and implement vital record keeping procedures, and (5) having supervisory capabilities. Knowledge of these programs and accurate records are important aspects of utilizing all of the federal and state funding programs available to the center. Further requirements for the kitchen coordinator include a minimum of an Associate Degree in Dietary Management plus two years of experience in an agency kitchen.

Once the kitchen coordinator is hired, work can begin immediately as plans must be coordinated to comply with sanitation regulations. Staff needs, pay scales, and scheduling requirements, as well as criteria for hiring must be determined.

Seminars and Workshops

Once all hiring is completed, the kitchen coordinator should arrange to attend a seminar or workshop concerning the daily operation of a not-for-profit agency food center. Such workshops are often available through the **School Lunch Program, Department of Public Education**. Primary benefits of such a program are: (1) sharing of information about available sources of food supplies, vendors and suppliers; (2) ways in which nutritional menus can be built around commodity items; and (3) learning a variety of low budget, appetizing recipes. Additional ideas can be incorporated into the training program for the kitchen staff from suggestions made at such seminars. Schedule staff members for attendance at workshops suitable for their needs. It may be possible to schedule these workshops on site for staff members and parents once the center is in operation.

Vendors and Suppliers

Using the list of vendors and suppliers obtained at the seminars and those in the Yellow Pages, contact these businesses to determine their schedule of operations, to request a price list, and to determine the line of credit the center can expect to receive.

Select the vendors who will be used from those who are willing to provide a price list, offer a line of credit, and whose schedules will meet your delivery needs. Some coffee vendors and dishwasher chemical vendors, will furnish, service and clean their equipment, which can cut down on the center's maintenance costs. It is important in the agency setting to know the price of food items necessary to complete monthly menus. Time is saved each month if the list is up dated and available at the center, rather than having to phone individual suppliers to determine prices. With a price list, the chance of a budget surprise at billing time should be eliminated. Further, the insistence upon having and using price lists helps to keep the operation of the kitchen on a sound business basis.

Dining Room Arrangement

Make the dining room conducive to a family feeling. Try to create an atmosphere of warmth and cheer by arranging this area for family type meals. There are limitations. The population and its ever changing census necessitates an area readily adaptable to a variety of table numbers and sizes. The area must be maintained in accordance with sanitation requirements of the SBH. Therefore, use furnishings and decorations which can be easily sanitized. Although carpeting may be used for a floor covering, it is more practical to use tile that can be scrubbed or congoleum flooring. Brightly colored or patterned commercial grade carpet could be used on the bottom portion of the walls. This is an effective way to create a cheery setting while incorporating sound reduction material and safety features in the dining area. For one upper wall surface of the room, use a type of material upon which pictures, menus, or nutritional information can be posted.

Because the population of such a center can vary overnight from minimum to maximum numbers or change from teens to toddlers, flexibility of the area is a primary goal. The type of facility on which this information is based is planned to accommodate twenty children and/or teens. The court mandated length of stay may vary from three to ten days. Breakfast for ten teens and one infant may become lunch for four teens, eight toddlers and two infants. These probabilities make change a constant factor in meal and dining area planning programs. Time required and ease of converting the area from use of adult sized tables and chairs to the smaller sized toddler tables and chairs are essential factors to take into consideration when planning the dining room. Keep on hand a variety of floor plans for table groupings to increase the efficiency of quickly arranging necessary tables and chairs. Remember to keep any one table from being isolated. Family style dining requires the use of movable two shelved carts for providing second servings. Therefore, the use of pre-planned charts will assure the necessary space requirements for these wheeled carts.

Generally, the children are assigned chores such as clearing their own plates, collecting trash, and wiping up the tables. For these purposes plan space for a movable receptacle for stacking dishes, flatware, glasses, and cups near the kitchen door. Such receptacle should have three shelves and be on wheels, making it easy to move soiled dishes directly to the dishwashing area. Equip the top shelf with a plastic dish pan for used flatware and another pan for cups and glassware. On the second shelf, two similar pans collect plates, bowls, and miscellaneous dishes. Place a large, plastic lined waste container at one end of this collection area. Have a storage space close to this area containing disposable bibs and disposable wet and dry towels for use with the babies in high chairs. Table X–III lists the dining equipment needed based on a population maximum of 20.

TABLE X-III
DINING ROOM EQUIPMENT

2- Thirty gallon trash containers, on wheels, with lids
2- Three tier carts, stainless steel, on wheels
8- Six foot folding tables
6- High chairs on wheels
48- Fiberglass stack chairs, full size
6- Toddler size tables, 20″ high
40- Toddler size fiberglass stack chairs, 11″ high
4- Room divider, preferably covered with burlap
1- water fountain
1- Small table for ice, drinks, etc.

In the family group setting, one adult will be seated at each table with the toddlers and one with the older children at the larger tables. Should the census require it, two adults can be seated at the larger tables. To further encourage family feeling, older children can help younger children in the clearing of the tables. Training in appropriate table manners and behavior is an ongoing educational process by the adults eating with the children.

Kitchen Arrangement

The kitchen arrangement depends on the physical size and layout of the space designated for this room. Figure X-1 is a sketch of a well-planned kitchen. Food deliveries are made through double doors. Either one or two work tables readily accommodates sorting, repackaging, and taking inventory of new items. These foods are then in convenient location for storage in their proper area, such as the freezer, the store room, or the walk-in refrigerator. To prevent cross contamination, SBH requires chemical and paper storage areas be separate from edible items.

The three compartment sink is used for washing and preparing foods, as is the counter space and either of the two work tables. The set up of

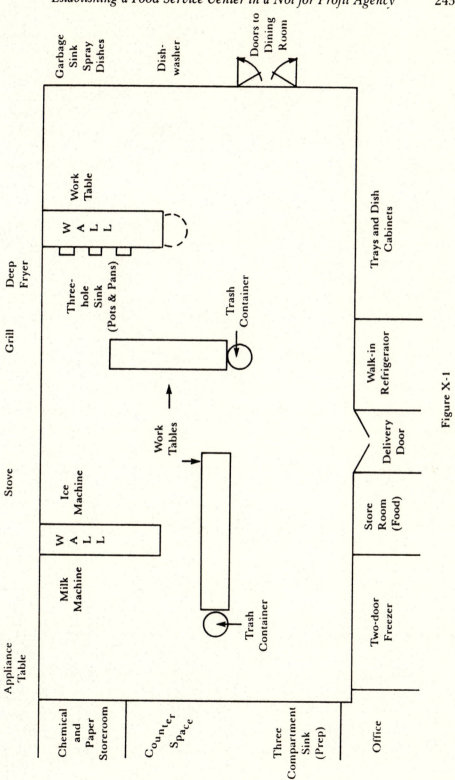

Figure X-1

appliances, stove, grill and deep fryer allows the division of work and activity in food preparation. After pots and pans are used, they are scrubbed, washed and then sanitized in the third pot and pan sink which is equipped with the required heat element to heat water to 180 degrees. This plan allows ample room for access to the dining room with serving carts and trays. The wheeled receptacle containing soiled dishes and utensils can be brought directly to the garbage sink and spray area before being loaded into the dishwasher. Once washed and dried, the dishes are close to the appropriate cabinet storage areas.

General rules from the SBH apply to the freezer and refrigeration areas. Both appliances must be kept at the appropriate temperature as specified by these SBH rules to prevent or retard spoilage of foods. Containers of food must be covered, labeled and dated. The refrigerator must be cleaned and sanitized once a month. This is a good time to inventory items in both the refrigerator and freezer. Light bulbs should be changed when necessary. Light covers should be cleaned regularly. Thermometers must be visible and must be kept clean. The freezer must be defrosted and cleaned at regular intervals.

Arrange items in the storage areas so that they are readily accessible on sturdy shelving in well lighted areas. Stock must be rotated as new orders or donations are received, assuring use of older items first. No food items may be placed on the floor, and bottom shelves must be high enough off of the floor so that the floor can be cleaned and sanitized regularly. Some ventilation should be provided in these storage areas. Covered plastic bins on wheels are convenient storage facilities for bulk cereal, flour, sugar, etc. The storage area should be locked with a limited distribution of keys in order to better control the inventory.

Inventory control is a vital part of the kitchen coordinator's job and responsibility. In both food and equipment areas, a strong inventory control system serves to:

1. keep up with rotation of food items,
2. keep coordinator familiar with products being used, aiding in decisions when reordering,
3. help prevent theft by making sure all employees know that stock and equipment are regularly counted,
4. help keep the coordinator aware of damage or breakage, order repairs or replacement,
5. alert the coordinator to possible misuse of equipment, and

6. schedule training sessions to educate staff in the proper usage of equipment.

OPERATIONS

Two weeks before the center is ready to open, plan a four month cycle of menus. Appendix X–A includes a month of menus and recipes for use of commodity foods. Review the list of food which will be donated. Check the date of distribution for those items which will be obtained through government commodity programs or from local food banks. If a fast food chain has pledged a once a month lunch, place that on the master menu calendar. Ask questions such as: (1) will additional food items be needed to complete that meal, and (2) are there meats or cheeses from the federal programs around which other meals can be planned? Check the date of use stickers on such items and plan to use them at the appropriate times. Check the list of donors for other food items. Are these foods precooked or in need of preparation? How often will such foods be available? A bakery might donate hot dog rolls every third week.

Checking these lists and answering such basic questions about types and quantities of food on hand is the first step in planning nutritionally balanced monthly menus. Planning on a four month cycle facilitates staying within budgetary allowances while providing nutritious, economical meals. Such a routine also carefully utilizes all donated and federally provided foods. Now order the first month's supply of food items, necessary staples, paper products, and chemicals. Include in the initial food order the required, three day emergency supply of canned food items. These supplies should be prominently labeled and stored in a special place.

Types of stored food may vary, but generally they will include at least 50 pounds of flour, 50 pounds of sugar, a supply of brown sugar and confectioner's sugar, dry cereals, and an assortment of pastas and dried beans. The kitchen coordinator will purchase fresh produce and fruits, breads and bakery items on a weekly basis.

It is not a good policy to check items while they are still on the delivery truck. Always check deliveries as they come into the kitchen; that way no item can be accidentally left on the truck. A consistent practice of counting items immediately, noting items shorted or missing, labeling and dating items, helps to prevent honest mistakes, misuse, and theft. Check the prices charged against the price list and run a quick addition of the numbers. It is simpler to correct a mistake at this point rather than trying to get satisfaction at a later date.

Once a year, an unscheduled inspection of compliance with sanitation requirements is made by a SBH examiner. The best way to be prepared for such an inspection is to initiate rigid sanitation procedures from the beginning of the operation of the center. The health of the children and the licensing of the center are dependent on this necessary routine. Because sanitizing is a routine repeated three times a day before and after meals, the kitchen coordinator must institute a standard of performance and an inhouse system of inspection to insure that procedures are consistently followed. Another routine necessary to establish is that of personal hygiene and cleanliness.

The rules by which the kitchen will be inspected are carefully and clearly written in the SBH booklet on **Food Service Sanitation Requirements**. The kitchen coordinator must know and enforce these rules. She must also establish the center's rules on personal hygiene and cleanliness. To aide the staff, a rotating schedule of sanitizing the major appliances, work areas, storage areas and trash containers will help to prevent monotony and carelessness. Work closely with the maintenance department in problem areas such as drain and grease trap sanitation and methods of insect control. A team effort concept can be encouraged through the ongoing inservice programs.

Planning regularly scheduled inservice programs is an additional responsibility of the kitchen coordinator. These meetings are an important means of keeping the staff up to date, of discussing and solving problems, or recognizing work well done. Generally, well informed, trusted, and included employees have higher morale and more enthusiasm for their work. Keep these meetings brief and well planned. Schedule speakers or films which will aide the employees in completion or improvement of their tasks, inform them about safety or health regulations, or add to skills for use in communication and support of the children. Contact sources outside the center such as the Fire Marshall, SBH department speakers bureau, Public Library or Library Film Department for programs and suggestions. Remember that state regulatory agencies are eager to assist in planning inservice programs. Make a tentative one year schedule of these programs, having the first six months of each year confirmed before the schedule is printed and posted. Table X–IV lists a sample of a year long schedule of inservice programs.

TABLE X-IV
INSERVICE SCHEDULE

Month	Subject	Presenter	Confirmed
January	Sanitation – 15 min. Film/discus.	SBH	Smith 12/16
February	Fire Safety – speech/demo.	Fire Marshall	Miller 12/16
March	Proper food storage – demo.	Home Demo.	Andrew 12/16
April	Maintenance/cooperation/problems	Maint. dept.	Peters 12/16
May	Sanitation – dish/food handling	SBH	Smith 12/16
June	Bacteria – cause and cures	Hospital staff	recall 3/88
July	Insights into welfare family life	Social worker	
August	Food preparation/temperature	Staff discus.	
September	Nutrition – the whys and hows	Univ. prof.	
October	Sanitation – tables/chairs/floors	Hands on review	
November	Personal hygiene	hospital staff	
December	Seasonal Blues – it happens to kids	psychologist	

One of the more difficult tasks for the kitchen coordinator is scheduling of the work force. Most not-for-profit agencies dealing with child care operate 365 days a year, 24 hours a day. However the kitchen is staffed on 7½ hour shifts for a total of 13 hours a day. One worker reports at 6:00 AM, finishing work at 1:30 PM. Another worker reports to the kitchen at 11:30 AM and stays until 7 PM. The third worker is a part-time employee, working twelve hour days both Saturday and Sunday. This employee ideally is available to help cover emergencies or vacation days, working up to 32 hours per week. There is a daily overlap at lunch time. As a rule, this is the time at which the largest number of people will be served because staff and volunteers are included. The typical schedule for dining hours are: breakfast at 7:45 AM; lunch at Noon; supper at 4:30 PM. Small snacks are provided for the children at 9:30 AM; 2:30 PM; and 7:30 PM. The evening snacks are left in a back room of the living quarters. This room has a small refrigerator and a microwave oven. Each evening before leaving, the kitchen personnel check to be certain ample snacks are available. An adequate amount of food is kept in the refrigerator to quickly prepare a meal for children who might come into the shelter in the evening or night time hours. An evening staff person would be responsible for this food preparation. With a small kitchen staff, reliability is vital. However, it is a good policy to allow the workers to plan to cover for one another and swap schedules if necessary.

The kitchen coordinator establishes the daily routine. A typical day begins at 6:00 AM with the appliances being turned on and coffee brewed in the employee lounge. Next a head count is taken from the child care supervisor and breakfast is started. After each meal the head count slip is tacked on the bulletin board by the coordinator's office. At the end of the day the total count is entered into record books in the coordinator's office. The accurate counting and maintaining of these records provides the documentation for reimbursement through the school lunch program. The center will be reimbursed for both the cost of meals and milk provided for any eligible school age child currently on the breakfast and lunch federally funded program. These funds go into the general operating budget of the not-for-profit center and are a substantial asset to the center. Therefore, it is important that accurate, honest, and complete records be maintained at all times. Inaccurate records could cost the center eligibility.

On Monday of each week the coordinator should call the private Food Bank Agencies for a schedule of their available food items. Such banks provide food supplies at a flat rate, for example 12 cents a pound. Careful planning of purchases can create considerable savings. At times such agencies may send along fresh vegetables rather than allow them to spoil. Once a year these agencies will review their services with the director of the center and the kitchen coordinator.

Commodity supply notices are received in the mail listing items and dates of availability. In order to take advantage of the free delivery, plan orders so that six cases of any food items are delivered at one time. The commodity agency will store food items in the freezer and hold for delivery. When food items come into the center, they should remain in the dated cases until ready for use. Personnel from the commodity agency will inspect your supply of their products to determine proper usage. If there are items not used by the center, the commodity agency will arrange for them to be used elsewhere, trying to find more appropriate foods for each of their clients. Menus for use of the commodity foods must be approved by a registered nutritionist. The agency often has menus which can be adapted for use by individual child care centers.

STRATEGIES

A well-nourished child . . . is usually happy and good natured; he is brim full of life and animal spirits and is constantly active, both physically and mentally (Mitchell).

A maximum of a ten day stay will not allow the kitchen coordinator to miraculously cure a child's nutritional imbalance. However, it is vital to keep in mind the opportunity to introduce these children to good eating habits, new foods, and to provide them with a relaxed, comfortable eating atmosphere.

An educational program can be casually included in menu planning and in the dining area with the use of easy A, B, C nutritional charts, bright cut outs of a new food being introduced, and cooperation of the adult table personnel. For example, there are many foods some of these children will not know or recognize, such as a pear. Displaying a variety of fresh pears, cans of pears, pear relish, pear preserves, and pear jelly can be coordinated to meals using each of these items. Breakfast can include pear preserves and jelly as toast or muffin toppings. Pear salad with grated cheese or cottage cheese would be on the luncheon menu and fresh pear would be served as the snack for that night. Rewarding younger children with a smiling pear stickler on a posted name chart encourages trying this new food item. Pictures of pear trees in blossom and with fruit could be posted as part of the dining area decoration for a week. The same type of program can be followed as foods such as raw vegetables or other fruits are introduced.

Similarly, ethnic foods can be used to build a week long menu, introducing the children to other cultures, their foods, and eating customs. A mexican tortilla, greek pita and crusty french bread can be the basis for building international sandwiches. If a particular country's food is chosen for a week of menus, invite natives of that country to be luncheon guests every day for the week, having them talk about their country. Have posters from travel agencies on the walls. If possible the major food words in English and the language of the country being introduced can be posted on the wall boards.

Be creative as menus are planned around programs such as this. A Mexican food chain might donate precooked special meals, or an ethnic Chinese food center might donate the ingredients and recipes for a Chinese speciality. Encourage the kitchen staff to contribute their ideas and suggestions, crediting the employee by featuring his or her picture in the dining area.

Ideally, getting parents to attend nutritional workshops and serving them a well-cooked, well-balanced, economical meal could be a long-term goal of the kitchen coordinator. Funding for such a program can be sought from outside sources and might include the work of the center's volunteer or auxiliary group in promotion and carrying out such workshops. Additional educational efforts include sending home a week's schedule of the center's menus with recipes, or a menu a particular child enjoyed. Such a program does demand cooperation by kitchen and child care staff and must have approval of the director of the center and the board of directors. It also takes a very dedicated kitchen coordinator.

One way to help promote such programs is to serve one of the **fun** ethnic meals to the board of directors on their scheduled meeting date. Include the wall decorations and other educational aids in their dining area. However, meals served to such outside guests should always be consistent with the meals actually being served the children. This helps board members and visitors understand the quality of food being served, the limitations of budgetary restrictions, and the value of a good kitchen staff.

Employees and volunteers at the center are encouraged to order their daily meals through the center's kitchen. Appropriate charges for food items are posted, with collections for such meals going into the **petty cash fund.** Petty cash is further increased whenever the center is donated a perishable item in large quantity. Kitchen staff may bake pies or bread with fruits or vegetables, such as apples or squash and sell them to staff members. These funds in turn are used to help purchase more fresh produce, often too expensive for the regularly budgeted funds.

In summary, the well-being of the child brought into the center for abuse and neglect is served through every department of the center, including the food service area. Nutritional values combined with appetizing food, served in a cheerful atmosphere is a goal which can be met by the kitchen coordinator and the kitchen staff.

REFERENCES

1. Indiana State Board of Health: *Food Service Sanitation Requirements.* Indianapolis, 1983.

2. Mitchell, Katherine: *Food in Health and Disease,* 6th ed. Philadelphia, Davis, 1958.
3. Natow, Annette, Heslin, Jo-ann: *No-Nonsense Nutrition for Kids.* McGraw Hill, 1985.
4. Robinson, C.H., Lawler, M.R.: *Normal and Therapeutic Nutrition,* 15th ed. New York, MacMillan, 1977.
5. Developing a nutritional surveillance system. *Journal of the American Dietetic Association, 65,* 1974.

APPENDIX X-A
WEEK OF MENUS

Week 1

Breakfast	Lunch	Dinner
Monday		
Scrambled eggs	1 c. Johnny Marzette	1 grilled cheese
1 slice toast/butter	1 c. green salad	sandwich
4 oz. orange juice	1 Tbs. french dressing	1/2 c. tomato soup
1/2 c. oatmeal	2 oz. broccoli	2 crackers
8 oz. milk	1 slice bread/butter	carrot sticks
	8 oz. milk	8 oz. milk
	1/2 c. ice cream	
Tuesday		
1 pancake/butter/	Hamburger on bun	2 oz. ham/ 1/2 c.
syrup	Lettuce, tomato salad	beans
1/2 c. applesauce	1 Tbs. french dressing	2 × 2 sq cornbread/
1 slice bacon	1/2 c. green beans	butter
1 oz. dry cereal	8 oz. milk	vegetables and dip
8 oz. milk	1/2 c. peaches	8 oz. milk
		1 slice pie
Wednesday		
Muffin egg	2 oz. fried chicken	Spanish hamburger
1 oz. cheese	1/2 c. mashed potatoes	1/2 c. mashed
4 oz. orange juice	1/2 c. carrots	potatoes

½ c. cream of wheat 8 oz. milk	1 biscuit/butter 8 oz. milk 1 slice pie	½ c. spinach 1 slice bread/butter ½ c. cole slaw 8 oz. milk ½ c. peaches

Thursday

Scrambled eggs 1 slice toast/butter 4 oz. orange juice ½ c. oatmeal 8 oz. milk	1 peanut butter/jelly ½ c. cole slaw ½ c. carrots 1 slice bread/butter 8 oz. milk 2 × 2 square choc. cake	1 c. tuna casserole ½ c. sliced tomatoes ½ c. carrots 8 oz. milk ½ c. ice cream

Friday

1 waffle/butter/syrup 1 sausage link ½ c. applesauce 8 oz. milk 1 oz. dry cereal	1 tuna salad sandwich carrot & celery sticks 1 oz. french fries 8 oz. milk ½ c. jello w/fruit	3 oz. chicken with ½ c. dressing ½ c. green beans 1 slice bread/butter 2 oz. jello 8 oz. milk 2 × 2 square cake

Saturday

1 fried egg
1 slice bacon
1 slice toast/butter
4 oz. orange juice
1 oz. dry cereal
	2 oz. fish sticks
	1 oz. french fries
	½ c. fresh carrot
	  salad
	8 oz. milk
	½ c. pears
		4 oz. meat loaf
		½ c. broccoli
		½ c. baked potato
		  with butter
		8 oz. milk
		½ c. jello/
		  whipped cream

Sunday

1 scrambled egg/
  cheese
½ Eng. muffin/butter
1 oz. dry cereal
	1 egg salad sandwich
	dill pickle
	½ c. macaroni/cheese
	8 oz. milk
		½ c. cottage cheese
		  with ½ peach
		celery sticks
		1 slice bread/butter

4 oz. orange juice	2 slices pineapple	8 oz. milk
8 oz. milk		

WEEK 2

Breakfast	Lunch	Dinner
Monday		
1 scrambled egg	2 oz. weiners	½ c. egg salad/bun
1 slice toast/butter	½ c. sauerkraut	½ c. slice tomatoes
1 slice bacon	½ c. mashed potatoes	½ c. carrots
4 oz. orange juice	1 slice bread/butter	½ c. jello
½ c. dry cereal	½ c. pears	1 slice pie
8 oz. milk	8 oz. milk	8 oz. milk
Tuesday		
1 pancake/butter/	3 oz. hamburger/bun	1 c. spaghetti/meat
syrup	1 oz. french fries	1 slice garlic bread
1 oz. sausage link	½ c. slaw	1 c. green salad
½ c. oatmeal	½ c. jello	2 × 2 sq. cake
4 oz. apple juice	8 oz. milk	8 oz. milk
8 oz. milk		
Wednesday		
Egg on ½ Eng. muffin	1 c. beef stew w/carrots	1 pork fritter/bun
½ c. dry cereal	celery, potatoes	½ c. macaroni/cheese
4 oz. orange juice	1 c. green salad/	½ c. pickled beets
8 oz. milk	1 Tbs. dressing	½ c. pineapple
	8 oz. milk	8 oz. milk
	½ c. ice cream	
Thursday		
1 scrambled egg	Grilled cheese	4 oz. meat loaf
1 slice toast/butter	sandwich	½ baked potato
4 oz. orange juice	1 c. tomato soup	½ c. green beans
½ orange	½ c. peaches	1 slice bread/butter

8 oz. milk	8 oz. milk	½ c. choc. pudding
	celery & carrot sticks	8 oz. milk

Friday

1 waffle/butter/syrup	Fish sandwich/bun	2 oz. roast beef
1 slice bacon	with tartar sauce	½ c. peas/carrots
½ c. dry cereal	½ c. potato salad	½ deviled egg
4 oz. orange juice	½ c. carrots	1 biscuit/butter
8 oz. milk	1 slice pie	½ c. pears
	8 oz. milk	8 oz. milk

Saturday

1 scrambled egg	2 oz. ham with	1 tuna salad sand.
1 slice toast/butter	½ c. beans	1 c. green salad/
½ orange	2 oz. cornbread/butter	1 Tbs. dressing
8 oz. milk	1 oz. celery sticks	1 oz. raw vegetables/
	½ c. spinach	dressing dip
	½ c. ice cream	½ banana
	8 oz. milk	8 oz. milk

Sunday

½ c. sausage gravy	2 oz. fried chicken	1 c. chili/crackers
1 biscuit/butter/jelly	½ c. mashed potatoes	2 celery stalks with
½ c. dry cereal	½ c. green beans	peanut butter
4 oz. orange juice	1 oz. hot roll/butter	½ c. slaw
8 oz. milk	2 × 2 sq. cake	½ c. jello/fruit
	8 oz. milk	8 oz. milk

WEEK 3

Breakfast	Lunch	Dinner

Monday

1 waffle/butter	1 c. tuna	Hamburger/bun
1 slice bacon	1 hot roll/butter	½ c. hash browns
½ c. dry cereal	½ c. spinach	1 c. green salad/

½ banana	½ c. slaw	1 Tbs. dressing
8 oz. milk	1 apple	½ c. ice cream
	8 oz. milk	8 oz. milk

Tuesday

1 scrambled egg	1 hot dog on bun	3 oz. Swedish meatball
1 slice toast/butter	½ c. potato salad	½ c. green beans
½ c. cream of wheat	½ c. carrots	½ c. apple salad
6 oz. apple juice	2 × 2 sq. cake	1 slice bread/butter
8 oz. milk	8 oz. milk	1 slice pie
		8 oz. milk

Wednesday

½ c. sausage gravy	4 oz. meat loaf	1 oz. ham sandwich/
1 biscuit/butter	½ c. mashed potatoes	1 oz. cheese
½ c. dry cereal	½ c. green beans	½ c. baked beans
1 orange	½ deviled egg	½ c. asparagus
8 oz. milk	1 slice bread/butter	½ peach
	1 slice pie	½ c. choc. pudding
	8 oz. milk	8 oz. milk

Thursday

1 scrambled egg	1 c. veg. soup/crackers	3 oz. sliced turkey
½ Eng. muffin/butter	celery & carrot sticks	1 c. potatoes/peas
½ c. oatmeal/	½ peanut butter sand.	1 slice bread/gravy
2 Tbs. raisins	½ c. ice cream	½ c. pears
8 oz. milk	8 oz. milk	8 oz. milk

Friday

1 fried egg	1 c. spaghetti pie	1 pork fritter/bun
1 slice bacon	1 c. green salad/	½ c. tomatoes
1 slice toast/butter	1 Tbs. dressing	½ c. spinach
½ c. dry cereal	1 slice bread/butter	1 slice cantaloupe
1 orange	½ c. peaches	8 oz. milk
8 oz. milk	8 oz. milk	

Saturday

1 pancake/butter/ syrup	Fish sandwich	3 oz. Fried chicken
1 sausage link	1 oz. french fries	1/2 c. potato salad
1/2 c. oatmeal	1/2 c. carrots	1/2 c. corn
4 oz. orange juice	1/2 cup fruit salad	1 biscuit/butter
8 oz. milk	8 oz. milk	1/2 c. ice cream
		8 oz. milk

Sunday

1 fried egg	2 oz. ham/1/2 c. beans	1 grilled cheese
1 slice toast/butter	1 oz. cornbread/butter	1 c. tomato soup
1/2 c. dry cereal	1/2 c. slaw	celery sticks
1/2 banana	1/2 c. greens	1/2 c. carrot salad
8 oz. milk	1 apple	1/2 c. coconut pudding
	8 oz. milk	8 oz. milk

WEEK 4

Breakfast	Lunch	Dinner
Monday		
1 fried egg	Hamburger/bun	1 c. tuna casserole
1 slice toast/butter	1 oz. french fries	1 c. green salad/
1/2 c. dry cereal	1/2 c. slaw	1 Tbs. dressing
1/2 orange	1/2 c. peaches	1/2 c. green beans
8 oz. milk	1/2 c. ice cream	1/2 c. pineapple
	8 oz. milk	8 oz. milk
Tuesday		
1 waffle/butter/syrup	3 oz. turkey/gravy	1 grilled cheese sand.
1 slice bacon	1/2 c. mashed potatoes	1 c. tomato soup
1/2 c. oatmeal	1/2 c. greens	4 crackers
4 oz. orange juice	1 biscuit/butter	1/2 c. carrot salad
8 oz. milk	1/2 c. peas	1/2 c. banana pudding
	8 oz. milk	8 oz. milk

Wednesday

1 scrambled egg	1 hot dog on bun	3 oz. roastbeef/gravy
1 biscuit/butter/jelly	½ c. baked beans	½ c. mashed potato
1 slice bacon	½ c. asparagus	½ c. peas
½ c. dry cereal	1 slice bread/butter	½ c. slaw
½ banana	1 slice cherry pie	1 slice bread/butter
8 oz. milk	8 oz. milk	½ c. ice cream
		8 oz. milk

Thursday

½ c. sausage gravy	Chicken salad	1 c. homemade beef
1 biscuit	sandwich	stew w/vegs.
½ c. hash browns	½ c. homemade veg.	1 biscuit/butter
½ c. oatmeal	soup w/crackers	½ c. carrot salad
4 oz. orange juice	1 oz. celery sticks	½ c. fruit salad
8 oz. milk	½ apple	8 oz. milk
	8 oz. milk	

Friday

1 scrambled egg	Fish sandwich/bun	BBQ on bun
½ Eng. muffin/butter	½ c. macaroni/cheese	1 oz. french fries
½ c. dry cereal	½ c. carrot salad	1 c. lettuce/dressing
½ banana	½ c. green beans	1 slice pie
8 oz. milk	½ c. ice cream/choc.	8 oz. milk
	8 oz. milk	

Saturday

1 fried egg	8 oz. chili/crackers	1 c. lasagna
1 slice bacon	2 oz. celery/peanut	1 slice garlic bread
1 biscuit/butter	butter	1 c. green beans
½ c. oatmeal	1 c. salad/dressing	½ c. slaw
4 oz. orange juice	2 × 2 sq. cake/icing	½ c. choc. pudding
8 oz. milk	8 oz. milk	8 oz. milk

Sunday

1 pancake/butter/ syrup	3 oz. Fried chicken	4 oz. slice pizza
1 slice bacon	½ c. sweet potatoes	1 oz. cheese sticks
½ c. dry cereal	½ c. spinach	1 c. green salad/
½ c. banana	½ c. apple salad	1 Tbs. dressing
8 oz. milk	1 hot roll/butter	½ c. ice cream
	1 slice pie	8 oz. milk
	8 oz. milk	

SNACKS

AM	PM	Bedtime
1 oz. pretzels	1 oz. cheese/4 crackers	3 cookies
4 oz. orange juice	8 oz. milk	8 oz. milk
4 oz. cheese/4 crackers	½ c. grapes	½ c. ice cream
8 oz. milk	8 oz. milk	8 oz. milk
3 cookies	1 oz. granola	½ apple
8 oz. milk	4 oz. orange juice	8 oz. milk
½ c. raisins	1 oz. raisins	1 krispie square
4 oz. apple juice	8 oz. milk	6 oz. apple juice
½ c. ice cream	1 oz. celery/carrot sticks	carrot/celery/dip
8 oz. milk	4 oz. apple juice	8 oz. milk
1 Tbs. peanut butter	1 Tbs. peanut butter	1 slice cheese
4 crackers	4 crackers	4 crackers
8 oz. milk	8 oz. milk	8 oz. milk
1 oz. granola	3 graham crackers	1 oz. granola
8 oz. milk	8 oz. milk	8 oz. milk

RECIPES

NUTTY PUTTY DANDY CANDY

1 c. nonfat dry milk powder
2 c. dry crispy breakfast cereal
½ c. raisins

1 c. honey or corn syrup
1 c. peanut butter

Measure out the dry milk powder, honey and peanut butter into a large bowl. Mix ingredients together thoroughly. Measure out raisins, add to mixture and mix well. Spread the dry cereal out on wax paper and roll the candy mixture in it to coat the outside. When the candy has been well coated, spread it out to about ¾ inch thickness. Cut candy into squares. You may wish to wrap each piece in wax paper if it is not going to be eaten immediately.

HONEY FRENCH DRESSING

1½ qts. oil
1 at. honey
¼ c. salt

1½ qts. vinegar
2 lb. 7 oz. sugar
¼ c. celery seed

1 qt. catsup
¼ c. paprika
½ Tbs. garlic powder

Blend all ingredients in a large mixer. Store in covered containers. Keep in refrigerator.

WALDORF RICE SALAD

2 qts. water
1½ lb. rice
1 Tbs. salt

Place boiling water in shallow pan. Add salt and rice. Cover tightly with foil. Bake at 350 degrees or steam at 5 lb. pressure for 30 minutes. Chill.

½ c. sugar
1 qt. celery, sliced
1½ c. chopped nuts

1½ qts. whipped
  topping
6 large red apples

1 qt. mayonnaise
2 c. raisins

Fold in whipped topping and sugar into mayonnaise. Fold in topping, celery, apples, raisins and walnuts into the chilled rice. Sprinkle with cinnamon before serving, if desired.

SPANISH HAMBURGERS

3 lbs. ground beef	2 c. bread crumbs	1 c. milk
4 Tbs. dried onion	salt to taste	

Mix meat mixture. Form into 18 patties.

28 oz. catsup	4 Tbs. chopped onions	1 c. water
4 Tbs. vinegar	4 Tbs. green pepper	1 c. sugar
4 Tbs. Worchestershire		

Combine sauce ingredients in pan. Bring to a boil. Gently put in patties. Simmer gently about one hour.

JOHNNY MARZETTI

3¾ lb. ground beef	¾ lb. noodles	⅓ chopped mango
¼ c. dry onions	1¼ Tbs. garlic powder	1¼ Tbs. salt
½ Tbs. pepper	23 oz. tomato soup	1 Tbs. oregano
23 oz. water	¾ lb. grated cheese	

Brown meat. Drain off excess fat. Cook noodles, drain, set aside. Add mango, onions, seasonings, soup and water to meat. Simmer mixture about 45 minutes. Add grated cheese. Add cooked noodles to meat mixture. **Note:** ⅔ of grated cheese may be used in recipe and remainder sprinkled on top during last 15 minutes of cooking time.

CHAPTER 11

INDIVIDUAL, GROUP AND FAMILY TREATMENT

JUDY MANNING KENDRICK

INTRODUCTION

The choice of who shall be the recipient of treatment for abuse and neglect of a child has much to do with the clinician's orientation, knowledge and beliefs about the problem. If one sees the child as a victim, needing protection and treatment, then it is likely the child will be the focus of intervention. Others may target the parent(s) and/or caretakers of the child, as those to whom service should be directed. Family intervention would be the treatment of choice for those who view the problem and its solution as being systemic in nature. The broader social network may also be involved in treatment, when the entire ecosystem is seen as contributing to and sustaining the problem. No one method of treatment is always correct, and oftentimes a combination of treatments is most effective.

In this chapter, a treatment model will be presented for individuals, groups and families. This model is not meant to be inclusive or exclusionary, but representative of some successful ways to approach the treatment of child abuse and neglect.

THE TREATMENT TEAM

The first person to be in contact with the child or family is the one who will set the tone for treatment, so when thinking about intervention, it must be appreciated that others may have already begun to work with the family prior to the clinician's involvement. Police, child welfare workers, teachers, nurses, doctors, lawyers, judges, day care personnel, family neighbors, etc., are all part of the treatment team that may be involved with the family. These may be people who are well versed in child abuse and neglect, skilled in risk assessment, and familiar with accepted and lawful procedures. They may also be people who have underestimated or overreacted to the situation. The family may have been subjected to treatment that has left them feeling angry, helpless and suspicious of those charged with providing treatment. The importance of a well-informed and trained team cannot be over emphasized.

Certainly, all are affected when confronted with children who have been hurt or ill-cared for. Children arouse the protective and nurturing instincts in all involved. It is natural to be sad or angry with those who do not protect and care for children. For these reasons it is vitally important that those charged in dealing with abuse and neglect have a good understanding of causation, as well as the potential of treatment, to ameliorate the problem.

Cooperation among the members of the treatment team is vital for successful resolution. Not only does this cooperation serve to support the treatment team, but also serves to engage the family in a more supportive and humane manner. Open communication between all those involved allows for more accurate sharing of information and goals, while narrowing the number of investigative contacts with the family. The facts need to be presented in an objective manner, despite sometimes strong subjective feelings. The reality is that objective evidence and observations are defensible and subjective opinions are not. Specific roles and purposes of all members of the treatment team need to be clearly defined and appreciated for their discrete role in the process. Child protective investigators and police are charged with uncovering the facts and often make difficult decisions in determining risk or prosecution. They are easy targets for others in the team. There needs to be an appreciation for the difficult decisions they are required to make on a daily basis, and a realization that those decisions are not free from error. Prosecution and adjudication of child abuse and neglect is also part of this team, and the reality is that many families would not receive treatment without the authority of the law mandating participation.

The clinician is likely not to be involved until some legal process has taken place. There may or may not be agreement on the manner in which a case was handled before it is referred for treatment, and the lack of appreciation for others' decisions about a case can present a serious impediment to treatment. Open communication between team members who have learned to work together helps to prevent conflict and allows for clinical treatment to begin more expeditiously.

In order for the team to work effectively together, efforts and time must be devoted to the development of a working relationship. Meetings and other contacts to discuss cases need to be built into schedules. Sharing of information regarding new knowledge and developments in the field of child abuse and neglect can serve to enhance skills as well as sustain commitment. Many workshops are now geared to all professions, and joint attendance helps to solidify the team approach.

PROGRAM MODEL FOR TREATMENT

The Comprehensive Family Life Education Program, (FLEP, 1984), was developed to respond to the demand for preventive and reunification services for abusive and/or neglectful families. Public Law 96-272 provided the mandate for these kinds of services to avert the need for placement of children outside their home and facilitate the reunification of families to avoid prolonged placement. The mission of the FLEP services is to meet this demand, thus avoiding the trauma of separation and reducing the costs for foster and institutional care.

The FLEP services and philosophy was modeled on programs like: The Saint Paul Project (1956), Families (1980) and Homebuilders (1977). The services offered through FLEP include:

1. Family counseling and case management provided by masters' level social workers who have advanced training in family therapy;
2. Monitoring and supervision by bachelors' level social workers;
3. Home education, homemaker and parent aid services, provided by a paraprofessional trained in child abuse and neglect;
4. Parent education classes, a four session group to cover the basic issues of discipline, child care, child development, protection and physical safety in a support group setting; and
5. Family advocate services, provided by trained volunteers to support and enhance the clients' efforts.

A family can receive one or all of these services, based on needs, but every family will have a counselor to supervise services and provide counseling when indicated, as well as perform the range of social work services. This might include enabling, advocacy, brokering and networking. Though the social workers have the title of family counselor, that may or may not be their primary function for a family.

The services are delivered with a frequency and intensity designed to meet an individual family's needs. One family may need only short-term counseling and parent education classes; another family may need the whole range of services, including counseling, seven day a week monitoring, home education, parenting classes and a volunteer family advocate. A family may need very intensive services for a time of crisis, and then less intensity. There is flexibility within the program to match service to needs.

The program is home-based, and the majority of service is provided in the client's home. The philosophy of the program has high regard for the integrity of the family and seeks to preserve its dignity, while seeking to promote health, growth and nurturance for children. The expectation is that most families, with education and support, can provide at least a minimally adequate environment for children to develop.

Homebuilders (1977) states that worker training begins at the attitudinal level, and FLEP subscribes to this belief. It begins with an awareness of the importance of the family and an acceptance that even the most dysfunctional families seek to provide for their members the basics of belonging, affiliation and nurturance, albeit in sometimes harmful ways. It is believed that separation of children from their families is usually more traumatic than living with their family, except in the most extreme life threatening circumstances. There is an understanding that services to families need to be delivered in the home using the milieu that is most comfortable for the family and which affords the clinician the most information for assessment and intervention.

This demands a shift for the clinician who is used to controlling their office environment. In the client's home, the family can provide distractions the clinician may find distressing. The resistance, however, is usually more blatant and therefore accessible. Issues regarding boundaries, alignments, etc., are more readily observable. Treatment can usually move more quickly in the client's own milieu.

There is also the message conveyed by visiting the client's home that says, "I am willing to reach out to you." One has to be willing to come often and stay long enough to allow the family to realize that this person will stay in there with them, through the rough times. Oftentimes, multi-problem families have succeeded in discouraging all forms of help which serves to reinforce for them the hopelessness of their problems and the inability of professionals to help them. The ability to join with the client in the home environment provides a firm foundation for a beneficial therapeutic alliance. This cannot be underestimated.

Melanie and I sat in her living/bedroom, interrupted at different times by one of her six children. It was my termination visit, and we were reviewing the progress Melanie had made in providing more stability and predictability for her children. She said, "You came every week and sat on my dirty couch." If called to define just why I was able to work with Melanie, I would have probably named some well-informed strategy on my part. But the client's alliance with me had more to do with my perceived acceptance of her, evidenced by sharing her couch.

ASSESSMENT

Assessment is probably the most critical piece of providing treatment to abusive and neglectful families. To overreact may mean needless separation of a family and to underact may place children in incredible danger. It is crucial that the clinician be knowledgeable about child abuse and neglect and cognizant of the incredible responsibility in assessing danger and risk. FLEP uses several tools in assessing problems and risks. The family interview, observations of parent/child interaction, hands on interaction with children, and paper and pencil instruments are all employed.

The family interview begins with the clinician's explanation of how he came to be involved, what his professional credentials and philosophies are, and how he might be able to help the family. The family needs a clear understanding of why the worker is there and what he may be able to do for them.

It is always useful to ask the family how they came to their present situation, what happened, when and where. It is usually not productive to ask why questions, as this may produce defensiveness. Let the family tell their story in their own way, as their perception of what has happened will usually identify if there is a denial of difference in regard to fact or responsibility. In talking about their problems, parents and children reveal much useful information about their situation, as well as how they live together. It can become very clear if there is a scapegoated or unfavored child, if the parent is in charge or overwhelmed with their responsibilities, and what stresses the family experiences. Experience dictates that the clinician originally accept the client's explanation of what the problem is and where it lies (inside or outside the family). This can be challenged later, when more information indicates other or additional problems.

On first meeting Darlene, she identified that she didn't have any problems with her kids. Her problem was her boyfriend's ex-wife, who kept reporting her to Child Protective Services. If she could get the ex-wife and CPS out of her life, she wouldn't have any problems. I empathized with how helpless she must feel when other people had so much control over her life, being careful not to deny her perception of the problem. I went on to talk about how difficult and challenging it is to raise kids even without people from the outside putting additional pressures on us. I talked about the incredible responsibility kids are and how little any of us are trained or supported in this difficult job. Darlene was finally able to say she could use some help in dealing with her children. As she came to trust me, we were able to work on a variety of issues, even though her initial stance did not indicate that she wanted or needed this kind of help.

In addition to the family's interpretation of the problem, there has usually been an investigation by Child Protective Services, and they have information about the family that is also useful in putting together a thorough evaluation. Other service providers the family may have been working with will also have input into the problem.

FLEP also uses a formalized risk assessment that resembles a checklist of problems. This assists the clinician in remembering to ask the important questions, and also serves as a cumulative tool to understand the complexity of the family's problems.

The Parent Stress Inventory (1983) and the CAP (1986) are two paper and pencil instruments that are also used to further assess risk and predict what type of intervention might prove most useful.

THE TREATMENT PLAN

After a thorough assessment, the clinician meets with the family to develop a treatment plan, or a contract for services. Problem areas are identified and goals to address the problems are agreed on. It is useful to make the goals as concrete and objective as possible, as well as realistic and attainable. This gives the family the greatest likelihood of success and therefore an increased sense of competence when they succeed. It is likely that by the time a family gets into treatment, they have accumulated a history of not being able to cope with, or solve their problems. There may be a strong feeling of learned helplessness, as the family was unable to successfully solve problems. Each failure built on previous failures, finally

TABLE XI-I
CHECKLIST OF FAMILY FUNCTIONS

Family Dynamics

SINGLE PARENT _____
CONFLICT INSIDE FAMILY _____
CONFLICT OUTSIDE FAMILY _____
BOUNDARIES: RIGID _____, LOOSE _____, CLEARLY DEFINED _____
GENERATIONAL BOUNDARIES: CLEAR _____, UNCLEAR _____
FINANCIAL PROBLEMS: YES _____, NO _____
EMOTIONAL PROBLEMS: YES _____, NO _____
UNEMPLOYMENT _____
HOUSING PROBLEMS _____
ALCOHOL AND/OR DRUG PROBLEMS _____
RETARDATION OF PARENTS _____
LITERACY _____
CRIMINAL PROBLEMS _____
DOMESTIC VIOLENCE _____
CUSTODY PROBLEMS _____
OTHER _____

Risks To Children

DISCIPLINE: HARSH _____, LACK _____, APPROPRIATE _____
EXPECTATIONS: REALISTIC _____, UNREALISTIC _____
KNOWLEDGE OF CHILD DEVELOPMENT _____
BONDED WITH CHILD/CHILDREN _____
NURTURING _____
HYGIENE _____
NUTRITION _____
PHYSICAL PROBLEMS _____
MEDICAL PROBLEMS _____
DEVELOPMENTAL PROBLEMS _____
SUPERVISION _____
CHILD CARE _____
SCHOOL PROBLEMS _____
CRIMINAL PROBLEMS OF CHILDREN _____
FREQUENCY OF CONTACT WITH PARENT(S) _____
EMOTIONAL PROBLEMS OF CHILDREN _____
OTHER _____

produces an attitude that reinforces the sense of being powerless to impact their lives. Setting achievable goals, helps the family to regain a sense of competence, until they gradually feel that they are able to confront problems toward resolution.

This is the stage of treatment we call overcoming the **yes butting**. Every suggestion is answered with "I already tried that, and it didn't work," or, "That might work for some kids, but mine are different." We confront the reality of not attempting to do anything and offer our support as new behaviors are tried.

In addition to identifying goals and methods to achieve them, it is also useful to put a time limit on treatment. This constrains both family and clinician to get to work and also does not seem completely overwhelming and intrusive. The family can look forward to being on their own. It must be understood that the length of their service commitment can also be shortened or lengthened, depending on circumstances or other events that impact treatment.

Sometimes an event will have brought the family to treatment that was situational or stimulated by a developmental phase. Several sessions with the family can open things up toward better understanding, and this may be all that some families need at a particular time to return to a homeostatic state that allows them to function.

> Tiffany's behavior had changed the year she began high school. She began running with a wild crowd and eventually became truant and was failing all her classes. Mother and dad had been divorced for six years and did not work together on behalf of the kids, in fact they used the kids to continue to fight with each other. Mom's frustration at being unable to control her usually compliant daughter resulted in a very abusive incident that required treatment. This brought the family's problem to the attention of the authorities and treatment was mandated. Mother and daughter responded well to counseling and mom also attended parenting classes. It became obvious that their previous level of functioning had been good and with increased awareness of better ways to communicate and discipline, they returned quickly to a functional unit. When there was another incident, where Tiffany violated the rules, mom was able to call me for a brief crisis intervention. As a result of our previous success in working together, she had somewhere to turn for help.
>
> This current uproar was seen by me as an attempt on Tiffany's part to get her mom and dad working together better, because she had involved him in this episode. I was able to have one session with mom, dad and Tiffany, where she was able to articulate how uncomfortable she was with their continued bitterness. They were all able to make their needs known and agreements were reached on how they would work together as parents. Tiffany was relieved to see them working together and said she felt she could now concentrate on "being a kid."

This is an example of a family who just needed a tune up. There were many issues that could have been worked on that would have involved long-term treatment, but the family's level of functioning was usually good. They were interested in and committed to brief therapy for the current crisis.

There are other families whose problems have been so chronic and ongoing that brief treatment is usually not possible. In fact, these may be families whose children are, or have been, removed from the home. These multi-problem families can present so many problems it is difficult to know where to begin. If indeed the problems are overwhelming to the clinician, one can only imagine how helpless the family must feel.

The service contract is a way to partialize the problems and identify a place to begin. Basic needs are a good starting place, because it would be foolhardy to attempt to work on discipline or communication if the family was so burdened trying to survive that they didn't even see these issues as problematic. Helping the family acquire needed resources to reduce stress is oftentimes the most helpful service that can be provided. This also makes the helping attempts of the clinician believable, because the help is more concrete and immediate. The relationship that develops as a result of being useful, tends to solidify the alliance and enhances the therapy that follows.

> Carrie was in danger of having her four children removed because of neglect and harsh discipline. She had written some bad checks and was also likely to face some criminal charges. She agreed to work with our program, rather than lose her children. We were providing monitoring and counseling services.
>
> Providing for her family's basic needs was one of the contract goals, and we discovered that Carrie had only paid a part of her monthly rent. She was on public assistance, so she had no means to pay the remainder, which meant there would be no home.
>
> In order to assure that housing would be maintained, we located a donor to pay the remainder of the rent. However, at the time we took this payment to the landlord, we devised an intervention to reinforce the seriousness of failing to provide for her family.
>
> My supervisor, the caseworker and myself planned a "good guy, bad guy" intervention. He was the bad guy who felt we should terminate services and pull out, because Carrie just couldn't make it. He painted a picture of her down the road, in jail, and all her children in foster care. He said that we should be providing our services to someone who could succeed, and that to waste our money on her was not good for our program or for her, because there was little likelihood of her succeeding.
>
> I said I disagreed with him and had been arguing with him about her potential to succeed. In fact we argued this in her presence. I said I felt change was difficult, and that new behaviors take time. I said I felt she

had the potential to succeed and that we needed to expect some backsliding.

The caseworker pleaded for the client, said she knew that she loved her kids, and asked us to stay involved.

The conclusion of this intervention was as we had expected. Carrie wanted to prove my supervisor wrong about her, and was encouraged by the caseworker's and my support. We were able to set up a very specific contract on this occasion and to build on the successes of these beginning goals. At the conclusion of services to this client, she had delivered her fifth child, maintained stable housing for a good period of time, was providing loving care for her children and finally went to work to provide better for her family. These successes occurred in steps and may not have been attained, had we not worked on the problems beginning with the most basic needs.

The service contract can be changed or added to as work progresses. It is useful to chart progress based on the assessment findings.

INTERVENTIONS

Family therapy is the primary treatment modality for the FLEP staff. There is an appreciation for the myriad of individual characteristics and difficulties that exist in the client population, but for the most part treatment is family focused.

Individual work is most often used when there is a single parent of children who are too young to engage in therapy. Some of the issues around which individual therapy with an adult might take place are: (1) abuse, sexual or physical, as a child or in adulthood; (2) parental abandonment or separation in childhood; (3) being the adult child of an alcoholic or violent family; (4) depression (with a psychiatric evaluation); and (5) dependency or relationship problems. When there is a chemical dependency or substance abuse problem, treatment for this is seen as primary to working on the parenting issues. When there is psychosis or other mental illness present, this is also seen as primary, and mental health services and medications must be maintained. Parents whose primary diagnosis is mental retardation need ongoing services from providers whose expertise is in the area of developmental services.

Children are targeted for individual therapy when it is deemed that they need treatment in addition to family therapy. Sometimes the child fears expression within the context of the family. In these instances, play therapy or therapeutic play may free them to express emotions that would be constrained in the family setting. It is the FLEP position, however, that individual treatment of the child, without family involvement, often leaves the child vulnerable to being a scapegoat for the family problems. Therefore, individual work may be indicated, but is usually done in conjunction with family work.

Group therapy is very useful in the treatment of abuse and neglect. It is recognized, however, that many parents who are abusive and neglectful are also very isolated socially and would not be ready for group work initially. It has been the FLEP experience, that after the family has come to know and trust the clinician, movement into a group is far less threatening. Experience would indicate that the group experience allows for much needed support and exchange of information, but the reality is that only the most highly motivated parents would select this modality as first choice.

Case examples are used to identify how different interventions are used and combined to treat some of the problems experienced by abusive and neglectful families.

Case 1: The C Family

The C Family was referred for treatment because of an abusive incident to the eight year old daughter, that came to the attention of the Child Protective Services. The mother was angry and frustrated with the child because she had been in trouble at school and brought home bad grades. The beating the child received left bruises. She was removed from the home temporarily while an investigation took place. The family was referred to FLEP and the mother to individual therapy at a Community Mental Health Center. The child was returned to the home and the mother agreed not to use physical punishment.

I set up an initial meeting with Mrs. C at her home. She was a bright woman from an Asian culture. When I asked her to tell me what the problems were, she responded in an open, often poignant manner. Mr. and Mrs. C had come to this country to make a better life for themselves and take advantage of the professional opportunities for their work. They had experienced many disappointments in this endeavor, and although they had been very creative in providing for themselves, their status was not what they had expected. This had created a high degree of stress in their lives. There was also a lack of social and familial supports for them.

They had dreams for their daughter, Missy, and wanted her to appreciate all the opportunities that were available to her. They placed great importance on obedience and education, thus Missy's misbehavior and lack of attention at school was shameful to them. It was also the domain of Mrs. C to provide the discipline for the child, and her knowledge of way to correct children were based on her own family of origin and a culture where children did not bring shame to their parents.

When you combined the high level of stress and the lack of knowledge about how to manage a child's behavior in a noncorporal way, the harsh physical punishment was almost inevitable. However, Mrs. C was sorry about the punishment, loved her daughter and was very eager to learn new ways to manage her behavior.

The individual therapy that Mrs. C was involved in was coming along well. Her therapist had a good understanding of the cultural issues and implications and was very supportive. Mr. C was not involved in this therapy, and politely declined my invitations to take part in our sessions. I would have liked his participation in order to spread out the parental responsibility for discipline and enforcing rules, because he enjoyed the role of "nice papa," but I realized my insistence on that could put Mrs. C in a difficult position.

I arranged to meet with Mrs. C alone three times and with her and Missy three times, as well as involve Mrs. C in FLEP parenting classes. The work with mother and daughter focused on identifying the three important rules, why they were important, and what the consequences would be if the rules were violated. It is my belief that even though it seems we have many rules, there are usually two or three things that are most important, and when these are not followed, we tend to get upset over everything. I also feel it is important that the rules and why they are important be spelled out clearly. This not only makes the rules public, but allows for some meaningful discussion about what is important to parents.

Mrs. C was able to identify two rules: (1) that Missy attend to her schoolwork and complete her assignments; (2) that Missy show respect for her parents by doing what she was asked. She explained the reasons for the rules and Missy expressed an understanding of their importance. I asked Missy for her opinion about what should happen if she violated these rules. She came up with suggestions about not getting to do fun things and we examined what those might be. Mrs. C agreed to take away privileges when the rules were broken. I let them know I would see how this worked and make suggestions or arbitrate if there were problems.

One of the advantages of getting parents and children together over an issue like rules is that the clinician has an opportunity to see how the family communicates and negotiates. In the process they may learn more about it and do more of it outside the therapeutic session. Another advantage is that there is an opportunity to assess the affective level of parent/child interaction. What I learned from Mrs. C and Missy was that they were able to talk openly with each other and that Missy did not fear her mother. The sharing that Mrs. C did about her own family history as she sought to explain herself was very important to their relationship.

In my individual sessions with Mrs. C, we worked on a variety of issues around being a parent as well as a person. Even though Mr. C was not present, I continued to emphasize how important it was for Missy to see her parents in agreement in regard to expectations and consequences for her behavior. She reported that he was being cooperative, and I had to rely on her taking the therapy to him.

The group experience of the parenting class seemed to help decrease Mrs. C's sense of isolation, in a social sense, as well as in sharing the challenges of raising children. She was able to take the alternative discipline techniques presented by the group leader and other parents, thereby increasing her discipline options. The group also served to normalize the frustrations of parenting, because she met many other parents who were experiencing difficulties with their children.

The C Family responded very well to relatively brief intervention. Their internal resources were good and they had a high degree of motivation to learn. This optimum climate is not always present, as the following case illustrates.

Case 2: The F Family

The F Family was referred for services after the children, aged two and four, were removed for neglect. Mrs. F was a single parent who had little stability in her life. She moved often, living with different people, and the children were often in an environment that included drugs and violence. After numerous reports, they were removed and placed in foster care.

When the case was first referred, I met with the mother, who was living with friends. She expressed that she loved her children and was committed to getting them back. She was very angry at the Welfare Department for taking her children and saw this as unjust. She had also sought treatment at a clinic for what she described as "bad nerves." They had prescribed medication as well as outpatient therapy. She went just often enough to get medication.

I saw her for several sessions, where she made some plans to get work and provide a home for the return of her children. She then failed to be home for out appointments, and eventually lost contact.

The case was reactivated when Mrs. F had gotten back with her former husband, the father of her oldest child. They had a place to live and said they wanted to provide for the children. The children were very bonded to both Mr. and Mrs. F, and the foster home placement was not good, so the children were returned. FLEP services of monitoring and counseling were started when the children returned.

The risks to the children were seen as: (1) lack of stability, and (2) a high level of conflict, within and outside the family, due to many people in and out of the home. We became very intrusive in their lives in an attempt to keep the environment as safe as possible for the children.

We met their family members, friends and acquaintances, and were continually aware of how dysfunctional the system was. Mr. and Mrs. F were ambivalent about our involvement and resented the intrusion, but they were aware that our presence allowed the children to be home. Mrs. F was needy and used the counseling time to talk about past experiences as well as asking for help in regard to current issues. She also used the monitor to help with resources and other immediate needs, but oftentimes was hostile to her presence.

I enjoyed the position of "good parent" with Mrs. F and was therefore able to confront some of the dysfunctional behavior in a way that did not elicit defensiveness or rebellion. I was doing a lot of re-parenting with her as I endeavored to make her more responsive to her own children's needs. The monitor was exclaiming one day that Mrs. F had said I taught her how to breathe. (I had taught her a deep breathing exercise in hopes of giving her more control over the panic and anxiety she continued to experience.) I realized that this was probably the only relationship Mrs. F had ever had with a functional person whom she perceived as being supportive and nurturing in an unconditional way. She learned that we would be there for her in a constant way, and she came to trust us.

Mr. F, on the other hand, went back and forth. I went to see the family one time when he was the only one there and he spent a lot of time talking about his childhood and what that experience was like for him.

Following this visit, he was not present for a couple of weeks. I think the experience of sharing those memories was frightening for him. He would also ask, "How long are people going to keep coming?" although he insisted that he did not mind our involvement.

The relationship between Mr. and Mrs. F slowly disintegrated. There was violence, drinking and drugs, as well as the reappearance of some bad characters in their lives. Mrs. F left the home with the children, and this move, coupled with the conflicting relationship, left the children increasingly vulnerable. Mrs. F was so emotionally distraught that at times she was not even attending to her children's basic needs. We also suspected she was abusing her prescription medication and only operating at a marginal level. During this time we encouraged her to use a local crisis shelter for the children to give herself some time to get herself together. It finally became clear that the potential risk to the children was too great to let things continue.

I agonized over planning an intervention that would force some movement. I realized that my relationship with her had never been challenged and that she trusted me. I also realized that I was being totally ineffective in producing change, so it did not matter that the relationship was good. In thinking about why change had not occurred, I tried to assess what the disadvantages or cost of change would be. When I began thinking about what change could mean for Mrs. F, I was able to plan an intervention based on the frightening nature of change.

I set up an emergency session at the DPW office. Mrs. F, the DPW caseworker, the FLEP monitor and Mrs. F's oldest child were present. I had told the caseworker and the monitor that I was going to reframe their behavior as "motherly," because the client was identifying them as critical or intrusive. I was going to take all the responsibility for lack of change, to avoid blaming the client and making her defensive.

When we assembled, I told Mrs. F how unusual it was for us to work with a family for six months and not have some change take place. I told her I had been trying to figure out what I was doing wrong. She jumped to my defense, but I insisted that I had not done my job. I told her it finally occurred to me what I was asking her to do be seeking change. I said, "I was asking you to give up everything and everyone." I went on, "I did not realize how dangerous change would be for you."

I pressed, asking if she had ever been lonely. She said she had, and I chastised myself for pressing change that I did not realize would probably leave her lonelier than she had ever been. I continued about how dangerous change would be and how inept I was for not being aware of this. I kept telling the caseworker and monitor how ineffective it was when they tried to "mother" her, and Mrs. F agreed that she did not need mothering. The reframing of their role stuck, which freed them up to be helpful instead of blamed or dismissed.

This session ended with Mrs. F asking that her children be placed in foster care, so that she could have time to get her life on a better track. I had a keen appreciation at this point of how vulnerable this request left her. All of her defenses were down and this request left the total responsibility for the decision with her. We were all aware of the cost of this honesty and that the people in her life would be unmerciful in their judgement of her. The only good identification of herself was in the role of mother, and she had voluntarily relinquished this role. It could be a long time before she was able to resume it.

I mention this case, because even with the few facts that I have provided, it is indicative of how difficult it can be to effect change. When change does not occur, I think it is the responsibility of the clinician to examine the cost of change for the client. We are oftentimes quick to blame the client and identify their behavior as resistant, when in fact we need to examine the costs and benefits, as perceived by the client. Looking at the level of dysfunction, it is easy to assume that the client will agree that change is better. However, even dysfunctional systems serve to meet the needs of their members because belonging to something may be preferable to belonging to nothing.

Case 3: The Q Family

The two Q Family children were at risk of being removed from the home because of extremely poor hygiene. The referral from the caseworker described the home conditions as deplorable. Living in the home was Mrs. Q, her sick and elderly mother, and two children, ages two and six.

The initial visit confirmed the caseworker's assessment of the home environment. I was not sure where to even sit, and the realization that people ate, slept and lived there was an assault on my values regarding minimum standards of cleanliness.

I discovered, however, when I began to explore where the hope for change might lie, that there was a great deal of caring and potential in this family. Mrs. Q was definitely lethargic and unmotivated at the present time, but her history revealed a woman who was capable of functioning at a much higher level. The immediate concern was the hygiene and I explored whether she was aware of the conditions and whether she wanted to do anything about them. I remember thinking, as I looked around, that it would be simpler to just vacate this home and begin somewhere else. That was my frustration in trying to figure out where to even start on the home. However, it became clear that the house, its location and space, was very important to Mrs. Q. I told her about the services we could offer and she said she could use them all. I arranged for the home educator and monitor to meet with her.

I was honest with the home educator and monitor about the condition of the home, and the home educator solved the problem about where to begin by picking a room in which to start, so that she was not overwhelmed. The family monitor was new to the program, and although energetic and committed, was not prepared for what she encountered on her first visit. Her purpose on that visit was to work on financial planning. However, the family all had the flu and diarrhea. The youngest child was not wearing a diaper or panties, so her feces was all over the floors of the house. I'll never forget her graphic description of that visit. Welcome aboard!

There were many frustrations for the workers with this family, and we spent a lot of staffing time supporting each other as we searched for the small gains that indicated improvement. There always seemed to be some backsliding that frustrated progress.

The home educator called me from the Q Family home one evening. She had gone for her visit and Mrs. Q had left town for the day with the youngest child. She found Mrs. Q's mother and the oldest child upset and worried. She went to work preparing dinner for them and engaged the child in doing homework and preparing for school the next day. When she left, they were relaxed and ready for bed. We later found out that Mrs. Q returned late that evening.

This family did eventually move into more suitable housing and hygiene was greatly improved. As that became less problematic, Mrs. Q began job training and got involved with a very supportive network. Her affection for her children was never an issue, but she became much more attuned to their physical needs. By the time she attended parenting classes, two months after initiating service, she was at a point where she was able to articulate her difficulties and give hope to other members of the group.

The Q Family is an example of a case where the counselor is only minimally involved in direct service. The greatest challenge here was in supporting the other team members and helping to devise strategies to overcome obstacles. We realized during the course of service that we were moving too fast for the client, and she let us know by her behavior to slow down. We need to pay attention to the pace at which change can happen, and realize that the client is the best judge of what they can deal with.

We know that families who abuse or neglect their children are almost always under stress. We feel the stress in the short time we are with the family and can only imagine what it must be like to live with the constant pressure some families are enduring. Sometimes if pressure can be relieved in one area of their lives, it helps to lessen the load, so they can begin to attack other problems.

Case 4: The B Family

Mrs. B is the single mother of two young children, ages two and four. There has been much chaos in her life, including the recent molestation of her children. The children are wild, and her threats and inconsistent discipline are doing little to improve their behavior. We know we can teach Mrs. B to use some behavior management techniques that will allow her to have better control over her children and find the role of mothering more rewarding. However, it is difficult to get her attention in the midst of all the craziness. We arrange for the children to attend a half-day program at a neighborhood center. This allows Mrs. B to have some quiet time and gives us the opportunity to work on a behavioral program. The added benefit is that the children have an opportunity to be in a structured environment, which makes it easier for mom to provide structure. This is only a beginning for Mrs. B, but it does reduce one stress which allows for work to begin on some of the other problems.

Case 5: The J Family

Mrs. J's mother was living with her husband and children. She had been extremely abusive to Mrs. J, and I suspected with Mrs. J's children. I determined that there would be little likelihood of the J Family providing a better environment for their children as long as grandmother remained in the home. I felt she would continue to undermine my efforts and keep the home in an uproar.

Our initial work focused on the need for adult children to have their own household, rather than identifying grandmother as a problem. Income supports were arranged to facilitate independent living and the transition was treated as a right of passage, rather than getting grandma out. There was still a lot of guilt and feelings of rejection to be reckoned with, but the task was accomplished. Work then proceeded with the parents in control of their home. Grandmother was no longer there to be used as a scapegoat or as an excuse for lack of progress. The responsibility clearly became the parents', and it was their choice whether or not to provide good care for their children.

Although we try to avoid encouraging parents to make a choice between a significant other person and their children, the reality is that the behavior of a person or the nature of the relationship can put children at considerable risk. An attempt is always made to engage the entire system, but if a person who is determined to be a threat to the child's well-being will not participate in treatment, the changes of maintaining the family unit are significantly reduced. I do not believe we can force someone to make a choice, but we are certainly called to be candid in telling a parent of our concerns about the impact of a person on the life and well-being of their children. Sometimes a parent will elect to maintain a relationship that is threatening to their children, and that is their right. However, it is our responsibility to inform the court and welfare system of our concern.

This case is illustrative of the use of power and authority in the relationship between client and clinician. To deny the power is a sham, because as clinicians we are called on to render opinions and recommendations that have great impact on families. Power is present in the client/therapist relationship in child abuse and neglect cases, and can be used to initially engage a client, as well as keep them working. This is, however, the flip side of power that can become destructive. We often impact access of parents in regard to their children, and it may be tempting to use that access to coerce parents to comply with our suggestions or demands. The relationship of parent and child is so vital, that we ought never to make the maintenance of that relationship a reward or punishment. The only time that relationship should be interrupted is when there is clear and present risk to children. In using our power and authority appropriately, a parent can learn more appropriate ways to use the power and authority in the parent/child relationship.

Issues and strategies for each family are different. There is no perfect solution to the problems that impact families in regard to abuse and neglect. However, it is helpful to be aware of interventions that are commonly used by FLEP workers.

Behavior Management Training

Discipline is probably the number one concern of all parents, and every FLEP family receives information on age appropriated, nonphysical ways to manage undesired behavior and encourage desirable behavior. Our policy is never to condone or encourage hitting children.

Parents are encouraged to identify the important rules in their family (usually less than five), make sure that everyone knows the rules and finally, to plan in advance what the consequences are for violating the rules.

It is our experience that parents need a lot of support and reinforcement in attempting to use new discipline techniques. It is a retraining process for the parents as well as the children.

Assertiveness Training

Abusive and neglectful families are not likely to be assertive in very useful ways. Parents may say, "I try all the time to be in charge, but my children never listen to me." What that may mean is that the parent does a lot of talking and yelling, but because of a lack of action or follow through, the children ignore the parent.

We emphasize the activist role of a parent. It is a demanding job and cannot be done from the arm chair. The smaller a child, the more hands-on work is required. A small child cannot just be told not to do something, he must be removed from the offense as he is told. Distractions must be offered. Parents are encouraged to understand that the child is not out to make their life miserable because he is curious.

The earlier in a child's life that a parent can become assertive in the parental role, such as making demands and following through, the more manageable a child will be because they can depend on their parents to be parents. Children will continue to challenge their parents as they increasingly exert their independence, but they seem comforted to know that their parents will set the necessary limits.

Assertiveness training is also useful for parents beyond the parental role. It can help them to be more demanding in what they expect from others in intimate, social and business relationships. Being assertive in asking for what you want and refusing to accept bad treatment can only help to enhance a person's sense of power and competency. The more competent a person feels, the more they can accomplish. So, this is an important intervention.

Modeling

Rather than just tell someone to do something, FLEP workers model behaviors they want clients to try. Instead of saying, "You've got to protect your child from danger," the worker will remove an unsafe object from the child's reach. The worker will talk to the child using tone and words that she would like the parent to use. By actually modeling good interaction with a child, the parent sees the new way of relating. It also enables the worker to appreciate the frustration of the parent in dealing with a difficult child.

Modeling also extends beyond the parent/child system into the large environment. Oftentimes our families are the most vulnerable, and taken advantage of by landlords or merchants. As workers negotiate and advocate for a client, the client observes new ways to approach problems. The more the client is present as we advocate in their behalf, the greater the likelihood he/she will be able to model the behavior at another time.

Problem Solving Training

If parents could pass on one skill that would allow children to lead productive lives, it would probably be the ability to deal effectively with problems. The ability to recognize when something is wrong, identifying the options in dealing with it, and recognizing when outside help is needed, are real survival skills. What happens in families where there are multiple problems is that they usually come from families that did not have good problem solving skills, and therefore, in an attempt to deal with difficulties, they create more problems.

It can seem overwhelming to a worker when there are problems with many areas of a family's life. There may be school problems, housing problems, financial problems, legal problems, criminal problems, etc., all in one family. By picking out one problem to work on initially, the family and worker are able to remain focused. Oftentimes, none of the available options is attractive, but doing nothing is less attractive and more problematic.

Most families have developed survival skills that have enabled them to meet their basic needs. It is important when we work on solving problems with the family that we do not just dismiss their present skills, but expand and refine them. It is amazing to learn of the ingenuity families have developed in order to cope and survive. We may see this and judge their efforts critically, when indeed, considering the circumstances, it required wit to develop some of the strategies. Their attempts at survival also reinforce for us the incredible lengths some families will go to in order to maintain the family.

Communication

There is often an assumption that because we are verbal, we communicate. What is astounding in working with families is how little direct communication takes place. Enhancing communication skills is an important intervention that is used with most families we treat.

Encouraging the use of "I" messages, instead of the judgmental "you" is useful and is a skill that can be modeled by the clinician. Parents are asked to become aware of how often they say things like, "you are an inconsiderate kid not to let me know where you are." Parents are encouraged to use more direct messages like, "I've been worried about where you were, and it's important to me that I know where you are." The first response is blaming and does little to inform the child of a parent's concern. The second message is more accurate in letting the child know the parent's concern and need.

Family sessions are wonderful places for families to learn and practice new and more direct communication. Blaming and incongruent messages can be rephrased. Family members can learn that it is safe to ask for what they want and need, even if it is something as simple as attention. Messages can be rephrased. Messages that are unclear or double binding can be explored. Because it is observable and immediate, communication problems are readily accessible and workable within the family sessions. Paying attention to a family's communication patterns gives the clinician useful information as well as an immediate place to intervene.

Focus on Family Strength

If we spent half as much time focusing on the healthy aspects of a family as we do identifying pathology and problems, we might be able to be more hopeful about their potential to change. We know that improvements will not come from the pathology, but from the goodness. Granted it is sometimes challenging to identify strength in the midst of chaos, but we believe if we are going to survive and be helpful to the family, it is vital to know what is right with them. This not only serves to make us more hopeful about a family's potential, but also allows the family to look at more positive aspects of themselves.

Because we are hopeful about the capacity of the families we work with to change, we can have a positive impact on others with whom they interact. I remember an attorney called one day who was representing the parents of a family where the children were in placement. As I began to talk about my experience with the family, she breathed an audible sigh and said, "I was dreading even calling you, because everyone has such a pessimistic view of these folks, and although I do not share that view, I was afraid you'd just be someone else who didn't believe they could succeed." It seems that everyone is anxious to share the bad news and labels that seem to follow families with problems. However, as people begin to hear another view of the problems and potentials, they can often become more hopeful and supportive of the family.

Support

This is an intervention strategy for the families as well as the staff who work with them. I always ask families if anyone ever told them they were doing a good job with their kids before they got in trouble. The answer is almost always no. Raising children is probably the most important job any of us will ever do, and yet we are expected to do it without training and with very little support. It is almost unacceptable to admit we do not know what we are doing as parents and even worse to say that sometimes we do not like doing it. And yet, the reality is that most of us are frustrated at times with the incredible demands of our children, and we wonder why we opted to become parents. Usually, the joys and fulfillment keep us engaged in our role as parent, but imagine how difficult it might be to function in this role if we had the stresses that some parents live with day in and day out.

We need to make it okay to say, "Yes, it is rough, and I need help," and to offer services to educate, encourage and support parents. I am always taken with the supportive atmosphere of the FLEP parenting classes. The participants are so relieved to know they are not the only people who have problems in caring for their children. They are also relieved to know there is no magic formula that is used by others to succeed at the tasks, but is somehow unknown to them. Increasing awareness of the needs of children and learning new ways to meet their needs is so much more effective in a supportive, nonjudgemental setting.

A supportive clinical staff serves to support and sustain workers engaged in treatment of abuse and neglect. Working outside the office means there is usually no one immediately available with which to share successes and frustrations. The team approach that FLEP uses helps to offset the feeling of being alone "out there". We also have a weekly, three hour staffing, where we can come together to talk about new cases and to share our problems and joys. We share a common commitment to the work we are doing and a respect for each other's knowledge and experience. This affords us our own consulting team to support each other as well as brainstorm creative strategies. The staff's needs are important if we are to work on behalf of our clients, therefore, time is allocated to support ourselves and each other.

Environmental Therapy

It would be futile to close this chapter without including one of the most important aspects of treatment, the societal problems that impact families and serve to put children at risk. We all have ideas about changes that would make the environment safer for children, and we who work with child abuse and neglect have a responsibility to advocate for them.

Income supports for families to adequately care for their children need to be expanded, so that increasing numbers of children are not reared in poverty and all the problems it creates. We pretend to be a nation who cares about children, and yet we are reluctant to provide the necessary social programs that will insure their development. Income does influence the care that children receive. We all know there are children who are being poorly supervised because there is not adequate subsidized child care for the working poor. We know there are families who are living in unsafe housing because they can afford no better. We must advocate for better conditions for families.

We live in a country that condones violence toward children. As recently as 1975, the U.S. Supreme Court in **Wright vs. Ingram** said we can use corporal punishment on children in schools. Adults in any segment of society are afforded more protection against violence than our children. As long as hitting children is an acceptable form of discipline, children will be hurt and killed because the hitting went too far. If indeed we believe that hitting children is an effective means to control their behavior (and I've never seen this evidence), then let us issue a cattle prod with the take home bag from the maternity ward. That way we can issue a jolt that can be measured and that can not kill. This may sound absurd, but hardly so when compared to the human hand or fist, which is not moderated by efficient controls. Mandating humane treatment for children is an issue that cannot be ignored by clinicians or others dealing with abused and neglected children.

In summary, treatment begins at the onset of identification of the problem. Working cooperatively as a member of the treatment team not only leads to more effective treatment, but helps to sustain those involved. Regardless of the conceptual framework that influences clinical practice, a good understanding of the dynamics of child abuse and neglect is vital to an amelioration of the problem. And finally, advocating for policies and programs that will prevent child abuse and neglect is essential.

REFERENCES

1. Abidin, R. R.: *Parenting Stress Index (PSI)*. Charlottesville, Pediatric Psychology, 1983.
2. Brit, C.: Family centered project of St. Paul. *Social Work, 1:*41–47, 1956.
3. Family Life Education Program: *Visiting Nurse Service*. Indianapolis, 1984.
4. Home-based family centered services, a basic view (eighteen minute slide/sound presentation). In Bryce, M. E. and Lloyd, J. C. (Eds.): *Home-Based Family Centered Services*. 1980.
5. Kinney, J. M., Madsen, B., Fleming, T., and Haapala, D.: Homebuilders: keeping families together. *Journal of Clinical and Consulting Psychology, 45:*667–673, 1977.
6. Milner, J. S.: *Child Abuse Potential Inventory (CAP)*. Webster, Psytec, 1986.

CHAPTER 12

PSYCHOLOGICAL MALTREATMENT
MEANING AND PREVENTION

PAUL A. TURGI
STUART N. HART

INTRODUCTION

This chapter addresses the psychological maltreatment of children as a highly pernicious and insidious form of child maltreatment responsible for detrimental long-term consequences. It stresses the imperative necessity for the development and implementation of prevention policies and programs.

Physical and sexual abuse are understood more easily, and consequently the need to rectify the situation is readily perceived. Greater public awareness, pictures of children with bruises, burns, and casts, and our pre-existing cultural mores relative to sexual exploitation of children, are sufficiently convincing. Psychological maltreatment typically is rarely susceptible to this type of instant recognition with a few exceptions, including cases of involuntary and prolonged confinement (see Corson and Davidson, 1987 for additional examples).

The chapter has five sections which cover: (1) specific definitions and associated problems in definition development, (2) relevant theoretical perspectives, (3) conceptualizing the child's world of psychological maltreatment, (4) prevention of psychological maltreatment, and (5) the parent, child, and sociocultural stressors as primary targets for intervention.

Many children incur a seriously detrimental level of psychological maltreatment on a daily basis. The devastating effects result in dysfunctional behaviors and attitudes for the victim which may interfere with successful development throughout the life span. Protection and intervention for these child victims is almost nonexistent. Only woefully blatant cases receive attention through coercive intervention by a court (Corson and Davidson, 1987).

Because budgets are strained to the extreme and caseloads are impossibly high, child protection service programs, workers, and their attorneys, generally refuse to move against cases based solely on psychological maltreatment. Legal definition issues and insufficient usable evidence relegate most cases unprovable under present judicial requirements. Consequently, the cases are viewed as a fruitless use of valuable time.

A situation such as a mother putting a diaper on her ten year old, bedwetting son and tying him by a leash to the clothesline, is a blatant act of psychological maltreatment. It would likely bear the necessary burden of proof for a court of law, especially if witnesses are available for court testimony. However, the majority of psychological maltreatment is more subtle and insidious; but very powerful, and strongly negative in its influence on children's lives.

Budgets, caseloads, definitions, evidence, and treatment problems may prove to be too serious a quagmire to expect any comprehensive and satisfactory level of corrective treatment in the foreseeable future. Prevention of psychological maltreatment provides a more promising alternative.

Economic factors provide additional rationale for the intervention and prevention of psychological maltreatment. Society incurs a severe economic drain from dysfunctional families, juvenile delinquency, and adult criminal behavior. It is probable that a multitude of individual and social problems, (e.g., aggression, theft, substance abuse, truancy, adolescent runaways, spouse abuse and suicide) are produced by child maltreatment.

The need for prevention and intervention of child psychological maltreatment is a pressing national problem. However, psychological maltreatment receives minimal attention from the professional community as well as the public, vis-a-vis the emphasis given physical and sexual abuse. Ironically, psychological maltreatment appears to be more prevalent and generally more detrimental than other forms of maltreatment (Hart and Brassard, 1987).

PERSPECTIVE OF PSYCHOLOGICAL MALTREATMENT

Psychological maltreatment is recognized as a universal detrimental component in child abuse (Hart and Brassard, 1987; Navarre, 1987). It can be considered from two perspectives: (a) as the core component of most physical and sexual maltreatment (Hart, Germain, and Brassard, 1987; Navarre, 1987), and (b) as a discrete form of maltreatment (Garbarino, Guttman, and Seeley, 1986; Hart, Germain, and Brassard, 1987).

Psychological maltreatment, whether a component of, or separate from physical and sexual abuse, appears to produce a spectrum of short and long-term harmful effects to the child (Hart, Germain, and Brassard, 1987). These effects are expressed in dysfunctional behaviors, and juvenile and adult criminal behaviors, including, but not limited to age inappropriate or unrealistic fears, enuresis, social retardation, failure to thrive syndrome, depression, impaired memory, runaway behavior, conduct disorders, prostitution, aggression, suicide, and homicide (Hart, Germain, and Brassard, 1987).

Authors' Perspectives

The knowledge base on the psychologically victimized child continues to expand. This combined with increasing sophistication relative to psychological maltreatment yields a clearer indication of its pervasive nature and the serious, long-term harm inflicted upon the victims.

Characterizing psychological maltreatment as the central component in maltreatment, allows for theoretical speculation. To wit: from an intergenerational perspective, psychological maltreatment may be considered as the primary causal agent for all forms of child maltreatment. If this is accepted, prevention of psychological maltreatment will be a keystone in breaking the intergenerational cycle of all forms of child maltreatment. Obviously, this position cannot be established through cause and effect evidence. Even so, the authors believe it to be the central etiological component for child maltreatment, and that psychological maltreatment will be recognized as such in time.

THEORETICAL PERSPECTIVES

Kurt Lewin has commented that there is nothing so useful as a good theory (Polansky, 1986). In the case of psychological maltreatment, many theories have value, particularly to guide explanation, prediction, program design and implementation. The theoretical perspectives of basic human needs, child development, and ecological systems are particularly relevant. These theories are to be examined individually in this section.

Basic Human Needs Perspective

The satisfaction of basic human needs is recognized as a significant contributor in the adequate psychological development of the human being (Gil, 1987; Maslow, 1970). Maslow's (1970) well-known hierarchy of human needs delineates an ascending order in which the satisfaction of physical and lower level psychological needs is necessary before the higher order needs can be met. Gil (1987) adds perspectives on the fulfillment of basic human needs. He views institutional abuse as the failure of society's social institutions, policies, and practices to fulfill the intrinsic needs of its members. Gil (1987) lists several human needs "essential to healthy development":

1. Regular access to life sustaining and enhancing goods and services.
2. Meaningful social relations, and a sense of belonging to a community involving mutual respect, acceptance, affirmation, care, and love.
3. Meaningful and creative participation in accordance with one's innate capacities, and stage of development in productive processes of one's community and society.
4. A sense of security, derived from continuous fulfillment of needs for life sustaining and enhancing goods and services, meaningful relations, and meaningful participation in socially valued productive processes.
5. Becoming all that one is capable of becoming, or, in Maslow's terms, self-actualization through creative, productive work (. . . Maslow, 1970), (Gil, 1987, p. 161).

Gil contends that to significantly reduce or eliminate institutional (human) abuse, the satisfaction of these basic needs is necessary. To implement the fulfillment of those needs, necessitates a major societal redirection; a change from an inegalitarian, competitive society, to an egalitarian cooperative society.

Developmental Perspective

The developmental perspective recognizes the child as a developing entity who progresses through several differentiated critical stages during childhood and adolescence. Specific stages of development are suggested to be more susceptible to particular types of maltreatment than other stages (Egeland and Erickson, 1987; Rosenberg and Germain, 1986); and what is judged to be abusive treatment of an infant may not be considered to be abusive treatment of an adolescent and vice versa.

For example, parental activity such as emotional unresponsiveness toward the child may be far more detrimental to the infant than to the adolescent (Erickson and Egeland, in press) because of the different developmental issues or challenges facing the victims of those periods.

Garbarino, Guttman, and Seeley (1986) have responded to the problem of defining psychological maltreatment by developing categories of psychological maltreatment, and delineating abusive acts within those categories relative to impact upon a stage of development. The developmental stages applied are infancy, early childhood, school age, and adolescence.

Ecological Perspective

The ecological perspective applied to child abuse was formulated by Garbarino (1977) as an adaptation of the ecological perspective developed by Bronfrenbrenner (1979). The ecological perspective in child abuse recognizes a multiple factor etiology that includes levels of environmental impact from a broad to a narrow focus, and various vectors that impinge upon these levels to produce the abusive environment.

The child as the base level is seen as a unit that functions within the environmental level of the family. The family is seen as a unit that functions within the level of the community, which in turn is perceived as a unit functioning within a regional or national culture.

The vectors are those abusive influencers that impact the maltreated child. Vectors can originate from a broad base such as a cultural or subcultural (e.g., religious or ethnic) set of attitudes toward parental expectations for children, or a narrow focus such as parent psychopathology, or somewhere in between such as poverty level finances. The ecological approach sees child abuse as a problem whose solution depends upon attention to multiple factors on multiple levels of influence (Garbarino, Guttman, and Seeley, 1986; Navarre, 1987).

Additional Theoretical Considerations

An important emerging theoretical perspective conceives psychological maltreatment as a major etiological basis for development of psychopathology or maladaptive deviancy, including juvenile delinquency and adult criminal behavior (Hart, Germain, and Brassard, 1987).

Levy (1986) has stated that after ruling out organic factors, child abuse is the etiological basis for most serious child psychopathology. Other authors, researchers, and practitioners agree that child abuse is a major contributor to the development of psychopathology (Coons, 1986; Egeland and Sroufe, 1981; Egeland, Sroufe and Erickson, 1983; Green, 1983; Hart and Brassard, 1987; Martin and Beezley, 1977; Bowlby, 1979; Miller,

1983; Rieker and Carmen, 1986; Sroufe, 1979; Steele and Pollack, 1974; Steele, 1986).

Strong connections between child abuse and delinquency have been noted. Steele (1981) reports on several studies of juvenile offenders who were interviewed just after they were apprehended and booked by the police. The studies indicated that between 76% and 85% of the subjects had a history of being abused or neglected. One study found that, "92 percent had been bruised, lacerated, or fractured by a parent within the year and a half previous to the pickup" (p. 96).

Coons (1986) in a review on the psychiatric problems associated with child abuse concludes that expert opinion agrees that child abuse is linked to juvenile delinquency and adult criminal behavior. The implications of recognizing child abuse as an etiological basis for psychopathology, juvenile delinquency, and adult criminal behaviors, should give direction to diagnosis and treatment, and most importantly, to promoting the prevention of child maltreatment.

CONCEPTUALIZING THE PSYCHOLOGICALLY MALTREATED CHILD

It is necessary to provide perspectives on psychological maltreatment in order to have a reasonable sense of the experience from a child's point of view. Following are sections describing: (a) **messages received** by the child, and (b) a child's life as a prisoner of psychological war to provide these perspectives.

Messages Received

When considering whether psychological maltreatment has occurred or is occurring, one needs to consider what message the child is receiving. Parents deliver many messages to their children. Some are intentional, such as is the case when a mother or father who had no desire for a child, convey that message by constantly sending the child out of the room and only interacting with the child to maintain his physical safety.

At other times, messages are unintentional, and may be diametrically opposite to a parent's intent. For instance, a parent with positive intent who feels it is necessary to improve a child's level of performance and responsibility in a task of chore, may consistently point out to the child what is wrong with the child's performance, and devote little or no attention to how much of the task the child has successfully completed.

Over time, consistent emphasis on what is wrong, easily results in the message that the child can never do anything right.

This persistent style of negative parental interaction may cause the child to give up in hopelessness, thinking, "what's the use, why try, I can never do anything right. I can never please them anyway." Obviously this can lead to feelings of low self-esteem, a lack of self-confidence and feelings of incompetence.

Some messages are as blatantly obvious as those sent by the mother or father who had no desire for a child. Their "go away kid, we don't want you," is clear. Others are subtle. The parent who only responds to the child with encouragement or praise when the child has done something exceptional, sets this child up for believing that he must do something exceptional to be worthwhile. This could be a tough burden to carry through life, and could be powerfully influential in shaping the reality of the individual as a child and an adult. The **messages received** by a child is the critical criterion in determining the effect the parental activity has on the child (Garbarino, 1980; Navarre, 1987).

Some parental actions, patterns, or statements are readily recognized as being almost universally detrimental to children. Cross-cultural research by Rohner and Rohner (1980) has established parental rejection to be universally detrimental in its wide variety of forms. More recently, Baily and Baily (1986) reported on a study designed to operationalize the definitions of child psychological maltreatment. The study used researchers and practitioners to delineate and concur on the actual types of situations and actions that embody psychological maltreatment. In addition to fulfilling the primary task, the participants responded in the majority that the message transmitted and typically received in relation to this set of operational definitions is so universally clear and destructive that regardless of the degree of the established effects on the child, these actions should be considered as acts of psychological maltreatment sufficient to meet the burden of proof necessary for establishing **mental injury** in a court of law.

Appreciation of the viewpoint of messages received is essential to conceptualizing the emotional and cognitive impact of psychological maltreatment upon the world of the child.

Childhood Environment; Prisoners of War

The abused child lives in a dangerous, stressful environment. Some experts (Benedek, 1985; Green, 1983; Rieker and Carmen, 1986) have drawn the comparison between the behaviors exhibited by abused children and those individuals manifesting the symptoms of posttraumatic stress disorder.

Benedek (1985) explains that posttraumatic stress disorder is a concept used to explain dysfunctional psychological reactions to encounters with violent, highly stressful situations such as attack, and natural disasters. It has evolved from the study of adult victims of acute psychological trauma. Recently, posttraumatic stress disorder has been recognized as occurring in children, but still far too few professionals have made the connection, especially with abused children (Benedek, 1985). Benedek has also postulated that posttraumatic stress disorder is the primary mechanism explaining child abuse as the etiological basis for the dysfunctional psychological sequelae manifested by abused children.

Relative to the posttraumatic stress disorder, the environment of the abused child has been described as similar to a combat zone such as in the Vietnam War (Rieker and Carmen, 1986). This characterization is designed to relate the difficult and traumatic living conditions of abused children.

But the family dynamics in severe cases of psychological maltreatment, produce a living environment for the child that is more similar to living as a prisoner of war. The child living in a psychologically abusive environment may be considered a captive (Segal and Yahraes, 1979), who is unable to avoid the psychologically pernicious conditions of degradation, terrorization, severe unpredictability, and isolation. Like the prisoner of war, s/he may not know from minute to minute whether to expect reasonable or harsh treatment. The child may also be subjected to extreme threat or fear through terrorization or made to endure degrading conditions and verbal attacks.

The parallel is applicable to the resultant effects of the maltreatment. Aberrant, and deviant antisocial behaviors frequently develop as a consequence of captivity as a prisoner of war, and as a captive, maltreated child. The prisoner of war will typically adopt **survival** behaviors in order to maintain himself physically and psychologically. Lying, cheating, stealing, insensitivity, brutality of others and self, aggressiveness, and withdrawal are a few of the common reactions to the environmental stresses imposed by psychologically brutal captivity during warfare.

The maltreated child develops similar **survival** behaviors (Lindberg and Distad, 1985; Rieker and Carmen, 1986) to withstand and copy with detrimental captivity. Hart, Germain, and Brassard (1987) have developed an extensive list of sequelae, with references, attributed to general and psychological maltreatment of children. Rieker and Carmen (1986) explain, "The psychological strategies that once ensured survival now form the core of the survivor's (child's) psychological illness."

Once a prisoner of war is released, he or she has at least four distinct advantages over the psychologically abused child. First, the ex-POW's environmental situation is usually a change for the positive. Once beyond the power of captivity, the POW is able to reflect back to earlier life experiences—experiences which may provide a more positive background supported by values, mores, societal expectations, and at least a semblance of appropriate, nonaberrant behaviors.

This provides a frame of reference enabling the individual to discriminate between the aberrant behaviors adopted for survival in a prisoner of war situation, and those behaviors appropriate for normal social interaction.

The psychologically maltreated child however, may have no such references depending upon the child's age and previous experiences at onset of the maltreatment. The child may have no idea his behaviors are aberrant adaptations to atypical living conditions. To the maltreated child, his experiences and environment are reality. The behaviors become an integral part of that reality.

Second, during the genesis of a POW's survival behaviors, the POW is not passing through critical stages of childhood development; as is the child. The maltreated child is developing and using aberrant survival behaviors as reality while simultaneously growing through critical stages of fundamental personality development. During these critical stages the child may incorporate what he considers normal (survival) behaviors and attitudes as integral parts of his personality. These personality characteristics will be manifested through childhood, through adolescence, and into adulthood, unless some personal realization or external intervention acts to initiate a change in behaviors and/or attitudes.

Third, the POW can understand the reasons for aversive treatment because the attacker is the enemy. This offers cognitive explanation for the maltreatment. The child is not allowed this cognitive necessity. The child may be profoundly confused because the attacker (parent) is supposed to love the child. The parent is supposed to be at least the one person in the world capable of loving the child, yet is the very person inflicting the maltreatment.

It is no wonder the typical maltreated child manifests low self-esteem, distrust, and other aberrant, survival behaviors (Green, 1978; Hart, Germain, and Brassard, 1987; Kinard, 1980; Reidy, 1977; Roscoe, 1985). In order to cognitively and emotionally reconcile being attacked by the person who is supposed to love him, it is easy for the child to rationalize that he is an unworthy person of the lowest stature, and to further rationalize he is deserving of the attack (Green, 1983).

Fourth, the prisoner of war is allowed to be angry and to hate the attacker, but the child is not. The victimized child is forbidden to express her rage or possible hate toward the attacking parent for the humiliation and degradation imposed. It is culturally unacceptable for the child to be angry with or to hate the parent. The message to the child may be, "your feelings are wrong, your feelings are unacceptable, your feelings are not real." Consequently, the child's negative feelings toward the attacker (parent) must be denied.

Recurrent denial of feelings in this style, referred to as disconfirmation (Bowlby, 1979; Rieker and Carmen, 1986), is psychologically devastating for many individuals. It is devastating to such a degree that a range of psychological dysfunction from mild disorders to psychoses can result depending upon the situation and the individual (Bowlby, 1979; Miller, 1984; Rieker and Carmen, 1986).

PSYCHOLOGICAL MALTREATMENT DEFINITIONS

Defining psychological maltreatment has been a difficult and elusive task for many years. Several factors have to be weighed when considering a definition of psychological maltreatment. Forms of maltreatment, semantics, cultural influencers and mediators, intensity, frequency and duration of maltreatment, and legal versus mental health perspectives all influence the development of an adequate definition of psychological maltreatment. In recent years these factors have been recognized and incorporated in efforts to give direction to development of more tangible definitions (Garbarino, Guttman, and Seeley, 1986; Hart and Brassard, 1987).

Psychological maltreatment has been discussed and referred to as **emotional abuse, emotional maltreatment, mental cruelty, maternal emotional deprivation, maternal deprivation syndrome,** and **mental injury.** The term psychological abuse is used because it "better subsumes all affective and cognitive aspects of child maltreatment" (Hart and Brassard, 1987).

Mental injury is a category of child abuse included in the 1974 Federal

Child Abuse Prevention and Treatment Act. However the federal statute does not define or clarify **mental injury**. The mental injury category is described in many state statutes, but because clarifying definitions are generally not provided, these statutes are essentially useless for child protective services and court intervention. Pennsylvania, Virginia, and Mississippi are exceptions. They have developed procedural guidelines which provide more clarity and usefulness to the definition for the intervention (Corson and Davidson, 1987; Garbarino, Guttman, and Seeley, 1986).

Efforts at defining psychological maltreatment have ranged from broad definitional categories (American Humane Association, 1980; National Center on Child Abuse and Neglect, 1981), to very specific acts of maltreatment such as scapegoating, ridiculing, and chaotic family environment (see Hart, Germain, and Brassard, 1987 for extensive coverage). These attempts have failed to "receive consistent support across researchers, child advocates, and the courts" (Hart and Brassard, 1987).

The 1983 International Conference on Psychological Abuse of Children and Youth developed eight domains of psychologically destructive acts or environmental conditions: (a) mental cruelty, (b) sexual abuse and exploitation, (c) living in dangerous and unstable environments, (d) drug and substance abuse, (e) influence by negative and limiting models, (f) cultural bias and prejudice, (g) emotional neglect and stimulus deprivation, and (h) institutional abuse (Proceedings summary of the International Conference on Psychological Abuse of Children and Youth, 1983). These domains addressed the breadth of types, independent forms, forms integral to other types of abuse, and directness of focus (Hart and Brassard, 1987). The conference succeeded in developing a "working generic definition" which garnered a broad level of support. It states:

> Psychological maltreatment of children and youth consists of acts of omission and commission which are judged by community standards and professional expertise to be psychologically damaging. Such acts are committed by individuals, singly or collectively, who by their characteristics (e.g., age, status, knowledge, organizational form) are in a position of differential power that renders a child vulnerable. Such acts damage immediately or ultimately the behavioral, cognitive, affective, or physical functioning of the child. Examples of psychological maltreatment include acts of rejecting, terrorizing, isolating, exploiting, and mis-socializing (Proceedings Summary of the International Conference on Psychological Abuse of Children and Youth, (1983).

Current Definitions

Attempts to develop necessary levels of specificity beyond generic definitions are currently focused on maltreating acts of an adult directed toward a child, such as: (a) rejecting, (b) degrading, (c) terrorizing, (d) isolating, (e) corrupting, (f) exploiting, and (g) denying emotional responsiveness. These and similar sets of acts of commission and omission are being used to develop operational definitions of psychological maltreatment (Hart, Germain, and Brassard, 1987; Garbarino, Guttman, and Seeley, 1986; Hart, Gelardo, and Brassard, 1986; Office for the Study of the Psychological Rights of the Child, 1985). Brief descriptions of each follow.

Rejecting

Psychological rejection is an act which sends a child the message he is unwanted. The message can be sent in the form of an outright statement such as, "I never wanted you anyway." It may also be sent in more subtle ways by the parent through a lack of attention, a lack of affection, or a failure to recognize a child's accomplishments. The degree of maltreatment severity depends upon the frequency with which the parent engages in rejecting behavior (Garbarino, Guttman, and Seeley, 1986; Rohner and Rohner, 1980).

Degrading

Degrading means essentially to put a child down. Degrading is accomplished by sending the message to a child that she is of low worth, or is faulty. It is a relentless process of undermining the child's sense of personal value which contributes to the detriment of the child's self-esteem. Calling the child a dummy, or stupid, or not much good for anything are examples of degrading (Hart, Germain, and Brassard, 1987).

Terrorizing

A child is being terrorized when a parent engages in activities that create a climate of intense fear or threat in the child. Observing violent actions such as: parents fighting, unreasonable parental expectations and the concomitant punishment, extreme or severe punishment for unwanted activities, and highly charged, vicious verbal abuse are examples of parental behaviors that are psychologically terrorizing to a child (Garbarino, Guttman, and Seeley, 1986).

Isolating

Psychological isolating occurs when the parent fails to provide or intentionally denies the child normal social relations. The child is deprived of the opportunity to develop social confidence and competence through the interaction with other children in normal situations (Garbarino, Guttman, and Seeley, 1986). Examples include locking a child in a closet, or setting extreme limitations on an adolescent such as not allowing interaction with friends outside of school.

Corrupting

Corrupting a child involves parental action that mis-socializes a child in directions which are in strong conflict with cultural, moral, or legal standards. Modeling, encouraging, and reinforcing antisocial behavior such as aggression, sexual activity, or substance abuse are examples of behaviors which can cause the child to be dysfunctional in normal social relations. The degree of dysfunction can vary from mild difficulty in interacting with others, delinquency, permanent social dysfunction as in frigidity, to addiction (e.g., a child is obviously being corrupted and possibly being turned into a childhood alcoholic by a parent who uses the child as a weekend drinking partner; or a young adolescent girl being corrupted by a mother who allows the mother's boyfriends to sexually molest her daughter).

Exploiting

Exploiting a child means using a child for financial or other gain by an adult in a manner detrimental to the child, (e.g., regularly using the child as a servant for the whim of the parent, or the parent trading the sexual favors of a thirteen year old daughter for money or attention from a male). The child is forced to perform highly inappropriate acts for the benefit of the parent at the expense of the child's health (Hart, Germain, and Brassard, 1987).

Denying Emotional Responsiveness

Lack of parental emotional responsiveness, which is also referred to as **ignoring** (Garbarino, Guttman, and Seeley, 1986), occurs when the parent becomes psychologically unavailable to the child. Egeland and Erickson

(1987) have provided research leadership in this area and have found the lack of emotional responsiveness by caregivers toward the infant to be one of the most devastating forms of psychological maltreatment. Failing to provide emotional responsiveness can occur by failing to attend or react to an infant's spontaneous actions and vocalizations, failing to protect a school age child from sibling or peer threat, or by failing to exhibit interest in an adolescent's activities and concerns (Garbarino, Guttman, and Seeley, 1986).

Lack of emotional responsiveness is frequently found in cases in which attachment between mother and child have not occurred and in cases diagnosed as nonorganic failure to thrive.

Operationalization of Definitions

Accurate identification of psychological maltreatment calls for something more definite than a generic definition and a list of acts supported by the dictionary or logically derived definitions. Progress required operational definitions which are unambiguous and meet the burden of proof necessary for successful court intervention.

The act categories just presented are a major move in that direction. These acts appear to have support from recently completed opinion research directed toward operationalization of emotional maltreatment jointly conducted in conjunction with the National Center on Child Abuse and Neglect and the appropriate departments in the states of Alabama, Maine, Mississippi, Vermont, and Virginia (Baily and Baily, 1986).

The sixteen categories of emotional maltreatment delineated by the study are:

1. The parent shows no attachment to the child and fails to provide nurturance;
2. The parent consistently singles out one child to criticize and punish, to perform most of the household chores and receive fewer rewards;
3. The parent has unrealistic expectations of achievement for the child and criticizes, punishes and ostracizes or condemns the child when s/he does not achieve far above his/her normal abilities in areas such as school, arts, sports, and social status;
4. The parent makes inappropriate demands on and exploits the child by expecting the child to take care of the parent, to be a

companion, to protect the parent from outsiders, and to perform household tasks/functions which the parent is unwilling to do;

5. The parent expresses no affection toward the child and avoids and resists all physical closeness such as hugging, touching, or smiling;

6. The parent confuses the child's sexual identity;

7. The parent provides no stability or security for the child;

8. The parent exposes the child to maladaptive and harmful influences;

9. The parent does not permit the child autonomy and independent learning;

10. The parent denies the child the opportunity to learn from others by prohibiting the child from participating in social activities, commonly engaged in by the child's peers, such as extracurricular activities or outside play;

11. The parent regularly denigrates and ridicules the child, stating without foundation, that s/he reminds everyone of a person who is totally offensive and unacceptable by the family;

12. The parent sexually exploits the child by permitting the child to watch pornographic materials;

13. The parent uses excessive threats and psychological punishments;

14. The parent uses excessive threats and physical punishments in an attempt to control the child;

15. The custodial parent undermines the child's attachment to the other parent by consistently refusing all legitimate opportunities or requests for visits between the child and the other parent, even when these are requested by the child; and/or

16. The parent has consistently refused to permit any professional to assess the child's problems and has also announced that the child is forbidden from participating in any remedial education or counseling services (p. 8).

Direct to Indirect Maltreatment

From the ecological perspective, the seven categories of psychological maltreatment and the sixteen examples presented above may be interpreted as emphasizing primarily the **person-to-person** level of intervention. The tight focus is prompted by the present ambiguous state of definitional development and the imminent mandate to stop psychological maltreatment in the lives of children presently being victimized.

Psychological maltreatment is not limited to direct **person-to-person** activity. It also occurs on a continuum from direct to indirect forms of psychological maltreatment.

Direct Psychological Maltreatment

Direct psychological maltreatment is an omission or commission from an adult targeted to a specific child or set of children. Direct forms are represented by any of the definitions. Successful legal action has been accomplished in cases of child psychological maltreatment when a child has been subjected to public humiliation and terrorization with threats of extreme violence. Direct forms are the base level of the ecological environmental framework and are conceived in the context of **person-to-person** maltreatment.

Intermediate Forms

Between direct and indirect psychological maltreatment is the situation in which the parent regularly subjects the child to surroundings that are detrimental to the child's development. It has been described as exposure to "influence by negative and limiting models" (Teizrow, 1987). Subjecting the child to witnessing violence or chaos in the lives of significant adults, modeling of substance abuse by significant adults, and promoting attitudes of racial prejudice (Jones and Jones, 1987) qualify as examples of influence by negative and limiting models. The child as a developing and malleable entity is potentially predisposed toward dysfunctional behaviors and attitudes resulting from exposure to this less direct level of ecological impact being presented as appropriated reality.

Indirect Psychological Maltreatment

The most indirect extreme of the continuum represents the broadest level from an ecological perspective. It refers to the negative psychological influences that impinge on the child's life as a result of community, cultural, and national attitudes; as well as values, mores, and goals. Indirect psychological maltreatment of the child results from society's unwillingness or inability to adequately address basic human needs (Erickson, 1968; Gil, 1987; and Maslow, 1970) necessary for the child's appropriate physical and emotional development.

The institutionalization of society for the majority (Gil, 1978) through the establishment of public policy, and the powerful influence of the mass media, has subjected children to a wide range of culturally accepted negative influences. Examples of such influences include the presentation of excessive violence and distortions of reality through public media, and constraints set on the range of individual talent development through limiting reinforcement in institutions such as schools and employment opportunities.

PREVENTION OF PSYCHOLOGICAL MALTREATMENT

By the time children are identified as abused or neglected, many have suffered substantial physical or emotional damage. Often the damage is irreparable. Unfortunately treatment programs for known abusing or neglecting families have not been notably successful. Thus, if we cannot (or will not) prevent abuse we may have no way of adequately protecting a child without separating the child from his or her parents (Wald and Cohen, 1986).

Ominous words. But this is the harsh reality for the hundreds of thousands of children involved. The prevention of psychological maltreatment or any child maltreatment, is one of the most critical areas requiring attention in our society.

Informed opinion argues for prevention of child maltreatment. Roberts (1984) states that, "Experts in many fields are calling for an expended awareness of prevention." Anne Cohn (1982), the executive director of The National Committee for the Prevention of Child Abuse, has stated that, "It is time . . . to apply what we know about child abuse to prevention." Joffe (1981) wrote, "Clearly, prevention . . . is an idea whose time has come." Finally, Starr (1979) concluded that, "The key to the elimination of child abuse is . . . prevention." These individuals advocate for the protection and edification of children.

Prevention generally is thought to be a process intended to avert the occurrence of some event or process. Prevention in the field of mental health and psychological maltreatment typically encompasses a somewhat broader scope, but this chapter will be limited to the narrower concepts of primary or **pure** prevention.

Organic Disorder Considerations

The primary orientation of this chapter addresses the psychological elements of maltreatment, but prevention of physical disorders through medical research merits brief attention because it is an important and promising consideration for the prevention of some child psychological maltreatment. Cumulative family stress level has been recognized as a significant component in the abusive family (Egeland, Breitenbucher, and Rosenberg, 1980). Congenital and disease associated disorders such as physical handicaps, physical dysfunction (e.g., diabetes), serious illness and mental retardation produce a **special needs** child or parent. These disorders also increase the probability of child maltreatment as a result of additional, detrimental family stressors (Kadushin and Martin, 1978). Additional family stressors can result from necessary additional coping, or from the problems of dysfunctional intrafamily interaction generated by inadequate knowledge **about** or **by** the **special needs** person. This could be a frequent situation if unreasonable developmental expectations are forced upon a child by an intellectually low functioning parent (Seagull and Scheurer, 1986).

From genetic research, an encouraging example is the **fragile X** syndrome. It is highly suspect as the causal agent for some incidence of a variety of problems including: mental retardation in boys (Gerald, 1983), autism (August, 1983), aggressive behavior, and arithmetic problem solving difficulty in girls (Bishop, 1986). Developing corrective procedures for genetic manipulation would restore impaired individual ability and eliminate a hereditary component for offspring.

Prevention of organic disorders will be a significant contribution toward reducing some incidence of psychological maltreatment, and toward what Kadushin and Martin (1978) term an "interactional event" between the parent and child.

Negative Ecological Influence

Eco-developmental theoretical perspectives and the models rooted in Bronfrenbrenner's (1979) work, have been proposed by Belsky (1984), Bitner and Newberger (1982), and Garbarino (1977). They conceptualize the following three common factors as contributing to child maltreatment: (a) dysfunctional parenting, (b) child vulnerability, and (c) sociocultural stressors.

One, inadequate knowledge of child developmental needs, poor parent interaction skills, modeling inappropriate behaviors, negligent parenting attitudes, and seriously unsatisfied parent psychological needs are recognized as major contributors to the psychological maltreatment of children.

Two, the child also needs to be perceived separately from her parents as an individual embodying certain characteristics and needs. The unfulfilled needs, the development of low self-esteem, and feeling uncared for are examples of conditions that undermine the child's adequate psychological development and set the child up for vulnerability to future social stressors. Social stressors are likely to be encountered by the child in increasing frequency as the child ages.

Three, sociocultural stressors impinge on the child from a wider and more indirect level of the ecological environment. Personally limiting cultural values can be stressors, for instance: (a) viewing the child as a possession rather than as an individual human being entitled to necessary developmental rights; (b) seeing the educational needs of the child strictly from the limited view of preparation for employment; and (c) not recognizing the educational needs for development of the whole individual. These conditions produce negative influences or stressors affecting the psychological development of the child.

PREVENTION TARGET AREAS

To address primary prevention from a proactive perspective the problems need to be reformulated. Based upon the concept that prevention activity is designed to develop or alleviate a situation or process, the three categories: (1) dysfunctional parenting, (2) child vulnerability, and (3) sociocultural stressors, can be reformulated into prevention target categories: (a) developing a responsible and effective parent, (b) producing a resilient (stress resistant) child, and (c) reducing negative sociocultural influences. Each of these three areas will be specifically addressed through recommendations for three domains of activity judged to be of critical importance in prevention (Office for the Study of the Psychological Rights of the Child, 1986): (1) satisfying psychological needs, (2) developing knowledge and skills, and (3) reducing negative stress.

Targeting the Parent

Parenting is a critical area for attention in the prevention of child maltreatment. The ecological approach recognizes the existence of maltreatment from many sources, but dysfunctional parenting is typically perceived as the primary contributing factor (Belsky, 1984). The eco-developmental theory recognizes the necessity for a parent to (a) understand child developmental needs, (b) understand age appropriate childhood expectations, (c) develop adequate skills for knowledge application, and (d) be sufficiently healthy and motivated to apply those understandings and knowledge. Following are the domains to be targeted in developing a responsible and effective parent.

Satisfying Basic Psychological Needs

Each individual requires some minimal level of satisfaction of basic psychological needs, and parents are no exception. Belsky (1984) has formulated critical determinants for parenting through the integration of disparate research information, and has concluded that, although several factors interact, the parent's personal psychological resources are the most important component in effective parenting. The psychologically needy parent is apt to use the child to satisfy his own needs and ignore the child's developmental needs; thus, contributing to the inadequate psychological development of the child, and sustaining the intergenerational aspect of child maltreatment. Helfer's (1978) W.A.R. Cycle (world of abnormal rearing) very effectively conceptualizes this type of maltreatment situation and the intergenerational succession between the parent and the child.

Basic parental needs exist in many forms, and prevention programs can occur in a variety of ways to assist parents to satisfy those needs. One important form is teaching people strategies to meet their own basic psychological needs through instruction and modeling. This can be accomplished through self-help or organized programs.

For self-study, many popular psychology books provide encouragement and processes for recognizing and meeting one's own psychological needs. Authors such as Eric Berne, Wayne Dyer, Albert Ellis, William Glasser, Scott Peck, and Gail Sheehey are some who provide self-help information for individuals.

Organized programs can provide more opportunity for directed and individually tailored learning processes. They can include: (a) providing pro-social skill and **human** psychological development as a regular and integral part of schooling, job training, and church programs; (b) providing individual and group counseling through employer programs and community agencies; and (c) developing dependable social support and helping networks in neighborhoods, churches, and places of employment.

Another form of prevention is the development of practical competencies and opportunities for meaningful work which can include: (a) preparing individuals in school years with learning tools, critical thinking and problem solving competencies necessary for general applications and for a variety of occupations; and (b) guaranteeing occupational opportunities for all through private and governmental cooperation.

Developing Knowledge and Skills for Parenting

Knowledge of child development and effective parenting skills are an essential activity for the prevention of child maltreatment. Preventive programs can be developed for a variety of needs, such as those designed to reach the parent-to-be, or the **high risk** parent identified by front line caregivers such as gynecologists, obstetricians, hospital maternal care staff, pediatricians, visiting nurses, and educators. These programs allow for early intervention with the parent through education and emotional support before maltreatment occurs, and includes ongoing monitoring by home health **visitors.**

Any parent could also participate in community educational programs in child development and parenting skills, which could be accomplished through books, videotapes, and parent training classes. Tax advantages could be provided as an incentive to participate. Prevention through necessary parenting education can be accomplished by schools at the secondary level providing hands-on, mentored experience in child development, and in parenting knowledge and skill development by offering a system-wide child care program to the community.

Reducing Negative Stress

The parental breakdown of impulse controls when under stress contributes significantly to the psychological maltreatment of children. Reducing negative stress in the parent's life is a primary goal for prevention programs. Prevention programs can be of a variety of forms which can include: (a) encouraging dependable and frequent extended family/social/spiritual support networks and interactions; (b) providing home visitor services; (c) providing tax advantages for employers providing on-premises or close proximity child care; (d) stressing management training provided by the community or the employer; (e) employer provided and encouraged physical/mental fitness programs; and (f) providing opportunities for spiritual and religious experience.

Producing the Resilient Child

Producing the resilient child is the second prevention target. The resilient or **stress resistant** child is one who, if he incurs psychological maltreatment does not manifest, either initially or delayed, any seriously dysfunctional behavior and attitudes. Mediating variables apparently intervene with maltreatment to reduce the level of child vulnerability (Hart, Germain, and Brassard, 1978). Garmezy (1981, 1987), and Werner (1986) have written about the occasional **stress resistant** child.

Research delineating the mediating variables is encouraging. Providing prevention programs to develop those variables offers the potential for reducing the child's susceptibility to direct and indirect psychological maltreatment. Findings to date strongly suggest that parenting or effective influence by another adult is extremely important in the development of the stress resistant child. Garmezy (1981) reports that, "the children . . . seem to have at least one adequate identification figure among the significant adults who touch their lives" (p. 220). The parent or significant adult as a mediating influence for resilient development is also supported by Feuerstein's (1982) concept of necessary mediating learning experiences (MLE's) being provided by adults for adequate child development.

Consistent with the developmental perspective of child psychological maltreatment, Rutter (Garmezy, 1981) proposes a **vulnerable age phenomenon** in relation to specific stresses and their consequences. The preventive implications indicate the need for program design at age specific periods of vulnerability such as teaching young mothers the crucial importance of adequate emotional responsiveness to their infant child (Egeland and Erickson, 1987).

Satisfying Basic Psychological Needs

The necessity for the satisfaction of basic psychological needs for child development has been well established by Maslow (1970), Erickson (1968), and Gil (1987). Such needs have been more specifically recognized by Egeland and Stroufe (1981); and Hart, Germain, and Brassard (1987) as necessary for a child's psychologically healthy development. The deprivation of these basic psychological needs can lead to a child exhibiting behavior and attitudinal problems that continue through adolescence and into adulthood. The needs vary from promoting positive enhancement such as the establishment of parent/child attachment and a psychologically responsive relationship (Bowlby, 1982; Egeland and Erickson, 1987), to the elimination of negative influencers (Garbarino, Guttman, and Seeley, 1986).

Developing prevention programs to promote the satisfaction of basic psychological needs of the child is an integral step in developing a child resistant to psychological maltreatment. Ecological and developmental stage considerations will have to be attended to in program development through programs aimed at the needs of children at different ages. Examples of prevention programs could be: (a) establishing bonding patterns between newborn and parent(s) before leaving the hospital; (b) establishing love and belonging as a child, sibling, friend and student; (c) assuring low child-to-adult ratios in child care and education; (d) using a **home visitor** program for **high risk** families to monitor and educate new mothers (Rosenberg and Repucci, 1985; Wald and Cohen, 1986); and (e) the establishment of a **child development** committee to oversee the process of meeting children's needs in school (Hart, 1987).

Develop Knowledge and Skills in the Child

A growing child will normally experience an increase in contact with society, and can be expected to demonstrate increased competency in school, home, and social settings. The more effectively the child may manage her external environment, the less susceptible she will be to detrimental **messages** from society that can damage her feelings of self-worth and ability to interact effectively with friends, peers, teachers, parents and other adults.

Prevention programming for the child needs to include self-efficacy programs that will improve the child's ability to function in society. Examples of such programs could be school programs to: (a) develop the ability to communicate feelings and needs to caring adults and peers; (b) develop critical thinking abilities; (c) prepare children to meet their own needs and to assert personal rights, such as current **say NO!** programs; (d) ensure mediating learning experiences (Feuerstein, 1982); and (e) to teach children pro-social behaviors, skills, and attitudes necessary to elicit and provide social support (Hart, 1987).

Reducing Negative Stress

Environmental stress impacts the child just as seriously as the adult. Reducing high negative stress situations can allow the child the psychological freedom to engage in a more developmentally beneficial way, such as through normal life experiences, and learning to interact appropriately with friends, peers, and adults.

Prevention programs designed to reduce negative stress for children can include: (a) provide home visitor service to at-risk newborns and families (Rosenberg and Repucci, 1985; Wald and Cohen, 1986); and (b) provide stress management, respite, social support, and personal development programs to at-risk parents (Hart, 1978).

Sociocultural Factors

Cultural and social psychological maltreatment is a form of influence on the child that is perpetuated from a broader ecological level. Cultural values and attitudes result in community, state, and national public policy that impinges upon every adult and child. Aspects of programs adequately designed to promote the prevention of psychological maltreatment will have to be addressed through public policy in order to effect satisfactory implementation. Likely, this will require not only the development and implementation of prevention programs, but also a change in cultural values toward children to provide the necessary public mandate.

Satisfying Basic Psychological Needs

The satisfaction of basic psychological needs requires addressing the problems on a broader, state or national level. Gil (1987) discusses the institutionalized psychological maltreatment resulting from the failure of our social institutions to recognize the developmental needs of the individual.

He recommends a change in cultural values is needed to develop a preventive mindset that values and supports the public policy necessary for implementation of broad based child maltreatment prevention programs. Establishing responsible human need fulfillment as the primary goal of our society (Gil, 1987), and establishing a positive ideology of the child for our society (Hart, 1987) are examples of changes essential for implementation.

Developing Knowledge and Skills

Developing knowledge and skills on a cultural or national level would need to address the requirements of both children and adults. Competence in parenting, and competence in living as a member of society can be addressed through cultural values and a public policy mandate to develop: (a) more knowledgeable and skilled parents, and (b) children who are better equipped psychologically to function in society.

Examples of public policies designed to accomplish are: (a) the establishment of child development and parenting skills as basics in education; (b) providing concrete advantages for participation in ongoing parenting/child development enhancement programs (e.g., tax advantages, release of time from work, child care respite); and (c) the modeling of pro-social behaviors and good parenting practices in popular media.

Reducing Negative Stress

A cultural and public policy mandate to assist in the development of psychologically healthy individuals by preventing psychological maltreatment can reduce negative stress in the lives of both parent and child. Two examples of such policies are: (a) providing child care at places of employment, and (b) providing concrete reinforcement for good parenting (e.g., paid leave from employment for either parent during the first two years of a child's life).

IMPLEMENTATION OBJECTIVES

Implementation of significantly broad based prevention activity will likely necessitate the following changes. First, the development of a preventive mindset is crucial to the successful establishment of broad based effective policy for prevention of psychological maltreatment. Therapeutically oriented administrators and resulting decisions, significantly impede the implementation of prevention activity, especially with current critical budgetary constraints. Even Bloom (1981), who is heavily invested in prevention concepts, bemoans in his book on primary prevention, the problems of the therapeutically oriented professional in attending to prevention amid the interminable day-to-day crises. Bloom also stresses the impossibility of significantly interrupting the intergenerational cycle of maltreatment with an after the fact, therapeutic, one-to-one process, and proposes that proactive process through prevention is mandatory.

It is important to consider that to implement a broad based prevention process it may be necessary to remove program and funding decisions from therapeutically oriented administrators by establishing organizations of individuals whose only mandate is prevention.

Development of a preventive mindset is critical for successful implementation. In other fields the concept is well established, such as safety in aviation. Because of complexity of operation and potentially serious consequences, pilots and supporting personnel are immediately taught to develop and continuously implored to maintain a safety (preventive) mindset. Raising a child in a psychologically healthy environment is no less complex a process with consequences equally as serious.

Second, the entitlement of children's rights is crucial to the prevention of psychological maltreatment. Entitlement recognizing that: (a) children presently have only few protection rights, (b) that children are more than just parental possessions, and (c) that children are human beings with specific developmental needs (Hart, 1982). Such a change will necessitate enactment of public policy change to recognize children as having needs that are worthy of special attention and whose fulfillment are necessary for development into an emotionally mature and competent adult (Gil, 1987; Hart, Germain, and Brassard, 1987).

Third, developing a prevention mindset, and establishing entitlement rights for children entail significant social change. Gil (1976) contends that child abuse (maltreatment) is a social issue and stated, "The primary prevention of child abuse . . . is a political rather than a professional issue." Social change implies public policy change which requires direction from strong effective leadership to unify disparate activity in support of a singular agenda of promoting the prevention of child psychological maltreatment.

Current systems of child protection and service are not adequately responding to prevention needs. System change necessary for adequate response may be unlikely without external organized pressure. James Lardie (personal communication, 1986), the executive director for the Association of Child Advocates, a national association of state based child advocacy organizations, believes the systems are unwilling to change and have to be prompted externally, because typical organizational process results in an increasingly homeostatic system. Unless the system's leadership is unusually objective and secure, the few within the system who speak out for change are either ignored, harassed, or terminated.

SUMMARY

Psychological maltreatment is a pernicious problem that is only now beginning to receive necessary attention, even though it is more widespread than either the physical or sexual maltreatment of children. Because many concepts in psychological maltreatment have not previously received adequate attention, and many of the essential considerations involved are closely related to maltreatment in general, some material in the chapter is referred to in more general maltreatment terms instead of strict psychological maltreatment reference.

However, the chapter is still designed to acquaint the reader with the psychological maltreatment of children. First, through presenting a means to conceptualize and define psychological maltreatment within a theoretical framework. Secondly, the prevention of psychological maltreatment is addressed by providing an organizational structure for the primary concepts of **pure** prevention activity directed toward the parent, the child, and the psychological environment. Third, the need for prevention is stressed and some recommendations for prevention implementation are presented to close the chapter.

For the reader who desires more comprehensive coverage on the psychological maltreatment of children, two highly recommended books have recently been released: (a) **The Psychological Maltreatment of Children and Youth** by Brassard, Germain, and Hart; and (b) **The Psychologically Battered Child** by Garbarino, Guttman, and Seeley. Both are included in the reference section for this chapter.

REFERENCES

1. American Humane Association: Definitions of national study data items and response categories. *Technical Report, 3,* 1980.
2. August, G. J.: A genetic marker associated with infantile autism. *American Journal of Psychiatry, 140*(6):813, 1983.
3. Baily, T. F., and Baily, W. F.: *Operational Definitions of Child Emotional Maltreatment: Final Report.* Augusta, Bureau of Social Services, Maine Department of Human Services, 1986.
4. Belsky, J.: The determinants of parenting: a process model. *Child Development, 55:*83–96, 1984.
5. Benedek, E. P.: Children and psychic trauma: a brief review of contemporary thinking. In Eth, S., and Pynoos, R. S. (Eds.): *Post-Traumatic Stress Disorder in Children.* Washington, American Psychiatric, 1985.
6. Bishop, J. E.: Genetic marker: chromosome linked to mental impairment raises abortion issue. *Wall Street Journal, November*(18):1–27, 1986.
7. Bittner, S., and Newberger, E.: Child abuse: current issues of etiology, diagnosis, and treatment. In Henning, J. S. (Ed.): *The Rights of Children.* Springfield, Thomas, 1982.

8. Bloom, M.: *Primary Prevention.* Englewood Cliffs, Prentice Hall, 1981.

9. Bowlby, J.: *Attachment and Loss.* New York, Basic Books, 1969, vol.I.

10. Bowlby, J.: On knowing what you are not supposed to know and feeling what you are not supposed to feel. *Canadian Journal of Psychiatry, 24*(5):403–408, 1979.

11. Brassard, M. R., Germain, R., and Hart, S. (Eds.): *The Psychological Maltreatment of Children.* New York, Pergamon, 1987.

12. Bronfrenbrenner, U.: *The Ecology of Human Development.* Cambridge, Harvard, 1979.

13. Cohn, A. H.: The prevention of child abuse: what do we know about what works. In Leavitt, J. E. (Ed.): *Child Abuse and Neglect: Research and Innovation.* Boston, Martinus Nijhoff, 1983.

14. Coons, P. M.: Psychiatric problems associated with child abuse: a review. In Jacobsen, J. J. (Ed.): *The Psychiatric Sequelae of Child Abuse.* Springfield, Thomas, 1986.

15. Corson, J., and Davidson, H.: Emotional abuse and the law. In Brassard, M. R., Germain, R. B., and Hart, S. N. (Eds.): *The Psychological Maltreatment of Children.* New York, Pergamon, 1987.

16. Egeland, B., Breitenbucher, M., and Rosenberg, D.: Prospective study of the significance of life stress in the etiology of child abuse. *Journal of Consulting and Clinical Psychology, 48*(2):195–205, 1980.

17. Egeland, B., and Erickson, M.: Psychologically unavailable caregiving. In Brassard, M. R., Germain, R. B., and Hart, S. N. (Eds.): *The Psychological Maltreatment of Children.* New York, Pergamon, 1987.

18. Egeland, B., and Sroufe, A.: Developmental sequelae of maltreatment in infancy. *New Directions of Child Development, 11:*7792, 1981.

19. Egeland, B., Sroufe, L. A., and Erickson, M.: The developmental consequence of different patterns of maltreatment. *Child Abuse and Neglect, 7:*459469, 1983.

20. Erickson, M. F., and Egeland, B.: A developmental view of the psychological consequences of maltreatment. *School Psychology Review,* (in press).

21. Erikson, E.: *Childhood and Society.* New York, Norton, 1968.

22. Feuerstein, R.: Intergenerational conflict of rights: cultural imposition and selfrealization. *Viewpoints in Teaching and Learning, 58*(1):4463, 1982.

23. Garbarino, J.: The human ecology of child maltreatment: a conceptual model for research. *Journal of Marriage and the Family, 39:*721735, 1977.

24. Garbarino, J.: Defining emotional maltreatment: the message is the meaning. *Journal of Psychiatric Treatment and Evaluation, 2:*105110, 1980.

25. Garbarino, J., Guttman, E., and Seeley, J. W.: *The psychologically battered child.* San Francisco, Jossey-Bass, 1986.

26. Garmezy, N.: Children under stress: antecedents and correlates of vulnerability and resistance to psychopathology. In Rabin, A. I., Aronof, J., Barclay, A. M., and Zucker, R. A. (Eds.): *Further Explorations in Personality.* New York, Wiley & Sons, 1981.

27. Garmezy, N.: Stress, competance, and development: continuities in the study of

schizophrenic adults, children vulnerable to psychopathology, and the search for stress-resistant children. *American Journal of Orthopsychiatry, 57,*(2):159174, 1987.

28. Gerald, P. S.: Chromosomal derangement and treatment prospects. In Menolascino, F. J., Neman, R., and Stark, J. A. (Eds.): *Curative Aspects of Mental Retardation.* Baltimore, Brookes, 1983.

29. Gil, D. G.: Primary prevention of child abuse: a philosophical and political issue. *Journal of Pediatric Psychology,* 54–56, 1976.

30. Gil, D. G.: Maltreatment as a function of the structure of social systems. In Brassard, M. R., Germain, R. B., and Hart, S. N. (Eds.): *The Psychological Maltreatment of Children.* New York, Pergamon, 1987.

31. Green, A.: Self-destructive behavior in battered children. *American Journal of Psychiatry, 135:*579582, 1978.

32. Green, A.: Child abuse: dimension of psychological trauma in abused children. *Journal of the American Academy of Child Psychiatry, 22*(3):231237, 1983.

33. Hart, S.: The history of children's psychological rights. *Viewpoints in Teaching and Learning, 58*(1):115, 1982.

34. Hart, S.: Psychological maltreatment in schooling. *School Psychology Review, 16*(2):169180, 1987.

35. Hart, S. N., and Brassard, M. R.: A major threat to children's mental health: psychological maltreatment. *American Psychologist, 42*(2):160–165, 1987.

36. Hart, S. N., Gelardo, M., and Brassard, M.: Psychological maltreatment. In Jacobsen, J. J. (Ed.): *Psychiatric Sequelae of Child Abuse.* Springfield, Thomas, 1986.

37. Hart, S. N., Germain, R., and Brassard, M. R.: The challenge: to better understand and combat psychological maltreatment of children and youth. In Brassard, M. R., Germain, R. B., and Hart, S. N. (Eds.): *The Psychological Maltreatment of Children and Youth.* New York, Pergamon, 1987.

38. Helfer, R.: *Childhood Comes First.* East Lansing, Author, 1984.

39. Joffe, J. M., and Albee, G. W. (Eds.): *Prevention Through Political Action and Social Change.* Hanover, New England, 1981.

40. Jones, R. L., and Jones, J. M.: Racism as psychological maltreatment. In Brassard, M. R., Germain, R. B., and Hart, S. N. (Eds.): *The Psychological Maltreatment of Children and Youth.* New York, Pergamon, 1987.

41. Kadushin, A., and Martin, J. A.: *Child Abuse: An Interactional Event.* New York, Columbia, 1981.

42. Kinard, E. M.: Emotional development in physically abused children. *American Journal of Orthopsychiatry, October*(1):686–696, 1980.

43. Levy, S.: *Evaluating the Reliability of Statements Made About Abuse.* Chicago, American Bar Association National Child Advocacy Conference Workshop, 1986.

44. Lindberg, F. H., and Distad, L. J.: Survival responses to incest: adolescents in crisis. *Child Abuse and Neglect, 9:*521–526, 1985.

45. Martin, H. P., and Beezley, P.: Behavioral observations of abused children. *Developmental Medicine and Child Neurology, 19:*373–387, 1977.

46. Maslow, A. H.: *Motivation and Personality.* New York, Harper and Row, 1970.

47. Miller, A.: *Thou Shalt Not Be Aware: Society's Betrayal of the Child.* New York, New American Library, H. Hannum and H. Hannum. Translation, 1983.

48. Miller, A.: *For Your Own Good: Hidden Cruelty in Child Rearing and the Roots of Violence.* New York, Straus-Giroux, H. Hannum and H. Hannum Translation, 1984.

49. National Center on Child Abuse and Neglect: *Executive Summary: National Study of the Incidence and Severity of Child Abuse and Neglect.* Washington, U.S. Department Health and Human Services, 1981.

50. Navarre, E. L.: Psychological maltreatment: the core component of child abuse. In Brassard, M. R., Germain, R. B., and Hart, S. N. (Eds.): *The Psychological Maltreatment of Children.* New York, Pergamon, 1987.

51. Office for the Study of the Psychological Rights of the Child: *Unpublished Research Information.* Indianapolis, Indiana University-Purdue University, 1985.

52. Office for the Study of the Psychological Rights of the Child: *Unpublished Prevention Model.* Indianapolis, Indiana University-Purdue University, 1986.

53. Patterson, G. R.: *Coercive Family Process.* Eugene, Castilia, 1982.

54. Polansky, N.: There is nothing so practical as a good theory. *Child Welfare, LXV*(1):3–16, 1986.

55. Office for the Study of the Psychological Rights of the Child: *Proceedings Summary of the International Conference on the Psychological Abuse of Children and Youth.* Indianapolis, Indiana University, 1983.

56. Reidy, T. J.: The aggressive characteristics of abused and neglected children. *Journal of Clinical Psychology, 33*(4):1140–1145, 1977.

57. Rieker, P. P., and Carmen, E. H.: The victim to patient process: the disconfirmation and transformation of abuse. *American Journal of Orthopsychiatry, 56*(3):360–370, 1986.

58. Roberts, M. C., and Peterson, L.: *Prevention of Problems in Childhood.* New York, Wiley & Sons, 1984.

59. Rohner, R. P., and Rohner, E. C.: Antecedents and consequences of parental rejection: a theory of emotional abuse. *Child Abuse and Neglect, 4:*189–198, 1980.

60. Roscoe, B.: Intellectual, emotional and social deficits of abused children: a review. *Childhood Education, May/June:*388–392, 1985.

61. Rosenberg, M. S., and Germain, R. B.: Psychological maltreatment: theory, research, and ethical issues in psychology. In Brassard, M. R., Germain, R. B., and Hart, S. N. (Eds.): *The Psychological Maltreatment of Children.* New York, Pergamon, 1987.

62. Rosenberg, M. S., and Reppucci, N. D.: Primary prevention of child abuse. *Journal of Consulting and Clinical Psychology, 53*(5):576–585, 1985.

63. Seagull, E. A. W., and Scheurer, S. L.: Neglected and abused children of mentally retarded parents. *Child Abuse and Neglect, 10*(4):493–500, 1986.

64. Segal, J., and Yahraes, H.: *A Child's Journey: Forces that Shape the Lives of Our Young.* New York: McGraw-Hill, 1979.

65. Sroufe, L. A.: The coherence of individual development: early care, attachment, and subsequent developmental issues. *American Psychologist, 34*(10):834–841, 1979.

66. Starr, R. H.: Child abuse. *American Psychologist, 34*(10):872–878, 1979.

67. Steele, B. F., and Pollock, C. B.: A psychiatric study of parents who abuse infants and small children. In Helfer, R. E., and Kempe, C. H. (Eds.): *The Battered Child,* rev. ed. Chicago, University of Chicago, 1974.

68. Steele, B. F.: Discovery of children at risk for juvenile delinquency. In Dutile, F. N., Foust, C. H., and Webster, D. R.: (Eds.): *Early Childhood Intervention and Juvenile Delinquency.* Lexington, Lexington Books, 1982.

69. Steele, B. F.: Notes on the lasting effects of early child abuse throughout the life cycle. *Child Abuse and Neglect, 10:*283–291, 1986.

70. Telzrow, C. F.: Influence by negative and limiting models. In Brassard, M. R., Germain, R. B., and Hart, S. N. (Eds.): *The Psychological Maltreatment of Children.* New York, Pergamon, 1987.

71. Wald, M. S., and Cohen, S.: Preventing child abuse—what will it take? *Family Law Quarterly, 20*(2):281–302, 1986.

72. Werner, E.: Resilient offspring of alcoholics: a longitudinal study from birth to age 18. *Journal of Studies of Alcohol, 47:*34–40, 1986.

CHAPTER 13

EVALUATION OF THE ALLEGED SEXUAL ABUSE VICTIM: BEHAVIORAL, MEDICAL AND PSYCHOLOGICAL CONSIDERATIONS

ROBERTA A. HIBBARD

INTRODUCTION

Media attention, school programs and community education continue to increase the public awareness of the problem of child sexual abuse. As a result, increasing numbers of children are presenting to professionals for the evaluation and management of possible sexual victimization (American Humane Association, 1981, Peters et al, 1986). This evaluation falls into several professional domains: (1) welfare, (2) criminal, (3) mental health, and (4) medical. There are few formal divisions of roles and few professionals have had the experience of working together or learning about other's roles (Finklehor et. al., 1985). Optimal evaluation of the alleged sexual abuse victim incorporates a multidisciplinary model with communication and understanding of the various components.

This discussion of the evaluation of the alleged sexual abuse victim will focus on the child. The child remains central in any investigation of allegations of possible abuse. It is important for professionals to understand a child's perspective in dealing with issues of sexual abuse. Children are not **little adults** and may perceive their environment or experiences in ways differing from usual adult expectations. Developmental perspectives with regard to the identification of possible victims, interviewing children, the medical evaluation, and children in the legal system will be emphasized.

EPIDEMIOLOGICAL CONSIDERATIONS

An understanding of the epidemiology of any problem includes knowledge of the definition and natural history, both of which are influenced by case identification and reporting. Both definitional and reporting issues are of paramount concern in the interpretation of the epidemiology of child sexual abuse because the statistics are significantly influenced by these factors.

To identify child sexual abuse, it must first be defined. Sexual abuse and sexual misuse are frequently interchanged terms that denote any sexually stimulating act that is inappropriate for a child's age, level of development, or role within the family (Brant and Tisza, 1977). Many definitions incorporate the desire for sexual gratification of one of the participants (Mrazek, 1981). This general definition does not always help in individual cases. Acts that may be considered sexually abusive by one individual in a given situation may not be considered as such by other individuals under differing circumstances. For example, kissing is certainly appropriate and expected in many family situations, but what about heavy kissing that leaves **hickeys** on the neck of a six year old child? There may be some dispute as to the abusive nature of such contact. There may be similar disputes regarding issues of nudity. When does nudity go beyond the accepted norm within a household and become flashing or exhibitionism? These are not issues that are easy to answer in a general sense but must be addressed individually.

There is a wide spectrum of parent/child sexual contact (Summit and Kryso, 1978). Incidental contact, as in play and wrestling, and explicit sexual education of the young child fall at one end of the spectrum and may be **normal**. Overt incest, child rape and child pornography are at the other extreme and are clearly inappropriate. It may be difficult to distinguish loving attention from lustful intrusion.

In examining child sexual abuse statistics, both the definition of abuse and characteristics of reporting must be considered (Hibbard and Orr, 1985). Statistics only reflect those cases that are reported and may be biased by the agency receiving the reports. Child protective services often only accept reports of intrafamilial or institutional abuse and may not include stranger abuse. On the other hand, cases reported to law enforcement agencies are more apt to involve stranger abuse. Hospital emergency rooms and medical records only reflect statistics on those children receiving medical examinations. It may be that children who are victims of less physically traumatic or more chronic abuse may not be receiving medical exams.

The age of victims included warrants consideration. Some studies consider children to the age of 16 years, other studies may consider children up to the age of 18 or 21 years of age. Such factors will influence the descriptive characteristics (i.e. average age) reported.

In general, what do the epidemiologic studies indicate? Children of all ages, races, socioeconomic strata and sexes may be victims of child sexual abuse. Several survey studies indicate that 19–38% of females and 9–17% of males may be victims of sexual abuse before reaching adulthood (Finkelhor, 1979, Russel, 1983, DeJong 1982, Ellerstein and Canavan, 1980). These sexually abusive experiences range from exhibitionism to rape and pornography. Younger children are more often abused by an assailant known to them in a familiar environment, and tend to have less physically traumatic experiences than older children (DeJong et al, 1982). Many children are subjected to repeated abuse. Violence or threat of force is a factor in 1/3 to 1/2 of cases but coercion and bribery are even more common, especially in young children. Children are abused in homes, schools, and public places.

IDENTIFYING ABUSE

In order to identify child sexual abuse, the possibility must be considered. It is all too easy to ignore subtle signs because we don't want to deal with the intense emotional feelings evoked by realizing a child may have been sexually abused. Those reactions, while natural, may interfere with the objective evaluation of an alleged abuse victim and may negatively influence a child's ability to disclose experiences. We all know that many children **read** adults very well and will not tell them things they believe adults won't like. It is necessary to deal with our own emotional reactions in order to function as child and family advocates.

There are many barriers to the identification of victims of sexual abuse. Misconceptions about what is involved in abuse and how children may react to it are common. Beliefs such as: (1) children cannot be abused, (2) boys cannot be abused, (3) children may get sexually transmitted diseases from sources other than sexual contact, (4) children make up reports of abuse in order to get out of trouble, (5) children are provocative and seductive bringing abuse onto themselves, and (6) normal everyday activity may cause significant trauma to the child's bottom, hinder identification of possible victims.

Each child may present to professionals in a different fashion. There is a spectrum of reactions: emotional, physical, behavioral and psychological. One child may be hysterical in reporting a history of abuse, while another child may disclose experiences as if reading a book. Children, like adults, have different styles in dealing with stress.

What should be **red flags** that alert professionals to consider the possibility of sexual victimization? It is important to recognize that indicators are just that, they indicate the possibility of sexual abuse and suggest the diagnosis needs to be considered. They **DO NOT** mean definitively that a child has been abused. Many of these signs and symptoms can be consistent with other etiologies but should make one think about the possibility of abuse. Physical and behavioral indicators in a child and behavioral indicators in the parents are listed in Table XIII–I These indicators reflect some of the many possible effects of child sexual abuse.

TABLE XIII-I

INDICATORS OF POSSIBLE SEXUAL ABUSE: SIGNS AND SYMPTOMS SUGGESTING SEXUAL ABUSE, BUT NOT PROVING IT

Child's Behavior	Child's Physical Complaints	Parent's Behavior
Changes in behavior: withdrawn depressed aggressive acting out	Difficulty walking or sitting Torn, stained or blood underclothing Pain or itching in genital area	Very protective or jealous of child Encourages child to engage in prostitution or sexual acts in front of caretaker
Regressive behavior: enuresis encopresis thumbsucking	Bruises or bleeding in genital or rectal area Vaginal, penile discharge	Excessive concern about venereal disease or pregnancy in child
Sleep disturbances: nightmares	Venereal disease Pregnancy	Concern about possible abuse of child
Sophisticated or unusual sexual behavior or knowledge		
Poor peer relationships		
Running away		
Delinquency		
Prostitution		
Suicide attempts		
Unwilling to change clothes for gym		
Reports sexual assault		

The Sexual Abuse Accommodation Syndrome describes a common sequence of behavioral reactions and adaptation in children who have been sexually abused by a trusted adult (Summit, 1983). It puts into a child's perspective the reactions and environmental influences are that related to coping skills. The components include: (1) secrecy, (2) helplessness, (3) entrapment and accommodation, (4) a delayed unconvincing disclosure, and (5) retraction.

Child sexual abuse is a secret. The child is usually told that this is a secret and is not to be shared. If the child does share this secret, it won't be believed. This secrecy becomes the source of the child's fear, but also a mechanism for safety. As long as the secret is not disclosed, there won't be harm. The child is helpless to react to such a situation. Vital relationships have been betrayed by this person that the child is supposed to trust; how can they get any help? The child does not have the authority or the power to stop the abuse. As such, the child learns to accept the situation and becomes entrapped. The child must adapt to survive.

This accommodation may take many forms. Some children may act out, runaway, become very clinging, or be afraid to leave their parents. Other children may become sexually provocative, turn to prostitution, or develop psychosomatic complaints such as abdominal pains, headaches and pseudoseizures. Some children react to the acute situation by vomiting; who wants to sleep in the bed of a child who has just vomited? Children may developmentally regress, wet the bed, soil their pants or suck their thumbs. Each child draws on their individual environment and own inner strength in an attempt to deal with the situation. If a child is able to disclose the abusive situation, it is often unconvincing and delayed.

Adults do not understand why the child didn't tell when it first happened. The disclosure often comes forth at a time when the child is more independent and is able to confront the perpetrator. Many cases are disclosed through sensitive outreach, as in educational programs in the schools. Some children may disclose when they are observed by a third party to be involved in such activity. Many children never disclose the abuse. At the time of the disclosure, all of the threats, fears and reasons for keeping it a secret may come true. The family is often disrupted, parents may be removed from the environment, or the child may be removed from the home. People do not want to believe the child. People blame the child. Without support and encouragement or understanding, children may retract their statements. Although the child may still be angry and maintain self-guilt about provoking the incident, there is often a sense of obligation to preserve the family unit. It is much easier to retract the statement and avoid problems rather than go through the emotional upheaval of disclosure. The child accepts full responsibility for the events, and with retraction, may reenter a vicious cycle.

Knowledge of the pressures faced and children's abilities to adapt to their environments is crucial in trying to understand or make sense out of a child's story and reaction to sexual assault. Adults often expect a child to behave in accordance with adult concepts of autonomy and self determinism. This is unrealistic. A child is generally dependent upon adults for the reality assigned to experiences.

A child is truly insubordinate in authoritarian relationships. It is incorrect to assume that an uncomplaining child is a consenting child; the child does not have the power to say **no** (Finklehor, 1979). Actions truly do speak louder than words for many children; children respond much more rapidly to the threat of removal of love or to silent finger counting on an upheld hand than they do respond to physical punishment. Thus, the child is not necessarily a willing accomplice even if there are no physical threats. It is difficult for a child to perceive a trusted adult as being bad, and a child may learn to be good by doing what the adult expects.

The cognitive development of children varies. Abilities develop at different ages in different children; no two children are exactly alike. Children do not develop the ability to reason (logical thinking) until 7 to 11 years of age (Ginsburg, 1969). That is why you cannot win an argument with a child. Abstract reasoning does not develop until the teen years, if at all. Children live in the present and have a very difficult time in considering the future, which is an abstract thought. They also have difficulty putting into reference past events. Older children may be able to put those events into perspective with the use of landmark days or special occasions.

Just like adults, children must feel comfortable in order to discuss a private or uncomfortable experience. Children are active and their attention spans are often short. They may change subjects frequently and may require a variety of activities in order to tolerate lengthy discussions. These aspects of child development must be considered when dealing with children.

INTERVIEWING THE CHILD VICTIM

The interview for child sexual abuse is lengthy because the issue is an emotional one and often difficult to discuss. It is important to take the time to prepare the child and the interviewer for the discussion.

Prior to the interview, it is helpful to have information, if possible, regarding who reported the assault, how it came to be reported, and when the assault occurred. The child should not be present during an adult's description of what happened. One does not want to influence what the child may tell. The child, too, should be interviewed alone. Many children are unwilling to disclose details in front of parents whom they might feel would be hurt by learning of such activities.

The professional must be aware that a child may exhibit a variety of emotional styles in disclosing abuse. The timing and frequency of the assault may affect the child's response. If the assault has occurred frequently, and/or over a long period of time, the details will probably be less accessible to the child's memory. Just as adults cannot often remember what they had for dinner a week ago, it is unreasonable to expect a child to remember what clothes a perpetrator had on. The child's reaction to the perpetrator may be varied. Affectionate behavior between the suspected perpetrator and the child does not disprove an allegation of sexual assault.

The interview should be performed in a comfortable, neutral setting. A child is less apt to disclose abuse in the environment in which it occurred. The child may not feel safe. It is important to see the child alone and with few distractions. The parents should be told what will be taking place and what interviewing aids might be used. If a child is unwilling or extremely uncomfortable about being interviewed alone, it is reasonable to permit the presence of an adult requested by the child. That adult should be asked not to interfere with the interview. The adult may sit next to or behind the child, out of the child's view, with the interviewer opposite both of them.

The first step in the interview is establishing rapport with the child. The child needs to know who you are and why you are speaking with them, what agency you represent and what your role is. You need to establish your credibility as a person this child should talk with. The child's expectations of the interview must be clarified. Does the child know why you are speaking with them? How does the child feel about it? An older child may need to know for what purpose the questions are being asked. The child should know that the information must be reported. Demonstrate an interest in the child and allow **get acquainted** time. Find out about the child's favorite activities, play games or draw pictures. Interviews are most successful when **safe** topics are approached first.

Throughout the interview, a relaxed, unhurried attitude is necessary. Positive reinforcement for cooperation, talking or behavior helps.

There are many approaches to discussing the topic of sexual assault. Discussing feelings, worries, secrets, and touching are all relatively nonthreatening approaches that may yield information. For example, "Do you know about secrets? Sometimes people have good secrets and sometimes people have bad secrets. What are some of the good secrets? What are some of the bad secrets? Sometimes grownups tell children to keep certain things secret because it may get them into trouble. Do you know about those kinds of secrets? What are some examples?" A talk about **touching** may sometimes be helpful and can often be made into a game. You can discuss touching or kissing on all parts of the body, ask if people are touched in these places, and who might touch them in such places.

The child may experience feelings of guilt, fear or anxiety regarding the abuse and the disclosure. It is important to allay those feelings as best as possible for example, "Sometimes things happen to children that aren't their fault. Some of the children I have talked to were afraid of somebody. Sometimes it is scary to talk about things. Do you know that sometimes things that happen to you aren't your fault?" This removal of blame is important to reiterate throughout the interview process. The child might hear these statements again and again, but often do not believe them for many, many months. The child may try to switch the subject to avoid some of the anxiety that goes along with disclosure. A brief digression may decrease the child's anxiety and permit a return to the discussion at hand with direction from the interviewer.

Age related tools, such as drawings and dolls, may be helpful. Drawings are a fun, very nonthreatening way to begin to get to know a child and establish rapport. Pencil and paper are often available. Children may be asked to draw a picture of a person, a picture of the family, or whatever they choose. It is important then, to ask the child to describe what has been drawn. This is particularly helpful when having children draw pictures of people, for example, "Who is this person? How old is this person? What is this person doing?" This will often service as a launching pad for discussion about what someone likes about the person, or dislikes; how the child may interact with that person; and do they know other people who do those things?

Whether or not the drawing elicits specific information about abuse, it is a very comfortable and easy way for a child to begin to open up and talk to an examiner. Some children prefer to draw pictures of the abuse when they do not want to verbalize what happened. It can be less threatening to draw the pictures than to discuss specifically what happened. Many children will verbalize as they draw without realizing it. Some drawings may be very explicit and provide graphic evidence for legal purposes. The spontaneous drawing of genitalia on a human figure warrants further questioning and investigation for sexual abuse. Alleged sexual abuse victims have been observed to draw genitalia more often than do presumably nonabused children (Hibbard et al, in press).

The figures in Appendixes XIII were drawn by an eight year old female victim of sexual assault. She did not want to talk about her experiences and asked to draw them instead. She first drew what she and her stepbrother looked like and how they felt at the time of the abuse. She completed the outline describing the genitals as "the worst part of his body." She then drew the things they did; the drawings speak for themselves. Such graphic evidence can be very convincing.

Anatomically correct dolls are often used in the evaluation of alleged sexual abuse victims. If they are to be used, it is important to have the dolls available and to indicate that they belong to you. The child's spontaneous interactions with the dolls should be observed. It can be helpful to note how the child plays with a single doll or chooses to have the dolls interact. The dolls may be used as a means of determining the child's knowledge of body parts and what those body parts are for. If the child does not initiate undressing, it may be remarked that the doll's clothes can be removed. Ask the child what is seen. Have the child name the body parts, starting with the head. It is important to let the child use his or her own words for body parts and to continue to use the child's terminology when you speak to him or her. Ask what the various body parts do. This may then be extended to ask about touching, for example, "Who touches different body parts? Where? How? What does it feel like when those body parts are touched? What body parts are used to touch other body parts?"

One purpose of the interview is to obtain a description of the assault. The child should be encouraged to tell the complete story from the beginning. Stating your own perception of the assault should be avoided. Open ended questions and reflective listening are most helpful, (e.g. "What happened next? And then . . . ?"). Time should be allotted for the child to volunteer information before questions are asked. The child should be interrupted only to clarify or encourage the child to continue.

Techniques to help clarify include drawings, dolls, asking the child to point to areas of his or her body, or the interviewer pointing to his or her own body.

It is easiest to move from general topics to more specific information. The duration and the type of assault should be determined if possible, for example, "What happened? Where did it happen? When did it happen? How often did it happen?" In addition, a progression of activity from less involvement to more intimate contact may be important to elicit, as are components of secrecy and coercion, such as, "What were you told? What would happen if you told?" It must be remembered that multiple interviews may be necessary to elicit a complete history. Pressuring a child to talk usually doesn't work.

The interviewer's response should be supportive. The child should be told repeatedly that it is appropriate to disclose what happened. The child should hear that the abuse was wrong and that the adult was responsible. Honesty regarding your obligation to report information is imperative. Promises should never be made regarding what will happen after the report is made. It is helpful to identify the child's perceptions of the consequences of telling and what the child would like the interviewer to do in order to help. Some aspects of the request should be granted if possible, but again, promises that cannot be kept should not be made. Information regarding what may happen next should be provided. The child should always be given ample opportunity to ask any questions.

In addition to the investigative components and description, the impact of the assault should also be addressed. This is done by focusing on changes in lifestyle or symptoms that have developed such as: (1) changes in eating and sleep patterns, (2) school performance, (3) peer relationships, and (4) emotional, behavioral and physical symptoms. Has the child reported sexual assault previously? Is there a concern over the child hurting himself? It is also helpful to assess the reaction of the family members. What is their reaction to the allegation, what actions have they taken, and who do they blame? How supportive is the family?

The child may not be the only victim. The child lives within the context of the family and environment, therefore parental concerns and expectations must also be addressed. It is helpful to be sensitive to parental reactions such as: (1) guilt regarding inadequately protecting the child, (2) failing to recognize abuse, (3) fear regarding consequences of the assault, (4) embarrassment and (5) others.

Parents must be informed about the obligation to report and that some investigation will take place. Parents can help their children by following up on medical and counseling appointments, having other children in the household examined or interviewed and being supportive of the child. They can encourage the child to express their reactions to the assault, but should be informed not to pressure or push the child to talk. They should allow the child to express both positive and negative feelings about the perpetrator. The parents can also help the child resume normal activities. Parents must be aware of the physical and psychological indications that the child might need further help or counseling. They then need to know whom they may contact should that help be needed.

THE MEDICAL EXAMINATION

The medical examination is a necessary component in the evaluation of every alleged sexual abuse victim. The purposes of the medical evaluation are: (1) to determine if there is physical injury or infection present, thus providing supportive evidence; (2) to determine the appropriate treatment for any injury or disease that may be present, such as pregnancy, venereal disease or trauma; and (3) to allow the opportunity to provide appropriate reassurance to the child and family regarding the integrity of the child's anatomy, reproductive function and the normal reactions to sexual victimization. Even if the type of abuse suggests that a child would have a normal physical examination, it is imperative that every parent have the opportunity to ask the physician questions or be told that the child is normal and can grow up to be a parent and have babies, if that is in fact the case.

All victims need a medical evaluation at some point in time. The timing of that examination will be dependent upon several factors, primarily the time since the child was last assaulted. The considerations are: (1) the possibility of supportive evidence being present, (2) the emotional state of the victim, and (3) the expertise of the examiner available.

Clothing, hair and physical evidence of sexual assault are most apt to be present immediately after an assault. In cases where such evidence might be obtainable, the child should be examined immediately, and before bathing or changing clothes. Sperm may be motile for as long as 24 hours and nonmotile for 24 to 48 hours (Boeckx, 1982). Acid phosphatase, another indication of ejaculation, may be detected for up to 72 hours after an assault.

Physical signs of trauma, such as redness, bruises, tears and bleeding, may be apparent immediately after an assault or may develop hours to days later. Thus, in an acute assault situation, the child needs to be examined immediately. If the assault has occurred within the past 72 hours, it is important for the child to be examined as soon as possible. In those cases where a child has been assaulted beyond 72 hours, the emotional state of the victim and the expertise of available examiners will influence the timing of the examination. It may be appropriate to hold off referral to an emergency room in the middle of the night if the evaluation can be done during the day or there is an examiner with more expertise who would be available to perform the examination within several days or even a week.

There are several components of the medical exam: the history, the physical examination, forensic specimen collection and treatment. It is necessary and appropriate for medical personnel to interview the child and family regarding the child's medical background, developmental history and current state of functioning. There is some debate among professionals regarding the need for medical personnel to interview a child regarding the history of abuse. It is the experience of this author that in the courtroom, the physician is invariably asked what the child told her about the abuse experience. Regardless of the source, the knowledge of the types of acts allegedly committed is necessary and may influence components or interpretation of the examination.

Assessment of the child's current functioning should include behavioral changes, nightmares, fears that have developed, new kinds of questions and play the child may be demonstrating. The review of systems must include an assessment of problems with: (1) choking, (children who have had oral sex may choke); (2) vomiting, (a child vomiting in his bed may be a good way to keep someone else out); (3) any form of somatic symptoms; (4) urinary tract symptomatology such as pain on urination or frequency of urination; (5) genital complaints; (6) vaginal discharge or stains in the underwear; (7) blood in the urine or stool, and (8) any form of sexual preoccupation.

It is also important to assess the kinds of questions the child has asked about sex, what education the child has had regarding sexual activity or unwanted touching, and how parents may deal with issues of nudity and modesty in the home such as co-sleeping and bathing practices. These questions may be important because the child's developmental back-ground in this regard may certainly influence what it is the child knows or understands about body parts and functions. A child's exposure to sexually explicit material (magazine, movies) may also influence apparent knowledge.

The child should have a complete physical examination. Most children are familiar with physicians and physician's offices. They expect their ears and heart to be checked as part of their examination. This helps to take abuse out of the realm of something very special. As part of the physical examination, the emotional state and reaction to the examination should be noted. Signs of trauma anywhere on the body should be observed and noted. Physical and sexual abuse do occur together.

It is imperative that the child be prepared for the examination. The medical examination is not harmful and with preparation, the majority of children tolerate it very well. It is important to explain why and what tests will be done, and to show the child all of the materials to be used. The child may want to hold and touch cotton swabs and gloves. The anatomically correct dolls can be useful in demonstrating to the child what will be included in the examination.

Many children can help in the exam. They can look, show you their anatomy, hold the labia apart, and do the touching with the cotton swab with guidance by the physician's hand. In addition, the child should be allowed to choose the position for the examination. Some children may prefer to sit on the mother's lap during the examination, or lie down on top of the mother who is lying on the examining table. Many children prefer to lie flat on the table and hold their knees apart, or sit in a frog-leg position, leaning backward.

During the examination of the genitalia, any signs of trauma should be noted: erythema, tears, bruises and scars. The vaginal opening should be examined and the integrity of the hymen noted. The introital opening size should be described in terms of millimeters of horizontal diameter. The characteristics of the hymen should be described: shape, vascular pattern, and any irregularity in the edges of the hymen (rounding or adhesions). Lesions that are identified should be reported by location with reference to the introitus as a face of a clock. The rectal examination should note rectal tone, blood, fissures, hemorrhoids, scars and tears.

A complete pelvic or internal exam is indicated if the child has vaginal bleeding or is post-pubertal. The pelvic examination includes cervical cultures for chlamydia and gonorrhea, a good look at the vaginal walls and cervix for signs of trauma or infection, and collection of forensic specimens, when indicated. The reason for an internal examination with vaginal bleeding is to identify the degree of trauma and bleeding. A child may have significant internal bleeding from such trauma and may need surgical repair. The pubertal or post-pubertal child needs a pelvic exam to identify infectious organisms. Both chlamydia and gonorrhea in the post-pubertal child will survive only in the area of the cervix. In a pre-pubertal child, the vaginal pH and mucosa allow growth of gonorrhea and chlamydia within the vagina itself. A speculum exam is not indicated if there is no external evidence of penetration and the cultures can be obtained from the vagina.

Colposcopy is a method of magnified visual inspection that employs a binocular system and may have photographic capabilities. The colposcope provides a mechanism for closer inspection for signs of trauma. It has been primarily used to study cervical pathology and carcinoma in situ in adult females, but has been recently used to investigate hymenal integrity and microtrauma after sexual intercourse (Teixeira, 1981).

It's potential for use in identifying and documenting microtrauma is under exploration in the normal and sexually abused child. Several studies report minor trauma, changes in vascularization, tears, fissures, bruising and interrupted hymen after sexual assault (Teixeira, 1981, Norvel et al, 1984, Emans et al, 1985). The concern remains, however, regarding interpretation of findings with the colposcope. There have yet been no published control studies examining presumably normal, nonabused children. Emans (1985), has recently reported preliminary data suggesting an increased presence of erythema, friability, adhesions and synechiae in sexually abused female children when compared with other populations; abrasions and fissures were seen only in abused children. Further studies using colposcopy in presumably nonabused control children will be necessary to further delineate the usefulness of this tool. It may be that some of the minor trauma identified only by the colposcope is not necessarily an indication of sexual assault. The colposcope, however, is very useful in further delineating trauma that is seen with the naked eye.

Forensic specimens are necessary when penetration or attempted penetration has occurred within the previous 72 hours. Permission from parents or others who are responsible for temporary custody (police) is required to collect evidence. Some states allow children 12 years of age and older to consent to the examination and the collection of evidence.

The chain of custody must be preserved if the results are to be admissible as evidence in court. Evidence to be collected would include clothing, fingernail scrapings, pubic or other hair, and blood or saliva that may be the assailant's. Sperm may be collected from the vaginal vault or cervical area and all suspicious areas should be swabbed (the mouth, the anus, labia, vagina and cervix) to detect acid phosphatase, another indication of ejaculation. Cotton swabs should be used to collect specimens from any suspicious areas. A blood and saliva sample from the child should be obtained as a control. All sites should be cultured if there is any history of loss of consciousness or drug use. Cultures are usually not performed by the police laboratory and must be processed separately. Specific directions in handling forensic specimens may vary from one area to another and should be clarified with law enforcement and district attorney's offices locally.

Whether or not there was abuse within the previous 72 hours, every child should be tested for gonorrhea and chlamydia in the vagina or penile urethra, the throat, and the rectal area. A serum test for syphilis should be obtained. A pregnancy test should be obtained in all post-pubertal females. Any other medical tests that are necessary based on the history and physical examination should be included. The treatment involves medical management of infection or pregnancy, and reassurance, if appropriate, to the parent and child regarding the integrity of the child's anatomy, the ability to resume normal functions and **grow up to be a parent.**

The findings of the medical examination are related to: (1) the time since the last abuse, (2) the duration and type of abuse, and (3) the degree of force used. Recent and acute trauma is more apt to leave marks that are evident, whereas remote abuse occurring months or years previously is less apt to be associated with physical findings. Certainly the type of abuse, be it fondling or intercourse, will leave different marks. It is important to identify other indications of physical trauma that may be associated with sexual assault. For example, a child who has been forcibly held down or chained may have marks on the extremities indicating such.

Chronic sexual molestation is suggested by physical findings of multiple hymenal transections, rounded hymenal remnants, vaginal dilatation, healed hymenal laceration at six o'clock, the ability to relax the pubococcygeus muscle and cervicitis (Blythe and Orr, 1985). Acute molestation is suggested by perineal contusion or bruising, erythema of the hymen, abrasions and lacerations, spasm of the pubococcygeus muscle and evidence of seminal products.

A NORMAL EXAMINATION DOES NOT EXCLUDE SEXUAL ABUSE. Twenty to fifty percent of victims of sexual assault have been noted to have a completely normal physical examination (Rimsza and Niggemann, 1982). This is one of the reasons that it is imperative that the other behavioral and psychological information be obtained as well.

The medical record should document detailed objective medical findings and a general impression. Both presence and absence of findings should be noted. It is important that the medical examiner not state, "There is no evidence of abuse." Such a statement may cause considerable problems in the courtroom, even though **no evidence** can be entirely consistent with sexual assault of a child. It is suggested that **normal exam** be used instead, or simply a comment that the physical examination is normal but consistent with the possibility of sexual abuse. All professionals must realize that in many cases the medical examination cannot specifically determine that sexual assault has or has not occurred.

THE PSYCHOLOGICAL ASSESSMENT

The psychological assessment and treatment of the victim and family become the core of any comprehensive community program and should begin at the time the child enters the system. It is generally assumed that the child is telling the truth and that sexual victimization will have some negative effects. This does not mean that all children suffer psychological sequellae either immediately or long-term. Because so little is known about those children who are either not followed-up or who never report, it is inappropriate to state that all victims of sexual abuse suffer long-term psychological damage. It is imperative, however, that each child and family be assessed and recognize that there may be some negative effects that would respond to treatment and intervention.

The degree of psychological impact seems to be affected by several factors: the relationship to the offender, the number of encounters, the duration of the abuse, the extent of the abuse, the degree of bribery or coercion, the family response, the nature of the court involvement and the ego strengths of the child. A study comparing women reporting dysfunction as a result of assault compared with women who were sexually assaulted but felt no dysfunction suggested that age at the time of assault, duration of the assault, and the relationship to the offender were significantly related to the long-term outcome of perceived dysfunction (Tsai et. al., 1979). Those women who did not perceive any dysfunction and felt themselves to be clinically normal, were assessed to be no different from nonabused control women with regard to clinical functioning and the Minnesota Multiphasic Personality Inventory.

The rape trauma syndrome describes reactions to a life threatening situation in adult women who were sexually assaulted (Burgess and Holmstrom, 1974). The acute phase components of this reaction include disorganization with fear, anxiety, anger and self-blame regarding the assault. There are often disturbances in sleep patterns and fear of physical violence or death. Phobic reactions, nightmares and psychosomatic symptoms may develop. It isn't unusual for women to change their addresses and phone numbers in order to readjust.

Sexually abused teenagers 12 to 17 years old were studied to determine self-reported stresses of adolescent rape (Felice et. al., 1978). Fear for their lives and bodily harm were the major concerns. Shame, self blame and guilt were more of a problem than anger at the perpetrator. Part of this may have been due to many parents actually blaming the child. Sexual anxieties about relationships with men and promiscuous behavior were of much more concern to the parent than to the victims. The most important thing for adolescents was to be accepted and treated like every one else. Teenage and adult victims may experience similar reactions to sexual abuse but some differences are notable.

Felice (1978) described the adolescent's responses to rape as distinct from the rape trauma syndrome. In adolescents, the rape led to phobias about leaving the home, interacting with strangers, or developing relationships with boys. A later stage of denial allowed them to begin to socialize, but was followed by psychosomatic complaints of headaches, dizziness or abdominal pain. Rather than a constellation of findings distinct from rape trauma, adolescent responses might be considered developmentally based manifestations of the same process (Hibbard, 1985).

Abusive experiences may predispose children to behavior and emotional problems, sleep disturbances, drug and alcohol abuse, school failure and suicidal ideation. Lower self-esteem, social isolation and delinquent runaway behavior are well known sequellae. Sixty-five to seventy-five percent of adolescent prostitutes report having been victims of forced sexual relations prior to their prostitution (James and Meyerding, 1977, Silbert and Pines, 1981). Sexually misused adolescents taking the

Offer Self-Image Questionnaire were found to have serious problems with sexual attitudes, family relationships and ability to master the environment (Orr, 1981). There are now several reports of hysterical seizures in victims of incest (Goodwin et. al., 1979, Gross, 1979).

Strong emotional and psychosocial supports are imperative for a good outcome. Later corrective sexual experiences and the attitudes of the family and community may temper adverse effects. Treatment plans should incorporate considerations for the age of the victim, the ego capacities, the relationship to normal growth and development and the environmental supports. Reassurance that the child is not responsible for the abuse and that it was right to reveal the abuse are important. Issues of protection by a trusted adult must be addressed.

Some victims and families may not feel the need for immediate psychological intervention, however, it should always be offered. Those children needing more extensive evaluation and treatment should be referred appropriately. It is often important to remember that in a young victim, the family or mother may need counseling and therapy more than the child. The child and family should be aware of potential problems that may surface later. If intervention is not deemed necessary immediately, it may be needed at a later point in time.

CONCLUSION

Any problem may have a different presentation or manifestation in a given individual. To identify that problem, it's possibility has to be considered. There is no difference in the problem of child sexual abuse. One must be willing to consider the diagnosis and recognize that the problem occurs in order to identify it. No two children may present in exactly the same way. It is important to understand the impact of sexual assault from the child's perspective in order to interpret the information obtained. One must be careful to not place adult expectations on childhood experiences and reactions. There are rarely absolute answers regarding what may constitute abuse and it's affect on a given child. Professionals must work together in order to best understand and coordinate efforts in evaluating a child for the possibility of sexual abuse. Communication and coordination can avoid duplication of effort while optimizing the overall evaluation and treatment.

REFERENCES

1. American Humane Association: *National Study on Child Neglect and Abuse Reporting*. Denver, American Humane Association, 1981.
2. Blythe, M. J., and Orr, D. P.: Childhood sexual abuse: guidelines for evaluation. *Indiana Medicine,* Jan, 11–18, 1985.
3. Boeckx, R.: Interpretation of tests for the detection of semen in vaginal fluid sample. In: *Training Materials, Division of Child Protection*. Washington, 1982.
4. Brant, R., and Tisza, V.: The sexually misused child. *Am J Orthopsychiatr,* Jan, 1977, pp. 80–90.
5. Burgess, A. W., and Holmstrom L. L.: Rape trauma syndrome. *Am J Psychiatri, 131*(9):981–985, 1974.
6. DeJong, A.: Epidemiologic factors in sexual abuse of boys. *Am J Dis Child, 136,:*990–993, 1982.
7. DeJong, A., Emmett, N. G. A., and Hervada, A. R.: Sexual abuse of children. *Am J Dis Child, 136:*129–134, 1982.
8. Ellerstein, N. S., and Canavan, J.: Sexual abuse of boys. *Am J Dis Child, 134:*255–257, 1980.
9. Emans, S. J., Woods, E. R., Flagg, N., and Freeman, A.: Genital findings in sexually abused girls. In: *Society for Pediatric Research*. Washington, 1985, Abstract 47.
10. Felice, M. A., Grant, J., and Reynolds, B.: Follow-up observations of adolescent rape victims. *Clin Pediatr, 17:*311–315, 1978.
11. Finkelhor, D.: *Sexually Victimized Children*. New York, Free, 1979a.
12. Finkelhor, D.: What's wrong with sex between adults and children? *Am J Orthopsychiatr, 49:*692–697, 1979.
13. Finklehor, D., Gomes-Schwartz, B., and Horowitz, J.: Professionals' responses. In Finklehor, D. (Ed.): *Child Sexual Abuse, New Theory and Research*. 1985, pp.200–220.
14. Ginsburg, H., and Opper, S.: *Piaget's Theory of Intellectual Development*. New Jersey, Prentice Hall, 1969.
15. Goodwin, J., Simms, M., and Bergman, R.: Hysterical seizures. A sequel to incest. *Am J Orthospychiatr, 49:*698–703, 1979.
16. Gross, M.: Incestuous rape: a cause for hysterical seizures in four adolescent girls. *Am J Orthopsychiatr, 49:*704–708, 1979.
17. Hibbard, R. A., and Orr, D. P.: Incest and sexual abuse. *Seminars Adol Med, 1:*153–164, 1985.
18. Hibbard, R. A., Roghmann, K., and Hoekelman, R. A.: Genitalia in children's drawings: an association with sexual abuse. *Pediatr,* (in press).
19. James, J., and Meyerding, J.: Early sexual experience and prostitution. *Am J Psychiatr, 134*(12):1381–1385, 1977.
20. Mrazek, P. B.: Definition and recognition of sexual child abuse: historical and cultural perspectives. In Mrazek, P. B., and Kempe, C. H. (Eds.): *Sexually Abused Children and Their Families*. New York, Pergamon, 1981, pp. 5–16.

21. Norvell, M. K., Benrubi, G. I., and Thompson, R. J.: Investigation of microtrauma after sexual intercourse. *J Repro Med, 29:*269–271, 1984.
22. Orr, D. P.: Psychosocial adjustment of adolescent sexual abuse victims. *Clin Res, 29:*105A, 1981.
23. Peters, S. D., Wyatt, G. E., and Finklehor, D.: Prevalence. In Finklehor, D. (Ed.): *A Source Book on Child Sexual Abuse.* Beverly Hills, Sage, 1986, pp. 15–59.
24. Rimsza, M. E., and Niggemann, E. H.: Medical evaluation of sexually abused children: a review of 311 cases. *Pediatrics,* Jan, 8–14, 1982.
25. Russel, D. E. H.: The incidence and prevalence of intrafamilial and extrafamilial sexual abuse of female children. *Child Abuse Neglect, 7:*133–146, 1983.
26. Silbert, M. H., and Pines, A. M.: Sexual child abuse as an antecedent to prostitution. *Child Abuse Neglect,* pp. 407–411, 1981.
27. Summit, R. C.: The child sexual abuse accommodation syndrome. *Child Abuse Neglect, 7:*177–193, 1983.
28. Summit, R. C., and Kryso, J.: Sexual abuse of children: a clinical spectrum. *Am J Orthopsychiatr, 48*(2):237–251, 1978.
29. Teixeira, W. G. R.: Hymenal colposcopic examination in sexual offenses. *Amer J Forensic Med Path, 2:*209–215, 1981.
30. Tsai, M., Feldman-Sumners, S., and Edgar, M.: Childhood molestation: variables related to differential impact on psychosexual funtioning in adult women. *J Abnormal Psychol, 88:*407–417, 1979.

Figure 1.

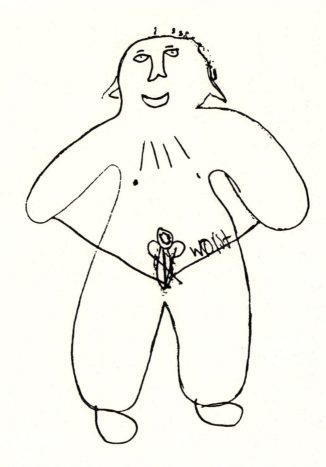

Figure 2.

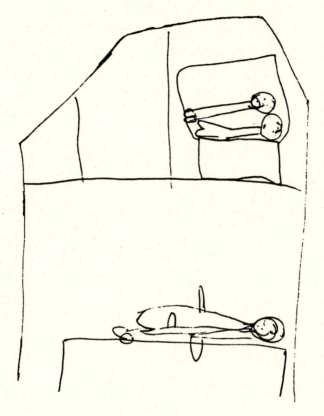

Figure 3.

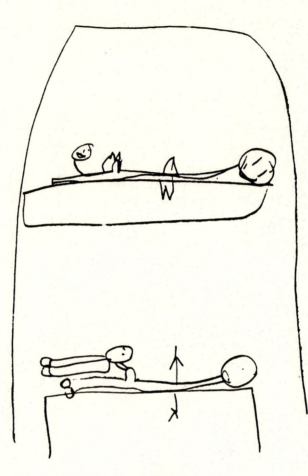

Figure 4.

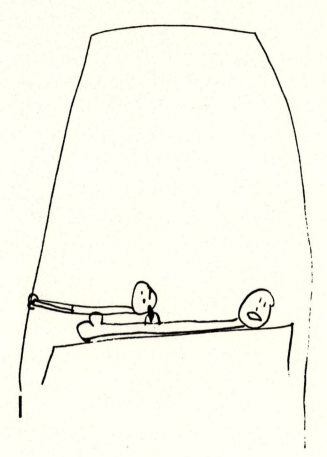

Figure 5.

CHAPTER 14

INTERVENTION AND TREATMENT
OF CHILD SEXUAL ABUSE

ANN H. TYLER
KEVIN J. GULLY

INTRODUCTION

The primary objective for delivering services to a sexually abused child is to eliminate the adverse effects of the sexual abuse in order to ensure normal emotional, cognitive, and behavioral development. Failure to help a victim can mean that immediate problems will fester for years. Often, the ultimate consequence is a new victim of sexual abuse. This consequence could have been prevented if successful intervention and treatment had been provided. Three cases highlight this point.

Case 1: Mary was sexually abused by her father for eight years. Mary had a daughter by her father at 15 years of age. The sexual abuse was never reported or addressed. Now, Mary's daughter is 9 years of age and she has been sexually abused by her father/grandfather.

Case 2: Henry was sexually abused by his father and forced by his father to have sexual contact with his sisters. During the ensuing years, Henry was placed in numerous residential treatment programs. At 18 years of age, Henry was convicted of rape. In jail, he was gang raped.

Case 3: John was sexually abused by a foster mother and by a teenage female on another occasion. There was no intervention or treatment and, subsequently, John began raping his sister until arrested.

The focus of this chapter is on the intervention and treatment of child sexual abuse since some issues (e.g., traumatic sexualization) are unique to this problem. Furthermore, it is important that concomitant problems receive attention and that services are provided for the prosecution and the treatment of the offender. However, this chapter is not directed specifically toward these related issues.

The complications associated with sexual abuse are numerous. The history of the sexually abused child may include additional physical abuse, emotional abuse, or neglect. The victim may be retarded or emotionally disturbed. The victim may have amnesia for the sexual abuse. Parents may be single, very rigid in their beliefs, isolated, alcoholics, poor, physically abusive with each other, or emotionally disturbed. Parents may minimize the problems because of the personal distress they feel due to the abuse and a belief that the abuse should be eliminated from discussion so that it will be forgotten. There may be no transportation or permanent home. Services may be required to shift from providing immediate treatment to the sexually abused child, to giving data to law enforcement, prosecutors, defense attorneys, the court, or protective services. Legal authority to work with the victim may not be clear. Custody disputes create additional confusion.

These interrelated problems are often significant and the resolution of these issues are critical if the intervention and treatment of the child sexual abuse is to be successful. These related aspects of child sexual abuse deserve a full review, but for the sake of clarity, the core of this chapter will focus on the central factors involved in the intervention and treatment of child sexual abuse.

The key elements for delivering services to a sexually abused child are: crisis intervention, assessment, diagnosis, and treatment. These components are not necessarily discrete and are often iterative. The final part of this chapter details training issues.

CONCEPTUALIZATION

Child sexual abuse is a complex problem with a vast number of issue domains and consequent problems can indeed be pervasive. These areas include: the type of abuse, victim, perpetrator, and context. Interactions among these variables create additional issues of concern.

The issues related to abusive acts can be discussed in terms of three dimensions. First, aspects of the sexual act vary from intercourse, attempted intercourse, fellatio, cunnilingus, analingus, and anal intercourse to less intimate unwanted kissing or touching of clothed parts of the body. Second, coercion or force versus manipulation or positive reinforcement for sexual behavior. Third, the duration and frequency of the abuse are important determinants of how the victims will be affected. Browne and Finkelhor (1986) conclude that more intimate contact and force are associated with more trauma, and that the duration and frequency of the sexual abuse are not necessarily related to the degree of trauma experienced by the victim.

The victim may be male or female, be prepubertal or postpubertal, and vary in emotional, cognitive, and/or behavioral dysfunctions. Browne and Finkelhor (1986) state that there is not a clear relationship between age of onset and trauma, but a possible trend for younger children to be more traumatized exists.

The perpetrator can be a male or a female, known or unknown, trusted or not trusted, intrafamilial or extrafamilial, and an adolescent or an adult. Sometimes, there is more than one perpetrator. Browne and Finkelhor (1986) note that sexual abuse by a close relative and male perpetrators may be more damaging. They contend that greater trauma occurs when the perpetrator is a father or father figure as compared to all other types of perpetrators. They state that data consistently suggest that being victimized by an adolescent perpetrator is less traumatic.

Contextual elements for the sexual abuse include such questions as: whether the abuse is reported, what are the parental reactions, has there been intervention by protective services, will there be involvement in prosecuting the perpetrator, and what are the treatment recommendations? The general clinical assumption is that reporting the abuse facilitates its resolution, but Browne and Finkelhor (1986) were not able to find studies to confirm that keeping the abuse secret results in greater distress. They did identify consistent results in two studies showing that negative parental reactions exacerbate the trauma. Another study revealed that children removed from their homes display more behavioral problems (Browne and Finkelhor, 1986). Involvement of the sexually abused child in the criminal process may have unique implications, for example, increased guilt or sense that control over his/her life has been regained (Terr, 1986; Claman, Harris, Bernstein, & Louitt, 1986).

Problems occur in emotions, cognitions, behaviors, and the family (e.g., Becker, Skinner, and Abel, 1983; Berliner and Ernst, 1984; Tyler and Brassard, 1984; Friedrich, Urquiza and Beilke, 1986; Jones, 1986; Lusk and Waterman, 1986). Browne and Finkelhor (1986) summarize the significant initial and subsequent effects of child sexual abuse:

> The empirical literature on child sexual abuse, then, does suggest the presence—in some portion of the victim population—of many of the initial effects reported in the clinical literature, especially reactions of fear, anxiety, depression, anger, hostility, and inappropriate sexual behavior. Empirical studies with adults confirm many of the long-term

effects of sexual abuse mentioned in the clinical literature. Adult women victimized as children are more likely to manifest depression, self-destructive behavior, anxiety, feelings of isolation and stigma, poor self-esteem, a tendency toward revictimization and substance abuse. Difficulty in trusting others and sexual maladjustment in such areas as sexual dysphoria, sexual dysfunction, impaired sexual self-esteem, and avoidance of or abstention from sexual activity have also been reported by empirical researchers. (p. 72)

Although a specific syndrome or cluster of problems caused by sexual abuse would be very useful for forming a conclusion that sexual abuse has or has not occurred when direct data are not available to substantiate sexual abuse (Nurcombe, 1986; Green, 1986), current information only demonstrates that many behavioral problems are consistent with childhood sexual victimization. Other possible explanations for problems that might suggest sexual abuse has occurred include interparental conflict (Emery, 1982), observations of spouse abuse (Wolfe, Zak, Wilson, and Jaffe, 1986; Jaffe, Wolfe, Wilson, and Zak, 1986), physical abuse and neglect (Aragona and Eyberg, 1981; Bousha and Twentyman, 1984; Main and George, 1985), or sibling violence (Gully, Dengerink, Pepping, and Bergstrom, 1981; Gully and Dengerink, 1983). Being a victim in nonsocial incidents (e.g., burglary) could form the basis for some apparent symptomatic behaviors (Kahn, 1984).

CRISIS INTERVENTION OF SEXUALLY ABUSED CHILDREN

Intervention with children who have been sexually traumatized should include intervention with the children's family; whether the abuse is intrafamilial or extrafamilial. Clinical experience and research noted previously indicate that the child's resolution of the abuse certainly is influenced by the parent's reactions. If the parents are so traumatized by the experience that they are not psychologically available to the child, then the child feels as if indeed the very worst thing in the world has happened to him/her. In addition to the parental reaction, the investigatory system's treatment of the case has a strong influence upon the child's perception of what has happened to him/her (Tyler and Brassard, 1984).

Again, clinical experience demonstrates that a child almost regardless of age, senses or knows that an act of sexual abuse is wrong. It confuses and usually frightens the child. In an effort to ameliorate this trauma, it is important to intervene quickly, with authority and as much community support as is possible. Of prime importance is ensuring immediate protection for the child. This would preferably involve removing the perpetrator from the home if it is an incest situation. If, however, the nonperpetrating parent of the child is physically or psychologically unable to protect the child, then removal of the child into protective services is necessary. Because the child already suffers from confusion, fear, anxiety, perhaps even guilt, it is certainly better to leave her/him with the family of origin if at all possible.

The crisis intervention and the assessment phase typically occur concurrently, with the latter usually taking around three appointments to assess the disruption and the dysfunction that occurs as a result of the sexual abuse.

There are five steps to consider so that the crisis intervention phase becomes integrated with the assessment and the treatment phases.

1. Although physical findings are not common in these cases, the first priority in the intervention is to assist the child to cope with the medical examination which is usually required for prosecution. Referral to a pediatrician with special training in this area is important since insensitive examination would cause further traumatization to the victim.

2. Helping the child cope with the investigative interview by police and protective service workers is important. In some communities, these interviews are consolidated and coordinated between law enforcement and protective services and a qualified psychologist. Reports of multiple interviews of children are not uncommon, resulting in report inaccuracies, inconsistencies, and further trauma to the child. The investigative interview, when videotaped can be useful in several ways: (a) it helps protect against later recantation of the child; (b) it reduces the number of times a child is interviewed; and (c) it can and has been used for court purposes in prosecution of the case. Careful use of the videotaped interview is important however, since there are some problems; for example, confidentiality and questions of videotape ownership.

3. If the perpetrator of sexual abuse is prosecuted, the child and the family may require assistance to understand the legal procedures involved. It is often recommended that a child be appointed a Guardian ad litum, particularly in cases wherein there is a custody or divorce proceeding.

4. When it is necessary to remove the child from the home, it is important that the psychologist support the child, helping him/her with expression of feelings related to the crisis. The victim needs one person who is available throughout the crisis period.

5. Depending upon the developmental level of the child, different strategies can be utilized to facilitate cognitive mastery of the abuse experience. A five year old child's perception is significantly different from an eight, twelve, or sixteen year old's perception of sexual abuse. It is necessary to help a child reframe his experience as his understanding of the event changes throughout his development.

Assessment of the child's functioning both before and after the crisis, should include the following areas: behavioral, affective, somatic, and cognitive.

ASSESSMENT GOALS, METHODOLOGY AND DIAGNOSTIC CONSIDERATIONS

The evaluation is important for determining treatment goals and corroborating the child's statements regarding the nature and scope of the abuse because child sexual abuse is a crime.

The general goals of assessment are to substantiate the parameters of the alleged sexual abuse, identify consequent and concurrent problems, and make recommendations for the treatment and safety of the child. Accomplishing these goals requires: (1) analyses of all relevant background information, (2) assessment of the child's ability to report the facts, (3) evaluation of the credibility of the child, (4) emotional and interpersonal problems, (5) health issues, and (6) documentation of all circumstances of abuse and neglect. Interviewing skills and competence to use psychological tests are fundamental components of the process.

Establishing the parameters and context of the sexual abuse promotes optimal protection of the child and provides necessary data for treatment recommendations. If the abuse included force on numerous occasions rather than a simple one time exhibition, then the perpetrator is more apt to be incarcerated and removed from the community where he/she could again sexually abuse the same child or other children. Without the parameters and context, there is the potential to incorrectly conclude the amount of danger presented by an alleged perpetrator. Failure to understand the total circumstances of the apparent sexual act might lead to the incorrect conclusion that sexual abuse occurred if the decision is based solely on information that a child touched the genitals of a parent, since touching is not uncommon (Rosenfeld, Bailey, Siegel, and Bailey, 1986). If the abuse involved violence or threats of harm versus subtle manipulation by a parent, then issues for treating the sexually abused child may be expected to vary respectively from anxiety and fear to trust and depression.

Concluding that a child is competent requires analyzing his/her ability to report the facts of the case accurately. Claman, Harris, Bernstein, and Louitt (1986) note two questions that require affirmative answers to determine that a child is a competent witness. The questions are:

1. Does the child have the intelligence and capacity to provide the facts about a case?
2. Does the child feel a duty to tell the truth, and can the child separate truth from falsehood? (p. 457)

Nurcombe (1986) discusses the idea that credibility is relative; that is, honest testimony may be incredible and fabrications can be convincing especially if the entire picture is not viewed as a whole. Nurcombe reports four criteria to consider when drawing conclusions regarding credibility: (1) constancy over time, (2) amount of detail, (3) expressive format, and (4) underlying motivation. Whitcomb, Shapiro, and Stellwagen (1985) have detailed four dimensions identified by Melton, Bulkely, and Wulkan (1981) to assess the competence of a child to testify:

1. Present understanding of the difference between truth and falsity and an appreciation of the obligation or responsibility to speak the truth;
2. Mental capacity at the time of the occurrence in question to observe or receive accurate impressions of the occurrence;
3. Memory sufficient to retain an independent recollection of the observations; and
4. Capacity truly to communicate or translate into words the memory of such observation and the capacity to understand simple questions about the occurrence. (p. 127)

Green (1986) lists the characteristics of true and false cases of child sexual abuse. The general focus is on conflict and reticence to discuss the abuse. False allegations are more common in particular instances. Green notes that about 6% of reported cases of sexual abuse are not substantiated when there is no custody dispute. In contrast, 36% to 55% of allegations of sexual abuse are false during court litigation involving custody and/or visitation.

The examiner, when interviewing an alleged child abuse victim, must have empathy, warmth, and genuineness. The following interviewing techniques are also important: (1) use vocabulary and age appropriate language that permit communication with a child, (2) control the duration of the evaluation tasks, (3) do not suggest memories, (4) use directive, specific questions only as a final attempt to secure information, and (5) understand the child's current mental status. The psychologist should be alert for any distortions of reality, any attempts by the alleged victim to lead to particular conclusions or passive acceptance of inaccurate feedback and the active integration of false information given by the psychologist. Attempts by the psychologist that fail to prove suggestibility can increase confidence in the allegations.

Many questions often need to be answered. Does the child know the difference between telling the truth versus a lie, and which is most valued? Can the child learn the difference? Is his/her affect consistent with the discussion of the allegation? Is the child reluctant or embarrassed to make the allegations?

It is important that the examiner not focus on one allegation, thereby neglecting to investigate additional physical or sexual abuse incidents. It is additionally important that the examiner not create unnecessary stress for the child so that it becomes a detrimental experience for the child.

Three common interviewing tools are: (1) play houses with figures, (2) **Red Flag and Green Flag People** (Rape and Abuse Crisis Center, 1985), and (3) anatomically correct dolls (White, Strom, Santilli, and Halpin, 1986). These aids can be powerful evidence, especially on videotape, when a child lacks the capacity to clearly communicate verbally the essence of the sexual abuse.

Psychological tests provide objective and projective data. Observation of the behavior of the child on structured tasks gives additional information. Coupled with background and interview data, these additional sources of information permit more comprehensive and definitive answers.

Many psychological tests are available. These tests can give relevant information regarding ability, credibility, emotional, interpersonal, and health problems. A core battery of tests might include a drawing of a man and woman, the Child Behavior Checklist (Achenback and Edelbrock, 1983), and a projective story test. The drawings can be converted to a standardized score of intellectual maturity (Harris, 1963), and affective information can be obtained by asking questions (e.g., How is this person feeling? What might make this person angry or sad?) The Child Behavior Checklist is completed by an adult who has frequent interaction with the child (e.g., parent, teacher, or foster parent).

Standardized scores for social competence and behavioral problems can be obtained for children (e.g., depression, social withdrawal, or aggression) ranging from 2 through 16 years of age. The Plenk Storytelling Test (Plenk, Hinchey, and Davies, 1982) consists of nine photographs from which affective themes can be determined (e.g., fear or sadness) and judgments can be made regarding whether the precepts of the child are bound by reality. Other frequently used tests include the Bender Motor Gestalt Test (Koppitz, 1975), the AAMP Adaptive Behavior Scale (Lambert, 1981; Lambert, Windmiller, Tharinger, and Cole, 1981; Gully and Hosch, 1979), the Stanford-Binet Intelligence Scale (Thorndike, Hagen, and Sattler, 1986), the Bayley Scales of Infant Development (Bayley, 1969), the Developmental Test of Visual-Motor Integration (Beery, 1982), the Children's Depression Inventory (Saylor, Finch, Jr., Baskin, Furey, and Kelly, 1984), or Robert's Apperception Test for Children (McArthur and Roberts, 1969). There may be reasons to use other tests if the circumstances and focus shift beyond the utility of the identified tests.

After substantiating the facts of the abuse, the psychologist is often required to formalize a diagnosis to establish treatment goals and the victim's prognosis.

Certainly most sexual abuse experiences can be defined as traumatic and emotionally damaging (DeFrancis, 1970) with common results such as: anxiety, intensive fears about bodily damage, fears of loss of loved ones if threats of death were made, isolation, sleep disturbances and other depressive phenomena, guilt, explosive anger, and misinformation (Brassard, Tyler and Kehle, 1983; Tufts, 1984; Goodwin, 1982; Yates, 1982). Many abused children's symptoms satisfy the **Diagnostic and Statistical Manual** of Mental Disorders (DSM–III, American Psychiatric Press, 1980) diagnostic criteria for Post-Traumatic Stress Disorder (PTSD):

1. Child sexual abuse constitutes a recognizable stressor that would evoke distress symptoms;
2. Reexperiencing of the trauma, as evidenced by recurrent dreams and intrusive recollections of the abuse;
3. Reduced involvement with the external world marked by signs of social withdrawal and contradiction of affect; and
4. Symptom formulation often manifested as sequelae of sexual abuse (i.e., hypervigilance, nightmares, avoidance of stimuli that might retraumatize, problems in concentrating or remembering, and symp-

tom intensification during exposure to events that resemble the abusive situation).

Three psychological evaluations depict the variability involved in completing an assessment. They reflect the diversity of approaches and issues. These reports have been modified to protect confidentiality.

Family Support Center
Psychological Evaluation
May 2, 1985

NAME OF CHILD: Jim Doe
DATE OF BIRTH: May 22, 1972
DATES OF EVALUATION: February 25 and 28. 1985: March 11, 18 and 25, 1985: April 1, 8, and 15, 1985.
AGE: 12
MOTHER: Ms. Doe
FATHER: Mr. Doe

I. REASON FOR EVALUATION

A. Mr. and Mrs. Doe want to verify that Jim Doe has been the victim of sexual assault.
B. They want to establish who committed the offenses.
C. They want to identify Jim's problems.
D. Finally, Mr. and Mr. Doe want Jim's problems to be treated.

II. BACKGROUND INFORMATION

The issue of sexual abuse was first raised with Mr. and Ms. Doe by people in their neighborhood. Initially, Jim was evaluated for sexual abuse by a local psychologist. Later Mr. Doe contacted Dr. Jones, of the Family Support Center requesting additional services.

Mr. and Ms. Doe provided information about the sexual abuse, alleged perpetrator(s), chronology of events, and problems that Jim has been experiencing. Aspects of the abuse include the use of drugs (orally and via injections), kidnapping, pornography, taking movies, attempts to force the consumption of feces and wearing of female underwear, threats of being shot with a gun, bruises around his groin, swollen glands, red marks near his groin, a back injury, and the demonstration of a doll having its penis cut off with the threat that the same would happen to him (Jim) if he told. The alleged perpetrator involved in all instances was John Smith, a man living near them for many years. A couple, the Sheds, were also possibly involved according to Mr. and Ms. Doe, since Jim reported that they looked like a couple that had been involved. There was an unknown many who took pictures of the sexual behavior. Mr. and Ms. Doe state that Jim was friendly and outgoing in the first and second grade, but that in 1980/1981

Jim was diagnosed as having an attention deficit disorder and started wanting to wear nylons and his sister's underwear. Copies of hospital records provide the history of three injuries and their dates: (1) "red welts on . . . (the) left leg (and) enlarged lymph nodes in (the) groin area: on November 7, 1982; (2) "lumbar contusion" on May 3, 1983; and (3) a "skinned knee . . . with tender nodules in (the) groin" on March 31, 1983. Problems noted by Mrs. and Ms. Doe include his attention deficit disorder, "cross-dressing," extreme fear of pain, fighting with his siblings, and attempts to grab other boys' genitals.

There is also an allegation that Joe Doe, Jim's younger brother, has been victimized by John Smith. No information suggests that Jim's older or younger sister have been sexually abused.

III. EVALUATION PROCEDURES

A. Clinical Interviews
B. Anatomically Correct Dolls
C. Plenk Storytelling Test
D. Draw-A–Person
E. Bender-Gestalt Visual Motor Test
F. Nowicki-Strickland Scale
G. Piers-Harris self-Concept Scale
H. Hopkins Symptom Check List
I. Achenback Child Behavior Checklist—Teacher Report Form
J. Achenback Child Behavior Checklist—Parent Report Form
K. Copies of Medical Records
L. An Educational Evaluation from May 30, 1984

IV. RESULTS

A. **Cognitive Functioning (Ability)**: Jim has the intelligence to perform adequately at grade level and understand the difference between reality and fantasy. His drawings suggest average intelligence. Similar conclusions can be drawn from the Wechsler Intelligence Scale for Children — Revised (WISC–R), Woodcock Johnson Psycho-Educational Battery, and Draw-A–Person administered and reported in a prior educational evaluation conducted by Drs. Hansen and Roberts in May, 1984. His current Bender-Gestalt and an earlier one discussed by Drs. Hansen and Roberts were deficient. His recent Bender-Gestalt was poorly planned and done quickly. The variability observed on his WISC–R and deficient Bender-Gestalt might be due to either his "reported" attention deficit disorder (ADD) or the sequelae of emotional trauma (e.g., anxiety and fear). Better academic performance is anticipated as his attention, impulsiveness, and conduct problems improve via the management of his ADD and/or resolution of his emotional trauma. No information indicated disorientation or brain damage.

B. **Reliability of Information (Credibility)**: Jim claims that the first person to know of his sexual abuse by John Smith was his mother, Ms. Doe, after she asked if he had been touched. He denied that his friends have ever talked about the case with him or that he has talked with them. Information that he provided seemed always to be firsthand knowledge, uncontaminated by second hand data or intimidation. He understands the importance of telling the truth.

Jim was very uncomfortable reporting the offenses, often trying to avoid the emotional pain. He was embarrassed frequently while discussing his victimization. Jim's verbal reports matched demonstrations with anatomically correct dolls. He readily corrected our mistakes about the case. His discussion of the case was concrete, very detailed, beyond the scope of knowledge expected for even a very sophisticated professional, factually consistent, matched by congruent emotions, embedded in the world of John Smith via his home, son, and condominiums, and further clarified without prompting. Unexpected complications were noted. Jim readily acknowledged that all of the events were not completely clear to himself. The events, Jim revealed, seemed to be understandable deviant sexual behavior. The apparent production of pornography seemed consistent with the information provided by Jim. Hospital records seem to corroborate what Jim states to be the facts of the case, including periods of time.

All information indicated that Mr. and Ms. Doe want their children to be happy and healthy. They seem to be concerned parents who would not coerce their children into testifying or fabricating a story, since it has been painful for them as well as their children.

C. **Emotional-Social Functioning**: Jim has a good self-concept, but experiences excessive fear and somatic problems. He is impulsive, lacks sustained attention, displays conduct problems, and acts immaturely. He may have generalized anxiety problems. There is some underlying sadness or depression.

D. **Health Issues**: Jim complains of back pain, dizziness, chest pains, sweating, low energy, nauseousness, sore muscles, and trouble getting his breath. Past hospital records indicate a lumbar contusion and swollen lymph glands.

E. **Instances of Abuse (Videotaped Interviews Available)**: Jim has been able to identify clearly four instances of sexual assault. The sequence represents a possible temporal order for the events. Other instances are possible.

Incident Number 1: According to Jim Doe, this alleged offense occurred in John Smith's bedroom after he (Jim) had been taken there by John Smith. Elements of the offense perpetrated by John Smith included being hit in the back with a belt, repeatedly hit in the back with a fist, told to ingest a red capsule, instructed to "go to the bathroom" while pictures were taken, locked in the room, shown adult and child pornography, and touched on his penis. Additionally, an "old guy with gray hair and a scar on his face," (Pete) took movies while John Smith touched Jim on his penis.

Jim said that this offense happened in May, two summers ago, after finishing the fifth grade. He explained his injuries to his mother as the consequences of falling off of a trampoline. One hospital record shows that Jim suffered from a lumbar contusion per a diagnosis on May 3, 1983.

Incident Number 2: Jim states that this offense transpired in a condominium in Anywhere, USA. He saw pictures of "naked boys and girls". A couple, "Micky and Suzy," performed intercourse in front of him (Jim). Jim and John Smith were naked; John Smith touched Jim's penis and tried to have Jim touch his (John's) penis. John Smith hit Jim in the face after Jim refused to lay on top of a "girl." Pete took movies.

Jim said that this incident occurred about noon, during the summer, after finishing the fifth grade. However, Jim was not sure about the years and suggested it could have been in 1981 or 1982.

Incident Number 3: This event is relayed by Jim as taking place in a different condominium with a swimming pool in Anywhere, USA. People included John Smith, Pete, Micky and Suzy, a male and female teenager, three children about four years of age, and some other children about five or six years of age. Mr. Smith told him to take off his clothes. Jim revealed that he and the other "kids" were given shots in the groin. Jim continued by saying "I couldn't move my legs" and "I felt sleepy." Jim noted that these marks looked like spider marks and were "puffy". He (John) hit Jim and touched Jim's penis. John Smith made the teenagers touch the little kids. John, the couple, and Pete "touched the little kids". John yelled at the "teenagers to touch" the children with their mouths. "The little kids were crying and... screaming". Mr. Smith put his mouth on a boy's penis and Pete put his mouth on a little girl's boobies". Micky put his tongue in Jim's anus and "it went in." "Mr. Smith put his mouth on my weaner." John Smith said, "Don't tell or I'll come and kill your mom."

Initially, Jim could not remember how he got to the condominium, but went on to describe how he (Jim) had been walking to his friend's house when "Mr. Smith pulled up" in a car and "pulled me in." Jim responded to my question about volition by articulating that he did not want to get into the car.

Hospital records indicate that Jim had enlarged lymph node in the groin and "mosquito looking red welts on . . . (his) left leg" on November 7, 1981. On March 31, 1984, Jim and "tender nodules in . . . (his) groin" and a "skinned knee."

Incident Number 4: This offense apparently happened in the same condominium as the second incident. In this instance, "I was playing behind our condominium, (when John Smith) pulled me into his car." "I was crying and screaming and said, 'let me go'." "He (John) covered my mouth and left", hence, taking Jim to the condominium. The people included John Smith, Pete, Micky, and Suzy. There were no other children. "I was on the bed . . . I didn't want to say 'no' anymore because I didn't want to get hit." Jim went on to report that Pete took pictures and John touched his (Jim's) penis.

The fact that Jim states that he had stopped fighting to avoid being hit permits the conclusion that this is a more recent incident.

V. DIAGNOSTIC SUMMARY AND RECOMMENDATIONS

A. Has Jim Doe been the victim of sexual assault?

There is no doubt that Jim Doe has been sexually abused and assaulted. Any confusion could be explained by the emotional trauma, poor attention, or drugs (e.g., benzodiazipines?) that might cause partial amnesia or confusion for events.

B. Who committed the offenses?

Men named "John Smith" and "Pete" were involved in every incident. A couple, "Micky and Suzy," who looked like the Sheds, were involved in some incidents. Specifically, "John Smith" has assaulted Jim with a weapon (belt), forced Jim to participate in the production of pornographic pictures and movies, touched Jim's penis, placed Jim in the position of watching the sexual abuse of other children, given Jim injections in the groin which caused paralysis in his legs, placed his mouth on Jim's penis, threatened to kill Jim's mother if he told, and kidnapped Jim for the purpose of sexually assaulting him. "Micky" penetrated Jim's anus with his tongue.

C. What are Jim's problems?

Jim experiences excessive fear and somatic problems. He is impulsive, lacks sustained attention, displays conduct problems, and acts immaturely. He may have generalized anxiety problems. There is some underlying sadness or depression and anger. All of these problems could be a consequence of the sexual abuse, although the attention deficit disorder might be independent, but exacerbated by the sexual assaults.

Jim is intelligent enough to perform adequately at his age-appropriate grade level, but he does not. Symptoms of an attention deficit disorder and emotional problems are sufficient to explain the underachievement. Jim's emotional problems may be at the core of his attention deficit disorder.

D. How can Jim's problems be treated?

1. Jim should be given a physical examination to identify any reasonable medical treatments that might reduce Jim physical problems. Signs of sexual abuse or disease should be identified and treated medically, if appropriate.

2. Jim should participate in individual therapy; behavioral treatment might work very well for some of his fears, anxiety, impulsiveness, and poor attention. Jim's school performance should improve with behavioral interventions for impulsiveness and attention, some social skills training, and the reduction of emotional problems.

3. Group therapy with other victims might help reduce his stress and give him opportunities to explore the trauma in a supportive environment.

4. Family therapy is important so that the whole family will become comfortable talking openly about the sexual abuse and its impact.

5. Sex education will be very important for Jim. Depending on Jim's sexual fantasies, visual and auditory material that depict healthy sexual behavior should be available for Jim so that he can replace his deviant experiences with socially appropriate images and models. The material probably should be explicit, if it is going to be effective.

6. Social isolation will be a danger sign. Healthy relationships with other male and female teenagers are critical.

Family Support Center
Psychological Evaluation
February 1, 1986

CLIENT: Sally Smith
DATES OF EVALUATION: December 19, 1985; January 2, 9 and 16, 1986
DATE OF BIRTH: October 29, 1980
AGE: 5
FOSTER PARENT: Sara
MOTHER (GUARDIAN): Mary Smith
FATHER: Joe Smith
CASEWORKER: Ms. Conti
COUNTY ATTORNEY: Mr. Johnson

I. BACKGROUND INFORMATION

Ms. Conti noted that Mary brought Sally to shelter, apparently months ago, reportedly because she was afraid that Joe would hurt Sally. However, according to Ms. Conti, Sally stated that the scrape on her chin was from her mother who had slammed her into a table. Other bruises were also observed. Ms. Conti added that there is a history of alleged neglect, nonsupervision, and sexual abuse in Joe's family.

Ms. Conti explained that Mary is certain that Joe has sexually abused Sally since Mary has observed his 14 year old niece (Cindy) give "head" to Joe at his direction and his familial history includes sexual abuse. Ms. Conti noted that Mary possibly believes that Cindy has sexually abused Sally, too.

The account given by Joe, per Ms. Conti, is that he is innocent, but that he thinks that Mary and a man (Tom) are the perpetrators, although she lives with another man (Ernie). Ms. Conti continued that she believes that Ernie is violent, contends that Tom has been in jail for molestation, and argues that Tom raped Cindy.

Mary talked about her problems as a parent. Initially, Mary blamed Joe for telling Sally that she did not have to obey and claimed that "when I really get mad, I walk away". However, Mary continued "she gets me a little bit mad and gets her butt whopped a little bit." Mary added, "I've never been consistent enough. She (Sally) knows how to pull my strings, she'll always be able to". Mary went further by describing Ernie as someone who lets her know if she is not being consistent or being "too restricting or lenient."

Mary admitted that she has slapped Sally possibly four times, but denied that there were ever any bruises or cuts. Mary contended that, "I had two choices, let Joe spank her or . . . I would have to do it . . . and he was so hard on her." Mary claimed to have seen Joe punish Sally by putting his hand over her mouth, hitting her with a belt which left strap marks on her thighs and arm, and hitting her on the head in a manner that hurt since "he was always wearing a big ring." Mary said that his "girlfriend" stated that she became scared because Joe was holding Sally's head under water. Mary noted that on one occasion she made an anonymous report, I believe, to Protective Services about the way Joe abused his two sons.

Mary stated that she knows that Sally "has been sexually molested directly or by witness . . . by the way she acts". "Sally is always trying to catch you . . . in the tub . . . peeing . . . or watch naked bodies." Mary denied ever witnessing Sally being sexually abused, but articulated that she was afraid that Joe "would try to get her to work." Mary added that Cindy is Joe's "steady bed partner", she observed Cindy with Sally wearing their clothes in a "69" position, Cindy "used to always beat Sally up," and Cindy was the daughter, I think, of Lucille (Lucy) Jensen, Joe's sister. Mary continued by reporting that Lucy is dead from AIDS, but that she had five children and would "bring home tricks . . . get in the tub with her syringe and spoon and let the kids take care of the (tricks)".

After one inquiry, Mary said that, "I had trouble with (Sally) masturbating all the time." In response to my question about where she learned that behavior, Mary stated that Sally "definitely (learned it) from Cindy and . . . Joe's family." Mary continued, "Joe didn't hesitate to give his sister face or get head from her in front of me . . . I'm sure (Joe) has AIDS."

Mary answered my question about baths by contending that Sally only has taken a bath with Joe and herself (Mary). Mary stated that on one occasion Sally asked to "kiss my boob". Mary believes that Sally only has seen Joe's penis. Mary denied that Sally has ever seen Ernie naked. Tom was discussed only after I mentioned him. At which point, Mary detailed that Tom raised Lucille (Lucy) Jensen's daughter(s). Mary denied that Sally could have seen his penis, since he is "so fat . . . his gut would cover him (while sitting in the tub)".

Mary stated that she stopped "shooting-up" drugs and being a "hooker" about one year ago and gives credit to Ernie. She contended that she stopped abusing alcohol when Sally went into the shelter.

Sara noted one conversation with Sally in which she described playing a "pinching game" with Ernie that entailed Sally pulling her pants down. (Note: Sara stated the possibility that this conversation was audiotaped over the telephone by a friend.)

Ms. Conti stated that Sally has unsupervised visits with Mary and Ernie but that Joe's are supervised. She explained that Joe always brings Harry who possibly was married to Cindy's mother. Mary and Joe are still married.

Ms. Conti described that Mary and Ernie get money by "dumpster diving" to obtain things to sell at the swap meet. Mary said, "according to Ms. Conti, Sally loves to 'dumpster dive,'" which was verified directly by Mary. Mary nor Ernie have jobs, but Joe does.

Ms. Conti explained that Sally is in treatment at the Children's Center. Mary is scheduled to start in January and Ernie is willing to go. There are no treatment plans for Joe.

Five appointments have been scheduled with Mary. She has missed two of them, plus been late for one meeting. Sally had an expectation that Mary would be at one meeting that she (Mary) missed. She did not complete the testing by the date to which she had committed herself.

Sara and Mary both contended that Sally has made significant improvements since she has been with Sara in the foster placement.

Ms. Conti articulates that Juvenile Court has ordered Sally, Mary, Joe, and Ernie to have psychological evaluations completed. Ms. Conti is interested in establishing whether Sally has been sexually abused, and by whom if she has been. Furthermore, Ms. Conti would like treatment recommendations for Mary and Sally. The county attorney, Mr. Johnson, identified the concerns regarding physical abuse and neglect by Mary and Joe. (Note: The Family Support Center is evaluating Sally and Mary. A separate report has been prepared on Mary. Apparently, the Juvenile Court Mental Health Unit is evaluating Joe and Ernie.)

II. EVALUATION PROCEDURES

A. Clinical Interviews and Behavioral Tasks
B. Draw-A–Person (DAP)
C. Plenk Storytelling Test (PST)
D. Developmental Test of Visual-Motor Integration (VMI)
E. Red Flag and Green Flag People
F. Anatomically Correct Dolls
G. Child Behavior Checklist (CBC) per Sara and Mary
H. Wahler Physical Symptoms Inventory per Sara and Mary
I. AAMD Adaptive Behavior Scale (ABS) per Sara
J. Sexually Aberrant Behavior (SAB–ABS) per Sara and Mary

III. CLINICAL OBSERVATIONS

Sally came to the first appointment somewhat clean. She was dependent on Sara. There was some laughter, but poor eye contact. It was difficult to keep her attention focused and to get her to respond to questions in a compliant or sensible manner. Once, she lifted her clothing up over her chest, although it was not clear if she was just stretching or trying to interact with me.

During one joint appointment, I asked Sally and Mary to play together and for Mary to terminate the play. Mary demonstrated competent parenting skills. She asked reasonable questions, gave clear instructions, provided some structure, was not too controlling, prompted the development of language by Sally, used social reinforcement, and was affectionate. Mary successfully negotiated a compromise to terminate the play although Sally wanted to continue. Mary used no coercion or threats. Sally interacted fairly well with Mary. Sally never became aversive or coercive. Sally appeared to enjoy the social reinforcement from Mary although Sally was not attending to Mary consistently. In one instance, she appeared to refuse to answer a question from Mary. They appeared to be bonded to each other. They laughed together, Sally named a figure after Mary, and they held hands.

During one visit, Mary tried to decide how to minimize her contact with Sally so that she would not get her (Mary's) "cold," although Mary obviously was sad about the situation and missed Sally.

On one occasion, Ernie and Sally minimally interacted in the waiting room. Sally was somewhat friendly with Ernie and did not exhibit any fearful behavior.

Sally referred to Joe as "mom's boyfriend."

IV. RESULTS

A. **Cognitive and Adaptive Functioning (Ability)**: It is difficult for Sally to process information and adapt to her environment. Her DAP was in the 2 to 4% range for her age. The VMI showed that Sally functions more like a 4 year old than a 5 year old. Her independent functioning, language development, and numerical/time skills were poor (respectively, 14th, 26th, and 24th percentiles). It was difficult for her to count to five and she called the color orange, "pink." In response to questions regarding the Red-Green Flag booklet, Sally usually responded that the child was receiving a "bad" touch, or even "no" touch, although the picture may have been depicting a smiling, happy child being hugged. She clearly demonstrated the difference between a soft and hard hit.

Some of her statements were detached from reality; for example, "naked in the wall . . . peering in the wall . . . I want to be alone in the wall . . . nice monster . . . killed me." However her description of pictures from the PST matched their basic content.

Sara rated the play of Sally as "below average," and Mary marked "above average".

B. Credibility: Initially, Sally was not able to explain the difference between the truth and a lie, although she learned to discriminate the truth versus a lie on simple tasks. On the ABS, Sara checked Sally as not trustworthy.

Sally consistently focused across questions and time on taking a bath with a "Tom." Attempts to gather detailed information were basically rejected by Sally. My impression was that she knew what happened, but was unwilling to tell or show me. While alone with me, Sally said that Sara had taught her not to say "bad words", and therefore, would not "tell." Furthermore, she said that she was unwilling to tell Sara or Mary privately and did not respond to prompts from Sara.

C. Emotional and Interpersonal Functioning: Sally has significant problems. Sara and Mary were asked to rate the current status of Sally on the CBC. Both women provided answers indicating similar perceptions of Sally, except Sara noted more internal problems. All scales were significantly elevated: (1) Somatic Complaints; (2) Depressed; (3) Schizoid or Anxious; (4) Social Withdrawal; (5) (poor relationships); (6) Aggressive; (7) Sex Problems; and (8) Hyperactive. Both Sara and Mary detailed that her behavior is worse than expected with peers. Mary views Sally as worse than average with parents versus Sara who marked "better." The problems identified by Sara on the ABS depicted that Sally has pervasive emotional and interpersonal problems compared to children her own age. Problems were significant in each possible domain: (1) Aggressiveness; (2) Antisocial Behavior; (3) Rebelliousness; (4) Trustworthiness; (5) Withdrawal; (6) Mannerisms; (7) Interpersonal Manners; (8) Acceptability of Vocal Habits; (9) Acceptability of Habits; (10) Activity Level; and (11) Symptomatic Behavior. A pervasive perception on the DAP and PST is that people feel sad which is something Sally indicated that people do not like to feel.

The SAB–ABs completed by Sara and Mary revealed that both women are aware that Sally frequently engages in masturbation, exposes her body improperly, displays homosexual behavior, and exhibits other unacceptable sexual behavior (e.g., "lifts or unbuttons others' clothing to touch intimately.")

D. **Health:** Sara and/or Mary noted various weekly physical problems on the Wahler such as, headaches, nauseousness, shakiness, stomach trouble, feeling tired, and difficulty with her appetite.

E. **Alleged Victimization (Videotaped Interviews Available):** Sally demonstrated a solid hit to the dolls face and stated that Mary has hit her in the same way. She denied that anyone else has hit her.

Sally labeled the labial area, "private"; anus, "bum-bum"; and penis, something like "pees." Sally stated that Ernie has a "pees." She reported that, "I took a bath with Tom before." "I took a bath with Joe." In another instance, Sally claimed that she has "baths just with Mary and Tom." She denied touching Ernie's penis. Touching Tom's penis seemed to be a more acceptable idea, while Sally denied the notion of touching with Joe or Ernie. She claimed not to have seen Cindy with her clothes off. Sally seemed naive about Jerry's anatomy. Jerry is Sara's husband.

During another interview, Sally continued to maintain her allegation with a demonstration by the dolls that she was in the bathtub with Tom. however, she refused to say or demonstrate what happened. Sally asserted, "nothing can happen . . . so I can't tell." She further stated, "(I) can't say bad words . . . (so I) won't tell because Sara said not to (say the bad words)." (As noted previously, Sally made no specific allegations after getting permission from Sara and with prompting from her.)

Sally described Tom as "mean and nice."

V. DIAGNOSTIC INTEGRATION

Independent of the background data, it's reasonable beyond any doubt that Sally has been sexually abused; one candidate is a person named Tom. Furthermore, Mary has very likely hit Sally excessively hard in the face. One very substantial hypothesis is that her history of sexual and physical abuse caused her extensive emotional and interpersonal problems. If Sally overcomes her emotional and interpersonal problems, her cognitive and adaptive functioning has a good chance of improving. Her unwillingness or inability to provide clear and generally consistent data are apt to be caused by her emotional and interpersonal problems interfering with her ability to think about her experiences and clearly report the information. The length of time since the alleged abuse and what she has learned in her foster placement create additional obstacles to getting reliable, detailed data. However, there is a minimal chance that better data can be collected as she improves.

The background data strongly suggest that the sexual and physical abuse is extensive. In conjunction with information from Sally and the tests, it is reasonable to conclude that Mary has not provided completely accurate data in regard to her knowledge of any abuse to which Sally has been subjected, or if she really does not know, she should have. It is very reasonable to conclude that Sally has been neglected and emotionally abused.

It appears that Mary and Sally love each other. Mary demonstrated a genuine concern for Sally and put Sally's health before gratifying her interest in being close to Sally. Mary seems to have the basic skills for raising Sally but she may lack insight and motivation to be a successful parent. (Note: More information is presented in Mary's psychological evaluation.)

VI. RECOMMENDATIONS

A. Sally needs to be protected from further abuse and neglect. Hence, she should not have unsupervised visits with Joe or Mary until it is clear that they are competent parents, willing and capable of protecting her.

B. Joe and/or Mary's lack of motivation (e.g., missed appointments) should be monitored and documented in a treatment plan.

C. Cindy and adults (i.e., Joe, Harry, Tom, Ernie and Mary) noted in the background data, should have their criminal and abuse registry histories checked. Referrals to law enforcement for prosecution may be important to protect children from other abuse. Any of these adults and Cindy wanting contact with Sally should first complete a psychological evaluation and demonstrate motivation to participate in a treatment plan. Evaluations of the men should include a penile plethysmograph to identify deviant patterns of arousal. This is not a suggestion that homosexual abuse has not occurred, rather it just reflects recognition of current technologies being primarily limited to men. All evaluations should include the direct observation of the particular adult interacting with Sally, if it is determined that she will not be traumatized seeing the particular person. Any of these individuals who want contact should be tested for sexually transmitted diseases, especially if the AIDS information is valid. Other family members or children should not be ruled out as potential perpetrators of physical and sexual abuse with Sally.

D. The children noted in the background data should be evaluated for sexual and physical abuse.

E. Sally should have a physical evaluation by a qualified physician with specific attention given to indications of sexual abuse or disease.

F. Sally should receive intensive treatment with due consideration given to typical issues often seen as the sequelae of physical and sexual abuse.

G. If Joe or Mary are to be competent parents, each will need to demonstrate above average skills and motivation since Sally has exceptional needs and problems.

Family Support Center
Psychological Evaluation
January 30, 1986

CLIENT: Jane Doe
DATES OF EVALUATION: January 9, 16, and 30, 1986
DATE OF BIRTH: April 20, 1961
AGE: 24
CASEWORKER: Judy
PLACEMENT SUPERVISOR: Jerry
PROSECUTOR: Jill
ALLEGED PERPETRATOR: John Smith (Stepfather)

I. BACKGROUND INFORMATION

The referral was received initially in October of 1985, but according to Judy, Ms. Smith (her mother) was preventing Jane from being evaluated. Apparently, the psychological evaluation became possible after intervention by the professionals involved in her case.

Allegations have been made that Mr. John Smith (her stepfather) has sexually abused Jane, her sister Mary, and other retarded child(ren) at the Special Olympics.

Data presented by Jerry, and Jane depict frequent situations in which Jane and Mary are still visiting at their parents home and staying overnight while Mr. Smith is there and Ms. Smith is the sole supervisor.

Jill reports that John Smith is currently on probation. Jerry indicates that he has been in previous treatment programs.

II. EVALUATION PROCEDURES

A. Clinical Interviews
B. Draw-A–Person (DAP)
C. Plenk Storytelling Test (PST)
D. Red Flag and Green Flag People
E. Anatomically Correct Dolls
F. Wahler Physical Symptoms Inventory—per Judy
G. AAMD Adaptive Behavior Scale (ABS)—per Judy
H. Rathus Assertiveness Schedule—per Judy
I. Wechsler Adult Intelligence Scale—Revised (WAIS–R)
J. Child Cognition Scale (CCS)
K. Thematic Apperception Test (TAT)
L. Prior Psychological Evaluation: 1-15-85 per Hansen

III. CLINICAL OBSERVATIONS

Jane presented herself as clean, friendly, and well groomed. While chewing gum, she popped bubbles. Jane cooperated, was able to maintain her focus, and approached tasks in a methodical manner.

IV. RESULTS

A. Cognitive Functioning (Ability): Jane's cognitive functioning is poor, but she is capable of describing her own experiences. Intellectually, she is mentally retarded with a full scale IQ of 60 which is nearly identical to prior test results. Her human drawings are poorer than the bottom 1% of 15 year old adolescents. They are most similar to the drawings made by the average 5 year old child. Jane remembered the date, my name, and the name of the agency. She read the time, signed her name, read the "Red Flag and Green Flag People" booklet, counted ten objects, knew that it was cold outside, and said that people wear shorts when it is hot outside. On the ABS, Jerry details that Jane has a grasp of very simple temporal and numerical concepts, but lacks a clear understanding of what the differences are between various temporal concepts. She was able to associate red and green crayons with "bad" and "good" touches, respectively. There was no evidence of a thought disorder.

B. Credibility: Jan's credibility varies with the task and is determined by her cognitive functioning. She seems most reliable while recalling her own experiences. Integrating experiences or dealing with general abstract ideas seems to reduce her reliability.

Jane discriminated between lies and the truth. She said that it is important to tell the truth to "prevent trouble." She created one story to a TAT card in which the person felt bad because someone told a "lie." However, Jane is rated by Jerry, as not trustworthy on the ABS.

Jane corrected me when I incorrectly used a different name for her, but did not readily dismiss incorrect numerical data. She corrected herself on one subtest of the WAIS–R, but quickly drew human figures without any erasures.

Information presented by Jane about the events involved in her alleged sexual abuse was very consistent and contained unusual circumstances. She depicted accurate factual data about sexual functioning, but she used naive terminology (e.g., "pussy" or "white stuff"), which suggests that she has not been discussing the allegations to any great degree that might bias her reports. Incriminating data had some limits, since she denied that her "dad" has never "hurt" her in response to my specific question. Yet she stated that John Smith was "hurting her" as part of an explanation about why she made the allegations. Similarly, Jane minimized the frequency of the alleged abuse by stating that it happened two times, but detailed and implied many more instances; for example, she described the alleged sexual abuse occurring "every morning." Jane said that she told someone other than her mother that (her dad) was "hurting her" and that she was "scared to tell her mother again because he (John Smith) said he'd do something terrible to me if I told." Her affect depicts that Jane was embarrassed to discuss the allegations. Lack of eagerness to present the allegations indicate that Jane was not too motivated to discuss the allegations. Jane denied that anyone told her what to say or not say during her evaluation with me.

C. **Emotional, Interpersonal, and Adaptive Functioning:** Jane has definite deficiencies in her adaptive behavior. Compared to 15 year old adolescents, she is equal to or less than the lowest 5% in independent functioning, physical development, economic activity, language development, prevocational activity, and self direction. Her adaptive behavior is most similar to that demonstrated by children 6 to 11 years of age.

Results from the ABS, PST, TAT, DAP, and Rathus, suggest that some undue emotional and interpersonal problems exist. Possible problem areas noted on the ABS include her attempts to control people, rebelliousness, trustworthiness, overestimating her own abilities, poor reactions to criticism and frustration, excessive demands for attention, somatic complaints, and her occasional mention of suicidal thoughts. Her Rathus score shows that Jane may be slightly less assertive than the average person. Projective data detail that Jane may view herself as shy and isolated, but optimistic. Although Jane's primary feeling is happiness, affective themes include anger and depression due to a view that she has been mistreated, justifiable anger if someone does something "wrong," and possibly, some denial of sexually laden percepts.

Jane details that the suicidal thoughts related to one instance when Ms. Smith came to Jane's apartment. "I had real bad headaches . . . I was under a lot of stress . . . I was going to take pills or something." Jane explains that the stress was due to her "concern about" Ms. Smith. In response to my question about what prevented her from committing suicide, Jane said, "I stopped when told lots of people love me." Jerry offered another perspective on the suicidal situation with which Jane agreed. Jerry describes that Jane was under "a lot of stress due to her mom being angry at her, since (Jane reported the sexual abuse) and (Ms. Smith) threatened to cut off all contact." There was a further statement that maybe a knife had been the medium by which the suicide had been threatened.

According to the CCS, Jane strongly opposes incest and the irrational thinking that might allow it to occur.

D. **Health:** Jerry rates Jane as healthy, except for "high blood pressure" for which she apparently receives medication.

E. **Alleged Victimization (Videotaped Interview Available):** Jane claims that she has been only sexually abused by John Smith. With prompting by Jerry, Jane states that she became pregnant previously by someone other than John Smith. These circumstances are not clear. Jane stated that she had been sexually abused on two occasions by John Smith commencing "when I was a little girl . . . before . . . in high school." Later, Jane asserted that she was sexually assaulted on more than two occasions. Although she maintained that it happened less than ten times, Jane implied that the frequency might have been much greater, by stating that the "(sexual abuse) happened every morning . . . (whenever) John Smith had to bring something to my apartment." Although she denied that the alleged abuse happened after high school, she noted at a later point that she resided in her apartment after high school. One notion of Jane's is that it was occurring while she was 22 years of age, but stopped by the time she was 23. Further attempts to target a time when the alleged abuse occurred, resulted in information about living in two apartments. The first alleged offense to transpire in the apartment(s) occurred after she had lived there for "one year," "cause I was home not doing anything." Jane further asserts that the alleged abuse at the apartment(s) first took place when it was "hot outside." She denies any allegations the first or last summer that she has lived in apartments', however, she does allege that she was sexually abused the second summer. Without independent information to help Jane have temporal anchors, she conveyed that she moved into one apartment for four months which included one summer when she was 22 years old, was in a new apartment for one summer while 23 years old, and was in the same apartment for one summer while 24 years of age. Through this process, Jane indicates that she was taken into the bedroom in her apartment for the first time and forced to have intercourse with John Smith during the summer of 1983.

Jane consistently details that she attempted to resist and stop John Smith from allegedly perpetrating what she clearly describes as intercourse. Jane notes, "I wanted to keep my clothes on, he took them off." Many other similar comments describing the use of coercion and force were stated by Jane. "I said no, then he took them off." "He (John Smith) would take me into the bedroom (and) . . . screwed me." "He grabbed my hands and put me into the bedroom." "He jerked my hand." Jane further explained that, "I told my mom once about it, (but I was) scared to tell again . . . because he (John Smith) said he'd do something terrible to me if I told." Jane says that she told someone (i.e., Jerry) other than her mother, because "(John Smith was) hurting us (i.e. Jane and Mary Doe), . . . we had to talk about it". Jane denied being scared or that John Smith had ever hurt her or her sister. Jane further detailed a specific instance while she lived at home and reports being 21 years old. In this case, Ms. Smith "caught him in the act," since they (John and Jane) were both in the bedroom together wearing no clothes. Jane does not believe that her brother would be able to protect her from her father.

Jane is aware of two other alleged victims: Mary Doe and a "girlfriend, . . . June Rogers." Jane says that Mary would say, "my dad tried to touch me." "She (Mary) was scared." Jane articulates that "I surprised them." Consequently, she says that she saw John "on top" of Mary with neither of them wearing clothes. After which, "my dad made me go out of the room." In regard to June Rogers, Jane claims that "my mother told me that (John) touched June Rogers in the wrong places."

V. DIAGNOSTIC INTEGRATION

Jane Doe provides credible and consistent information that she has been coerced and forced to have sexual intercourse with John Smith. Furthermore, the data strongly suggest that she has been sexually abused for many years and on many occasions by John Smith. It further appears that Ms. Smith has not been able to protect her. Additionally, there are data indicating that John Smith has sexually abused her sister (Mary) and another female. It is consistent with her cognitive functioning that information derived from questions focusing on dates, frequency of instances, or nonspecific (general) references may be unreliable. Information is much more apt to be reliable if she relates specific experiences or someone provides temporal anchors which she can use to help her recall events.

Jane has moderate emotional and interpersonal problems. She shows deficits in adaptive functioning. Combined with her cognitive functioning, these additional problems indicate that Jane is mildly mentally retarded. It is difficult to sort which problems are a consequence of the abuse versus what might be expected to be exhibited by someone with similar cognitive functioning. Her level of cognitive, emotional, interpersonal, and cognitive functioning reduces (reduced) her ability to competently defend herself against Mr. Smith.

VI. RECOMMENDATIONS

A. Jane Doe must be protected from John Smith. It is not reasonable to assume that her mother or brother are competent to protect her. It is not reasonable to assume that Ms. Smith will always act in the best interest of Jane. Therefore, people (e.g., Jerry, Judy, Jill and John's probation officer) working with Jane and John Smith must meet to determine how she will be protected. Initially, Jane and John should not be together without nonfamilial supervision. John's probation officer should expect him to be extremely accountable for his time. Before contact resumes, John should demonstrate that he is accepting personal responsibility for the alleged sexual abuse, not blaming Jane, and showing to a licensed clinician with experience working with sex offenders that he is capable of helping Jane overcome her victimization. If he chooses to go home for visits rather than Jane that would be a sign that he is placing his needs before Jane's. If John has actually sexually abused femaled in his family and outside of it over the course of many years and previously been treated, it is reasonable to assume that he is apt to be dangerous and may not be very amenable to treatment. At this point, Jane may choose to be at home while John is there with the real potential for additional sexual abuse. Hence, Jane may not be able to act in her best interest in this area.

B. Jane needs continued supervision and training to help her make daily decisions. Training in assertiveness and sexuality will be important. She should learn ways to prevent and cope with depression and have options (e.g., telephone numbers) to handle crises. When John and Ms. Smith demonstrate that they can help their daughters, family meetings with a therapist will be important. However, all members of the family should complete psychological evaluations before treatment plans are implemented for the family. This may require that pressure be placed on John Smith by the court and that guardianship of family members may need to be awarded to someone other than the mother.

C. It may be possible to obtain more reliable time frames for the alleged sexual abuse if someone provides accurate temporal anchors that Jane can use to prompt her memory.

TREATMENT

Following the initial crisis intervention, assessment, and diagnostic period, goals for short-term therapy (up to six months) are established.

Treatment modalities are predicated by the age of the child, the nature and scope of the abuse, and the level of the child's functioning in the areas of affect, cognition and behaviors. For the young child, play therapy is the typical treatment approach using drawings, a sand and water table, storytelling, clay sculpting and behavior modification techniques (especially when working upon reduction and elimination of regressive behaviors such as encopresis and enuresis).

For older children the treatment approach includes play therapy, art work, dramatics, education, and some talk therapy with a minimum of interpretation. Individually or in groups, structured tasks can facilitate the development of empathy, social skills, assertiveness, and negotiation skills. Opportunities to express feelings to the fantasized perpetrator can help reduce the disruptive intensity of those feelings.

Ten treatment issues, as defined by Suzanne Sgroi (1982), are often typical in child sexual abuse. They are;

1. **Damaged goods syndrome,** when a child has been hurt he/she fears being hurt or is stigmatized by the abuse;

2. Guilt, which occurs most often after disclosure when a child may feel responsible for what has happened;
3. Fear of harm, separation from parent, even death of a loved one if threats have been utilized;
4. Depression which can take any of several forms, (the child may be suicidal, withdraw from friends and family, refuse to eat, or somaticize his feelings of sadness);
5. Low self-esteem and poor social skills;
6. Inability to trust, especially when the perpetrator is a family member of a close friend or neighbor;
7. Anger and hostility, sometimes repressed, sometimes overt;
8. Role confusion, most often seen in intrafamilial sexual abuse cases where a child takes on a parental role;
9. Failure to complete developmental tasks, when inappropriate sexual stimulation interferes with the step wise progression of emotional development; and
10. Problems of control and self-mastery occur when psychological and/or physical coercion has been used to exploit the child. All of the different treatment approaches can be used to work on all of the treatment issues, however, it is often important to start therapy sessions with nonthreatening, nonverbal material. Watercolor paintings used to describe correct feelings at each therapy session are often quite revealing, not only in content but also in color, demonstrating sequentially the progress in treatment. Important to remember is the fact that children's therapy, though labeled play, is actually very difficult work for a child. Therapists must be sensitive to the fine balance between taking the lead and structuring the play while making interpretations versus sitting back to allow the child to set the pace and structure the task.

Determining when the child and his/her family are ready for termination is dependent upon several factors. When the child's symptoms have decreased sufficiently so that he/she is able to function emotionally, psychologically, cognitively and behaviorally at least as well as before the abuse, termination can proceed if the child's family is capable and willing to provide the emotional support that may be necessary. Both children and their families need to appreciate that future treatment may be needed, particularly at the onset of new developmental levels, when the understanding of the abuse and its effects may need to be reframed.

The long-term effects of abuse have been described in the literature as often resulting in two contrasting adaptive styles in children who have been sexually abused. One style results in the victim becoming the victimizer, seeking resolution through reenactment, or mastery through repetition (McVicar, 1979; Yates, 1982; Brassard, Tyler, and Kehle, 1983). The contrasting style of coping or adaptation is described as avoidance of sexual stimuli, resulting in adult social dysfunction characterized by phobic reactions and sexual inhibition (Stelle and Alexander, 1981; Tsai and Wagner, 1979).

The current literature indicates that individuals who sexually or physically abuse their children were often victims of child abuse themselves. In a comparison study of physically abusing, sexually abusing and nonclinical fathers (Tyler, 1986), the most statistically significant predictor variable was the history factor of the perpetrator having been abused himself as a child. If indeed the child is father of the man, then treatment of the child victims of abuse assumes great importance in mitigating the generational effects of child abuse.

TRAINING ISSUES

Unfortunately, well meaning people can jeopardize the prosecution and resolution of a child sexual abuse case if they are not adequately trained. The consequences of the abuse investigation can be devastating for the victim, his/her family, and even the community (Tyler and Brassard, 1984). Because child sexual abuse is both a social problem and a criminal justice problem, the general issues in assessment, intervention and treatment are complex and often interrelated.

Child sexual abuse is a crime which results in serious penalties when the perpetrator is found guilty. The investigating officer, protective service worker, physician, and psychologist must cooperate and coordinate in their efforts to protect the child, attend to the trauma, and document data sufficiently. Extreme care must be taken that witness statements are not contaminated by repeated interviews, leading questions, and evaluations. Careful examination by highly trained professionals will help to ensure that questions are not discussed outside of the professional investigation. Care must be exercised during the intervention and treatment stages to preserve the victim's initial recall and to prevent, if possible, recantation of the abuse.

Following individual statements, group therapy is very useful, particularly in the treatment of a case involving multiple victims. However, this group treatment should not be done until the court case is completed if the first objective is prosecution of the case. The possibility of witness contamination and suggestibility is too great. Even if the victims' testimony remained virtually unchanged, defense attorneys could use the fact that the children talked about the experience together to discredit their testimony.

The role of the psychologist as an expert witness in court is an extremely important one. Because of the **Hearsay Statute** in many states, prosecution may depend almost entirely upon the expert witness for documentation of the abuse. For this reason, it is imperative that the witness be: (1) well educated and trained in the field of child sexual abuse; (2) prepared with sufficient data to make informed statements; (3) knowledgeable about court procedure; (4) prepared to withstand a barrage of questions from the defense that is often intended to impeach or impugn the credibility of the witness; and (5) capable of discussing the reliability and validity of the assessment results. As an example of the unique aspects of this process, sixteen standards offer what must be done to videotape the clinical interview:

1. No attorneys may be present;
2. The tape must be visual and aural;
3. It must be an accurate record of the interview of the child;
4. It must be filmed by a competent operator;
5. Voices of each person on the tape must be identified;
6. The interviewer must be available to testify;
7. The videotape cannot have been edited in **any way**;
8. Only the videotapes of child victims under age 12 may be utilized in lieu of appearance;
9. Only one child may be in the room at a time;
10. Quality lighting must be used;
11. The videotape must be secured when complete to insure no one could alter, lose, copy or mar the tape;
12. The interviewer must meet statutory requirements and be able to meet the test as an expert;
13. The interviewer must be certified by the County Attorney's Office as a qualified interviewer or the tape must be screened by the County Attorney's Office to determine if all of the elements are adequately addressed;

14. The videotape must have a determination of the ability of the child to determine truth and falsity;

15. The videotape must have specific details of the acts in question; and

16. The tape must not have any other recording on it, over it, or under it.

Because the entire area of investigation, treatment and prosecution of child sexual abuse cases is relatively new, there is much that needs to be done in research, education, and training. As the incidence of child sexual abuse reports increase and as experience and research defines new parameters, the university programs and continuing education for professionals are essential if knowledge is to be perpetuated, refined, and expanded.

REFERENCES

1. Achenbach, T. M., and Edelbrock, C.: *Manual for the Child Behavior Checklist and the Revised Child Behavior Profile.* Burlinton, Queen City, 1983.

2. Aragona, J. A., and Eyberg, S. M.: Neglected children: mother's report of child behavioral problems and observed verbal behavior. *Child Development, 52:*596–602, 1981.

3. Bayley, N.: *Manual for the Bayley Scales of Infant Development.* New York, Psychological, 1969.

4. Becker, J. V., Skinner, L. J., and Abel, G. G.: Sequelae of sexual assault: the survivor's perspective. In Green, J. G., and Stuart, I. R. (Eds.): *The Sexual Aggressor: Current Perspectives and Treatment.* New York, Van Nostrand Reinhold, 1983.

5. Beery, K. E.: *Revised Administration, Scoring and Teaching Manual for the Developmental Test of Visual-Motor Integration.* Cleveland, Modern Curriculum, 1982.

6. Berliner, L., and Ernst, E.: Group work with preadolescent sexual assault victims. In Stuart, I. R., and Green J. G. (Eds.): *Victims of Sexual Aggression: Treatment of Children, Women, and Men.* New York, Van Nostrand Reinhold, 1984.

7. Bousha, D. M., and Twentyman, C. T.: Mother-child interactional style in abuse, neglect, and control groups: naturalistic observations in the home. *Journal of Abnormal Psychology, 93:*106–114, 1984.

8. Brassard, M. R., Tyler, A. H., and Kehle, T. J.: Sexually abused children: identification and suggestions for intervention. *School Psychology Review, 12:*93–97, 1983.

9. Browne, A., and Finkelhor, D.: Impact of child sexual abuse: a review of the research. *Psychological Bulletin, 99:*66–77, 1986.

10. Claman, L., Harris, J., Bernstein, B. E., and Louitt, R.: The adolescent as a

witness in a case of incest: assessment and outcome. *Journal of the American Academy of child Psychiatry, 25:*457–461, 1986.

11. DeFrancis, V.: *Protecting the Child Victim of Sex Crimes Committed by Adults.* Denver, American Humane, 1970.

12. Emery, R. E.: Interparental conflict and the children of discord and divorce. *Psychological Bulletin, 92:*310–330, 1982.

13. Friedrich, W. N., Urquiza, A. J., and Beilke, R. L.: Behavior problems in sexually abused young children. *Journal of Pediatric Psychology, 11:*47–57, 1986.

14. Green, A. H.: True and false allegations of sexual abuse in child custody disputes. *Journal of the American Academy of Child Psychiatry, 25:*449–456, 1986.

15. Gully, K. J., and Dengerink, H. A.: The dyadic interaction of persons with violent and nonviolent histories. *Aggressive Behavior, 9:*13–20, 1983.

16. Gully, K. J., Dengerink, H. A., Pepping, M., and Bergstrom: Research note: sibling contribution to violent behavior. *Journal of Marriage and the Family, 43:*333–337, 1981.

17. Gully, K. J., and Hosch, H. M.: Adaptive behavior scale: development as a diagnostic tool via discriminant analysis. *American Journal of Mental Deficiency, 83:*518–523, 1979.

18. Harris, D. B.: *Children's Drawings as a Measure of Intellectual Maturity: A Revision and Extension of the Goodenough Draw-A-Man Test.* New York, Harcourt, 1963.

19. Jaffe, P., Wolfe, D., Wilson, S. K., and Zak, L.: Family violence and child adjustment: a comparative analysis of girls' and boys' behavioral symptoms. *American Journal of Psychiatry, 143:*74–77, 1986.

20. Jones, D. P. H.: Individual psychotherapy for the sexually abused child. *Child Abuse and Neglect, 10:*377–385, 1986.

21. Kahn, A. S. (Ed.): *Final Report: American Psychological Association Task Force on the Victim of Crime and Violence.* Washington, D.C., American Psychological Association, 1984.

22. Koppitz, E. M.: *The Bender Gestalt Test for Young Children: Volume II—Research and Application, 1963-1973.* New York, Grune & Stratton, 1975.

23. Lambert, N.: *AAMD Adaptive Behavior Scale: Diagnostic and Technical Manual.* Monterey, McGraw-Hill, Publishers Test Service, 1981.

24. Lambert, N., Windmiller, M., Tharinger, D., and Cole, L.: *AAMD Adaptive Behavior Scale: Administration and Instructional Placing Manual.* Monterey, McGraw-Hill, Publishers Test Service, 1981.

25. Lusk, R., and Waterman, J.: Effects of sexual abuse on children. In MacFarlane, K., Waterman, J., Connerly, S., Damon, L., Durfee, M., and Long, S. (Eds.): *Sexual Abuse of Young Children: Evaluation and Treatment.* New York, Guildford, 1986.

26. Main, M., and George, C.: Responses of abused and disadvantaged toddlers to distress in agemates: a study in the day care setting. *Developmental Psychology, 21:*407–412, 1985.

27. McArthur, D. S., and Roberts, G. E.: *Robert's Apperception Test for Children: Manual.* Los Angeles, Western Psychological, 1982.

28. McVicar, K.: Psychotherapy of sexually abused girls. *This Journal, 18:*342–353, 1979.

29. Melton, G., Bulkley, J., and Wulkan, D.: Competency of children as witnesses. In Bulkley, J. (Ed.): *Child Sexual Abuse and the Law.* Washington, D.C., American Bar Association, 1981.

30. Nurcombe, B.: The child as witness: competency and credibility. *Journal of the American Academy of Child Psychiatry, 25:*473–480, 1986.

31. Plenk, A. M., Hinchey, F. S., and Davies, M. V.: *Plenk Storytelling Test.* Salt Lake City, Children's Center, 1982.

32. Rape and Abuse Crisis Center: *Red Flag and Green Flag People.* Fargo, Rape and Abuse Crisis Center, 1985.

33. Rosenfeld, A., Bailey, R., Siegel, B., and Bailey, G.: Determining incestuous contact between parent and child: frequency of children touching parents' genitals in a nonclinical population. *Journal of the American Academy of Child Psychiatry, 25:*481–484, 1986.

34. Saylor, C. F., Finch, Jr., A. J., Baskin, C. H., Furey, W., and Kelly, M. M.: Construct validity for measures of childhood depression: application of multitrait-multimethod methodology. *Journal of Consulting and Clinical Psychology, 52:*977–985, 1984.

35. Sgroi, S. M. (Ed.): *Handbook of Clinical Intervention in Child Sexual Abuse.* Lexington, Heath, 1982.

36. Steele, B., and Alexander, H.: Long-term effects of sexual abuse in childhood. In Mrazek, P., and Kempt., C. (Eds.): *Sexually Abused Children and Their Families.* New York, Pergamon, 1981, pp. 223–234.

37. Terr, L. C.: The child psychiatrist and the child witness: traveling campanions by necessity, if not by design. *Journal of the American Academy of Child Psychiatry, 25:*462–472, 1986.

38. Thorndike, R. L., Hagen, E. P., and Sattler, J. M.: *The Stanford-Binet Intelligence Scale: Fourth Edition — Technical Manual.* Chicago, Riverside, 1986.

39. Tsai, M., and Wagner, N.: *Incest and Molestation: Problems of Childhood Sexuality.* Medical Times, Special Section, pp. 16–22.

40. Tyler, A. H.: The abusive father. In Lamb, M. E. (Ed.): *The Father's Role: Applied Perspectives.* New York, Wiley & Sons, 1986.

41. Tyler, A. H., and Brassard, M. R.: Abuse in the investigation and treatment of intrafamilial child sexual abuse. *Child Abuse and Neglect, 8:*47–53, 1984.

42. Whitcomb, D., Shapiro, E. R., and Stellwagen, L. D.: *When the Civtim is a Child: Issues for Judges and Prosecutors.* Washington, D.C., U.S. Government, 1985.

43. White, S., Strom, G. A., Santilli, G., and Halpin, B. M.: Interviewing young sexual abuse victims with anatomically correct dolls. *Child Abuse and Neglect, 10:*519–529, 1986.

44. Wolfe, D. A., Zak, L., Wilson, S., and Jaffe, P.: Child witness to violence between parents; critical issues in behavioral and social adjustment. *Journal of Abnormal Child Psychology, 14:*95–104, 1986.

45. Yates, A.: Children eroticized by incest. *American Journal of Psychiatry, 139:*482–485, 1982.

CHAPTER 15

ESTABLISHING COOPERATION WITH COMMUNITY AGENCIES TO FOSTER THE LEGAL RIGHTS OF CHILDREN

ROBERT S. NEVIN
ALBERT R. ROBERTS

INTRODUCTION

In many communities, the rights of children in instances of child abuse and neglect are not being addressed sufficiently. Due to the lack of communication and absence of formal mechanisms between the representatives of law, child protection services, medicine, education, and essential community agencies, a very uneven delivery of services is provided to these children and families in stress. More states are passing laws and more local communities are actively developing programs to communicate more promptly and act more effectively in these instances for both the child and their family in a comprehensive manner. This chapter will focus upon: (1) the influence of legislation for community cooperation, (2) a means by which agencies may more adequately address the legal rights of children, (3) conceptual models for community action, and (4) the role of the criminal justice system in protecting the best interests of the child victim. Special emphasis will be placed on vulnerable populations in the community, and the nature and responsiveness of child protection, medical, and criminal justice systems.

LEGISLATION'S INFLUENCE ON THE DEVELOPMENT OF COMMUNITY SERVICES

In 1963, no state legislation existed to require the reporting of suspected child abuse. Today, each state has passed a reporting law. We have seen that many more reports are being made and that local communities have set up their own specialized child protection services (CPS). Despite these improvements, numerous professionals (i.e., physicians, nurses, teachers, social workers, child care workers, and police officers) fail to report more than half of the incidents of child maltreatment that they encounter (Besharov, 1985). The laws, in many instances, are very clear regarding the penalty for failure to report, but fail to clearly spell out the protection afforded the individual making the report. Many of the state laws are vague about their purpose, such as when the child's "environment is injurious to his welfare," when the child "lacks proper parental care," or when the parents are "unfit to properly care for such child." Besharov (1985, p. 23) notes:

> Other statues are blatantly tautological, calling for intervention when a child has been "abandoned or physically, mentally, or emotionally abused or neglected or sexually abused" without further defining these terms. In an attempt to be more specific, some recent statutes address the failure to provide "adequate" or "necessary" or "proper" food, clothing, shelter, medical care, education, supervision, or guardianship. But, again, these statues do not define the key—but ambiguous—words: "adequate," "necessary," or "proper."

Besharov believes that laws should be redrafted so that the two major child protective interventions are authorized only when the parents have already engaged in abusive or neglectful behavior. The most common child protective intervention is involuntary supervision of the home situation and provision of treatment services. Besharov (1985), recommends that laws be changed to recognize two categories of seriously harmful parental behaviors: **immediately** harmful behavior and **cumulatively** harmful behavior. He identifies and provides definitions for eleven seriously harmful parental behaviors. These are:

(1) physical battering, (2) physical endangerment, (3) physical neglect, (4) medical neglect, (5) sexual neglect, (6) sexual exploitation, (7) emotional abuse, (8) developmental neglect, (9) improper ethical supervision, (10) educational neglect, and (11) abandonment.

Over the past twenty years, foster care, as the second major child protection intervention, has seen a dramatic increase. Utilizing the legal processes, far too many children have been removed from their homes and placed in foster care arrangements. CPS workers have often used this intervention, but have had no legal standards to guide their foster care decisions. Besharov (1985, p. 27) recommends that:

> Child protective laws should prohibit the removal of children from cumulatively harmful situations unless: the parents refuse to accept or cooperate with efforts to provide needed compensatory services; the

child needs specific diagnostic or remedial services that are available only through residential care; foster care is used in response to an otherwise irreconcilable conflict between the parent and an adolescent child; or foster care is a planned precursor to the termination of parental rights and a subsequent adoption.

These recommended changes could minimize unreasonable expectations about what social workers and judges can accomplish. The result would be more manageable caseloads due to fewer unfounded reports being made, smaller numbers of children being placed in foster care (which may place them in a less desirable environment), and improve the reporting of and services to children in serious danger.

Koerin (1980, p. 546), believes that the history of the child abuse laws over the last twenty years has reflected punishment versus treatment themes.

> The first child abuse reporting laws were protective of the professionals reporting suspected incidents and punitive in the measures dealing with abusive and neglecting families. The new laws included provisions for reporting incidents to law enforcement bodies, with an underlying stress on removal of children and prosecution of parents ... between 1967–1970 most state laws were revised on the basis of research related to therapeutic work with families, on the recognition that a large majority of abuse and neglect cases are handled successfully by agencies without court action, and on the understanding of the increased damage to child and family that a punitive approach often has (especially when prosecution of parents fails and a child suffers from the parents' heightened hostility).

Koerin urges that more preventive programs be established to maintain family integrity by treating, rather than punishing, such families.

Gottesman (1981, p. 42–43) has summarized the five key provisions of many state statutes:

1. A list of designated professionals who are required to report suspected abuse or neglect to the Police Department of Protective Services;
2. A section encouraging all other citizens to report suspected incidents of abuse and/or neglect;
3. A statement that all records maintained in accordance with the statute will be confidential;
4. Establishment of a central registry of names of child abusers; and
5. A section which ensures that those who report in good faith cannot be successfully sued for libel and/or slander by the accused parent.

These reporting provisions are designed to make professionals more willing to perform their duty in reporting. As can be seen, the state laws have included various legal safeguards designed to protect the reporter from potential liability for filing a child abuse report.

Expanding on this analysis of state laws is Bremner's listing (1974, p. 881–889) of thirteen basic elements in the laws: (1) statement of purpose, (2) age limits for reportable children, (3) definition of reportable abuse, (4) nature of report, (5) who reports, (6) how reports are made, (7) to whom reports are made, (8) mandate to agency receiving report, (9) immunity, (10) waivers, (11) the penalty clause, (12) central registry, and (13) special clauses, such as those related to child abuse as a crime and those exempting cases of children receiving religious healing. As states have enacted reporting laws, we find that the nature of the legislation largely influences and determines a community's response to a victim of child abuse and neglect. The clarity of these laws help professionals cooperate more readily, whereas, the lack of clarity in these laws impedes this process.

COLLABORATIVE STRATEGIES, INTERAGENCY THEORIES, AND COMMUNITY PREVENTION PROGRAMS

Needs in Communities

The multidisciplinary management of child abuse and neglect, as well as obtaining the mutual cooperation of various professionals and disciplines in communities is very difficult. Numerous problems exist, according to Newberger (1978, p. 16–18), and include the following:

1. Lack of understanding by the members of one discipline of the objectives, standards, conceptual bases, and ethics of the others;
2. A lack of effective communication from members of one discipline to members of another;
3. Confusion as to which personnel can take what management responsibilities at what times;
4. A kind of professional chauvinism about the domain of services to the child and the family;
5. Too much work for everybody and a sense of hopelessness and despair in the face of overwhelming problems and unsympathetic colleagues;

6. Institutional relationships which limit effective interprofessional contact;

7. Prevailing punitive attitudes and public policies about child abuse; and

8. A lack of confidence and trust on the part of personnel from one profession toward colleagues in the others.

In communities, it is a very large challenge to address these issues in an effective manner. The development of the public child welfare system has resulted in a bureaucratization of the services. What has resulted is a highly organized system of agencies of multilevel authority, extremely specialized functions, elaborate rules governing eligibility, and rigid jurisdictional divisions.

In the development of model systems for the prevention and control of child abuse and neglect, Newberger (1978), has identified these essential attributes:

1. Underlying support through public policies which strengthen family life;

2. Incorporation of child advocacy and child development education; and

3. Commitment of adequate resources to assure that a successful program is possible.

A model program in a community needs to: (1) see child abuse as a symptom of family crisis; (2) recognize the values and traditions of child rearing in its community; (3) maintain protection of information about people; (4) include citizen supervision of professional policies and practices; (5) evaluate the outcomes of the services provided; (6) maintain the family as the unit of practice and not fragment health, social, and psychological problems into separately provided services; (7) provide 24 hour services; (8) assure adequate legal representation for all parties in any court proceeding relating to child abuse; and (9) respond creatively to individual family's problems with services suited to their needs (Newberger, 1978).

In a slightly different manner, Schmitt (1978), has identified the needs in a community as a range of treatment options that are essential for case management. A carefully planned combination of treatment options is the most useful means of intervening with parents and children. These include: (1) treatment interventions for the parents (individual psychotherapy, lay therapy, marital therapy, group therapy, and crisis hotlines);

(2) treatment interventions for children (therapeutic playschools, individual play therapy, and group therapy); and (3) treatment interventions for families (crisis nurseries, family therapy, family residential treatment, and parent/child intervention).

Problems occur when the community's system of services do not seem to be as coordinated as they should. The characteristics of problems that occur in communities are identified by Cohen (1980), as including: unclear rules of interaction, lack of agreement on the system's purpose, ambiguous roles of professionals, an unclear and changing arena of action, and lack of mechanism for surfacing or resolving any of these dilemmas!

Collaborative Strategies

Trohanis (1980), has presented an effective framework for designing a communications campaign and planning guide for building acceptance within a community. His guidelines to encourage community acceptance of efforts to build support and increase participation within the community include:

1. Solidifying support for the communication effort within the program staff and agency before going public;
2. Collaborating with other local programs;
3. Building community awareness as a long-term proposition;
4. Building up a community awareness program over time and not having it **shot all at once;**
5. Identifying and using people with credibility in communications efforts to serve as spokespersons or chairpersons;
6. Being straightforward in approaching controversial topics or issues;
7. Wherever and whenever possible, striving for active participation and avoiding passivity;
8. Using a mix of delivery methods;
9. Communicating the message simply, honestly and concisely, with sensitivity to audiences;
10. Being positive in your approach, and prompt in delivering services; and
11. Finally, being creative!

Interagency Theories

These strategies for community communication by Trohanis are helpful pointers in facilitating interorganizational activities. Interagency theories revolve around aspects of three theoretical perspectives: (1) **Interorganizational Theory** which deals with the size and complexity of structure, power, status, communication, leadership and roles; (2) **Systems Theory** which deals with interaction of people and the effects of boundaries; and (3) **Exchange Theory** which is built upon reciprocity and gift exchange aspects of giving, receiving and repayment. This gift exchange implies obligations and strengthens social bonds. Coordination of services can occur as one of three types: (1) an **ad hoc** case (handled by the individual practitioner), (2) a **systematic** case (handled by rules and procedures agreed upon by administrators of the agencies involved), or (3) a **program** case (seen by joint projects, mutual assistance, and joint planning). Cooperation has the necessity of not being too much or too little, but just right.

This range of interorganizational relationships can be seen in five stages: communication (sharing information and ideas only), cooperation (working together informally), confederation (when relationships are formalized and tasks defined), federation (when a joint structure is created by the agencies and each gives up a certain amount of autonomy), and merger (when agencies give up their identities and become one new organization).

The process by which interagency cooperation occurs is very complex. Factors that **facilitate** the occurrence include: an interest in cooperation in one agency, a history of cooperation between the agencies, a mutual desire to decrease overlap in services, a scarcity of resources crucial to adequate delivery of services, funding reductions necessitating a more efficient operation, consumer or public demand for new services or improvements in old one, and a gap in services. Various factors that **hinder** interagency cooperation include: fears of changes in the level or a loss of funds, lack of information about the other agency, the distance between the agency and the project is too great, ideological differences, competition for clients or other resources, incompatible goals, and a legal structure which may prevent changes needed for cooperation. Resources are available for developing a structure to build better cooperation through: initial contact preparation, gaining access to and establishing the contact, maintaining and directing the interaction, interpersonal techniques, getting the commitment and expediting contacts, relating to role behavior needs, and keeping one's perspective. Key thoughts to keep in mind are: cooperation doesn't happen overnight, your first effort may not work out, expect the unexpected, timing is important, and don't expect to reform your entire community!

Community Prevention Programs

Osborn (1981), has proposed a model plan for the coordination and management of child abuse programs, which was developed in San Mateo County, California. This model structure is composed of five basic components:

Component I: Advocacy/Legislation. This component includes children's rights, public relations, media involvement, the reporting law, the issue of corporal punishment, and State Department involvement.

Component II: Prediction and Prevention. This component includes such areas as Bonding Studies, High Risk Identification, Hotlines, Parenting classes, Respite Care, and Information and Referral Services.

Component III: Detection and Prevention. This component includes a Multidisciplinary Team (MDT) effort, 24 Hour Crisis Service, Schools (Public and Private), Police Departments, Mental Health, Medical Services, Social Services, and Public Health.

Component IV: Intervention and Treatment. This component includes the Multidisciplinary Team (MDT), Foster Care, Adoption and Permanent Planning, Individual Therapy, Group Therapy, Self Help Groups, Friendly Visitors, Teaching, Homemakers, and the Court System.

Component V: Education and Training. This component includes public education for the lay community and training for professionals involved in the field, including a library and dissemination of materials.

Within all communities, Osborn believes that a committee or program needs to be established that is representative of the entire child abuse community and to have vested in it some measure of power or authority. Jenkins, MacDicken and Ormsby (1979) see the functions of this group to be: (1) encouraging policies of cooperation, (2) surveying and analyzing needs and resources, (3) developing community awareness of needs and resources, (4) making program recommendations, (5) developing new community resources and programs as needed in primary and secondary prevention, (6) providing service evaluation, (7) facilitating child abuse and neglect case consultation teams, and (8) serving as advocates for children and families.

Three levels of prevention can be found in most communities' prevention programs. **Primary prevention** (Jenkins et al., 1979), can be carried out in the following ways: (1) Programs designed to make society more supportive to effective child rearing. This applies to all adults who care for children (i.e., current parents, adolescents presently in school, and anyone considering parenthood); (2) Programs which help children to develop the skills they will need in order to function effectively as adults. Examples of this are programs in day care centers or schools that aid the child's psychological, intellectual and physical growth; and (3) Advocacy for changes in the role of children in society, for support of the family structure, and for alleviation of basic social problems re— lated to unemployment, poor housing, poverty, or discrimination.

Secondary Prevention programs (Jenkins et al., 1979) should be geared to prevent child abuse and/or neglect in those families who are identified to be at risk or in crisis and who may become abusive or neglectful. These programs may include: a crisis telephone line or hotline, crisis center, homemaker service, parent aide program, foster grandparent program, big brother or big sister programs, parents anonymous groups, visiting health nurses, and parents' day out programs.

Tertiary Prevention programs are geared to deal with the child who has actually suffered child abuse and/or neglect. Programs which deal with the child removed from parental custody may include these options: (1) temporary evaluation of injuries in a health care facility's pediatric unit; (2) temporary substitute parental care in a foster home; (3) longer term adoptive placement; and (4) group care services through emergency shelter and care, group homes, residential treatment homes, training schools for delinquents, and institutions for the physically, emotionally or mentally handicapped (Kadushin, 1980).

Shireman, Miller and Brown (1981, p. 420), have completed research with three different samples of child abuse and neglect complaints, which were drawn from the Juvenile Court files, child welfare agency intakes and police intakes. They found, "... a consistently higher rate of emergency placement of children when the police first investigated the complaint. Children left at home tended to remain at home ... Clearly the decisions made in the original investigation had a continuing impact." Many professionals are beginning to question the use of foster care because too often, temporary situation have turned into long term placements.

Case disposition was studied by Craft and Clarkson (1985) between attorneys and social workers. They found that attorneys recommend court interventions and foster care more frequently than CPS workers. The social workers appeared more concerned with unwarranted intervention into family affairs and less convinced of the therapeutic nature of early, limited, or coercive intervention than attorneys. However, there was greater intragroup agreement on cases by CPS workers when the child abuse situation was a low risk situation, while the highest accord for attorneys was in high risk situations.

CONCEPTUAL MODELS FOR COMMUNITY ACTION ON CHILD ABUSE AND NEGLECT

Four key conceptual models for community action on child abuse and neglect reports have been identified in the literature: child protection, medical, legal and interdisciplinary models. Each of these approaches has a unique orientation to investigation, case planning, treatment, use of court action, and level of involvement in prevention activities.

Child Protection Model

Bremner (1974, p. 851) quotes the rationale for CPS work, provided by the American Humane Association, as an obligation of society to assure to every child the standard of care and protection below which the state does not wish its children to live. CPS should stand ready to act on behalf of children who are abused or neglected, and should take suitable action in regard to those causing such neglect or abuse, or contributing to delinquency. Standards for CPS work have been further developed by the Child Welfare League of America (Bremner, 1974, p. 851). They defined CPS as a specialized social service for children who are neglected, abused or exploited. These standards state: (1) the focus of service is:

> . . . a child whose parents, or others responsible for him, fail to provide, either through their own efforts or through the use of available community resources, the love, care, guidance and protection a child requires for healthy growth and development; and whose condition or situation gives observable evidence of the injurious effects of failure to meet at least his minimum needs.

(2) the purpose of protective service; (3) distinctive characteristics of protective service; (4) agency responsibility in protective service such as powers and duties (to act on each report and offer help to the family) and removal of a child from his own home (not be done unless M505parental consent is given or a court order is secured); (5) authority of social worker in protective service (derived from knowledge, skills and status as a professional and as a representative of an agency with defined legal powers and responsibilities; and (6) provision of emergency care or shelter

care (desirable for the agency to provide emergency care itself in foster family boarding homes, subsidized group homes, or a group care facility).

DeFrancis (1975, p. 6–7) sees the need for CPS to do more work in prevention, casefinding, and examination and assessment of practices in dealing with an identified case of child abuse. He has succinctly expressed the CPS orientation as:

> ... attempts to rehabilitate the home ... for the most part, we are dealing ... with acts resulting from parental incapacities and parental inabilities. These are situations where parents need to be helped to do a better job; they need to be helped to understand their responsibilities; they need to be taught to resolve the many difficulties which they find too difficult to cope with. ... We are frequently dealing with parents who are so overwhelmed that they become unmotivated to seek help voluntarily. They become immobilized; and do not, themselves, voluntarily seek help. Help has to be brought to them ... This is the focus of child protective services! It reaches out to the family to offer services to remedy the situation; to offer the services which will make a good home out of a "bad home" and make "responsible" parents out of "less than responsible people."

In order for CPS workers to function, Carroll (1978), states appropriate professional qualities need to be present, such as: knowledge of child development, understanding of abuse and neglect dynamics, knowledge of pertinent legal process and skill in court procedure, ability to take referral information, ability to communicate through writing, competence in interviewing techniques, and the ability to integrate areas of knowledge and skill.

Deutsch (1983), has summarized the key issues of CPS work in a most effective manner as it relates to the broader community. She identifies the importance of support systems, both informal and formal, in reporting child maltreatment. However, the overreporting problems resulting from the public awareness campaigns of the 1970's caused a reduction in CPS help. No follow-up actions were taken because additional personnel were not provided, thus, the system became overburdened.

A second dilemma concerns the issue of confidentiality. Many people are hesitant to initiate a report because they may be violating the confidentiality of another person close to them. They fear the situation may not be handled in the most sensitive or competent manner. Even though this concern should not be an issue, there have been enough situations publicized that supportive corrective intervention may be undermined.

The remaining key issues of CPS work presented by Deutsch include:

(1) the case determination and management issues concerning case substantiation, coping with realities, the need for referrals, and removing children from homes; (2) the case treatment and evaluation concerns related to the need for lay oriented services and the effects of stress on CPS workers; (3) the institutional maltreatment of children who are wards of the state, residing in detention facilities and residential treatment institutions for the mentally retarded, emotionally disturbed, physically handicapped or delinquent; and (4) the alternative intervention models for supportive assistance to families at risk from the informal support system and the CPS professionals either through a consultation model or team approach. Deutsch raises the concern that CPS work has greatly expanded and been more broadly defined, but may need to return to a more narrow, focused mission.

Collaboration with other resources and agencies is identified by Carroll (1978, p. 90–91) as a very important component:

> . . . if a child needs to be taken into protective custody, it is necessary to involve the police or juvenile court . . . Other professionals with whom the worker may need to share information and discuss plans are mental health workers, medical personnel, and various attorneys involved in a case. The parent's attorney can be a key person to smooth case-flow.

In social workers' work with law enforcement and juvenile court, protocols of action need to be clearly developed. When working with law enforcement, social workers should work in partnership with an officer, who preferably has child abuse and neglect as a specialized assignment. Their work together encourages a collaborative response to a report of suspected child abuse and neglect; jointly conducted investigations, each according to appropriated agency requirements; cooperative decision making about the next steps in a case situation; and mutual agreement on a referral, if there is confirmation of child abuse and neglect (Broadhurst & Knoeller, 1979, p. 51). Sometimes CPS workers and officers have had difficult experiences while attempting to work as a team. This frequently happens when one of the parties distrusts or hold a low opinion of the other discipline. However, this trend is changing as more CPS and law enforcement agencies upgrade their services through increased staff training and development of a more enlightened attitude regarding the benefits of learning to work more cooperatively together. According to Carroll (1978), social workers need to cooperate with the judicial system and need to know: (1) the protocols and guidelines about all aspects of court (criteria for filing court petitions and court report outlines for each type of hearing); (2) the correct style used by a professional when testifying in court; and (3) pitfalls to avoid (lack of resources, misleading evaluations or over-identification with the parent, child, or community).

Statutory or administrative guidelines that specify standards of sound professional practice help CPS and law enforcement personnel in more effective management of child abuse and neglect cases. In their absence, actions may be taken on the basis of exhaustion, emotionalism, or personal values about child rearing (Craft & Clarkson, 1985).

Medical Model

Newberger and Bourne (1978, p. 597) have seen medicine's expansion, after the formulation of the **battered child syndrome** and the related laws that were passed requiring the syndrome to be reported, as a basis for a new proper and legitimate concern. They define this process as **medicalization** of child abuse so that it is seen:

> . . . as the perception of behavior as a medical problem or illness and the mandating or licensing of the medical profession to provide some type of treatment for it.

Schmitt, et. al. (1979, p. I–1) developed a manual of guidelines for hospitals and clinics and identified the objectives of the health care facility in addressing child abuse and neglect (CA/N) as the following:

1. **Identify** those children seen in the hospital setting who have been abused and neglected;
2. Provide adequate **medical care** for the injuries sustained;
3. Carry out the legal obligations of **reporting** CA/N cases according to state law;
4. Collect data in a comprehensive manner so that if these data are needed later in court as evidence, they will be adequate to **document the diagnosis** of CA/N; and
5. **Remain therapeutic and helpful** to the parents of the abused child so that parents will remain receptive to long-term treatment.

This manual (Schmitt et al., 1979), spells out very clearly for health care facilities: the requirements for personnel, laboratory and x-ray facilities, policies and procedures, responsibilities of nonmedical CA/N personnel, legal policies and procedures, emergency room protocols, hospitalized cases of physical abuse (physician's guidelines to management), incest and other family related sexual abuse cases (physician's guidelines to management), failure to thrive secondary to nutritional deprivation (physician's guidelines to management), newborn nursery, identification of and intervention with high risk families, child protection team protocols, and physical and behavioral indicators of child abuse and neglect. In this manual, the discussion related to legal policies and procedures focuses upon: (1) legal definitions to be put in state laws (proposed language is offered and/or samples of various state laws are provided) for physical abuse, sexual abuse, neglect, emotional abuse or mental injury; (2) hospital policy on reporting and investigating all cases of suspected CA/N; (3) reporting CA/N by phone and obtaining emergency (child welfare) services; (4) reporting CA/N in writing; (5) police or health hold orders; and (6) court order to provide medical care when parents refuse to consent.

Heindl and Associates (1979), have articulated the reasons for nurses, as well as doctors, being involved with child abuse and neglect as: (1) nurses work with and for children and their families; (2) the law mandates nurses' involvement and professional responsibility dictates it; and (3) nurses have a personal commitment to the health and well-being of children and their families. Some of the reasons that nurses have encountered difficulties in reporting or continuing to be involved in child abuse and neglect are personal feelings (i.e., people don't want to get involved or parents have a right to treat children in any way they wish); relationships with the parents (i.e., fear that they may betray someone's trust in them); problems internal to the employing organization (i.e., a doctor or school principal may discourage reports); and difficulties with child protection services (i.e., they feel nothing will be done or they had a previous unfortunate experience when reporting). However, all health professionals need to report what they observe, for if no report is made, a child may continue to be in danger.

Legal Model

Newberger and Bourne (1978, p. 598–599) have identified the **legalization** of child abuse and neglect cases.

> The legal response to child abuse was triggered by its medicalization. Child abuse reporting statutes codified a medical diagnosis into a legal framework which in many states defined official functions for courts. Immunity from civil liability was given to mandated reporters so long as reports were made in good faith; monetary penalties for failure to report were established; and familial and professional-client confidentiality privileges, except those involving attorneys, were abrogated.

Professional autonomy for lawyers was established, and status and power accrued to legal institutions.

The role of law enforcement has been developed in all of the 50 states. Each have identified for the police department, some role in the investigation of child abuse and neglect cases. Bockman and Carroll (1978), have a number of suggestions for a methodology to increase the amount of coordination that could occur between community agencies, and both the police and county attorney offices. These suggestions for police include: (1) having specially trained police officers who are familiar with the psychology of child abuse and the procedures for reporting it; (2) having law enforcement officers who are fully informed about services available through community agencies and who have a telephone referral list of appropriate agencies/individuals to call in times of crisis; (3) developing a working agreement between the law enforcement agency and the department of social services, which clearly defines roles, responsibilities, and delineation of cases where the police should take an active lead role and those where they should defer to another community agency; and (4) anticipating criminal action and involving the police from the earliest moment possible.

A most effective communication system was developed between the Social Service Department and the law enforcement agencies in Adams County, Colorado. This system had selected reports of nonserious child abuse sent to the Police Department labeled, "for information only". If the police, when they received the report, agreed with the statement that no police intervention was necessary, they did not make contact with the family (Brockman et al., 1978). In those cases where the police did not feel comfortable with the statement, they made contact with the CPS social worker for more information. Such communication allowed for frequent updates and clarification regarding previously reported cases, in addition to reporting new dispositions and referrals made by each agency.

Sometimes the law enforcement efforts may be complicated by jurisdictional issues, such as the variety of arrangements existing about the appropriateness of action in dealing with reports of child abuse and neglect situations on Indian reservations and military installations (Broadhurst et al.). Law enforcement officers encounter various difficulties in their work on child abuse and neglect complaints such as: (1) personal feelings of not wanting to get involved of interfering with the parent's rights; (2) distinguishing between appropriate discipline versus abuse in families; and (3) difficulties with CPS workers since they feel nothing will happen or be handled to their satisfaction.

For a more detailed discussion of the role of the criminal justice system, see the following section in that literature on "Child Abuse and the Criminal Justice System."

Interdisciplinary Model

Jenkins, MacDicken and Ormsby (1979, p. 1–14) see that a broad community response is necessary for child abuse and neglect situations because, " . . . no single individual, agency, or professional discipline has the necessary knowledge, skills or resources to provide all the services needed by families. . . . " A coordinated community is better equipped to intervene with the most appropriated services and minimize duplication of services. A formal community coordinating committee should fulfill the following functions:

1. Encourage policies on the part of community agencies which demonstrate a capacity and willingness to work together;
2. Survey and analyze awareness of needs and resources;
3. Determine community awareness of needs and resources;
4. Make program recommendations;
5. Develope new community resources as needed;
6. Review service delivery;
7. Establish and/or facilitate multidisciplinary child abuse and neglect case consultation teams; and
8. Serve as advocates for children and families.

Representation on this committee will vary widely, depending upon the community. According to Osborn (1981, p. 291), San Mateo County is one of the California counties that has a multidisciplinary team to review all serious cases of abuse and neglect. This San Mateo team operates in the following manner:

> The MDT meets on a regular basis and functions from within the Health and Welfare Department. Its purpose is to review cases of physical, sexual, and emotional abuse of children as reported to Children's Protective Services. The team is in its second year of existence and includes a pediatrician, child psychiatrist, clinical psychologist, district attorney, public health nurse, day care and foster care placement specialist, and representatives of Children's Protective Services. The team is used for ongoing cases, as well as for diagnosis. Mandatory referrals for discussion and review include all cases of physical abuse to

children under 2 years of age, serious physical abuse of a child of any age, sexual abuse and serious neglect, such as failure to thrive, which may endanger a child's life, safety, or health.

The MDT tries to look at specific issues such as the type of injury or neglect a child has sustained, distress and problems of the parents, the resources that could be used to allow the child to remain safely in the home, or the factors that would safely allow a child to return to his home. The less pleasant, but vital function of the team, is to work with those situations where services already provided to a family have been either rejected or ineffective and the best course of providing some hope of a meaningful life for the abused child would be through court ordered termination of parental rights. The MDT process can bring to bear a collaborative influence on cases which can be influential, especially in the juvenile court.

A similar MDT effort is reported by LeBlang (1979), about the success of their community-wide cooperative venture called the Springfield (Illinois) Family Stress Consultation Team. Their program operates with community professionals who serve on rotation at weekly consultation sessions. Coordination of their process is handled by a Team Coordinator with the representatives of the following disciplines: child psychiatry or psychology, social work, medicine (pediatrics or family practice), public health, and law.

All too often the role of mental health professionals and educators are overlooked. Lauer, Lourie, and Salus (1979), report that a number of mental health facilities have established policies and procedures regarding child abuse and neglect as well as appointed a staff member to act as a liaison to the local CPS program. Some of the difficulties mental health professionals may have focus on personal and professional feelings about jeopardizing their therapist/client relationship, procedural problems internal to the agency, and their belief that nothing will be done even if they report. Many of these issues can be addressed and resolved as mental health professionals collaborate with the community CPS program.

Likewise, Broadhurst (1979), states the reasons that educators get involved in child abuse and neglect are that: they work with and for children, law and policy command educator involvement, professional responsibility demands it, and educators have a deep sense of personal commitment to the children in their care. Some of the difficulties that schools need to overcome include: principals who may discourage teacher involvement by refusing to take teacher's reports seriously, central administrative staff who provide no backup to line staff, and superintendents who fail to provide inservice training to staff in order to inform them of their legal obligations. Barth (1985, p. 42–44) has identified additional difficulties that private schools may have.

> Most private schools are inexperienced in helping children who are economically disadvantaged, and these schools are largely unprepared to work with foster children and identify child abuse. At times, because of the pressures to please their paying customers, private schools may fail to report abuse to public authorities and instead attempt to handle such cases on their own. Similar pressures from educational consumers operate in all alternative schools and may block unpopular but needed assistance to children.

Thus, the professionals in both mental health and education need to be included in the community's plan to provide comprehensive services.

Jenkins, MacDicken and Ormsby (1979), have addressed the essential components in the operation of a community child protection coordinating committee, which include: (1) roles and responsibilities of committee members; (2) suggestions in getting the committee started and creating a plan of action; (3) ideas for effective coordinated effort, fostering community awareness and support, and gaining cooperation and participation from agencies and organizations; (4) ideas for operating effective meetings of the committee and barriers to avoid; and (%) the functions of the committee, both external (community policies, needs assessment, prevention, advocacy) and internal (open communications, planning, evaluation procedures and accountability). As mentioned earlier, the committee has to deal with barriers, such as: getting **bogged down** in theoretical issues, power struggles between member groups, confidentiality questions, and long-term issues such as leadership or turnover.

CHILD ABUSE AND THE CRIMINAL JUSTICE SYSTEM

Personnel from the social service, medical, law enforcement and legal professions need to develop mutual respect and work cooperatively to help victims of child abuse and child sexual abuse. Individuals who work with abused children can gain greater understanding of the responsibilities of the other disciplines through participation in multidisciplinary training sessions. It is also important for social workers, law enforcement officers and prosecutors to conduct a joint investigation of child abuse cases.

Children who have been abused (physically and/or sexually) may be subjected to a double trauma; the victimization itself and a secondary victimization brought on by inexperience, insensitivity, and a lack of coordinated efforts from individuals in the criminal justice system. However, contact with the justice system does not necessarily have to be traumatic. In this section the interaction between the child victim and the criminal justice system will be discussed, with emphasis on the ways in which interdisciplinary cooperation can and should be utilized to serve the best interests of the child.

Role of the Police

In every community, it is the law enforcement agency which is most likely to be available at any hour of the day, seven days a week, to respond to a report of child abuse or neglect. Therefore, it is vital that all police officers (not just juvenile officers) receive extensive training in identifying children who have been abused and in referring them to the appropriate agency (e.g., Child Protective Services). A police officer may be called to a home for a reason unrelated to child abuse but, if properly trained, the officer may be able to detect signs of previously unreported abuse.

Police department should have a specialized child abuse or family abuse unit which is alerted to and investigates every reported abuse case in that community. It is particularly important that the police exhibit sensitivity when investigating a case of suspected child sexual abuse. To help them acquire the knowledge and skills to be effective interviewers, specialized training workshops on child sexual abuse should be developed, which include the following components:

1. A film which describes the physical and psychological effects of sexual abuse on children and adolescents;
2. Lecture and discussion, including the opportunity for small group discussion; and
3. Case studies which depict the different dynamics of sexual abuse, including an examination of different methods for interacting with the child and the family (Stone et. al., 1984).

Some police specialists advocate using audiotapes and videotapes of actual interviews for the training sessions. If this technique is used, it is recommended that confidentiality be protected by disguising the identities of the involved parties.

In addition to receiving information on the dynamics of child abuse,

police officers need training (including role playing) on interviewing
children who have been sexually and/or physically abused (Graves and
Sgroi, 1981; Stone et. al., 1984). The location of the interview is an
important factor in helping the child to feel less anxious. Graves and
Sgroi (1981) suggest conducting the interview in a quiet room in a
neutral setting with comfortable chairs and no interruptions. The interview should not be conducted in the home if there is reason to suspect
that the assault took place there or that a family member is involved in
the abuse.

The child may feel more comfortable if the police interview is conducted
in the presence of a person the child trusts, preferably a social worker or
counselor. The third party should not be a family member, even if that
individual is not suspected of being involved in the assault. Some relatives might attempt to suppress information (through verbal or nonverbal cues) which might incriminate another member of the family or a
close friend. It is suggested that prior to the interview, the police officer
contact the supportive and trusted adult to gather background information regarding the abuse of the child. The officer can advise the other
adult about the way in which the interview will be handled and establish
ground rules on the officer's eliciting comments or clarification from the
adult during the interview (Graves and Sgroi, 1982).

Many communities have developed child abuse teams and task forces
in an effort to create a coordinated service delivery system. One example
of a successful coordinated approach was established in Tucson, Arizona
in the mid-1970's. Sadly, the impetus for creating the coordinated system
was the death of a young boy. The boy was taken to a hospital emergency
room after being beaten into a coma.

> He was treated and sent home with his mother. But a few days
> later ... he was back, again severely battered. This time, the social
> workers released him to his grandparents. But a judge allowed the
> mother to take the little boy home as long as the mother's boyfriend,
> who had been doing the beating, was not allowed to be alone with him.
> The next day ... the mother left the house, and the boyfriend killed
> the child. The boyfriend was charged with murder but contended that
> the child fell out of his high chair. At the trial, the judge instructed the
> jury to acquit the boyfriend because the prosecution could not prove
> the child died from a beating. Had there been a more complete
> investigation, which could have been accomplished through better
> coordination among different agencies, a conviction would have resulted
> (Bernstein, 1978, p. 59).

Before the development of a coordinated approach in Tucson, the police, social workers and physicians were distrustful of one another. Rather than sharing information and coordinating services, each group maintained its own records using **confidentiality** as an excuse for refusing to work together. The obvious tragedy of the above cited case and numerous others is that innocent children may be killed when professionals, who should be maintaining open line of communication, refuse to work cooperatively.

The Tucson police department began its child abuse unit in 1976 with one specially trained law enforcement officer. Following the development of the coordinated system, physicians who suspected that a child had been abused contacted the police child abuse unit and the social worker simultaneously, and both became involved in the case. A police officer from the child abuse unit trains other police officers in the proper way to respond and communicate in suspected child abuse cases. He also speaks to medical and nursing students about the need for a coordinated approach (Bernstein, 1978).

One reason for social workers' reluctance to share information on abuse cases with the police was their belief that the police were mainly interested in arresting the parents rather than being concerned about the welfare of the child. In Tucson during an 18 month period (after the coordinated system was underway), there were nearly 400 abuse cases and only 15 prosecutions. In most of the cases, the abuser agreed to participate in counseling as an alternative to arrest (Bernstein, 1978). Thus, if the situation in Tucson is representative of other cities, social workers need not be concerned that coordination with the police will result in too many abusive parents being prosecuted while too few parents receive counseling.

Guardian Ad Litem

Most cases of child abuse which go to court are heard in the juvenile court. Generally, the judge appoints a guardian ad litem to represent the best interests of the child. (The Child Abuse Prevention and Treatment Act of 1974 requires states to assign a guardian ad litem in order to receive federal monies.) This individual's responsibilities include counseling the child, providing information on legal procedures, and accompanying him or her to court and to a medical examination (if it is needed). The guardian ad litem is also expected to evaluate the case and may offer recommendations to the court. Opinions vary on whether this role should be filled by an attorney or a lay person. The obvious advantage of using attorneys is their knowledge of the legal process. But there are drawbacks as well, the most significant being: (1) prosecutors who serve in this capacity may be insensitive to the needs of the abused children and place emphasis on obtaining a conviction and harsh sentence at the expense of the children's feelings and needs; and (2) many attorneys are too busy to devote sufficient time to working with child victims (Whitcomb et. al., 1985).

Prosecuting Attorneys

There is a need for improved collaboration between attorneys and personnel working in the child protective services field. Child protective workers are testifying in court with greater frequency and with less time for preparation. Attorneys can be of assistance in advising child protective workers on collecting and presenting to the court **competent evidence** to justify their recommended interventions. Barth and Sullivan (1985), use the term **competent evidence** to refer to, "evidence that is court admissible, reasonably reliable and valid, and convincing."

Child protective services workers may also need to consult with an attorney regarding the following types of issues:

1. Whether a child can legally be removed from home;
2. The use of voluntary parent/agency service agreements;
3. Whether a court proceeding should be initiated; and
4. Relations with the other attorneys in the proceedings (Horowitz and Davidson, 1981).

There are also areas in which prosecutors need to seek the advise of social workers and other mental health professionals, for example: conducting interviews with child victims, choosing potential jurors, and preparing statements of introduction and summation to the court (Whitcomb, 1986). Finally, all attorneys who prosecute cases of child abuse should receive training in such areas as child psychology and family dynamics as well as case precedent and state law (Whitcomb et. al., 1985).

Reducing the Stress of Multiple Interviews

The Attorney General's Task Force on Family Violence (1984) has reported that, during the course of criminal justice proceedings, a child who has been sexually abused has an average of twelve investigative interviews. Therapists, attorneys, judges and police officers agree that being required to discuss the events so many times may be one of the most upsetting aspects of the entire ordeal (Whitcomb et. al., 1985). There are several ways in which the lengthy interview process can be consolidated:

1. By conducting some form of **joint** interview among two or more of the agencies involved;
2. By assigning specilaists within each agency, so there is only one interviewer per agency;
3. By videotaping the child's first statement;
4. By eliminating the need for the child to appear at one or more of the formal proceedings; and
5. By coordinating the juvenile and criminal court proceedings (Whitcomb et. al., 1985).

The following are two examples of interagency cooperation which have been successful in reducing the number of times a child needs to be interviewed. In Seattle, Washington, staff from all involved agencies have weekly meetings to examine the status of their cases. To reduce the number of interviews, one person is selected to interview the child; the others view the interaction from behind a one way mirror (Whitcomb, 1981). In Huntsville, Alabama, all cases of child sexual abuse are acted upon in one building, known as the Children's Advocacy Center, which has offices for representatives from the involved agencies. Interviews are handled by a team consisting of a prosecutor, a police officer, and a child protective worker (Whitcomb et. al., 1985).

Court Proceedings

Efforts are underway in all parts of the United States to alleviate stress for child victims when the case against the abuser goes to court. Changes in the proceedings focus on ways in which victims can be spared the stress of testifying personally in court. Two of the primary areas in which statutory reforms are being made are; reducing the number of times a child provides testimony (e.g., permitting hearsay), and recording the child's recollections on videotape.

In addition to the above mentioned reforms, there are techniques to reduce children's anxiety prior to giving testimony that do not require statutory reform, such as:

1. Enhancing the child's communication skills through dolls, artwork, and simplified vocabulary;

2. Modifying the physical environment by providing a small chair for the child, having the judge sit on a level with the child, and wear business clothes instead of a judicial robe;

3. Preparing child victims before their courtroom appearances by briefing them on the roles of people in the courtroom, introducing them to the judge, taking them for a tour of the courtroom, and allowing them to sit in the witness chair and speak into the microphone (Whitcomb, 1986).

Judges should take on a more active role when hearing a child's testimony. Whitcomb et. al. (1985) offer the following recommendations to enhance the involvement of judges:

1. Advise the attorneys before the trial on appropriate behavior, (e.g., caution them to maintain a specific distance from the witness chair, instruct them not to talk in a loud or angry tone of voice);
2. Be prepared for questions that may be intimidating to the victim;
3. Be observant of a child becoming embarrassed or upset and if the child's emotional state appears to be distorting the testimony, be prepared to call a recess to enable the victim to calm down;
4. Grant a continuance only if it is urgently needed; and
5. Ensure that every child is accompanied by a supportive adult friend.

The above mentioned issue of a child having a supportive adult nearby in court would seem to be a matter of common sense but, in fact, it may be difficult to carry out. In an effort to lessen the trauma of the court proceeding, the juvenile court may prevent anyone who has not witnessed the crime from being in court. Though the intentions are good, the result may be increased stress for the child who must endure the proceeding without the benefit of reassurance from a supportive adult (Rogers, 1982).

In cases of child sexual abuse, the National Legal Resource Center for Child Advocacy and Protection (1981) recommends coordination of the proceedings scheduled by the criminal and juvenile courts. The child may become confused if the two courts hear the case at the same time and make conflicting rulings. It is not uncommon for the judge in the criminal court to be unaware that the same case is simultaneously being heard in the juvenile court and vice versa. Testimony being provided by the child victim should be made available to both courts.

To expedite scheduling of trials involving victims of child abuse, the Attorney General's Task Force on Family Violence (1984) has recommended having a special docket for cases of domestic violence (which would also handle elder and spouse abuse). The defendant's lawyer may try to delay the proceedings in the hope that the child will forget the details of the victimization. Numerous postponements are very stressful for the child and should be avoided.

The stressfulness of requiring a child to repeatedly describe the events surrounding the victimization has already been discussed. In some jurisdictions, the child is required to testify at the preliminary hearing, the grand jury proceeding and the trial. A child's anxiety at testifying during all of these proceedings could be alleviated if judges permitted **hearsay evidence** prior to the trial. Allowing hearsay at the pretrial stages would result in fewer children being required to give formal testimony because a considerable number of cases never come to trial; many cases are dismissed or handled through pleas (Rogers, 1982).

Videotaping

Videotaping a sexually abused child's recollections soon after the assault has been endorsed by victim advocates as an effective means of lessening the trauma of testifying in court. This technique has been approved by the Attorney General's Task Force on Family Violence (1984) and by the National Conference of the Judiciary on the Rights of Victims of Crime (1983). In at least 14 states, videotaped testimony is admissible in court. It is recommended that all videotapes of children's statements be placed under **protective orders** to ensure privacy (Whitcomb et al., 1985).

There are many advantages to videotaping the child's first formal statement following the victimization. They are as follows:

1. The child's memory may fade over time;

2. In intrafamilial cases, family members often pressure children to retract their stories, thereby sapping their strength and weakening their testimony as their cases progress;

3. Videotaping can help to reduce the number of interviews children must give, thereby allowing them to get on with their lives and minimizing the prospect of testimony that is so well rehearsed that it loses credibility;

4. In states that permit hearsay evidence at the preliminary hearing or before the grand jury, the video could preclude the need for the child's live testimony at these proceedings;

5. Many prosecutors have observed an unanticipated, yet welcome

side effect of videotaping . . . it tends to prompt a guilty plea when viewed by defendants and their attorneys (Whitcomb et. al., 1985).

It is important to distinguish between videotaping of the first formal statement (as described above) which is generally recommended, and videotaping a deposition which is considered to have too many drawbacks. In taping a deposition, the victim and the defendant are brought together in a small room; a much more confined space than in a courtroom. Furthermore, "the judge may not be there to monitor the behavior of the defendant or his counsel, and victim advocates may not be permitted to attend" (Whitcomb, 1986, p. 4). In some jurisdictions, a finding of **emotional trauma** is necessary before the judge will permit a videotape to substitute for live testimony. Thus the victim may be required to undergo a series of medical and/or psychiatric tests (Whitcomb et. al., 1985 and Whitcomb, 1986).

Conclusion

There has been an increased awareness among professionals of the need for early intervention, treatment planning, and the provision of services to physical and sexually abused children. There has also been a growing emphasis on diagnosis and consultation by multidisciplinary teams, law enforcement agencies, prosecutor's offices, and the courts. Many of the problems of the past such as lack of planning, lack of interagency coordination, fragmentation, duplication of services, and failure to effectively intervene on behalf of the abused child, are gradually being remedied. In this regard, model collaborative interagency efforts including community strategies, multidisciplinary teams, specialized training models, interagency consultation and collaboration, and improved coordination between social workers and criminal justice professionals offer much promise for successfully intervention on behalf of abused children.

The need for training and familiarity with other relevant disciplines and their terminology is the premise of the book titled, **Interdisciplinary Glossary on Child Abuse and Neglect: Legal, Medical, Social Work Terms** (Haeuser, 1978). Many communities are incorporating inservice education through interdisciplinary workshops and seminars attended by various professionals as well as volunteers from the community. More public education needs to be initiated within the community. The recent public television series dealing with child sexual abuse is evidence of some tentative steps in this direction. However, in many communities some of the more conservative individuals were offended and have used the editorial pages of the local newspapers to protest the broadcast of programs dealing with such topics. It is too soon to assess the impact of such protests.

Certainly, social workers and law enforcement personnel need to establish collaborative strategies to work more effectively on behalf of physically and sexually abused children. As greater avenues of communication occur, the professional community's response to a child abuse report will become more individualized and helpful, offering the best possible intervention for each child's situation. More interdisciplinary communication and decision making will ensure consistency and uniformity in the initial response of a community's child abuse reports. Hopefully, more deliberation will then be given to cases to determine the course of action, whether it be CPS investigation, counseling services, supportive assistance, concrete needs, foster care, full police investigation, and/or prosecution.

REFERENCES

1. Attorney General's Task force on Family Violence: *Final Report.* September, 1984.
2. Barth, R. P.: Collaboration between child welfare and school social work services. *Social Work in Education,* 8(1):32–47, 1985.
3. Barth, R. P., Ash, J. R., and Hacking, S.: Identifying, screening and engaging high-risk clients in private non-profit child abuse prevention programs. *Child Abuse and Neglect,* 10:99–109, 1986.
3. Barth, R. P., and Sullivan, R.: Collecting competent evidence in behalf of children. *Social Work,* 30(2):130–136, 1985.
4. Bassuk, E. L., Fox, S. S., and Prendergast, K. J.: *Behavioral Emergencies: A Field Guide for EMTS and Paramedics.* Boston, Little Brown, 1983.
5. Baxter, A.: *Techniques for Dealing with Child Abuse.* Springfield, Thomas, 1985.
6. Bernstein, D.: Police vs. child abuse: protecting the victim comes first. *Police Magazine,* 59–63, 1978.
7. Besharov, D.: Child sexual abuse: incest, assault and sexual exploitation. In Kirschner Associates (Eds.): *Child Abuse & Neglect: The User Manual Series.* Washington, National Center on Child Abuse and Neglect, USDHEW, 1978.
8. Besharov, D. J.: Right versus rights: the dilemma of child protection. *Public Welfare,* Spring, 19–27, 1985.
9. Billingsley, A., and Giovannani, J. M.: *Children of the Storm: Black Children and American Child Welfare.* New York, Harcourt, 1972.
10. Bockman, H. R., and Carroll, C. A.: The law enforcement's role in evaluation.

In Schmitt, B. D. (Ed.): *The Child Protection Team Handbook: A Multidisciplinary Approach to Managing Child Abuse and Neglect.* New York, Garland, 1978.

11. Borgman, R., Edmunds, M., and MacDicken, R.: Crisis intervention: a manual for child protective workers. In Kirschner Associates (Eds.): *Child Abuse & Neglect: The User Manual Series.* Washington, National Center on Child Abuse and Neglect, USDHEW, 1979.

12. Bremner, R. H. (Ed.): *Children & Youth in America: A Documentary History, 1933-1973.* Cambridge, Harvard, 1974, vol. III.

13. Broadhurst, D.: The educator's role in the prevention and treatment of child abuse and neglect. In Kirschner Associates (Eds.): *Child Abuse & Neglect: The User Manual Series.* Washington, National Center on Child Abuse and Neglect, USDHEW, 1979.

14. Broadhurst, D., and Knoeller, J.: The role of law enforcement in the prevention and treatment of child abuse and neglect. In Kirschner Associates (Eds.): *Child Abuse & Neglect: The User Manual Series.* Washington, National Center on Child Abuse and Neglect, USDHEW, 1979.

15. Broadhurst, D., and MacDicken, R.: Training in the prevention and treatment of child abuse and neglect. In Kirschner Associates (Eds.): *Child Abuse & Neglect: The User Manual Series.* Washington, National Center on Child Abuse and Neglect, USDHEW, 1979.

16. Bulkley, J. (Ed.): *Innovations in the Prosecution of Child Sexual Abuse.* Washington, American Bar Association, 1981.

17. Byles, J.: Problems in interagency collaboration: lessons from a project that failed. *Child Abuse and Neglect, 9:*549–554, 1985.

18. Carroll, C. A.: The protective service social worker's role in treatment. In Schmitt, B. D. (Ed.): *The Child Protection Team Handbook: A Multidisciplinary Approach to Managing Child Abuse and Neglect.* New York, Garland, 1978.

19. Carroll, C. A.: The social worker's evaluation. In Schmitt, B. D. (Ed.): *The Child Protection Team Handbook: A Multidisciplinary Approach to Managing Child Abuse and Neglect.* New York, Garland, 1978.

20. Carroll, C. A., and Schmitt, B. D.: Improving community treatment services. In Schmitt, B. D. (Ed.): *The Child Protection Team Handbook: A Multidisciplinary Approach to Managing Child Abuse and Neglect.* New York, Garland, 1978.

21. Child Abuse Prevention and Treatment Act. *P. L. 93-247,* 1974.

22. Close, M. M.: Child welfare and people of color: denial of equal access. *Social Research & Abstracts, 19*(4):13–20, 1983.

23. Cohen, B. J.: Coordination strategies in complex service delivery systems. *Administration in Social Work, 4*(3):83–87, 1983.

24. Compher, J. V.: The case conference revisited: a systems view. *Child Welfare, LXIII,*(5):411–417, 1984.

25. Craft, J. L., and Clarkson, C. D.: Case disposition recommendations of attorneys and social workers in child abuse investigations. *Child Abuse and Neglect, 9:*165–174, 1985.

26. DeFrancis. V.: Child protection—a comprehensive, coordinated process. In

The American Humane Association Children's Division (Eds.): *Fourth National Symposium on Child Abuse.* Denver, AHA, 1975.

27. Deutsch, F.: *Child Services on Behalf of Children.* Monterey, Brooks/Cole, 1983.
28. Duquette, D. N.: The expert witness in child abuse and neglect: an interdisciplinary process. *Child Abuse and Neglect, 5:*325–334, 1981.
29. Etherington, C., and Stephens, K.: The police officer and the sexually abused child: developing an approach to a critical problem. *The Police Chief,* 44–45, 1984.
30. Fisher, N.: Reaching out: the volunteer in child abuse and neglect programs. In Kirschner Associates (Eds.): *Child Abuse & Neglect: The User Manual Series.* Washington, National Center on Child Abuse and Neglect, USDHEW, 1979.
31. Frank M. (Ed.): *Child Care: Emerging Legal Issues.* New York, Haworth, 1983.
32. Fraser, B. G.: The court's role. In Schmitt, B. D. (Ed.): *The Child Protection Team Handbook: A Multidisciplinary Approach to Managing Child Abuse and Neglect.* New York, Garland, 1978.
33. Frederickson, H., and Mulligan, R. A.: *The Child and His Welfare.* San Francisco, Freeman, 1972.
34. Gabay, G. N. M.: Neither adversaries nor co-conspirators: creating a dialogue between attorneys and child care professionals. In Frank, M. (Ed.): *Child Care: Emerging Legal Issues.* New York, Haworth, 1983.
35. Gottesman, R.: *The Child and the Law.* St. Paul, West, 1981.
36. Graves, P., and Sgroi, S.: Law enforcement and child sexual abuse. In Sgroi, S. M. (Ed.): *Handbook of Clinical Intervention in Child Sexual Abuse.* Lexington, Lexington, 1982, pp. 309–333.
37. Grosz, C. A., and Lenherr, M. R.: The coordinator's role in evaluation. In Schmitt, B. D. (Ed.): *The Child Protection Team Handbook: A Multidisciplinary Approach to Managing Child Abuse and Neglect.* New York, Garland, 1978.
38. Haeuser, A. A. (Ed.): *Interdisciplinary Glossary on Child Abuse and Neglect: Legal, Medical, Social Work Teams.* Washington, National Center on Child Abuse and Neglect, Midwest Parent-Child Welfare Resource Center at the University of Wisconsin-Milwaukee, 1978.
39. Heindl, C., Krall, C., and Salus, M.: The nurse's role in the prevention and treatment of child abuse and neglect. In Kirschner Associates (Eds.): *Child Abuse & Neglect: The User Manual Series.* Washington, National Center on Child Abuse and Neglect, USDHEW, 1979.
40. Hochstadt, N., and Harwicke, N.: How effective is the multidisciplinary approach? A follow-up study. *Child Abuse and Neglect, 9:*365–372, 1985.
41. Horowitz, R.: Policy: child welfare: an evolving legal bases. In Frank, M. (Ed.): *Child Care: Emerging Legal Issues.* New York, Haworth, 1983.
42. Horowitz, R., and Davidson, H.: Improving the legal response of child protective agencies. *Vermont Law Review, 6:*381–402, 1981.
43. Jenkins, J., MacDicken, R., and Ormsby, N.: A community approach: the child protection coordinating committee. In Kirschner Associates (Eds.): *Child*

Abuse & Neglect: The User Manual Series, Washington, National Center on Child Abuse Neglect, USDHEW, 1979.

44. Kadushin, A.: *Child Welfare Services,* 3rd ed. New York, Macmillan, 1980.

45. Koerin, B.: Child abuse and neglect: changing policies and perspectives. *Child Welfare, LIX*(9):542–550, 1980.

46. Krieger, M., and Robbins, J.: The adolescent incest victim and the judicial system. *American Journal of Orthopsychiatry, 55:*419–425, 1985.

47. Lauer, J., Lourie, I., and Salus, M.: The role of the mental health professional in the prevention and treatment of child abuse and neglect. In Kirschner Associates (Eds.): *Child Abuse and Neglect: The User Manual Series.* Washington, National Center on Child Abuse Neglect, USDHEW, 1979.

48. LeBlang, T.: The family stress consultation team: an Illinois approach to protective services. *Child Welfare, LVIII*(9):597–603, 1979.

49. Martin, H.: Treatment for abused and neglected children. In Kirschner Associates (Eds.): *Child Abuse & Neglect: The User Manual Series.* Washington, National Center on Child Abuse Neglect, USDHEW, 1979.

50. Morgan, G. G.: Practical techniques for change. In Frank, M. (Ed.): *Child Care: Emerging Legal Issues.* New York, Haworth, 1983.

51. Newberger, E. H.: Interdisciplinary management of child abuse: problems and progress. In The American Humane Association Children's Division (Eds.): *Fourth National Symposium on Child Abuse.* Denver, AHA, 1975.

52. Newberger, E. H., and Bourne, R.: The medicalization and legalization of child abuse. *American Journal of Orthopsychiatry, 48*(4):593–607, 1978.

53. Nightingale, N., and Walker, E.: Identification and reporting of child maltreatment by head start personnel: attitudes and experiences. *Child Abuse and Neglect, 10:*191–199, 1986.

54. Osborn, P.: A model plan for coordination and management of child abuse services. *Child Abuse and Neglect, 5:*287–297, 1981.

55. Paul, J. L.: Advocacy program development. In Paul, J., Neufeld, G., and Pelosi, J. (Eds.): *Child Advocacy Within the System.* Syracuse, Syracuse, 1977.

56. Paul, J., Neufeld, G., and Pelosi, J. (Eds.): *Child Advocacy Within the System.* Syracuse, Syracuse, 1977.

57. Pelosi, J. W., and Paul, J. L.: Advocacy in home, school, and community: child advocacy system design. In Paul, J., Neufeld, G., and Pelosi, J. (Eds.): *Child Advocacy Within the System.* Syracuse, Syracuse, 1977.

58. Pelosi, J. W., Taylor, D., and Paul, J. L.: Child advocacy in government: a statewide program. In Paul, J., Neufeld, G., and Pelosi, J. (Eds.): *Child Advocacy Within the System.* Syracuse, Syracuse, 1977.

59. Riddle, J. I., and King, L.: Advocacy in an institution. In Paul, J., Neufeld, G., and Pelosi, J. (Eds.): *Child Advocacy Within the System.* Syracuse, Syracuse, 1977.

60. Rogers, C.: Child sexual abuse and the courts: preliminary findings. *Journal of Social work and Human Sexuality, 1:*145–153, 1982.

61. Schmitt, B. (Ed.): *The Child Protection Team Handbook: A Multidisciplinary Approach to Managing Child Abuse and Neglect.* New York, Garland, 1978.

62. Schmitt, B., Bross, D., Carroll, C., Gray, J., Grosz, C., Kempe, C., and Lenherr, M.: Guidelines for the hospital and clinic: management of child abuse and neglect. In Kirschner Associates (Eds.): *Child Abuse & Neglect: The User Manual Series.* Washington, National Center on Child Abuse and Neglect, USDHEW, 1978.

63. Selinske, J.: Practice: models for implementing child abuse and neglect legislation. In Frank, M. (Ed.): *Child Care: Emerging Legal Issues.* New York, Haworth, 1983.

64. Selinske, J.: Protecting CPS clients and workers. *Public Welfare, 4*(3):30–35, 1983.

65. Shay, S.: Community council for child abuse prevention. In Kempe, C. H., and Helfer, R. E. (Eds.): *The Battered Child,* 3rd ed. Chicago, University of Chicago, 1980, pp. 330–346.

66. Shireman, J., Miller, B., and Brown, H.: Child welfare workers: police and child placement. *Child Welfare, LX*(6):413–422, 1981.

67. Stone, L., Tyler, R., and Mead, J.: Law enforcement officers as investigators and therapists in child sexual abuse: a training model. *Child Abuse and Neglect, 8:*75–82, 1984.

68. Tower, C. C. (Ed.): *Questions Teachers Ask About Legal Aspects of Reporting Child Abuse and Neglect.* Washington, National Education Association, 1984.

69. Trohanis, P.: Developing community acceptance of programs for children. *Child Welfare, LIX*(6):365–373, 1980.

70. U.S. Department of Justice. National Institute of Justice: *Statement of Recommended Judicial Practices,* adopted by the National Conference of the Judiciary on the Rights of Victims of Crime. Rockville, National Criminal Justice Reference Service, 1983.

71. Valentine, D., Acuff, D., Freeman, M., and Andreas, T.: Defining child maltreatment: a multidisciplinary overview. *Child Welfare, LXIII*(6):497–509, 1984.

72. Whitcomb, D.: *Assisting Child Victims of Sexual Abuse.* Washington, Government Printing Office, 1982.

73. Whitcomb, D.: Prosecuting child sexual abuse: new approaches. *NIJ Reports,* Department of Justice, National Institute of Justice, 1986.

74. Whitcomb, D., Shapiro, E., and Stellwagen, L.: *When the Victim is a Child: Issues for Judges and Prosecutors.* Washington, Government Printing Office, 1985.

75. Wolfe, D., MacPherson, T., Blount, R., and Wolfe, V.: Evaluation of a brief intervention for educating school children in awareness of physical and sexual abuse. *Child Abuse and Neglect, 10:*85–92, 1986.

CHAPTER 16

SUMMARY, EVALUATION, AND PROSPECTS

Oliver C. S. Tzeng
Jamia J. Jacobsen
Roger Ware

SUMMARY

The sixteen chapters presented in this book deal with the child abuse and neglect issues from a broad spectrum on content, ranging from a theoretical conceptualization to establishing a child crisis center for assisting in prevention, evaluation, and treatment of child maltreatment. In this chapter, effort will be made to integrate the fifteen content chapters in reference to the theoretical conceptualizations presented in Chapter One. Before such integration is attempted, a summary of the major determinants addressed in the theoretical model is presented.

In the first chapter, the Psychosemantic Process Model of Human Aggression adopts a continuous approach to categorize social aggressive behaviors in terms of four hierarchical typologies: competitiveness, intrusiveness, domination, and violence. Although these four types of behaviors are on the same continuum, they do not necessarily reflect a sequential movement from one level to the next. In fact, these types of behaviors can independently and/or simultaneously appear in an individual's behavioral patterns. For example, a domineering parent may also be intrusive in interactions with friends and/or relatives. This may not be the case, however, across different situations or social interactions. For example, a parent may be dominant at home, but submissive in the workplace. The parent's inability to determine his/her role of dominance or submissiveness in different situations may pose a threat to the harmony of family relationships with children. The theoretical model attempts to address these and related issues in terms of ten components in four behavioral phases.

Phase I addresses the supporting baseline characteristics of individuals which is made up of two components: (1) background characteristics in

411

subjective and objective cultures; and (2) long-term stressors (real or imaginary) that have an impact on adjustment and social behaviors. These two components have a direct relationship with child abuse and neglect problems, especially when insufficient baseline characteristics and inadequate coping with long-term stressors exist. In these situations, a neglectful parent may not pay attention to the needs and activities of the children.

The model further characterized these two components in terms of five ecological systems: the idiosyncratic idiosystem of individual characteristics, the microsystem of family conditions, the exosystem of community environments, the macrosystem of cultural characteristics, and the geopolitical system of international interactions. These five systems can further be categorized in terms of objective indicators (such as age, sex, ethnicity, geography, and national origins) and subjective cultures (e.g., self-concept, family values, community standards, and national heritage).

Phase II addresses the characteristics of short-term stressors that require the immediate attention of the individual in forming reactions and/or strategies. These stressors may be subjective or objective in nature from one or more ecological systems. The immediate causal (trigger) factors of child abuse usually fall in this domain of short-term stressors.

Phase III describes the mechanisms involved in human behavior adaptations to the short-term stressors. These mechanisms are integrated processes that consist of the following five components: (1) **trend coping mechanisms,** behavioral responses that are acquired historically through social learning situations; (2) the **cognitive evaluation system,** mental assessment of situations (directly as well as indirectly); (3) the **affective evaluation system,** emotional and motivational behavior judgment process that will help decide if behavior will be positive (approach), aggressive (attack), or passive (retreat) in each situation; (4) **behavioral dispositions,** internal reactions that are the combined effects of trend coping mechanism and evaluation systems; and (5) **behavioral habits,** intervention of habits in control of intended behavioral dispositions.

Phase IV addresses two components: (1) the **overt coping behaviors** which characterizes each aggressive act in terms of various factors in relationship to individuals or situations at the five ecological systems; and (2) the **social institutional consequences** which refer to the "appraisal" of each overt behavior in terms of institutional standards or social norms. The result of such appraisal, either implicitly or explicitly, by self or others, will generate direct or indirect effects on the adult's, as well as the child's, characteristics under other components of the model.

In summary, the Psychosemantic Model for Human Aggression and Violence emphasizes the comprehensive, parallel, and concurrent study of all components in dealing with human aggressive behaviors. In application to the child abuse and neglect problems, the model addresses seven operational service domains: **identification, intervention, treatment, prevention and education, evaluation, follow-up,** and **dissemination.** These seven service domains should be integrated with the individual components in the model such that an overall network system can be developed to conduct a comprehensive analysis of the issues and concerns of child abuse and neglect problems for each geographical region.

In planning programs to combat the problems of child abuse and neglect for any geographic region, the Psychosemantic Process Model emphasizes the importance of a comprehensive evaluation of the current and past circumstances of child abuse and neglect, such that the etiology and prospect of these conditions can be delineated. Based on comprehensive and integrated profiles of the present and the past, it is then possible to plan an overall system model for the region that will effectively perform the equivalent role of "social engineering" in evaluating, redesigning, and implementing an ideal program to restore better human ecology for the future.

Evaluation

The last section of Chapter One presents a plan for subsequent chap—ters. Chapters are divided into three general categories: (1) organizations of care facilities, (2) missions and functions, and (3) legal foundations and the role within the community service system. In this portion of the text, the contents presented in Chapters Two through Fifteen will be summarized.

Chapter Two presents a historical overview of child abuse from the beginning of human society to the present time. In ancient times infanticide was condoned, not only for deformed and atypical children, but also for those born into poor or very large families. Fathers frequently abused children and were more likely than the mother to neglect or abandon them. The father made the final decision to keep or to kill his children, and government supported his decision. Evidence of child abuse can be found in the scriptures and in the history of Ancient Greece where children were seen as an economic drain on the culture. Child abuse was also condoned in Rome where, by law, a father had the legal right to sell, abandon, kill or offer in sacrifice some or all of his children.

In Europe, the advent of Christianity brought about a slow change. By 400 A.D., infanticide was considered murder that was punishable by death, however, it was difficult to enforce. Foundling hospitals to care for unwanted babies became a popular charity, but many asylums were overloaded and few infants survived.

The plight of children in Great Britain was no less, and in the first four years, the London Hospital took in 14,934 children, most of which died. Few adults were ever brought to trial for infanticide and the practice continued into the industrial revolution era. Parliament passed the Infant Life Protection Act in 1872 which forced the registration of all children and reporting of all deaths.

In the United States, the first case of child abuse was fought by the American Society for the Prevention of Cruelty to Animals who said the abused child was a part of the animal kingdom and was entitled to the same justice as an animal. Only in recent years has the life of children become recognized as a precious possession. All societies consist of diverse social phenomena that are closely linked with abusive practices toward children. It is a paradox that the accumulated knowledge for a solution to human suffering has not made a reduction of suffering. In no other area of human activity has man's ignorance or indifference been as lamentable in its consequence as that of rearing children; the future parents in society.

In **Chapter Three**, known typologies of child abuse and neglect are presented (i.e. physical abuse, physical neglect, sexual abuse, and emotional or psychosocial abuse and neglect) and five general categories of maltreatment are summarized (i.e. physical injuries, sexual maltreatment, deprivation of necessities, emotional maltreatment, and other maltreatment).

This chapter presents summaries of official statistics on reported cases of child abuse and/or neglect in the United States between 1976 and 1986. Statistics includes three types of issues: (1) the nature and volume of reporting to child protective agencies, (2) the characteristics of the reported cases, and (3) the responses from child protective agencies concerning reported cases. An overall look at statistics is presented and the emerging patterns are described. In general, data suggests a growth in knowledge and cooperation between state data systems and protective agencies in investigation, reporting, and legal provisions about cases.

However, the rate of reporting has increased 158 percent since 1976, but resources have not increased proportionally to meet the service demands.

The negative impacts of child abuse and neglect are multifaceted and are discussed from three perspectives: (1) **family unity** and **development** are frequently affected by abusive cycles that accompany a variety of problems existing in individual and/or family, (e.g. parent modeling, mental illnesses, past abuse within the family, inadequately explained deaths of children, isolation from outside family contacts, marital discord, rigid expectations for children, harsh punishment, or unwanted children that are seen as a burden); (2) **psychosocial perceptions of family dysfunctions** can be presented jointly by a psychological and a sociological model, because child abuse is a collection of symptoms that has no single etiology and abusive families vary greatly in terms of characteristics; and (3) **societal problems** are presented in terms of juvenile delinquency, violent behavior, and aggressive behavior in younger children.

In **Chapter Four**, state laws for protecting child victimization are analyzed and organized into 31 categories which are categorized in the following 7 general sections: (1) purposes and definitions, (2) reporting child abuse/neglect, (3) administration, (4) protection, (5) evidence and examinations, (6) penalty for child abuse, and (7) court procedures. These categories represent an overview of the legal systems role in child abuse/neglect intervention and protection.

The purpose and definition sections outline the statutory procedures for preventing child abuse from occurring and for dealing with incidents that occurred. The reporting category delineates procedures for filing an alleged abuse report in terms of the contents of the report and to whom it should be filed. Explanations were made regarding the penalties for not complying with the mandatory report as well as liabilities that are exempted from false reporting under good faith.

The administration section outlines the duties and cooperation requirements of various departments that receive alleged reports of abuse/neglect. This section also summarizes responsibilities of maintaining a central registry including; filing of reports, investigations, planning rehabilitative treatment, and keeping all reports strictly confidential. The protection section addresses intervention of abuse and also protection from further abuse in terms of regulations of: protective custody, provisions for teams to assist agencies in report investigation, and implications of reunification of abusive families. The rights of suspected perpetrators are also included.

The evidence section summarized the issues concerning what constitutes abuse and what evidence can be collected and used in court. Photographs and/or x-rays of physical abuse, and emergency medical examinations are usually accepted when done according to stipulations. Privileged communications are admissible evidence in most states except for the lawyer/client privilege. Many states also include an exemption for spiritual treatment for a child's illness or remedial care.

The penalty of committing child abuse/neglect is defined in most states as intentional or negligent. Indictments may range from Class A misdemeanor (negligence) to Class E felony (intentional). Two states specifically will not prohibit ordinary punishment by a parent or teacher. Finally, the court proceedings section addresses the issues regarding the right to counsel for a victimized child and also for the alleged perpetrator. Some of the responsibilities of the guardian ad litem are also specified. Provision that may terminate parental rights are outlined. General court proceedings, such as original jurisdiction, petitioning, adjudicatory hearing, and disposition hearing are also identified.

In Chapter Five, child abuse prevention is advocated as being the best strategy for dealing with potentially violent or unstable families. The major purpose in preventing child abuse is to spread knowledge to the community, parents, children, social service workers, law enforcement officials, or anyone that may come into contact with child abuse. Other prevention strategies presented in this chapter include training child protection workers, implementation of hot lines, new and better investigative procedures, treatment programs and self-help groups.

Approaches to prevention can be found on three levels: (1) **primary,** which refers to efforts aimed at positively influencing caregivers before abuse or neglect occurs; (2) **secondary,** which is the supportive services offered to parents at risk; and (3) **tertiary,** more often referred to as treatment, which is in the form of keeping families from developing abusive cycles.

Various prevention approaches to providing child services are delineated in this chapter. They include child crisis centers, drop-in centers, home-based family services, support groups, extended family centers, live-in treatment centers, emergency homemaker services, and comprehensive emergency services.

Because of the complex nature of child abuse and neglect, the prevention of all cases should be based on community-wide coordination of child protective service staff and various social service agencies. This teamwork could enhance all services for children and families with a focus on prevention. The remaining sections of this chapter address prevention strategies from the perspectives of various social services including law enforcement agencies, educational systems, health (including mental health) facilities, communities, and the media.

Chapter Six presents the summary results of a nationwide survey that was designed to evaluate the facilities and programs available for crisis intervention/treatment of child abuse and neglect problems. The goal is to provide information on national trends as to how to optimize future service functions and crisis intervention. Major concerns addressed in this chapter include:

1. Types of facilities, clientele, effectiveness, and range of services;
2. Services available and clientele referral rate;
3. Residential/nonresidential treatment and length of services per client;
4. Staff composition such as volunteer vs. paid, and extent of positions;
5. Evaluation of services such as how often, contents, and criteria;
6. Referral rates, both to and from other agencies;
7. Financial sources and budgetary considerations; and
8. Major problems and suggestions for improvement.

The sources of information are a cameo study of 53 crisis centers in 26 states collected through phone interviews, a questionnaire developed from these results, and literature research. Some of the results include: (1) major services offered include emergency/medical, counseling/therapy, foster care, residential 24 hour crisis nursery care, referral to crisis management, and aid to parents; (2) staff size varied from 5 to 185 with an average of 52; (3) evaluation in most agencies had occurred in the past year; (4) referrals showed the highest frequency for both sources and outreach were child protective service; and (5) issues of concern included financial difficulties, staffing problems, and service limitations.

The conclusions of this study were that education and training of parents are keys to reducing child maltreatment and it is very important to concentrate on **prevention** and **intervention** rather than treatment only. There is a need for more volunteers, more assistance programs for the adult population. To assist in this needed expansion of services, improvement of cost-effeciency can be obtained by developing network systems to share strategies and resource information. For example, an increase of referrals through a network of agencies would assure more effective services. It follows that, a major goal should be to develop a community-wide comprehensive system for treatment, prevention and education.

Chapter Seven provides guidelines to establish a child crisis center. A spectrum to focus on include: (1) stressing community-wide coordination and cooperation; (2) setting goals such as ages of children and length of stay; (3) devising a clear and appropriate name for the center; (4) raising funds with a statement of need letter; (5) keeping careful records of all donations, (6) keeping accurate records of all income and expenses for an annual report, (7) planning strategically to keep the program activities going while organizing, and (8) gaining recognition and funding through the news media, newsletters, brochures and speakers.

Hints for raising funds to support a crisis center include designing a project that: (1) takes as little time as possible for the most dollars raised, (2) requires no large financial risk, (3) is relevant to the aims of the center, (4) helps publicize the center, and (5) is fun and facilitates friendships. Utilizing different sources to request donations may involve government funds, foundation funds, corporate money, church money, grass roots money, and United Way funds.

Most nonprofit centers rely on a hierarchical structure involving a Board of Directors which appoints an Executive Director. The staff of the center reports to the Director who in turn reports to the Board. All personnel and Board members should be involved in planning and creating ideas for the center. Planning is a tool to guide the crisis center, to solve problems, and to get results. Evaluating resources for each segment of the center such as administration, child care, volunteer corps, kitchen, counseling, medical and maintenance should be done one to five years in advance.

Staffing involves finding a competent team leader, hiring the staff, training, and evaluating employees. Before hiring staff, total cost should be evaluated and each person hired should have the goals of the center explained to him/her and team work should be stressed. Criteria of performance should be explained to the staff before evaluation and positive suggestions should be the basis in discussing problems.

In summary, the complex phenomena of family violence and child abuse causes a need for intervention programs such as crisis centers. The general public may not be aware of the extent of child maltreatment, therefore one of the jobs of the child crisis center is to make people aware of needs and what can be done to make life safe and healthy for children.

In **Chapter Eight**, facilities and functional requirements of a comprehensive child crisis intervention shelter are presented that are practical and useful suggestions for an effective center. Examples of admission forms and records such as health, family background, and emergency information are shown and suggestions are given of the type of data that should be collected when the child is first admitted to the center.

Important consideration for the physical environment when designing the facility are presented such as safety factors and state regulations. Special plans and room arrangements are needed for children with special needs such as the physically handicapped or mentally impaired child. Six factors to consider in designing the interior of the environment are color, lighting, acoustics, floor coverings, ventilation, and room arrangements. Child play is an essential learning medium, and to develop a quality facility, many special materials are needed to provide children with good tools. Table toys are divided into four activity categories; coordination, construction, reconstruction, and classification activities. Examples of materials and good ways to substitute for items out of budget range are given for table toys such as sensory, construction, dramatic play, large-muscle, and art materials.

The types of personnel and needed qualifications are suggested as well as recommended adult/child ratios. Meeting the needs of the abused or neglected child is a difficult task because of the wide rage of ages and types of children that seek assistance at the crisis center. The special needs of infants (0 to 12 months), toddlers (1 to 2½ years), preschoolers (3 to 5 years), school age children (6 to 12 years), and adolescents are discussed such as personal attention, feeding or toileting assistance, privacy needs, opportunities for socialization, and understanding. Suggested program schedules are given for four to five year olds and infants in particular. Providing a calm and relaxed daily routine will help alleviate stress in children as well as make them feel more secure and in control of their situation.

The last section of this chapter discusses financial planning for a crisis program. Options for types of support are given as well as a list of start-up costs that are needed before the facility opens its doors and operating costs to maintain a quality program.

In **Chapter Nine**, guidelines for establishing or maintaining an effective volunteer corps within a child crisis center are presented. A good volunteer program can expand services for abused and neglected children and increase community knowledge and support for crisis centers, but careful planning and analysis of agency needs is necessary. Volunteers have existed throughout history, however, their role has changed somewhat in present times. A program must understand and meet the needs of volunteers to be successful. Areas covered in this chapter include volunteer administration and recruitment, responsibilities and roles of volunteers, and volunteer training and motivation-building techniques.

The field of volunteer administration is being recognized as a viable profession. In order to successfully manage a corps of volunteers, there must be careful objectives set forth for the program, approval for and available salary funds for a program coordinator. This volunteer coordinator must be flexible and also the type of person who demonstrates initiative, can focus on the effects that decisions will have on the community, and can make solid, wise decision. Responsibilities of the volunteer coordinator include planning, organizing, staffing, directing, controlling, interpersonal roles, informational roles, and decisionmaking.

Staff should be involved with the volunteer program because everyone must work together as a team. In recruiting, the type of volunteer that is needed should be pinpointed and that type should be targeted to become involved. In order for people to be motivated to volunteer, the crisis center must offer something in exchange for the time the volunteer donates, such as trust and friendship, or feeling important and needed. Each volunteer should fill out an application and go through an interviewing process. This will give an opportunity to explain to them their rights as volunteers and what is expected of them.

Chapter Ten outlines the importance of planning the kitchen program in a child crisis center. The establishment of a proper nutritional program is to create a positive learning experience and a balanced diet that will contribute to the physical, mental, and emotional well-being of all who seek assistance at the center. This chapter includes a dining room and kitchen floor plan, a list of equipment and utensils needed, and menu suggestions complete with recipes.

Planning strategies include: (1) contact the State Board of Health to obtain a list of requirements for food service and storage areas and for food purchasing; (2) make initial contacts with possible contributors or donors of food items; (3) shop for equipment, utensils and furnishings in compliance with requirements; (4) apply for the appropriate authorized credentials to receive commodities from the local food bank; (5) hire a supervisor or kitchen coordinator; (6) attend a seminar or workshops with the supervisor provided by the School Lunch Program Department or similar agency; and (7) select vendors and suppliers needed to establish a credit line.

The well-being of the maltreated child brought into a crisis center is served through every department, including the food service area. Nutritional values combines with appetizing food, served in a cheerful atmosphere is a goal which can be met by the kitchen coordinator and the kitchen staff.

Chapter Eleven discusses ways to approach the treatment of child abuse in terms of who should be the main recipient of services. Treatment models are presented that focus on: (1) individuals (i.e. the victimized child, parents, and caretakers), (2) families, and (3) groups (social network). Co-operation among treatment teams is vital and includes: (1) defining and respecting specific roles of all treatment team members, and (2) sharing information and goals through open communication. Treatment is an ongoing process that involves many people (i.e. medical professionals, lawyers, police, and neighbors) who may or may not have previously experienced child abuse. Each family has individualized circumstances and emotional levels may be highly aroused.

The Comprehensive Family Life Education Program (FLEP) attempts to provide services needed to avert placement of children outside the home and facilitate the reunification of families. Services offered include: (1) family counseling and case management, (2) monitoring and supervision, (3) home education, homemaker, and parent aid services, (4) parent education classes, and (5) family advocate services.

Proper assessment is crucial and family interviews help by explaining the role of the worker to the family and allowing the family to interpret their story. After assessment the clinician meets the family to develop a treatment plan (or contract for services).

Family therapy is the primary treatment modality for the FLEP staff. Individual therapy is used most often with single parent families with very young children, but individual therapy for the child is usually done in conjunction with family therapy. Group therapy is useful, but many abusive/neglectful parents are isolated socially and may not be ready for group work initially. Five case examples are presented in this section to identify interventions used to treat some abusive/neglectful family problems. Interventions commonly used by FLEP workers include: (1) behavior management training, (2) assertiveness training, (3) modeling, (4) problem solving training, (5) communication, (6) focus on family strength, (7) support, and (8) environmental therapy.

Chapter Twelve addresses the psychological maltreatment of children as responsible for detrimental long-term dysfunctional consequences including: (1) theoretical perspectives conceptualizing the child's world of psychological maltreatment; (2) specific definitions and problems in development of definitions pertaining to child abuse; (3) prevention of psychological maltreatment; and (4) the need to target the parent, child, and sociocultural stressers.

Defining psychological treatment has been a difficult task and mental injury is described in many state statutes but not clarified, thus they are useless for child protective services and court intervention. Eight domains of psychologically destructive acts or environmental conditions have been developed which are: mental cruelty; sexual abuse and exploitation; living in dangerous and unstable environments; drug and substance abuse; influence by negative and limiting models; cultural bias and prejudice; emotional neglect and stimulus deprivation; and institutional abuse.

Psychological maltreatment can be considered from two perspectives: (1) as the core component of most physical and sexual abuse, and (2) as a discrete form of abuse. Either way it appears to produce a spectrum of short and long-term effects to the child. Theoretical perspectives are valuable to guide explanation, prediction, and program design and implementation. Theories discussed include perspectives from the viewpoint of basic human needs, developmental, and ecological considerations.

To address prevention it is necessary to have a perspective of: (1) the messages the child receives, and (2) the child's life as a prisoner of psychological war. Prevention involves: (1) **organic factors** including prevention of physical disorders in the child or parent which could increase the probability of child abuse, and (2) **non-organic factors** contributing to child abuse include dysfunctional parenting, child vulnerability, and sociocultural stressers. Based on the concept that prevention is designed to alleviate a stressful situation, these three categories can be reformulated into prevention promoting target categories as follows: (1) targeting the parent, (2) producing the stress resistant and invulnerable child, and (3) addressing sociocultural factors. Each of these categories can be addressed in terms of: (a) satisfying basic psychological needs, (b) developing knowledge and skills for parenting, and (c) reducing negative stress.

Chapter Thirteen addresses the problem of child sexual abuse. Public awareness in this area continues to increase and as a result, more children are presented for evaluation of possible sexual victimization. Professionals must develop perspectives with regard to: (1) identification of possible victims, (2) interviewing children, (3) the medical evaluation, and (4) children in the legal system. A general definition of sexual abuse does not always help in individual cases as there may be a difference of opinion as to what constitutes an abusive act. It is important to recognize indicators of sexual abuse, they **may** mean abuse has occurred and suggest diagnosis.

Interviewing is an emotional issue and difficult to discuss. Techniques are presented to make the process easier for the child. The purposes of the medical evaluation are: (1) to determine if there is physical injury for evidence, (2) to determine treatment for any disease present, and (3) to reassure the child and family of integrity of the child's anatomy and reproductive function.

When the medical exam takes place depends upon the recency of the sexual assault, the victims emotional state, and the expertise of the examiner. Medical history, physical examination, treatment, and forensic specimen collection are all part of the medical exam, including an interview with the child. The findings of the medical exam are related to: (1) the time since the last abuse, (2) the duration and type of abuse, and (3) the degree of force used. Recent, acute trauma is more likely to leave evident marks while chronic molestation is suggested by physical findings. A normal examination does not exclude that sexual abuse occurred and professionals must be careful with statements in medical records that will be presented in court.

Psychological assessment and treatment of the child and family should begin at the time the child enters the community service system. The degree of impact is affected by factors such as: (1) the relationship to the offender, (2) the number of encounters, (3) the duration of the abuse, (4) the extent of the abuse, (5) the degree of bribery or coercion, (6) the family response, (7) the nature of the court involvement, and (8) the ego strengths of the child.

In summary, diagnosis and recognizing the problem occurs are necessary to identify sexual abuse. It is important to understand the impact of assault from the child's view in order to interpret information. This must be done with caution not to place adult expectations on childhood experiences and reactions.

Chapter Fourteen pertains to the intervention and treatment of sexually abused children. Because child sexual abuse is both a social problem and a criminal justice problem, the general issues in assessment, intervention and treatment are complex and often interrelated. Besides sexual abuse, there may be additional physical abuse, emotional abuse, or neglect; the victim may be retarded or emotionally disturbed; the victim may have amnesia about abuse; parents may be single, isolated, alcoholics, poor, or emotionally disturbed; and there may be a lack of transportation or a permanent home.

Domains of child sexual abuse include the type of abuse, characteristics of the victim and perpetrator, and the context of the abuse. Reasons for abusing children sexually may stem back to childhood problems such as parental conflict, observations of spouse abuse, physical abuse or neglect, or sibling violence. Effects on children of sexual abuse include fear, anxiety, depression, anger, hostility, and inappropriate sexual behavior.

Key elements for delivering services to a sexually abused child are: (1) crisis intervention which includes stages of medical examination, investigative interviews, assistance in understanding legal procedures involved, assignment of psychologist, and application of age-appropriate strategies to facilitate cognitive mastery of the abuse experience; (2) assessment, methodology and diagnosis including goals to substantiate the parameters of the alleged sexual abuse, identifying consequent and concurrent problems, and making recommendations for the treatment and safety of the child; (3) case histories in which three (anonymous) psychological evaluations are presented to depict the variability involved in completing an assessment; and (4) treatment modalities that are chosen according to the age of the child, the nature and scope of the abuse, and the level of the child's functioning in the areas of affect, cognition and behaviors.

Training issues are described for the actions of professionals during legal examination to ensure that questions are not misleading, detail is carefully recorded, and the abuse is not discussed outside of the professional investigation.

Chapter Fifteen is the link between all preceding chapters in the Sourcebook because it describes the need for cooperation between community service agencies in the fight against child maltreatment. The rights of abused or neglected children are not sufficient due to lack of communication between child protection services, medical professionals, community agencies, and the justice system. More states are passing laws and more local communities are developing programs to communicate more promptly and efficiently to provide an even delivery of services to the child victim and the family.

Each state has made gains in passing laws concerning child abuse/neglect reporting, but many key words are not clearly defined. Five key provisions in state statutes and thirteen basic elements in the laws are presented. Legal caseloads and utilization of foster homes has greatly increased. Efforts to streamline caseloads, keep more children with their families, and reduce unfounded reports could provide better services to children in serious danger. Child abuse laws have reflected punishment versus treatment themes and more preventive programs must be established to maintain family integrity (Koerin, 1980).

Community needs include: (1) multidisciplinary management of child abuse/neglect between professionals and community disciplines, (2) development of model systems and the essential attributes involved, and (3) development of a range of treatment options that are essential for case management and appropriate for a community's system of services. Guidelines are included for: (1) collaborative strategies for solidifying support before going public, building community awareness, and approaching controversial topics straightforwardly; (2) interagency theories; and (3) community prevention programs. Model systems presented include a child protection model, medical model, legal model, and an interdisciplinary model.

There has been an increased awareness among professionals of the need for early intervention, treatment planning, and the provision of services to abused children. As greater avenues of communication occur, the professional community's response to a child abuse report will become more individualized and helpful, offering the best possible intervention for each child's situation.

PROSPECTS AND RECOMMENDATIONS

The problems cited in various chapters of this book clearly demonstrate the pervasiveness and prevalence of maltreatment of children across the county. These chapters also described an increased awareness of the child abuse and neglect problems in the general population as well as in governmental institutions. Over the past decade, millions of dollars have been spent for the purpose of the intervention and treatment of child abuse and neglect victimization. Literature has shown the existence of numerous programs available to assist victimized children and their families in the majority of the cities in the nation.

As a result, many scientific approaches have been adapted to establish programs for studying etiologies of victimization, including medical, social, and psychosocial models. Evaluation of the current phenomena and conditions of child abuse and neglect through any of these models should, in theory, offer sufficient fundamental knowledge and working experiences that are necessary for continuing efforts to combat the abuse and neglect of children.

Unfortunately, it is an undeniable fact, as mentioned by all authors of this book, that the contemporary state of affairs in dealing with child abuse and neglect issues is by no means perfect, nor is it likely to be ameliorated in the near future. Due to the complex nature of the issues involved, the strengths of various programs of intervention and treatment have frequently been limited by: (a) a narrow focus on some specific issues, (b) the orientation of a single discipline, (c) separate or disjointed efforts in services, (d) partial and frequently biased knowledge and skill in performance, and (e) a fragmental nature in program implementation. The authors of this book repeatedly pointed out that these limitations have severely undercut the efficiency and efficacy of existing service efforts.

Addressing these deficiencies, the Psychosemantic Process Model developed in Chapter One integrates these concerns into a theoretical framework. This model calls for the following fundamental principles: (1) identification of comprehensive contents to overcome narrow focuses, (2) multidisciplinary orientation to overcome individual, separate efforts, (3) systemization of knowledge to link all individual components and issues related to child abuse and neglect, and (4) operationalization of program development to overcome fragmental and partial program focuses. Based on these principles, the literature about child abuse and neglect can be delineated in terms of the ten culture-by-ecology units.

For future combatting of child abuse and neglect problems, the Psychosemantic Process Model calls for a "social engineering" approach that will gather comprehensive, detailed information of the past and present social conditions, plan the future correction mechanisms and destinations for all ecological systems, and implement "engineering constructing" plans in a systematic and concrete fashion for a better future of this society. This "social engineering" work requires thorough preparation, planning, implementation, and evaluation. Currently, the child abuse and neglect service system has done little work in the evaluation and follow-up domains called for in the model.

The problem of child abuse and neglect is profound; social institutions have spent much time trying to tackle this problem. The work accomplished thus far has provided enormous background materials for "social engineers" to evaluate and design a new and comprehensive system that will simultaneously perform the seven service domains: identification, intervention, prevention and education, treatment, evaluation, follow-up, and dissemination. Without such integration, the continuation of current efforts can only drain more of the public and private monies with little hope of attaining maximum levels of healthy social ecologies for our children to develop and enjoy.

The United States is rich in material goods and human resources that have armed our nation to overcome many crises in objective as well as subjective ecologies in the past. Abuse and neglect of children are undeniable social tragedies and humiliating facts in the contemporary civilization. Fortunately, the rich resources of this country, with definite goals and destinations, can overcome these challenges by unified efforts of all individuals and institutions involved. Let us hope that the time of instigating united new efforts is today.

INDEX

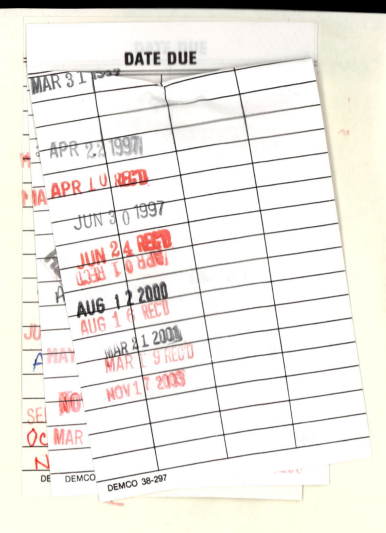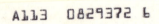